Progress in Language Planning

Contributions to the Sociology of Language

31

Editor
Joshua A. Fishman

MOUTON PUBLISHERS · BERLIN · NEW YORK · AMSTERDAM

Progress in Language Planning

International Perspectives

Edited by
Juan Cobarrubias
Joshua A. Fishman

(1983)

MOUTON PUBLISHERS · BERLIN · NEW YORK · AMSTERDAM

Library of Congress Cataloging in Publication Data

Main entry under title:

Progress in language planning.

(Contributions to the sociology of language; 31) Bibliography: p.
1. Language planning – Addresses, essays, lectures. I. Cobarrubias, Juan,
1936–
II. Fishman, Joshua A. III. Series.
P40.5.L35P76 1983 404 82-22310
ISBN 90-279-3358-8
ISBN 90-279-3388-X (pbk.)

Typesetting: Asian Research Service, Hong Kong. – Printing: Druckerei Hildebrand,
Berlin. – Binding: Lüderitz & Bauer Buchgewerbe GmbH, Berlin. – Cover design:
K. Lothar Hildebrand, Berlin.   Printed in Germany.

Contents

Introduction

JUAN COBARRUBIAS

Language Planning: The State of the Art

THEORETICAL FRAMEWORK

A glance at the titles of the essays contained in this book will reveal to the trained reader the jargon of at least two sources in language planning: Haugen's (1966) language planning model and Kloss's (1969) distinction between language *status planning* and *corpus planning*. The conceptual framework used in the gathering of the essays published here draws on both of these sources, although the authors have naturally used their personal insight.

Haugen's well known fourfold model (1966, 1966 [1972], 1969 [1972]), describes the stages of language planning thus: (1) norm selection, (2) codification, (3) implementation, and (4) elaboration. Haugen (1966 [1972]: 252) initially conceived these stages as four aspects of language development... as crucial features in taking the step from "dialect" to "language," from vernacular to standard.

Norm selection involves choosing a language or variety for specific purposes frequently associated with official status or national roles. Norm selection is, in an important sense, making official policy. In Morocco, Tunisia, and Algeria, for instance, prior to independence, French dominated the educational system, while Arabic was relegated to a secondary position. After independence, the question of what language was to be chosen as the official language and what language was to be used as the language of education became questions of fundamental importance. Two trends emerged, one led by those who favored an immediate and total Arabization, the other led by those who recognized the importance of Arabization but considered more immediately urgent the maintenance of an efficient educational system with basic education in French. The first trend prevailed and the Ministry of Education's plan for 1956-1957 determined that the first grade was to be completely Arabized. The resulting lowering in the quality of education and shortage of qualified teachers motivated other policy changes later (Altoma 1970 [1974]). The officialization of Quechua in Peru and the regulations providing for bilingual education in the U.S.A., Canada, or Finland, with due differences, offer examples of norm selection and language policy. Although in many instances norm selection involves choice among competing languages or varieties, they need not be competing in every instance.

Codification is related to the stabilization of the norm selected. Codification presupposes norm selection and is related to standardization processes. Standardization has involved at least two distinct language strategies, one requiring the elaboration and adoption of one variety among others, the other consisting in the creation of a new variety composed of some main dialects. The situation of Pilipino in the Philippines illustrates the first. Aasen's strategy for achieving a national language using the dialects as a raw material for a new Norwegian illustrates the second. The standardization process involes, among other things, the production of dictionaries, grammars, spellers, style manulas, punctuation and pronunciation guides, specialized glossaries, etc., and it is carried out in many instances by language academies or individuals who do the work of academies, like Aasen or Samuel Johnson.

Implementation or, as Haugen also calls it at times, acceptance, involves the activities of governmental agencies, institutions, and writers in adopting and using the selected and codified norm. Activities such as the production of newspapers, textbooks, books, and other publications, as well as the use of a language for mass-media communication, are part of the implementation process.

Elaboration involves the expansion of language functions and the assignment of new codes, such as scientific and technological. Language modernization is one of the most common activities requiring elaboration. Examples can be found in the modernization of Arabic (Altoma 1970 [1974]), Hebrew (Fellman 1974), Pilipino (Sibayan 1971 [1974]). Production and dissemination of new terms is one of the most typical activities of language modernization and elaboration.

Neustupny suggested (1970 [1974]) a model that differs from Haugen's in emphasizing language cultivation as a separate stage or process. Cultivation involves functional differentiation of one variety from another within a given code through identification of registers that will determine 'appropriateness,' 'coorectness,' or acceptable 'style.' Fishman, in a lucid comparison of both models (1973 [1974]: 80), finds the differences between Haugen and Neustupny reconcilable. Thus, the latter's emphasis on cultivation fits in Haugen's model, whereas the former's emphasis on implementation fits in Neustupny's model. Whether or not such reconciliation eliminates differences between the two models depends, in the ultimate analysis, upon our understanding of concepts still in need of further clarification.

Haugen's model has been the focus of attention of an important part of the literature on language planning. Others have added new dimensions to the model, such as evaluation (Rubin 1971), but in general the model has been widely accepted. Only in the essay included in this volume has Haugen attempted to revise the original model and offered, as he calls it, his own harmonization, although the basic structure of the model is still similar to the original. Interestingly enough, Haugen attempts to show that his new version harmonizes also with Kloss's distinction between status planning and corpus planning. Although some associations between Kloss's distinction and Haugen's model are fairly straightforward, such harmonization may be a matter of controversy for those who see status vs. corpus as a blurred distinction (see the summary of Rubin's paper in this volume).

The distinction, however, has heuristic value, and although Kloss's first presentation of it needs refinement, it seems illuminating. Discussions of language rights, language policy, language allocation, language legislation, for example, become more enlightened when seen through the distinction. The distinction also permits us to see where the attention of planning research has been concentrated. Several authors (Ferguson, this volume; Rubin, this volume) have observed that most of the research on language planning has been concerned with corpus planning. The problems related to status planning are not so clearly defined and seem to entail a greater degree of complexity. But it seems clear that we need to know more and do more in the area of status planning. A semantical analysis of the concept of language status can be found in the first part of my paper in this volume. One of the interesting aspects of this collection of essays is that, in addition to a number of papers focusing upon language-corpus issues, it includes a number of others focusing on language status.

It is important to note that neither Kloss's distinction nor Haugen's model, nor a combination of the two, is going to do the job of sound language-planning theory. Haugen himself recognizes that even the revised version of the original model he presents here does not 'amount to a theory of language planning'. He also points out that 'our discipline remains largely descriptive and has not reached a stage of "explanatory adequacy"'. This is an important realization shared by a number of other language planners and socially minded linguists. In order for language planning to provide adequate explanations, a paradigm shift is required, a gestalt switch on the language planning processes. Part of this gestalt switch is incipient in the realization that the task of language planning so far has been largely descriptive rather than explanatory. But in order to provide explanations we need well-confirmed hypotheses. A theory of language planning will consist, like any other theory, of a set of such hypotheses. A new paradigm will regard explanatory power as one of the fundamental goals of language planning, and the search for confirmable, sound hypotheses will be an essential part of theoretical development in language planning. A substantial amount of sociolinguistic information is already available, although it seems that the formulation of explanatory hypotheses will require a much more extensive gathering of data than we yet have. The task of hypothesis formation has barely begun. We are in a pretheoretical stage, in a 'sociological paradigm', 'a locus of professional commitment, prior to the various concepts, laws, theories' (Kuhn 1970 [1962]: 11). 'That commitment and the apparent consensus it produces are prerequisites for formal science'. Although the word 'paradigm' is an accordion word that by expansion and contraction generates too much philosophical music, Kuhn distinguishes the concept of 'sociological paradigm' from paradigm as 'a concrete scientific achievement' containing a problem-solving set of confirmed hypotheses (for a discussion of the intricacies surrounding the concept of paradigm, see Masterman 1970). A paradigm in the latter sense would be an 'artifact paradigm' or 'construct paradigm'. A theory of language planning would involve such an artifact paradigm, i.e. would supply the tools to provide reliable explanations.

Haugen thinks that a theory of language planning 'would surely have to be one that takes a stand on value judgements' (last paragraph of part one of his paper). It is understandable that language-planning issues relate to value judgements. However, a theory of language planning does not necessarily, *qua* theory, have to take a stand on value judgement. Explanations resulting from economic theory, for instance, may entail quite diverse value judgements, but these are not the direct result of the theory itself. Although theories may show different forms of theoretical and methodological commitment, no theory to my knowledge takes, as part of its own task, a stand on value judgements. Thus, Haugen raises the question: 'Where norms conflict, shall we plan for unity or for diversity, for "transitional" bilingualism or for maintenance?' His concern is quite legitimate. But I do not think that we should conceive of a language-planning theory committed to transitional bilingualism and another language-planning theory committed to maintenance. The theory should include hypotheses that explain and describe the regular consequences of both possible language strategies, but the theory as such should be a unified body of knowledge. It is because we may anticipate with the help of the theory desirable consequences that we may want to affect given conditions to bring about expected results or try to prevent centain events from happening. The epistemic value of the theory does not rest upon the results that we or other groups favor. Haugen's concern is quite legitimate since language-status decisions are affected by ideological considerations of powerful groups and counteracting forces. However, we should not saddle the theory with ideological considerations. I have attempted to show in my paper in this volume that language-status issues are entangled in ideological matters, and I submit now that the future theoretical foundation of language planning depends upon our greater understanding of status and policy issues so that we may separate objective knowledge, stated in well-confirmed hypotheses, from partisan inclinations and ideological sympathies.

The formulation of language-planning hypotheses seems to depend more heavily upon clarification of status than of corpus matters. Also, in this sense, the distinction status vs. corpus seems illuminating.

STATUS-RELATED PAPERS

Without attempting to do justice to the contributions assembled here and their authors, it seems worth noting some similarities and differences that give us an overall idea of the state of the art.

Language change as an independent topic of study has attracted the attention of socially minded linguists for a long time, and the references on diachronic studies of language evolution and language change are too numerous to be listed here. However, most of the existing research has approached language change as a natural or spontaneous phenomenon. The first essay that approached language change from the perspective of language planning, to my knowledge, was Rubin's (1977). Ferguson takes up the same approach and shows, with several examples, how non-'natural' language change relates to language planning. He observes that 'efforts devoted to language planning and studies of language-planning processes have generally been well separated from systematic studies of language change'.

And, on the other hand, the strong tradition of the study of language change in 19th and 20th century linguistics has typically distrusted language planning or assured that language-planning efforts were irrelevant to the fundamental processes of change.

Ferguson believes that a theory of language change will be incomplete if it does not take into consideration the influence of language planning. In order to make his point, Ferguson considers two perspectives: one, change and planning within a speech community; the other, change and planning in the structure of the language itself. There are changes in the functions of different varieties in the speech community and changes in the language structure. Again the distinction status vs. corpus reappears.

Heath and Mandabach study the way in which language-status decisions have been reached in the Anglophone-mother-tongue world. They find significant similarities between the achievement of the status of English in England and in the U.S.A., at least until the nineteenth century, i.e. 'without official declaration and without the help of an official academy.' The status of English in England does not come about through statute, but through cultural and societal forces. The United States inherited the reluctance to mandate language choice.

Heath and Mandaback sketch the history of the status of English in

England and show how after the Norman Conquest, 1066, Norman French became the language of the Parliament, the courts, and the upper class. Latin was the language of universities, scholarship, and legal writings. English was the popular tongue of the people. English and French were competing languages in regard to specific language functions from the Norman Conquest, 1066, at least until 1362, i.e. about 300 years. For at least a century and a half after the Conquest it was doubtful which of the two languages, French or English, would ultimately triumph. The two languages kept sullenly apart all those years, in a diglossic situation, refusing to intermingle. The Norman Conquest established in England a court and an aristocracy, and French, in its Norman dialect, became the only polite medium of intercourse. English was despised at first as the language of a subject race, used by boors and serfs. A study of the changes in the functional distribution of the two languages and the intervening forces should illuminate our understanding of diglossic situations.

Heath and Mandabach assign only a meager importance to Henry III's Proclamation of 1258, in improving the status of English. This milestone in the race of the two languages for linguistic supremacy may, however, be open to different interpretations. It is true that it is not the only event that may account for the triumph of English over French. The latter is marked, in fact, by a series of events, such as the loss of Normandy in 1204, that separated England from France and broke the connection between French aristocracy and Anglo-Norman aristocracy, allowing the possibility for a new English aristocracy to emerge. It was a combination of English and Norman barons that forced King John in 1215 to sign the Magna Charta. And it was in 1258 that English was used officially, for the first time since the Conquest, in the proclamation in the name of Henry III for summoning a parliament of barons from all parts of England. This, in my view, clearly shows that French had ceased to be the only language spoken and read by the Anglo-Norman nobles. But the race between English and French continued. In 1349, three years after the victory of Crecy, it was ruled that the teaching of Latin should no longer be conducted in French, as had been the practice until then, but in English. French continued to be used as the language of the courts until 1362, when it was ruled that all pleadings in the law courts should be conducted in English. The reason as stated in the preamble to the Act was 'that French has become much unknown in the realm'. The use of French by 1400 was considerably reduced, and a vast English literature had sprung in the interim and became popular not only among noblemen but also among knights and burgesses. Heath and Mandabach emphasize the literary use of English in achieving higher status and maintain that 'status promotion through increased use came about as poets, preachers, and some officials of the law quietly used English in their writings'. However, one may have the impression that the situation of English was linguistically more homogeneous than it was. It is not that the status of English per se was promoted through increased use by poets, writers, etc., but in fact it was a specific variety of English that was more strongly promoted than others, the Midland dialect, not the Northern or the Southern dialects, although each of them had had their own period of glory. These dialects also stood in a somewhat competitive relation. It is important to understand the emergence of Modern English from a number of language changes associated with language-planning processes. We recognize three periods in the evolution of Modern English: Old English (450-1200), Middle English (1200-1500), and Modern English (1500 to the present). But Old English consisted of at least three different dialects: the Northumbrian (Northern), the Mercian (Midland), and the Wessex (Southern). The latter is now better known as 'Anglo-Saxon', a name given by sixteenth-century scholars who wished to revive the language of Alfred the Great, whose subjects were known as 'West Saxons' or Wessex men. Curiously enough, the Northumbrian and the Mercian literatures prior to the Norman Conquest are fragmentary, while the Anglo-Saxon is, in contradistinction, significative and stretches from 700 to 1200. The 200 years from 700 to 900 are the years of the language of Alfred the Great, born in 849, who superintended the translation from Latin into the Wessex dialect of the *History of the World* by Orosius, *Church History* by Bede, *Consolations of Philosophy* by Boethius, and the *Pastorales* by St. Gregory. He was also responsible for the compilation of early portions of the *Old English Chronicle.* The period 900-1100 is the period of the language of Elfric, who wrote a collection of *Homilies* and other works; and the period 1100-1200 is that of the language of Layamont, who wrote *Brut,* a poem on the kings of England. This poem, written during a transition period in which English and French were competing languages and completed a century and a half after the Norman Conquest, shows how little influence French held over English at the time. *Brut* contains about 56,000 lines and has scarcely 150 French words in it, and about 200 Latin words. It was not until at least 1362 that French words began to be incorporated into English in substantial numbers, and, by this time, the status of English was secure, while French was more and more passing out of daily use.

The rivalry among the three dialects lasted practically until 1400. The supremacy of the Midland dialect can be explained by a number of reasons: it was the dialect in which the *Old English Chronicle* was completed up to the year 1154 (the *Chronicle* was written in the Wessex dialect up to the time of the Norman Conquest). It was the dialect used by Henry III in his 1258 proclamation for summoning a parliament from all the counties of England. It was the dialect used by Wycliff, the first translator of the Bible into popular language, and Chaucer, a Londoner, who raised the literary quality of the dialect in an unparalleled way. The Midland dialect was the only one patronized by Caxton when he introduced printing into England, in 1477. The decadence of the Southern dialect was sudden; it practically ceased to be used for literary purposes after 1400. The Northern dialect, however, includes a distinguished line of poets at least until 1555, including James I of Scotland, Henryson, Dunbar, Gavin Douglas, and Lyndsay. Burns is perhaps the last great poet who used this dialect. The diachronic description of the status of English should ideally include not only the competitive relation with French but also the rivalries existing among varieties of English. I recognize that this may indeed be the topic for a separate paper in itself, and that the increased use of English by poets and writers in status promotion is well taken.

The status of English in England seems well established at the beginning of the fifteenth century, and there will be little surprise that no academy had assisted in the process since the first academy we are aware of, the Accademia della Crusca, was established in 1582, the French Academy in 1635, the Spanish in 1713, the Swedish in 1739. It is at this time, as Heath and Mandabach note, that an academy for the English language in England was proposed. The difference is that such a proposal found no support in England. Thus the effort toward language codification of preparing a dictionary was undertaken by an individual.

Concerning efforts toward language codification of English, it is also interesting to note that the first English grammar on record seems to be the grammar by William Bulokar published in 1586, that is, almost a century after the Spanish grammar by Nebrija. By 1586 there were grammars in at least 17 languages other than English, including a Tarascan grammar (1558), an Inca grammar (1560), a Nahuatl grammar (1578), and a Zapotec grammar (1578) (Rowe 1974). Perhaps once more the somewhat prescriptivistic nature of most grammars of the time accounts for the reluctance to regulate language choice suggested by Heath and Mandabach.

Efforts to establish a language academy also failed on the other side of the Atlantic, and history repeated itself with the efforts by Webster toward language codification.

Heath and Mandabach find important similarities between the unregulated, decentralized language policies in England and the U.S.A., at least until the nineteenth century, concerning the status of the English language. This is undoubtedly a point of great interest in the history of the status of the English language. The degree of liberalism implied by the authors may nonetheless sound a little too optimistic to some Cherokee speakers, whose ancestors were driven away from their homelands, or to Afro-American speakers and many other language minority groups, whose ancestors suffered unregulated and decentralized linguistic discrimination, although it is also true that many other language groups enjoyed liberties commensurate to their socio/political power. The fact that the linguistic liberalism that existed prior to the late nineteenth century was greater than the degree of tolerance existing today should not be construed to indicate that prior to the late nineteeth century there were no coercion or restrictions on the allocation of language functions of minority languages. The characterization of the present status of English is quite accurate: '[It] is based not only on the British custom of no legal restrictions on language, but also on an intolerance to linguistic diversity akin to that which has been prevalent throughout British history'.

Mackey advises us not to draw general theories based on Canada's case study on language policy. He attempts to elucidate the concept of language status and finds that there are several aspects of status: demographic, economic, cultural, social, political, and juridical, as the status of a language depends 'on the number of people using it, their relative wealth, the importance of what they produce and its dependence on language, their social cohesiveness, and the acceptance by others of their right to be different'. Mackey makes a number of interesting comparisons between the language-status situation of French in Canada and that of Spanish in the U.S.A. as he develops the aspects of language listed above. Important differences are found, first in the very foundation of the country by two founding peoples: the French, who settled in Quebec, and the English, who settled in Ontario, in nearly the same proportions; second, in the official status of French, now protected by an Official Language Act, whereas no similar act is to be found in the U.S.A., except sporadic local status gains and losses as in Miami, where Spanish reached the status of 'officially promoted language', to use Kloss's terminology, in 1973. In all other cases we actually observe a loss of official status, for example, of Spanish in New Mexico, French in Louisiana.

The role of language in education is clearly perceived by Mackey as the way in which family vernaculars are transformed into vehicles for scientific, cultural, and professional advancement. In the U.S.A., 'English holds the status' in education. The fact that Spanish-speaking students go to college does very little for the advancement of the status of the Spanish language, since most courses are offered in English. The recent efforts in bilingual education at lower educationcal levels do not seem so significant, particularly in view of the scarcity of qualified teachers. The situation in Quebec is different, as it has always had education in French at all levels.

The section on juridical status reveals contrasting policies in Canada and the U.S.A. One interesting difference is the difference between symbolic bilingualism and functional bilingualism, practically nonexistent in the U.S.A. and significantly widespread in Canada. Symbolic bilingualism implies a qualitative difference in language status. Mackey's account sounds somewhat less optimistic than Heath and Mandabach's regarding the degree of tolerance toward language diversity. Mackey rightfully points out, for instance, that the evolution of language status of Spanish in the U.S.A. is quite different from the situation of French in Canada, in spite of the fact that Spanish was also 'a colonial language which was official over much of the United States Southwest before that area fell under the jurisdiction of an English-speaking population'. He also refers to the fact that in the Guadalupe Hidalgo Treaty, Article 9 promises the people all the political rights of U.S. citizens in addition to free government. The article contrasts this with the fact that it took New Mexico 66 years to achieve statehood. The reason, which surfaced in the 1902 Congressional Committee, was clearly reluctance in Congress to create a state in which most citizens were able to function in Spanish only. Statehood was granted only after intense encouragement of English-speaking settlers changed the majority of the population toward English. This does not look like a good example of granting the rights promised in Article 9 of the Guadalupe Hidalgo Treaty (on this issue see also Kloss 1977).

Mackey raises a crucial question on language status toward the end of his paper.

Just as in Canada French is official from the Atlantic to the Pacific in all matters under federal jurisdiction, is it also conceivable that Spanish or any other language will be so recognized from coast to coast and from the Rio Grande to the Canadian border?

This is a complex question and Mackey decides to answer it in the form of a condition.

If indeed another language should become official in the U.S., it supposes two things: the right of the citizen to use the language of his choice, and the corresponding duty of the government official to use that same language. Should the government official fail to comply, the citizen may take the government to court for violating his rights.

This condition may be viewed by some as too strong, for it may not necessarily be a *duty* of the official to *use the same language,* but rather to provide someone who will assist the citizen in achieving full participation in the system. Whether or not such degree of officialization will ever be achieved for any minority language in the U.S. is a matter open to debate.

The main thrust of Daoust-Blais' paper is to describe the series of legislative decisions that led to the existing *Charter of the French Language,* or Bill 101, issued in 1977. This piece of legislation makes French the official language while restricting some of the language functions of English to specific activities without official status. Thus Bill 101 shifts a bilingual tradition in Quebec into a monolingual French official status, with specific objectives such as the francization of even business firms, and restrictions on the use of English in schools. This situation, according to Daoust-Blais, bypasses status planning and can be viewed as a type of what Laporte has called 'labor-market planning', in so far as it impacts the potential labor force who will be required to use French.

Now, it is true that restrictions imposed upon English use will have an impact on social planning. But this is the case with most status planning. The fact that such an impact upon social planning is achieved mainly through the reallocation of language functions should not prevent us from seeing that from the language-planning standpoint this is a form of status planning, although the changes that obtain are not exclusively linguistic.

The *Charter of the French Language* contains provisions concerning scientific and technological terminology, and in this sense relates to the corpus of the language. However, the main focus of Daoust-Blais' paper is on status planning, as it deals mostly with legislative decisions that affect the reallocation of language functions.

Chronologically, there are at least three different pieces of legislation that lead to the *Charter*:

1. The *Education Department Act* (Bill 85) (1968).
2. The *Act to Promote the French Language in Quebec* (Bill 63) (1969).
3. The *Official Language Act* (Bill 22) (1974).
4. The *Charter of the French Language* (Bill 101) (1977).

Each one of these pieces of legislation changes the status of French, starting with the support of bilingualism and ending up with the support of French monolingualism.

The *Education Department Act* was basically geared to protecting the right to choose the language of education of linguistic minorities in Quebec. It ensures that English-speaking children and immigrants into Quebec will acquire a working knowledge of French. This Bill never became a law, but it helped to promote other pieces of legislation. The *Act to Promote the French Language* in Quebec reaffirms the rights recognized in Bill 85 and adds the parents' right to choose either French or English as the language of education for their children.

The *Official Language Act* is perhaps the most important piece of legislation in the history of the status planning of French in Quebec. It is this piece of legislation that makes French the official language of Quebec, and declares that the French text of Quebec's statutes will prevail over the English version in controversial situations. Thus, this piece of legislation adopts a very straightforward defining characteristic as to what gives a language its official status. It allows for bilingualism but includes measures to ensure that professional bodies and public utilities offer their services in French and that all official texts be printed in French.

The *Charter of the French Language* replaces the *Official Language Act,* partially as the result of the triumph of the new *Parti Quebecois* in an election held less than a year before the passage of the *Charter* (1977). While the *Official Language Act* allows for bilingualism, the *Charter* does not, stating that only French texts of laws, decrees, and regulations are official. It also decrees that every public utility and business firm is required to obtain a 'francization certificate' that will secure for French the highest status in the company. Public or subsidized instruction at the elementary or secondary school levels should also be in French. Three supervisory boards are established to monitor the implementation of the *Charter.*

CORPUS-RELATED PAPERS

Kachru's paper focuses upon a subject of growing interest, to which existing literature has not paid the attention it deserves: the origin and codification of non-native varieties of English (Kachru, forthcoming). Kachru gives a series of conceptual definitions and offers a number of articulated distinctions that permit analysis of broader problems of language spread and the development of non-native varieties in general. The proliferation of such varieties 'is not unique to English; to a lesser degree Hindi, Persian, French, and Spanish have also developed such transplanted varieties'. Thus, there is more to be learned from this paper than the development and codification of varieties of English as a second language, although the situation of English is complex and interesting in its own right.

A question arises naturally: how do these varieties emerge? However, this is a complex question. First, we must understand that there are a number of different varieties that satisfy different functions. Thus, Kachru suggests that there are mutually nonexclusive ways in which these varieties can be analyzed: we may consider them 'in *acquisitional* terms, in *sociocultural* terms, in *motivational* terms'. Each of these categories can also be analyzed further.

An important addition to the distinction between English as a *second* language and English as a *foreign* language is that second-language varieties are *performance* varieties. This helps us to understand the differential roles that English has in education, public administration, and sociocultural contexts in countries of West Africa and South Asia, where English has been institutionalized as a second-language variety, and countries like Japan and Korea, where English is studied as a foreign language but is not an institutionalized variety.

It is also interesting to understand how specific varieties of English, native or non-native, become a model. This will increase our understanding of how non-native varieties emerge and take shape and will also enable us to understand what varieties should be taught, what should be the role of bidialectalism in education, and how certain varieties become standardized.

Kachru rightly suggests that in the absence of an academy, models of English do not obtain the authority of codification from a body of scholars or from government, and submits that in fact 'the sanctity of models of English stems more from social and attitudinal reasons than from reasons of authority', although he observes that 'these models are more widely violated than followed; they stand more for elitism than for authority'. In regards to the questions of what is a standard (or a model) for English and what model should be accepted, Kachru answers the first question skeptically, borrowing a response by Ward to this problem: 'no one can adequately define it, because such a thing does not exist'. He does not answer the second question. In fact, it is difficult to imagine what the answer to it should be.

In looking at the origin of non-native models (standard varieties) of English, Kachru points out not only that they are institutionalized but also that they possess specific characteristics, such as extended use in the sociolinguistic context, extended register and style range, and others, in spite of the fact that institutionalized varieties start as performance varieties. Non-native models, like any other variety, do not acquire status until they are recognized and accepted. Recognition is manifested in attitudinal terms and in the adaptation of teaching materials to the sociocultural context.

Non-native English varieties may have different functions: as a medium of instruction (instrumental function), as administrative and legal language (regulative function), as a means for intergroup communication (interpersonal function), as a medium of creative writing (imaginative function). These functions vary in *range* (sociocultural scope) and *depth* (degree of linguistic competence at various societal levels). The degree of nativization of a given variety is related to both range and depth.

Two properties can be attributed to non-native models, showing the way in which they differ from native models: they may be either 'deficient' or 'different'. The former refers to 'acquisitional and/or performance deficiency within the context in which English functions as L_2'. The latter refers to the structural features that distinguish an educated language variety from another educated variety. Kachru concludes that although non-native models of English are 'linguistically identifiable, geographically definable, and functionally valuable, they are still not necessarily attitudinally acceptable'.

The acceptance of a model depends on its users. . . . The users of non-native varieties also seem to pass through linguistic schizophrenia, and cannot make up their minds whether to accept a mythical non-native model or to recognize the local functional model.

The unique position of English in the international sphere as a language of cross-cultural communication poses demands and responsibilities on those who use it as their *first* language and those who use it as their *second* language, in regard to what Kachru calls the need for 'attitudinal readjustment' on the part of both groups. These readjustments include things such as dissociating English from the colonial past, not regarding its influence as evil, accepting literature produced by writers who use it as a second language, and the like. Two questions are raised in regard to the possibility of implementing such attitudinal readjustments; first, whether there is a coordinating agency which has a realistic view of the international and national functions of English, and, second, whether non-native users of English feel at the moment that agencies in the U.S.A. or England involved with the teaching and diffusion of English can offer any significant leadership. The answers to these questions are not simple, and they are certainly not the objective of Kachru's present paper.

Milán's paper focuses on codification issues of Spanish and considers four models: Nebrija's, which he calls classical; the Academy's, neoclassical; Bello's, functional; and Lenz's, critical. In fact, only the last two are models of New World Spanish; the first two are an important part of the historical background on codification of the Spanish language.

Nebrija's Grammar shows a structural parallelism with Latin. Nebrija had some explicit objectives, such as reducing variability in the written language; facilitating the learning of Spanish, the language of the most powerful empire at the time, by speakers of other languages; helping in the process of dissemination of the Catholic faith; and making it easier for Spaniards to learn Latin. Quite an ambitious project, as Milán points out.

Milán's paper sketches the historical antecedents of language policy in the New World and suggests that, although Spanish conquerors had a complete language plan, Nebrija's program to teach Spanish to the conquered population was not followed; in fact, there are indications to the contrary, in that Charles V and Phillip II as well

. . . favored religious instruction in the native language for the sake of expediency; this policy made the acquistion of the Amerindian languages by Spanish missionaries a priority; the teaching of Spanish to the conquered population became secondary; the Jesuits undertook the task of studying, learning, and even codifying these languages.

Examples of such codifications include the following: Maturino Gilberti,

Arte de la lēgua de Michuacā, Mexico 1558, on Tarascan; Domingo de Santo Tomás, *Gramática o arte de la lengua general de los indios de los reynos del Perú,* Valladolid 1560, on Inca; Alonso de Molina, *Arte de la lengua mexicana y castellana,* Mexico 1571, on Nahuatl and Spanish; Juan de Cordova, *Arte de la lengua zapoteca,* Mexico 1578, on Zapotec; Antonio de los Reyes, *Arte en lengua mixteca,* Mexico 1593, on Mixtec; Ludovico Bertonio, *Arte y gramatica mvy copiosa de la lengua aymara,* Rome 1603, on Aymara. Perhaps the titles of three grammars prepared by Luis de Valdivia are more explicit about their intended use: *Arte y gramática general de la lengva que corre en todo el reyno de Chile, con vn vocabulario, y confesionario . . . Ivntamente con la doctrina christiana y cathecismo del Concilio de Lima en español y dos traducciones del en la lengva de Chile,* Lima 1606, on Araucanian. The titles of his two other grammars, one on Millcayac, 1607, and another on Allentiac, 1607, are roughly equivalent (Rowe 1974). It was not until 1767, with the expulsion of the Jesuits, that their work in the area of native languages and religious instruction imparted in them came to an end. But religious instruction had to continue, and Charles III imposed Spanish in 1770. A number of other grammars were produced before 1770. Considering these events one may choose to disagree with Heath and Mandabach's implication (second paragraph of the section on the U.S. legacy) that the Castilian empire viewed language as an instrument of forced assimilation. Although, in general their contention seems to be true, it obviously needs clarification. The cultural differences were significant and so were the demographic ones; one may feel tempted to make a comparison among the most widely spoken Indian languages in the area conquered by the Castilian empire and the areas of North America. Compare, for example, the seven million speakers of Quechua located in Peru (5 million), Bolivia (1.5 million) and Ecuador (500,000), with about 150,000 speakers of Navajo, even though the Navajos have been privileged when compared with other American Indian groups (actually, there were only 7000 Navajos a century ago); or 1.5 million speakers of Aymara, or 1.75 million speakers of Guarani with 10,000 speakers of Cherokee, or 30,000 speakers of Cree. These figures may not be very telling if taken in isolation without considering other sociopolitical factors. There is at present as it probably was during the conquest, a larger number of Indian language speakers in the Spanish World and this is in no way a justification of some of the atrocities committed by Spanish conquerors.

Many of the Indian languages used in Spanish America today are spoken by significantly more speakers than there were at the time of the Spanish conquest, and the numbers are still increasing. There are certainly more speakers of Quechua today than there were in the sixteenth century. The thesis that in fact in many areas the new conquerors promoted or contributed to maintaining the native languages could be argued for. In the case of

Quechua, for instance, all the literature prior to the Spanish conquest was handed down orally. In spite of their great technological skills, the Incas never developed a writing system. The records they kept were through the *quipus* (Quechua for 'knot'), consisting of cords of different colors knotted in a very complicated way. The Spanish conquerors introduced the Roman alphabet and although spelling has not been standardized even today, it stimulated literary production in many of the native languages; the drama *Ollantay,* about the life of the Inca courts, is without any question the best-known work of ancient Quechua literature, written anonymously in 1470 and most probably preserved until now because of its transcription into the Roman alphabet. Perhaps the most outstanding example is the *Popul Vuh,* sacred book of the Mayas, which describes Maya history and traditions, beginning with the creation of the world. It was also written down in the Roman alphabet in the middle of the sixteenth century. In contradistinction to the Incas, the Mayas possessed a fully developed writing system, which has posed a formidable challenge to linguists and scholars since the sixteenth century.

The release of the Academia's *Gramática* in 1771, one year after Charles III's decree, was timely. The Spanish Academy was modeled after the French Academy and founded in 1713. In 1730 it produced a *Diccionario,* and 41 years later a *Gramática.* The influence of classical grammars is still apparent, as Milán points out, for instance in the articulated, though unrealistic, case system for Spanish, which follows the Latin cases: nominative, genitive, dative, accusative, ablative.

The first codification of Spanish in America was Andrés Bello's *Gramática,* in which he attempted to offer a grammar for Spanish speakers of the New World. His organismic and evolutionary approach provided the theoretical justification for a departure from the traditional grammar offered by the Academy. Milán gives a clear account of the warm reception Bello's *Grammar* received in America, and in Spain as well. He also describes its impact on future efforts toward codification. The last example discussed by Milán is Lenz's *La Oración y sus partes,* also highly respected in Spain and in America, although it never equalled Bello's codification in prestige or influence.

Keller maintains in his paper that there are four main areas of Spanish official-language use in the U.S.: voting, the mass media, the classroom, and the courtroom. He actually claims that Spanish enjoys 'official status' in these areas. He contends that in order to answer the question that serves as a title to his paper, it is necessary to know how language planners have actually worked, how they have chosen between different alternatives, and what they have recognized as their goals in all the areas in which Spanish has been used. The thrust of the paper is 'the corpus planning of Spanish as the language of instruction in the United States classroom'. More specifically, the issue discussed is which varieties of Spanish should be used in the classroom. Without any doubt, this is an issue of great importance but it seems more an issue related to 'selection of norm', to used Haugen's terminology, in education, i.e. language status rather than corpus.

Keller distinguishes three language policies in regard to language use in the classroom, advocated by three different groups: (1) those who exalt the use of the vernacular and denigrate 'world standard Spanish', (2) those who exalt 'world standard Spanish' and denigrate the use of the vernacular, and (3) those who foster bidialectalism by adding the 'world standard variety' to the vernacular the child brings into the classroom. Keller enlists himself in the third group.

He also reports that in 1974 there were eight types of Spanish used in bilingual-education programs. I will omit the details of the typology here. Keller himself seems to endorse what he describes as type 8 and says: 'a number of programs have been written in type 8, including one of my own'. This type uses 'controlled "world standard Spanish", using only language in the standard for which there are no alternate regionalisms or ethnic varieties'. This may scarcely sound to some readers like 'fostering bidialectalism', and, if it does, it needs further clarification. I can conceive of a form of bidialectalism (adding type 9 to the list) consisting of 'controlled' bidialectalism, i.e. restricted use of the vernacular specific to a region and restricted use of 'world standard Spanish' (whatever this may mean). Naturally, this may only be advisable in situations where linguistic homogeneity obtains, at least with regard to the use of the vernacular within the school population. But this is not always the case. A solution of these problems can hardly be universally valid. What is advisable in a given context may not necessarily be so in another sociolinguistic context, and what may be advisable for one group may not necessarily be so for another group.

Another source of puzzlement for some readers may be the understanding of the very concept of 'world standard Spanish'. What kind of standard variety is it?

Keller is right in saying that 'there are as yet no grammars of United States Spanish'. There is, however, a wealth of material related to language codification, including phonology, lexicon, and grammar (see Solé 1970; Teshner et al. 1975), which is relevant to a description of the corpus of United States Spanish(es).

A good portion of Keller's paper deals with status planning and claims that the status of U.S. Spanish is 'only partially realized, or is temporary, indirect, crypto, or quasi'. He claims that 'the official status of Spanish is a very recent phenomenon, traceable back to the Voting Rights Act of 1965 and the Bilingual Education Act of 1968'. One should be reminded of the official status of Spanish in New Mexico around 1860 and at least until the

Constitution of 1912, which ensured the publication of Spanish versions of the laws for the first 20 years of statehood and was then extended (see note 4 to my paper, this volume; Kloss 1977: 125-140). I personally do not believe that either the Voting Rights Act of 1965 or the Bilingual Education Act of 1968 give Spanish an official status. To say that U.S. Spanish 'has now acquired an official status in certain areas of public life, particularly suffrage and education' runs up against the use of the term 'official' in the sociolinguistic literature (Kloss 1977, especially p. 140; 1971, especially p. 259; Bell 1976; Dittmar 1976), and obscures the difference between officially sponsored, supported, or promoted, and official language proper.

Spolsky and Boomer offer a lucid account of the issues surrounding the modernization of Navajo. The study not only is informative concerning the development of Navajo but also casts some light upon a number of related sociolinguistic issues. Athabascan languages, as noted already by Sapir in 1921, have been less susceptible to language borrowing from the languages they have been in contact with, mainly Spanish and English, than other languages. The authors explain this fact on the basis of structural differences: 'it is not easy to fit an alien word into the grammar of Navajo'. Lexicostatistics reflect that increased contact with English results in increased borrowings: from fewer than 40 words borrowed from English in 1945 to over 500 in 1971, identified through taped interviews with children.

The essay provides a clear account of the different stages in language codification, from the work of missionaries in the preparation of an Ethnological Dictionary in 1910 and a Grammar in 1926, to the subsequent work by Fred Mitchel, and then by Sapir and many others. Sapir's work in orthography has been perhaps the most influential. The authors note that extensive contact began to occur in the 1940s with a number of Navajos leaving the Reservation to be drafted or to take jobs. Modernization brought roads to the area, and the mineral and energy resources found on the Reservation caused a number of changes. The Navajo Reservation, controlled by the federal government, has never had a formal, explicit language policy. In spite of the facts that the 1868 Treaty was published bilingually, that voting regulations were issued, that Congressional bills were passed and translated into Navajo, and even, more recently, that bilingual education programs were sponsored, Navajo is not an official language. All official writing, as the authors note, is English. Even more, the draft resolution requiring the recognition of the existence of written Navajo which is to be presented to the Navajo Tribal Council is still available only in English. Spolsky and Boomer characterize the situation as diglossic, with Navajo preferred for oral use and English being used in writing.

Modernization efforts began in the mid-1930s and included the areas of 'medicine, parliamentary procedure, modern transportation and communication systems, federal and chapter governments, legal proceedings, and agriculture'. Medical dictionaries were developed in 1941 and 1956 under the auspices of the Bureau of Indian Affairs. 'Both were intended to list and standardize common medical terms used in interpreting'.

In a more general area, it is interesting to note the role of interpreters in language modernization. The Navajo Tribal Council has conducted its affairs in Navajo. In order for the Bureau of Indian Affairs and other officers who do not speak Navajo to communicate with the Tribal Council, interpreters have been needed. Spolsky and Boomer point out that the 'Tribal Council interpreters have had a key role in creating terms to explain and describe the various concepts presented to BIA officials and other specialists who appear before the Council'. The Council has insisted that interpreters do not use borrowings, so they have been forced to participate in the process of coining new words. A number of linguists, notably Young and Morgan, were employed by the BIA as Navajo linguists and were involved in projects that required terminological development. More recently, the development of new terminology has come through four schools with bilingual programs. The Native American Materials Development Center, funded by the Office of Education, has been involved with some formal control of the terminological development. One of the prevailing problems in modernization of Navajo has been the lack of commitment that teachers showed in regard to the process itself. Regarding the need for standardization, Spolsky and Boomer note that, although there is lexical and phonological variation on the Reservation, it is difficult to track down. Language variation does not seem to make standardization an urgent need. The most significant efforts on standardization are related to the work of Young and Morgan, whose revised edition of their dictionary is forthcoming. The attitudes toward modernization among Navajos are still ambivalent, as they seem legitimately concerned with passing down to future generations the rich legacy of the Navajo language and culture, perhaps more concerned than with modernization. Clearly, corpus planning is a delicate job, as Fishman says in his essay. For,

Corpus planning is often conducted within a tension system of changing and conflicting loyalties, convictions, interests, values, and outlooks. On the one hand, authentification/indigenization of the new is admired and courted but, on the other hand, it is often too limiting in reality and too rural/old-fashioned in image to serve or to be acceptable if uncompromisingly pursued. Successful corpus planning, then, is a delicate balancing act, exposed to tensions and ongoing change.

IMPLEMENTATION IN CHINA AND THE SOVIET UNION

Two contributions to this volume describe eloquently the issues of implementation of language planning in the two Communist superpowers. Barnes offers an informative historical account of language policy decisions in China and the attempts at implementing them. He notes that the question of a national language program coincides with the first steps of the Ch'ing Dynasty to start a program of mass education in 1903. The plan was to require that the spoken language of Peking, used for a long time as the language in which state affairs were conducted, be incorporated into required courses in Chinese literature. It was intended as a policy more than as a mandate, and the implementation of the program was to be dependent on the initiative and resources of local educational agencies. The result, as could be expected, was not very significant, and the national language program did not survive the revolution. An interesting observation is that Pekingese did not enjoy great prestige *vis a vis* the other regional languages, in spite of its geographic and demographic dominance. The yardsticks for the relative prestige of the Chinese languages were more cultural than linguistic. Even the officers to be appointed in the imperial service had to possess thorough knowledge of the classical Confucian literature, which was evaluated through imperial examinations. As Barnes says,

A regional language derived and perpetuated its status as an oral medium through which universal wisdom was acquired. This status was enhanced by the fact that much of this venerated early literature could in some regional pronunciations still be intoned in an approximation of the original sound, while, in North Chinese, regular processes of phonological change had made this impossible.

North Chinese, *putonghua*, or Mandarin, has been taught for cross-language communication nationally since 1956. In the southeastern inland and coastal areas, the first language is a regional variety other than *putonghua*. Thus a national program is likely to achieve cross-language communication between the two-thirds of the Chinese who speak some form of *potonghua* as a national language, and the other third who speak a regional variety other than *putonghua*. As Barnes reports, dialectologists have pointed out that the main source of unintelligibility between *putonghua* and the other regional languages is phonological. Nevertheless, the differences are great. On the other hand, these languages 'share a common word order and lexicon'.

The conflicts of prestige that existed between regional languages older than North Chinese, which could claim to represent more authentically the culture of ancient teachers, took a significant turn in 1913, when the Ministry of Education of the new republican government at a conference recommended the promotion of North Chinese as a phonological basilect to which several other significant regional sounds would be incorporated. As is conceivable, this trend met with opposition at different stages. It was in 1956 that the People's Republic of China adopted a policy of nationwide use of North Chinese 'as the medium of education in schools and as the principal medium for communication among speakers of other regional languages'. Two significant documents were issued concerning the national language program: (1) 'The Directions of the State Council Regarding the Promotion of the Common Language' of 1956, and (2) 'The Directions of the Ministry of Education of the People's Republic of China Regarding the Promotion of the Common Language in Elementary, Middle, and Normal Schools' of 1955. Both of these documents formulate plans for the incorporation of *putonghua* in public activities. The language was also to become 'the medium of instruction for Chinese language and literature classes in grades one through seven in the fall of 1956'. A teacher-training center was established in Peking to assist teachers that were to begin to teach in *putonghua*. The government has not taken an authoritarian attitude in imposing *putonghua*; it has acted as a facilitator. Barnes points out that

Marxist theory nowithstanding, the *putonghua* policy does not necessarily imply the decay of the regional languages. . . ; what is interesting is to note the apparent acceptance in regional-language areas of the need for bilingual competence by those whose grandfathers, just two generations earlier, would have balked at the choice of North Chinese to fill this role.

The essay also contains a lucid description of the vicissitudes of the implementation of *pinyin*, or the Chinese phonetic alphabet. This has been, without any question, a major language-planning problem in China.

Lewis's paper elaborates on the last chapters of Lewis (1972) and offers a comprehensive account of the implementation of language planning in the Soviet Union. Lewis suggests that language planning in the Soviet Union does not escape from the requirements of the 'national plan'. He says that 'for the Soviet regime, language planning is important because it is part and parcel of the work of the Communist Party; language planning leads to literacy and so opens the way to an understanding of Marxism; Lenin maintained that an illiterate person is outside politics and has to be taught his ABC; without this there can be no politics'. However, although the supremacy of Russian is important, the Soviet Union has an undeniable multiethnic, multilingual tradition that goes back to the Tzarist administration and to some degree still prevails. Lewis points out that as early as 1802 the Tzarist administration of education 'gave two of its six Commissioners of education responsibility for the education of national minorities', and in 1869 Ilya Ulyanov, Lenin's father, was appointed as 'school inspector for the multiethnic province of Simbirsk in the educational district of Kazan; he introduced native languages as media of instruction into very many of the 450 schools', although, in fact, student enrollment in those schools was low.

Lewis reminds us of the combined social forces and changes that affect the Russian language favorably and the minority languages negatively, such as migration, geographic spread, etc. Thus, although multilingualism prevails in many areas, the Soviet Union, like France, has indulged in what he calls 'negative planning' and has sought to eliminate dialects in view of the fact that they may hinder political unification. In any event, there is little doubt that 'upward mobility, and particularly status within the ruling hierarchy, depends on the acquisition of Russian'. Language planning and sociopolitical ideology in the Soviet Union are closely intertwined. Literacy is a fundamental goal of language planning, and literacy requires a national language; this is defined as 'exemplifying the most highly developed, stable, and socially acceptable linguistic norms'.

Lewis describes the development and standardization of some regional languages and observes that 'perhaps the most important criterion used in code selection is the degree to which the proposed dialectal base represents the norms of the spoken language'. Basically, the same holds concerning language elaboration, since 'the historical development of a literary language, whether "folk" or "national", is characterized by closer approximation to colloquial forms'. Cencerning language modernization, a basic rule has been that 'the maximum possible should be made of native resources'. There has been some degree of ambivalence concerning borrowings from Russian by the local languages, particularly during the 1920s and 1930s, although more recently 'Russian influence is more pervasive . . . since the Russian language has become the accepted model as well as a main source of lexical enrichment'. Russian is nowadays the intermediary for non-Soviet words coming from English, French, or German.

Another problem of language planning in the Soviet Union is script reform, in view of the fact that the Soviet Union is not only a multilingual conglomerate but multigraphic as well, including at one time the Arabic and Cyrillic alphabets as the most important, and Latin and some Finno-Ungaric varieties, using modified Russian scripts, as secondary. The demand for script reform became widespread with the inauguration of the Soviet regime.

Schools and the mass media, according to Lewis, have been the main agencies involved in language planning. A significant increase in formal education, including literacy programs for adults, and concurrently a development of printing and publishing in Russian and in the national languages, took place between 1914 and 1969. A substantial increase in the level of literacy in both the national languages and Russian followed. However, Lewis reports, opportunities to use the skills available to those who are literate in non-Russian languages remain ambiguous.

CONCLUDING REMARKS

Much remains to be learned in language planning from case studies. However, I submit that it is time to change the scope of the discipline and produce a real change of paradigm. One of the issues surfacing in many of the essays gathered here is the fact that language-planning processes take place in a sociocultural context and respond to ideological considerations and loyalties; this goes for status and corpus planning as well. Notwithstanding, there seems to be no good reason why language planning should be less explanatory than other social sciences, whether history or economics, with a degree of ideological contamination at least equal to that of our discipline. Explanation should definitely be a methodological goal of future language planning, leading to a theory of language planning in which hypotheses will form a network of testable assumptions and a unified body of cumulative and objective knowledge open to future refinements.

The role of evaluation, as I see it, is crucial in this endeavor. The work of both Rubin and Jernudd is unquestionably laudable. What they do is both useful and important. The surveys on status-planning and corpus-planning activities they offer give a highly professional account of what has taken place in the field. However, I see evaluation not merely as restricted to a determination of the effectiveness of decisions according to some sort of decision-making prototheory, be it rational-comprehensive, disjointed-incrementalist, or mixed-scanning (Faludi 1973a; 1973b: 217 ff.); I see evaluation as a metatheoretical reflection through which hypotheses can be generated.

REFERENCES

Altoma, Salih J. (1970 [1974]), 'Language eduction in Arab countries and the role of the academies', *Current Trends in Linguistics* 6: 690-720. (Also reprinted in *Advances in Language Planning*, ed. by J.A. Fishman. The Hague, Mouton, 1974).

Bell, Roger T. (1976), *Sociolinguistics*. New York, St. Martin.

Dittmar, Norbert (1976), *A Critical Survey of Sociolinguistics, Theory and Application*. New York, St. Martin.

Faludi, Andreas (1973a), *Planning Theory*. Oxford, Pergamon.

_____, editor (1973b), *A Reader in Planning Theory*. Oxford, Pergamon.

Fellman, Jack (1974), 'The Academy of the Hebrew Language: its history, structure, and function', *International Journal of the Sociology of Language* 1: 95-103.

Fishman, Joshua A. (1973 [1974]), 'Language modernization and planning in comparison to other types of national modernization and planning', *Language in Society* 2 (1). (Also reprinted in *Advances in Language Planning*, ed. by J.A. Fishman. The Hague, Mouton, 1974).

——————, editor (1974), *Advances in Language Planning*. The Hague, Mouton.

Haugen, Einar (1966), 'Linguistics and language planning', in *Sociolinguistics*, ed. by William Bright. The Hague, Mouton.

—————— (1966 [1972]), 'Dialect, language, nation', in *The Ecology of Language*, ed. by E. Haugen, 237. Stanford, Calif., Stanford University Press.

—————— (1969 [1972]), 'Language planning, theory and practice', in *The Ecology of Language*, ed. by E. Haugen, 287. Stanford, Calif., Stanford University Press.

Kachru, Braj B., editor (forthcoming), *The Other Tongue: English Across Cultures*. Champaign, University of Illinois Press.

Kloss, Heinz (1969), *Research Possibilities on Group Bilingualism: A Report*. Quebec, International Center for Research on Bilingualism.

—————— (1971), 'Language rights of immigrant groups', *International Migration Review* 5 (2): 250-268.

—————— (1977), *The American Bilingual Tradition*. Rowley, Mass. Newbury House.

Kuhn, Thomas S. (1970 [1962]), *The Structure of Scientific Revolutions* (second revised edition). Chicago, Chicago University Press.

Lewis, Glyn E. (1972), *Multilingualism in the Soviet Union*. The Hague, Mouton.

Masterman, Margaret (1970), 'The nature of a paradigm', in *Criticism and the Growth of Knowledge*, ed. by Imre Lakatos and Alan Musgrave. Cambridge, Cambridge University Press.

Neustupny, Jiri V. (1970 [1974]), 'Basic types of treatment of language problems'. *Linguistic Communications* 1: 77-98. (Also reprinted in *Advances in Language Planning*, ed. by J.A. Fishman. The Hague, Mouton, 1974.

Rowe, John Howland (1974), 'Sixteenth and seventeenth century grammars', in *Studies in the History of Linguistics*, ed. by Dell Hymes. Bloomington, Indiana University Press.

Rubin, Joan (1971), 'Evaluation and language planning', in *Studies in the History of Linguistics*, ed. by Dell Hymes. Bloomington, Indiana University Press.

Rubin, Joan (1971), 'Evaluation and language planning', in *Can Language Be Planned?*, ed. by Joan Rubin and B. Hernudd. Honolulu, East-West Center and University of Hawaii Press.

—————— (1977), 'New insights into the nature of language change offered by language planning', in *Sociocultural Dimensions of Language Planning*, ed. by B.G. Blunt and M. Sanchez, 253-269. New York, Academic Press.

Sibayan, Bonifacio (1971 [1974]), 'Language policy, language engineering and literacy in the Philippines'. *Current Trends in Linguistics* 8. (Also reprinted in *Advances in Language Planning*, ed. by J.A. Fishman. The Hague, Mouton, 1974).

Solé, Carlos A. (1970), *Bibliografia sobre el español en America*. Washington, D.C., Georgetown University Press.

Teshner, R.V., G. Bills, and J.R. Craddock (1975), *Spanish and English of United States Hispanos, A Critical Annotated Linguistic Bibliography*. Virginia Center for Applied Linguistics.

PART ONE

Decision Making in Language Planning

CHARLES A. FERGUSON

Language Planning and Language Change*

Let me begin with a discussion of the case of Faeroese, with due apologies *Faeroese*
to Einar Haugen, analyst of the Faeroese situation (cf. Haugen 1979). My
decision to begin with this example comes from the fact that a distinguished
Danish scholar, a medievalist and philologist, spoke at Stanford on the rise
of Standard Faeroese. I found that colloquium an especially interesting
exercise. What the speaker had to say was interesting and the reaction of
American linguists in the audience was interesting.

I can say that the Faeroese example is an outstanding success story in
language planning. A small number of people, at most 40,000 of them, living
on a group of islands belonging to Denmark, in the middle of the North
Atlantic, about as far away from anyplace else as you can get, have evolved
their own standard written and spoken language which has extensive use
throughout the community. For example, Standard Faeroese is used as the
medium of instruction in the school system, and they publish lots of books
in it. The literacy rate in the Faeroe Islands is high, and when they publish a
new novel in Faeroese, they print at least 2,000 copies, which are promptly
snapped up. It is as though language planning had really succeeded, and, in
fact, if you think about it, it is hard to find comparable speech communities
elsewhere in the world — communities of such small size with their own well-
recognized standard languages which are in wide use and serve as the object
of language planning. I would like to look at that success story from two
points of view as an introduction to what I will be saying in general: first, the
history of the Faeroese speech community, and, second, the history of the
Faeroese language.

What happened in the sociolinguistic history of the Faeroe Islands? How
did the sociogeographic distribution and functional allocation of different
languages and varieties of language change over time? First, a group of Norse-

* This talk is dedicated to William G. Moulton. I had wanted to include a more formal
paper of this same title in the Festschrift prepared for him but was unable to complete
it in time. The talk covers some of the same ground as the intended paper, and I am
pleased to be able in this way to offer him my personal appreciation.

men came and settled there, speaking a variety of the common Scandinavian language called Old Norse or Old Icelandic. After a long time Faeroese became linguistically quite separate from the other varieties of the language, simply because it was communicatively isolated for such a long period; that is, it came to be its own kind of Old Norse or Old Scandinavian. Then, of course, Christianity came and brought with it Latin as the language of the Church and of education. Eventually came the Reformation and some political changes, and then Danish replaced Latin. Danish came to be the language of education and of the Church.

For a long time after that, it was unthinkable to almost anyone in the Faeroe Islands for Faeroese to be the written language, the medium of instruction in schools, or even in any significant sense a national language. It was obvious that Danish filled those roles. But eventually some people got the idea — some Faeroese and some enthusiastic young Danes — that Faeroese could be made into a 'real' language and extended to other purposes. Someone devised a way to write the language, and gradually Danish came to be used somewhat less and Faeroese somewhat more.

Nowadays the Faeroese language is used throughout the society, although everyone studies Danish as a subject in school; and if they want to go to a university, it is taken for granted that they will go to a university in Denmark (or possibly Norway), where they will need to know Danish. So Danish still has a role in the society but a very different one from what it used to be. And Icelandic now has a special role too, because in recent times the Faeroese have discovered that Icelandic is the language most like theirs. If the Faeroese want to borrow words, for example to supply particular technical terms, they can now turn to Icelandic instead of Danish as a source and find words that are not so Danish-sounding and that also sound Faeroese rather than international.

The only point that I want to make here is that over a period of 1,000 years or more the distribution of functions of different languages in the Faeroe Islands has changed considerably. First was Old Norse, which became Faeroese; next there was Latin with Faeroese; Danish gradually replaced Latin; and finally Faeroese took over most of the functions of Danish, and Icelandic was added in a very limited function.

Now let us turn to the history of the language itself. Faeroese, like all other languages, developed dialect variations, and the first time a text in Faeroese (other than old ballads) was written down, someone translated the Gospel of Matthew into Southern Faeroese. That turned out to be a mistake. Most people thought that Southern Faeroese — the language of 'those backward people down in the southern part' — could not possibly be used for anything serious like the Word of God. Actually, most people apparently felt that the Word of God really came in Danish, but if it had to be in Faeroese it should not be in Southern Faeroese. Then as time passed someone else, more wisely, picked the kind of Faeroese spoken in a more central area — what can be called the capital. (The 'capital', however, probably never had more than 500 residents until very recent times).

People accepted the new written variety more willingly and thus they began the process of standardization whereby a particular form of the language became accepted throughout the Faeroe Islands as a supradialectal norm. During the standardization process the question of what spelling to use repeatedly arose, a relatively etymological spelling versus a more phonetic spelling. Eventually the question was resolved and people agreed on an orthography. Then there was the question of what to do for new terminology in the processes of elaboration and modernization: where should they get suitable loan words and how should native terms be coined? Once again decisions were made, in general, to reject certain sources of loan words, to make up certain kinds of native Faeroese ones. Sometimes there have been exceptions to the general policies. For example, 'sad to say' (as the Danish scholar put it), the word for 'telephone' is *telefon*, pronounced Faeroese style, not a made-up Faeroese word, perhaps based on an Icelandic source since the Icelanders have a pure Icelandic word for 'telephone'. The only point that I want to make is that all these problems were settled one way or another, so that one particular variety of the language was extended and accepted, an orthography was adopted, and ways of enriching or elaborating the vocabulary and forms of discourse were established.

Language planning was definitely involved. These changes did not just happen by chance, 'naturally', without conscious intervention. Some of the change was unconscious, no doubt, but there were individuals who said, 'let's do this' or 'let's do that'. Institutions were involved, decisions were made in Denmark and in the Faeroes, in churches and in schools, and so on. At every stage there was language planning and the language planning had some effect. That is, it constitutes a part of the explanation of what happened.

As I said, it is a success story for language planning. Many of us tend to think in those terms, but at the Stanford colloquium I mentioned earlier, I noticed that my fellow American linguists were squirming. Sometimes they just sat still, but at other times you could actually see them squirm. One of the troubles was that the lecturer kept saying, in effect, 'and so then people made the decision to change the language in such and such a way, and then they changed it'. American linguistis cringe at that. And then, what is more, the Danish scholar would occasionally say something which revealed his own point of ivew. Once he commented that it was fortunate that a particular kind of spelling went out of favor. A little bit later he said 'and you realize, with a language that has case endings like that, you can do a better job of planning'. Every time he made a personal evaluative comment like these, the American linguistis would squirm. I thought that gave a good indication of the problems American linguists have in relating language planning to language change. By a nice coincidence, all the American linguists present at that meeting had attended, several weeks before, an international conference on historical linguistics (cf. Traugott et al. 1980) at which about 60 papers were given. Not a single paper mentioned language planning, and the American linguists felt at home in that kind of setting, whereas they did not feel at home in a setting which mentioned planning in connection with change.

Efforts devoted to language planning and studies of language-planning processes have generally been well separated from systematic studies of language change.[1] In fact, language planners are typically impatient with attempts to understand processes of change or even to study the effects of planning. And, on the other hand, the strong tradition of the study of language change in nineteenth- and twentieth-century linguistics has typically distrusted language planning or assumed that language-planning efforts were irrelevant to the fundamental processes of change. Yet it must be clear to even the most casual students of either phenomenon, if they think directly about the question, that language planning is useless if it does not have an effect on language change, and that a theory of language change is incomplete if it does not allow for the possible influence of language planning. That is really the point of what I want to say. In the remarks that I make, however, I want to make that point again and again from two perspectives, both of them familiar to this group.

One is the perspective of change and planning in a speech community, and the other is the perspective of change and planning in language itself. Let me give some examples, in case Faeroese has not been enough. Change has taken place in the language situation in the English-speaking world in many ways over the centuries. The most obvious example, the one that comes to mind to most of us, is the period of the fourteenth to sixteenth centuries, when the distribution of languages in the British Isles changed drastically. At the beginning of that period English was the ordinary conversational language, French was the language of Parliament and the courts, and Latin was the language of education, the church, and science. By the end of that period, English was the language of conversation, the courts, Parliament, and most education; Latin still had a small but honored place in education and science, and the only remnants of the use of French were the numerous French expressions in the language of the law (Jones 1966). So over a period of several centuries a great change came about in the allocation of different language varieties in that speech community.

A second example of change in the language situation is the twentieth-century shift in the functional allocation of language varieties in the Chinese-speaking world. Early in the century, say around 1920, an archaic form of literary Chinese, often called *wenli,* was the normal variety used in writing, in contrast with the usual spoken form of the language. Spoken Chinese shows deep dialect cleavages, but a variety of spoken Mandarin based on North Chinese dialects, particularly educated Peking usage, was already in wide use as a kind of spoken lingua franca. The written language, also originally based on the Chinese of Peking, was even more widely recognized as the norm of written communication throughout China, although it was usually read with the pronunciation of the local dialect or in a special local traditional pronunciation. Major local varieties such as Cantonese were sometimes used as media of instruction in the schools.

By the end of the 1970s, the use of *wenli* has retreated to a small fraction of its former distribution, and a kind of Mandarin referred to as *Putonghua* ('common speech') is widely used for both spoken and written purposes. While written Chinese is often still read with local dialect phonology, the traditional local reading pronunciations are rapidly disappearing and the use of local dialects in the schools has decreased markedly. *Putonghua* has spread extensively as the national language, both spoken and written, being superposed on the everyday spoken Chinese of those areas which do not have North Chinese dialects as mother tongues. Thus, in the space of 50 years, a radical change has come about in the functional allocation of language varieties in China: not only is there a much higher proportion of literacy in the population, but one commonly written variety has lost functional ground and one commonly spoken variety has gained.

These are typical examples of what is happening over and over again in speech communities, and I chose them because they are so typical and familiar. Yet linguists interested in language change have not examined this kind of change very systematically, fundamental though it is to understanding the facts of language.

The other perspective of language change is the study of the structure of the language or language variety itself. Let me again give two examples: (1) in Middle English and continuing through the present day, there has been a dramatic change in the organization of the English vowel system, that is, the old 'e's became 'i's, and the old 'a's became 'e's, and so on − the incredible, fascination phenomenon called the 'great vowels shift'. The shift is still continuing, and the cycle has not run its course. These structural changes and their present-day synchronic echoes have been the subject of many phonological studies (e.g. Chomsky and Halle 1968; Wolfe 1977). A tremendous influx of French loan words into English changed the whole nature of the English vocabulary, so that within a relatively short period (a couple of centuries) the English lexicon was inundated with a different kind of vocabulary, which irreversibly altered some of the phonological and morphosyntactic characteristics of the language.

Once again, such processes of change have to be understood; they occur in all languages. One of the most general classifications of language change is a three-fold division which dates back to the neogrammarians of the nineteenth century and was widely accepted among American linguists of the Bloomfiled tradition. All changes are (a) exceptionless sound laws making their way through the language, or (b) borrowings either from another language or from another dialect in the same language, or (c) analogical new formations. This classification has proved of value as a guide for research and a stimulating framework for analysis, but it has many shortcomings. Even if modified to include syntactic laws and such notions as 'conspiracies' of different changes which lead to similiar outcomes, the 'drift' of related languages changing in the same ways for long periods of time, and the development of 'areal' characteristics, the classification is still inadequate, because most changes seem to involve all three aspects and because it gives no understanding of the processes of change in actual language behavior.

Labov's classification (1972) of 'changes from above' and 'changes from below' is better, especially as it is fleshed out with detailed descriptions of actual trajectories of change. But this has mostly been applied only to phonological as opposed to lexical, syntactic, orthographic, or other changes. Other classifications that are better for phonology than for syntax, lexicon, etc., are Hoenigswald's classification (1960) by outcomes: split, merger, replacement, etc., and Kiparsky's simplification vs. addition of rules (1968).

What is probably needed is not a small exhaustive list of nonoverlapping categories of changes but rather an identification of basic tendencies which are operative in all changes, and then careful delineation of many specific changes in terms of these tendencies, so that general principles of classification and explanation can be found. For example, some time ago I hazarded an identification of tendencies of that sort and I named three types: physiological constraints, which are based on perceptual and articulatory characteristics of human beings; cognitive processes, based on natural human processes of memory, comparison, classifcation, and the like; and social processes, that is tendencies related to human social behavior and communicative processes in general (Ferguson 1975). I am only trying to use this classification as an example. With this approach, every change is assumed to have the possibilities of involving all three types of tendencies, and more specifically, it is assumed that in the short term, social tendencies are able to outweigh the other two, but in the long term, the other so-called natural changes will tend to win out. Also, with this approach it is assumed that in any change, conflicting tendencies of the same type may be operative, that some tendencies may be more powerful than others, and that in the long term, under different circumstances and in different languages, there will be a significantly larger number of some outcomes, so-called 'universals', rather than others.

Status/corp

I have been talking about types of language change, that is, changes in allocation of language functions in the speech community and changes in the structure of language itself, both of which, it seems to me, are the proper object of study of linguists even though linguists customarily look much more at the second. How about types of language planning? They can be looked at from the same two perspectives. You can plan changes in the functions or the use of different varieties within the speech community, and you can plan changes in the structure of the language or language variety itself. These are, of course, the familiar categories of language planners that have been mentioned in this volume, essentially what we call 'status planning' and 'corpus planning', or other similar names. Thus far, the former has received less attention from language planners than the second.

U.S. Jews

Let's now take some examples of language changes of the two types that are taking place right now in American language behavior. Let's take a case of change in use of language varieties, the changes in allocation of languages among American Jews. In using this example I must make due apologies to Joshua Fishman, the outstanding expert in this field. Some time ago English was used for certain purposes by the Jewish community; Yiddish was used for other purposes; and Hebrew had its special functions; as did various other Jewish languages. And now, several decades later, there is a very different distribution of those three. Yiddish, on the whole, is used less and for somewhat different purposes. English is used more and for more purposes, and Hebrew is used, probably, somewhat more, but for different purposes, and different kinds of Hebrew are used. This set of changes can be talked about in terms of various social factors and historical events, but I specifically want to ask, What does language planning have to do with it?

We have to admit right away, I think, that most of these changes did not result in any direct way from language planning, but we also have to recognize that there was an important language-planning component in these changes. To take the most obvious one: the fact that there is a different pronunciation of Hebrew used by many Jews today in America has resulted from the influence of the modern Israeli pronunciation of Hebrew, and that pronunciation was a result, essentially, of language planning. In fact, if we want an example of language planning, the best example in the world is the existence of modern Hebrew as a mother tongue. When my linguist friends tell me you can't even change a case ending by language planning — that language structure is unconscious and built in — I can always say, 'How about the whole language that got planned and came into existence as a mother tongue, which hadn't been there as a mother tongue for centuries before?'

The changes in the use of Yiddish and English were to a great extent part of the general Americanization process of American Jewry, whereby many features of Eastern European Jewish life were replaced by American counterparts — in this case American English. The changes that took place in Yiddish pronunciation, grammar, and vocabulary, however, resulted not only from the natural dialect leveling of immigrants from different places of origin but also from conscious efforts of standardization and modernization. (Fishman 1965).

Let's take another example of change in the functional allocation of varieties of language in the overall — — — speech community, the disappearance or replacement of the religious register in American English. For over 100 years, there was a well-established way of speaking religiously, in public, in America. It did not much matter whether Catholics, Jews, Protestants, or some other group were speaking. You said 'thou' to the Deity, there were certain turns of phrase and an extensive set of different forms and details of pronunciation, and a different lexicon. If you turned on the radio, you only had to hear a sentence to know that religious talking was in progress. The language revealed that, even if the listener could not fully understand the content. Then, in the last 15 years, there has been a very rapid change, so that now most of the major church bodies have changed their worship books from 'thou' to 'you'. Many constructions that were common in religious languages have rather suddenly gone out of use, to be replaced by constructions nearer to ordinary conversation and writing. One could look at all kinds of influences that have led to this and we could talk a great deal about the nature of the changes, but I want to point out here the element of language planning that is involved.

Many religious denominations, responding in part to changes already begun, have spent hours and hours of committee work trying to figure out exactly how the language use should be changed; exactly how prayers and nymns should be reworded; and we see this happening throughout public use of the religious register in American English. There has been a substantial change in the pattern of the distribution of registers and the characteristics of the religious register. In fact, a new religious register of American English seems to be emerging. Within a few years we will probably see the restabilization of a religious register, with a different functional distribution and different characteristics. In some instances the outcome will be in line with the conscious planning of religious institutions and in other instances it will be different, but language planning will have been part of the complex of language factors leading to the changed patterns of language use.

Now let us turn briefly to examples of change in language structure, specifically in American English. Among the various vowel changes underway, the tensing of short 'a' has been studied in the greatest detail (cf. Labov et al. 1972) and will do nicely. In many parts of the United States the common low front vowel of 'bad' and hundreds of other words is getting longer, higher (i.e. toward the 'e' of 'bed'), 'tenser', and more diphthongal. This change, which is also in process in other parts of the English-speaking world (Ferguson 1980), is proceeding along the course of a typical 'change from below' (Labov 1972). The new pronunciation is more frequent in casual speech than in careful speech, and more frequent in working-class speech than in upper-middle-class speech.

Such changes in progress are shown by alternative pronunciations that are differently evaluated, such as the pronunciations [bæd] and [bɛəd] in Philadelphia. For some respondents the [æ] pronunciation will seem natural or 'correct' and the [ɛə] pronunciation somewhat uneducated or unpleasant; for others the [æ] will seems affected or school-teacherish and the [ɛə] natural. In fact, there is a complex web of evaluations for such alternatives, a web in which regional, social, and idiosyncratic factors have an effect. This web is largely unconscious and tappable only by indirect means — and the relationship between the users' evaluations and thier actual behavior is not as direct as might be expected — but some part is conscious and this part can play a role in the shifting preference for alternatives which constitutes language change.

Thus, in the [æ]   [ɛə] variation of *bad* and the short-'a' words, the choice of [æ] tends to go along with evaluations of its correctness, supra-dialectal neutrality, formality, and carefulness, as opposed to the choice of [ɛə] which serves to mark one's regional or social identity and to represent an unstudied naturalness of expression and a resistance to bookish correction. Thus a shift toward greater frequency of [bæd] than [bɛəd] on the part of a given speaker or social group of speakers in the Philadelphia area will tend to reflect such phenomena as an increased upward social mobility orientation, a de-identification with Philadelphia norms of speech, or the effectiveness of a particular model of speech such as that of a local teacher or leader whose pronunciation has a greater proportion of [æ] to [ɛə].

The present distribution of [æ] and [ɛə] in Philadelphia English represents the current stage of a highly complex series of vowel changes in the short-'a' area: raising, fronting, lengthening, and breaking processes which began at least as far back as the Anglo-Frisian 'brightening' but apparently began to assume their complex modern manifestation in the seventeenth century (Lass 1976: 122). The most obvious pattern of change over long periods of time is the spreading of [ɛə] values to new environments, the raising of the [ɛə] values, and at some point in the process the phonemic split of original short-'a' into [æ] and [ɛə]. Over short periods of time the most obvious patterns of change are the correcting, 'upward' shift of [ɛə] to [æ] and the adjustments in either direction by speakers whose sociolinguistic identity is shifting (e.g. New Yorkers moving into the Philadelphia area, cf. Payne 1976).[2] The language users' evaluations of the laternative phonetic values play a role in these patterns of change, and on occasion the evaluations may be made explicit and may even be dealt with by overt implementations of language planning. Thus, a given school district may decide to include among its goals the 'improvement' of pronunciation of words such as 'bad', 'ask', 'half', or the removal of a New York accent. The power of a deliberate orthographic change here could be quite dramatic; if under conditions of societal stress a politicized decision were taken to use a special symbol for [ɛə] in the spelling of a newly promulgated norm of English pronunciation, the effects on pronunciation, although unpredictable in nature and extent, given our present understanding of such processes of change, could be substantial.

As a second example of language change in American English we can think of the multitude of lexical innovations taking place in our speech. Let me take just two instance: the increased use of 'go' to mean 'say' and the increased use of 'black' in place of 'negro' and 'colored'. I choose these two because they are very different in their paths of diffusion and in their relation to conscious planning. The new use of 'go' is clearly an extension of the childish use in reference to inanimate objects and animals: 'How does the whistle go?' 'How does the kitty go?' for 'What noise or sound does the whistle or the cat make?' The use of 'go' in reference to human communication ('Then he went "———"; then I went "———" ') is now widespread among American teenagers, where the innovation seems to have taken place, and is apparently spreading into other sectors of the population. This change seems to be completely unconscious and unplanned, and it is likely to meet resistance from upholders of standard norms. The use of 'Black', however, is just as clearly conscious and planned. Some individuals and groups expressed a strong preference for this alternative, and both the preference and its rationale appeared in print in many places as a definite attempt to change this feature of American English. The change spread rapidly in the mass media and among groups sympathetic to the rationale offered. It has now become the most used of the three alternatives. The effect of planning on change was clear and powerful even though the initial institutional agency of change was neither a language academy nor a parliament.

Let me point out now the need for research on the relationship between language planning and language change. In fact, let me suggest three obvious projects for research here in the United States. First, graphization of American Indian languages. In a number of places in the United States groups of Indians have decided to use their ancestral spoken language in written form or are considering such a change in their patterns of language use. This is a perfect chance to observe with care the processes of conscious language planning and to try to relate the outcomes to the hundred-and-one variables involved. If we make careful studies during the next few years we will have a wonderful set of data to help us understand the process of introducing writing into a community.

Second, the standardization of Spanish in the United States. Spanish is the second most important language in this country, and it is attaining increased national prominence. It seems to me inevitable not only that there will be some dialect leveling among Puerto Rican, Chicano, and other Hispanic groups, but also that some individuals and groups will make conscious efforts at standardization. I realize that I am treading on dangerous ground, since many would be opposed to any attempt to dilute or change Puerto Rican identity in Spanish. I am not taking sides, but simply pointing to the availability of this very promising area of study to help us understand the still largely mysterious processes of language standardization.

Third, the 'plain English' movement in the United States. In government, banks, insurance companies, and elsewhere, a movement to increase the comprehensibility of English in certain contexts is gaining force and resulting in the rewriting and simplification of certain kinds of documents. Investigation of the origins, course, and outcome of this movement would be very revealing of the social matrix and linguistic effects of language-planning processes.

I do not wish to conclude on the note that further disinterested research is needed. I prefer to point to the need for active language planning. Even in our present state of ignorance of the complex relationship between language planning and language change, I want to emphasize the usefulness of two strategies. One is to undertake language-planning activities now when we perceive a significant language problem and then to monitor our actions and the changes that seem to result from them. The other is to search for recent and documentable instances of language planning and then to interpret the apparent results and apply them to other planning tasks. In both cases we will learn directly about the processes of planning and change. I am happy to see that many of the papers in this volume are devoted to these two strategies.

NOTES

1. There are, of course, exceptions to this general statement, such as Rubin 1977, which is a spirited attempt to persuade students of language change that language planning may affect outcomes of language variation.
2. For some groups entering the Philadelphia scene, the use of the shifted pronunciations may mark upward social mobility, as when Puerto Ricans select them in preference to pronunciations reflecting Puerto Rican Spanish or vernacular black English identity (Poplack 1978).

REFERENCES

Chomsky, N., and M. Halle (1968), *The Sound Pattern of English*. New York, Harper & Row.

Ferguson, C.A. (1975), 'Universal tendencies and "normal" nasality', in *Nasalfest,* ed. by Gerguson, Hyman, and Ohala, 175-196. Stanford, Calif., Stanford University Department of Linguistics.

_____(1980), 'Long "short *a*" in Australia and America'. Paper presented at the Linguistics Seminar, Monash University.

Fishman, J.A. (1965), *Yiddish in America; Socio-Linguistic Description and Analysis.* Bloomington, Indiana University Press.

Haugen, E. (1979), 'Language ecology and the case of Faroese,' in *Linguistic Method; Essays in Honor of H. Penzl*, ed. by Rauch and Carr, 183-197. The Hague, Mouton.

Hoenigswald, H. (1960), *Language Change and Linguistic Reconstruction.* Chicago, University of Chicago Press.

Jones, R.F. (1966), *The Triumph of English.* Stanford, Calif., Stanford University Press.

Kiparsky, P. (1968), 'Linguistic universals and linguistic change', in *Universals in Linguistic Theory*, ed. by Bacj and Harms, 170-202. New York, Holt, Rinehart & Winston.

Labov, W. (1972), *Sociolinguistic Patterns.* Philadelphia, University of Pennsylvania Press.

_____, M. Yaeger, and R. Steiner (1972), *A Quantitative Study of Sound Change in Progress.* Philadelphia, University of Pennsylvania Press.

Lass, R. (1976), 'What kind of vowel was Middle English /a/?', in *English Phonology and Phonological Theory*, 105-134. Cambridge, Cambridge University Press.

Payne, A. (1976), 'The acquistion of the phonological system of a second dialect'. Unpublished Ph.D. dissertation, University of Pennsylvania.

Poplack, S. (1978), 'On dialect acquistion and communicative competence: the case for Puerto Rican bilinguals', *Language in Society* 7: 89-103.

Rubin, J. (1977), 'New insights into the nature of language change offered by language planning', in *Sociocultural Dimensions of Language Change*, ed. by B.G. Blount and M. Sanches, 253-269. New York, Academic Press.

Traugott, E., R. Labrun, and S. Shepherd, editors (1980), *Papers from the Fourth International Congress of Historical Linguistics.* Amsterdam, John Benjamins.

Wolfe, P.M. (1977), *Linguistic Change and the Great Vowel Shift in English.* Berkeley, University of California Press.

JUAN COBARRUBIAS

Ethical Issues in Status Planning*

In this article I will attempt to show that certain tasks of language planners, language policy makers, educators, legislators, and others involved in changing the status of a language or language variety are not philosophically neutral. Changing the status of a language implies the allocation or reallocation of the functions of such language in a speech community. Language functions may change as a result of a spontaneous historical process or as a result of decisions involving concerted or planned changes. It is particularly the latter that raise ethical issues not dealt with, to my knowledge, either in the socilinguistic discussions or in the philosophical literature. I believe it is time that we start talking about such issues and their repercussions.

The first section of the paper is devoted to an exploration of the distinction between corpus planning and status planning. A review of the pioneer analyses by Kloss and Stewart related to language status is presented. The second part contains a discussion of the concepts of language function and language status. The concept of ethoglossia, as referring to the communicative character or strength of a language, is introduced in this section to facilitate subsequent discussions on language rights. Brief accounts of the difference between ethoglossia and language status and of their relation with other concepts such as diglossia and diglossia with or without bilingualism are given. The role of the language planners and agencies involved in language policy is outlined before the issue of language rights is taken up. An attempt is made to distinguish language rights from other types of rights. Language rights are also distinguished from claims to retaining certain language functions within a speech community. It is suggested that the retention of certain language functions cannot be guaranteed without specific legislation. The issuing of specific legislation should ideally follow certain ethical criteria, e.g. universalizability, reversibility. In turn, the ethical criteria a given society is willing to adopt seem to depend upon certain ideologies the group in control wishes to endorse. Language-status planning is ultimately contingent upon such ideologies.

*This article is dedicated to my colleagues John Callan and Bernard Duffy.

THE CORPUS VS. STATUS PLANNING DISTINCTION

The distinction between 'corpus planning' and 'status planning' was first introduced by H. Kloss (1969) to differentiate two basic aspects of language planning, the former referring to changes in structure, vocabulary, morphology, or spelling, or even to the adoption of a new script. In other words, 'these innovations have one thing in common, that they modify the nature of the language itself, changing its corpus as it were'. On the other hand, 'status planning' is concerned not so much with chaning the structure or corpus of the language but rather with its standing with respect to other languages or to the language needs of a national government.

'Those concerned with this type of language planning take the corpus of the language for granted; they are primarilly interested in the status of the language, whether it is satisfactory as it is or whether it should be lowered or raised'.

This distinction, like other well-known distinctions in linguistics (e.g. *langue* vs. *parole,* competence vs. performance), is not without its problems and has been occasionally criticized.[1] However, it has heuristic value, and for our purposes here it is convenient insofar as it permits us to isolate an area of language planning from which a number of ethical issues arise. Basically, the distinction, as it was first presented, amounts to a distinction between linguistic innovations that relate to the *allocation of language functions* of a language or of a language variety in a given speech community (status planning) and linguistic innovations that relate to the *structure* of a language or of a language variety (corpus planning). The allocation of language functions responds generally to extralinguistic factors that may often result in or necessitate changes in the corpus of a language in order for it to fulfill a specific function or a number of functions. However, in most instances, decisions that result in allocation or reallocation of functions are prior to decisions pertaining to changes in the corpus. By and large, linguists have paid more attention to changes in the corpus than they have to changes in the status of a language. This is one more reason why the distinction between 'status planning' and 'corpus planning' is important. More needs to be done on the study of factors that produce innovations in the allocation of language functions. We need to know more about the extralinguistic variables that reduce or eliminate language conflicts by making it possible or necessary for a language variety to be adopted as a regional official language, as a joint official language, or as the sole official language in a nation; or by increasing the scope of communication of a language variety or by adopting a language variety as a language of instruction at a specific stage of the education process; or by allocating or reallocating specific functions, such as religious, legal, etc., to a language variety. It must be noted that Kloss's presentation of the distinction in the 1969 monograph is rough and sketchy. It is also fair to say that the concept of 'language status' is a complex and elusive one. The status of a specific language is context-dependent and changes through time, and the functions of a language can be looked at from a number of different perspectives.

In 1968 Kloss dealt marginally with the concept of language status while attempting to establish a language-nation typology.[2] Kloss recognizes four categories that relate to language status: (1) the origin of the language used officially with respect to the speech community; (2) the developmental status of a language; (3) the juridical status with respect to the speech community; and (4) the ratio of users of a language to total population.

First, with regard to the origin of the language used officially, we may find that the national official language is an 'indigenous language', i.e. a language 'spoken natively by a sizeable segment of the population', or an 'imported language'. This determines in turn that the state is *endoglossic* if the national official language is an indigenous language, e.g. the United Kingdom with English as the national official language (although an endoglossic state may include indigenous linguistic minorities, such as the Welsh and the Gaelic-speaking Scots). An *exoglossic* state uses an imported language as the national official language, e.g. Ghana, Nigeria. Most exoglossic states are highly heterogeneous linguistically, with a large number of nonstandard indigenous languages often related to tribal groups and deemed unfit for the functions of modern government. Under these circumstances an excolonial language is often chosen as the national official language, although regional official status may be granted to one or more local languages. *Mixed states* from a separate category and are partially exoglossic or partially endoglossic. Mixed states may also be reclassified into a number of subcategories, depending upon what languages are indigenous, what language or languages are official, and how many languages are used in a given speech community.

Second, Kloss distinguishes six types of language status, according to what he labels 'development' or degree of 'elaboration' of the language:

1. A fully modernized, mature, standard language, through which modern scientific and technological knowledge can be imparted at both the secondary school and the college level, e.g. English, French, Spanish.

2. A small-group standard language, which, due to the relatively small number of users, has a limited scope of interaction and communication, e.g. Faroese.

3. An archaic standard language, which flourished prior to industrial development and is thus unfit for the teaching of modern science and technology, e.g. Latin, classical Greek, Hebrew, Sanskrit, or Tamil.

4. A young standard language, recently standardized for some specific

purpose such as religious training, political indoctrination, or education for the early years of elementary instruction, e.g. Luganda in Uganda.

5. An unstandardized alphabetized language, in which a writing system has recently been developed but no standardization has yet taken place. Writing is, again, pretty much restricted to elementary instruction. Examples can be easily found among some American Indian languages. Somali in Somalia is another.

6. A preliterate language; there is a considerable number of languages with no writing system, e.g. Gallah in Ethiopia.

Third, with regard to juridical status, a language may be:

1. The only national official language, such as French in France, English in the United Kingdom.

2. A joint official language, coequal with at least one other in terms of use for governmental functions, e.g. English and French in Cameroun; French, German, Italian, and Romansh in Switzerland; Pilipino, English, and Spanish in the Philippines; English and Afrikaans in South Africa; Sinhalese, with Tamil for some purposes, in Sri Lanka. The situation in this categoy, as the examples suggest, may vary depending upon whether the joint languages used for official purposes are both imported, both indigenous, or alternatively one indigenous and one imported.

3. A regional official language, i.e. the official language of a constituent state or region of a federal state, e.g. lbo in Nigeria; Marathi in Maharastra; German in the Alto-Adige region of Italy; Armenian, Byelorussian, Ukranian, Georgian, and Azerbaijani, among others, in Russia.

4. A promoted language, lacking official status in a country or in one of its regions but promoted by public authorities at the municipal, state, or even federal levels for some specific purpose. This generally means that the language is permitted and used for certain levels of instruction in some public schools, that it is represented in some public libraries, that some governmental reports, laws, and proclamations are translated into such a language at the expense of the state, e.g. West African Pidgin English in Cameroun, where this language is used by the government for specific communication purposes related to health, agriculture, and the like; Spanish currently, in New Mexico[3] and, to a lesser degree, in other regions of the U.S.A.

5. A tolerated language, i.e. it is neither promoted by public agencies or the government nor is its use or cultivation restricted; in other words, it is not proscribed by the authorities; its existence is recognized but officially ignored, e.g. the languages of migrants in the United Kingdom; some American Indian languages in the U.S.A., such as Tanoan, Taos, or Ute.

6. A proscribed language, whose speakers are not permitted to use it in

communal activities, social clubs, religious congregations; nor may it be cultivated in the schools or used for printing. The degree of proscription may vary from discouragement to active suppression on the part of the authorities. Examples can be found in the banning of Basque during the first years of the Franco regime, the banning of Scots Gaelic after the 1745 rising, and the banning of Norman-French patois during the German occupation of the Channel Islands during World War II.

Fourth, the status of a language will be contingent upon the ratio of users to total population. Kloss admits that determination of what statistical increments should be set as criteria to differentiate language status is somewhat arbitrary even though a language that is spoken by only 3% of the population will have a status quite different from that of a language that is spoken by, say, 70 or 80%. What seems important here is to note that there is a correlation of some sort between the ratio of speakers of a language and its status, even though it is difficult to establish demarcation criteria between one statistical increment and the next. It is also important to point out that the criterion of *ratio* of speakers should not be used in isolation to determine language status, but rather in combination with other factors such as those discussed previously or others. Also, even with respect to the ratio of speakers as a criterion for determining language status, it seems clear that the there will be a difference in status depending on whether the language in question is an indigenous language or an imported language. Furthermore, it is also important to know whether the users themselves are native-born inhabitants or immigrants and, if immigrants, whether they hold citizenship or not. In addition, the distribution of the population is important to the claims for language use and language maintenance and/or recognition of the language by a speech community for specific functions. A group that is concentrated in one region will be able to excercise more pressure and manifest more power than a group that is spread over a large territory. However, numbers are not the only source of power; social organization and resources are also needed.

Kloss's account, though fragmentary, clearly shows the complexity of the concept of language status. Kloss also leaves out of his account a number of important specific language functions related to status, such as education, religion, court proceedings, and the like. It would be unfair to Kloss to construe this as a criticism. However, it seems clear that different uses of a language in education in a given speech community bear upon the status of such language. A language may be widely taught, for instance, as part of the education process, but not be used at any stage as a medium of instruction. A good example of this is Latin in the United Kingdom. Second, a language may be used as a medium of instruction at the elementary level only, either because it is later replaced by another language or because there are no materials available at a given particular time for a higher level of instruction. Examples may differ greatly in these cases, but think, for example, of the way in which English is used in Ghana or Kenya, or some of the American Indian languages in the U.S.A. Third, a language may be used as a medium of instruction at the secondary level after having been studied as a subject at the elementary level; for example, there are several East African countries where English is taught first as a subject at the elementary level and later replaces L_1 as a medium of instruction at the secondary level. Fourth, a language may be used as a medium of instruction in college, or in higher education in general, and replace some vernacular language not fully equipped, or modernized, to serve as a medium of instruction at such a level, e.g. English in Tanzania where it replaces Kiswahili, the medium of instruction up to the secondary level. Fifty, a language may also be used for publication of advanced research, or for post-graduate-level instruction, e.g. English in nations where the national language is not a language of wider communication, such as in the Scandinavian countries.

Naturally, the status of a language will differ according to the level of instruction for which it is being used. Thus, the educational function of language bears upon language status in a significant way.

Another function related to language status is public worship. The language used for religious purposes may be the same as the official language, or a classicial language, or one of the indigenous languages. Also, a number of different languages, both indigenous and traditional, may coexist in a country where freedom of religion, and freedom of conduction of religious services in the language chosen by a given community, prevail. Thus, High German may be used by the Amish in Pennsylvania; a traditional language such as Polish may be used by certain communities of the Lower East Side in New York; and classical Hebrew may still be used by a number of other communities. Yet a decision by the Catholic Church in favor of the use of vernacular languages in lieu of Latin has had unintended results in a number of states, where even Creole varieties of English, rather than standard English, have been used, after the Vatican decision, as the basis of prayer books, catechisms, and Masses, e.g. Papua New Guinea and Cameroun. Also, a number of local language varieties have been used in folk-music Masses, such as the *Misa Luba* in Africa or the *Misa Criolla* in Argentina, to name only two.

Thus, there are a number of functions related to language status which Kloss does not deal with in his 1968 study; and, on the other hand, some of the categories he considers, such as 'developmental status' of a language, may actually involve several functions, not just one. The concepts of 'language status' and 'language fucntion' certainly need further clarification. However, Kloss was, in his 1968 study, more interested in language-nation taxonomy than in the conceptual clarification of such concepts. Certainly,

Kloss was not alone in dealing with taxonomy problems related to language status. A similar concern is also shown by Stewart, for example, who, in the same year (1968) developed a typology of multilingualism using categories that are also related to language status.[4] Stewart recognized that social characteristics of languages 'can have an effect on the role which a particular language system may assume in the linguistic makeup of a multilingual polity' (1968: 533). Language systems will, according to their attributes, 'fall into different categories of intrinsic social value' (language status).

Stewart classifies multilingual communities according to four attributes of each language involved: (1) degree of standardization, characterized as the acceptance, within the community of users, of a formal set of norms defining 'correct' usage; (2) degree of autonomy, characterized as the function of the linguistic system as a unique and independent one; (3) historicity (language tradition); and (4) vitality, depending on whether or not the language is used as a spoken language by an unisolated community of native speakers.

Depending on whether a language scores positively or negatively under each one of these categories, we can determine whether a language is a standard language, a vernacular, a classical language, an artificial language, a dialect, or a pidgin or creole.

Each of the preceeding language types may be further specified according to function. Stewart lists ten language functions as follows: (1) official; (2) provincial; (3) wider communication; (4) international; (5) capital city (national capital and its surroundings); (6) group; (7) educational; (8) school subject; (9) literary; (10) religious.

So far, a number of similarities (and differences) between Stewart's approach and Kloss's could be pointed out. Such an analysis is, however, beyond the scope of this paper. One important point of agreement between these two authors that I should like to mention is the fact that both stress the importance of establishing a correlation between other variables and the ratio, or percent, of users of a given language. Both authors distinguish six classes of statistical distribution, but they differ in the percentages at which a language falls under one category or another. Thus, according to Kloss, the first class is determined by the fact that 90% or more of the speakers use the language, and in a decreasing order, 70-89%, 40-69%, 20-39%, 3-19%, and less than 3%; whereas, according to Stewart, the classes are determined by the following percentages: 75%, 50%, 25%, 10%, 5%, and less than 5%. It seems obvious that a certain degree of arbitrariness has to be accepted in differentiating these classes from one another, at least if the difference is to be based on the number of speakers alone. But perhaps when the ratio of speakers is combined with other variables, numbers or percentages may show a clearer relation. We need more empirical research regarding this issue.

There is a degree of ambiguity in both Stewart's and Kloss's accounts.

Stewart, for example, uses the concept of language function as referring to specific functions, such as literary, educational, religious, that are complementary specifications of language types he has previously distinguished. On the other hand, the concept of language function is also used to characterize language types. But it seems clear to me that the term 'function' does not mean the same thing at both levels. This concept, however, is important. Kloss (1968), on the other hand, uses the concept 'status' ambiguously and characterizes the 'developmental status' of language according to whether it is being used for specific functions, e.g. a mature standard language is a language that can be used for scientific and technological communication (1968: 78). Also, juridical status is characterized more broadly, mainly according to governmental attitudes toward language. If these accounts are to be accepted, some additional explanations are needed as to how these key concepts relate to each other. Obviously, the authors of these two important pioneer contributions to the field had more pressing problems to attend to in their treatments than conceptual elucidation, although such may not necessarily be less meritorious.

ETHOGLOSSIA AND LANGUAGE STATUS

The concept of language status and the concept of language function seem to be clearly related. Language status sometimes corresponds to one language function, such as the language of religion, the language of education, the language of newspapers, radiobroadcasting, and the like. On the other hand, language status often corresponds to a combination of functions, as in the case in which the vernacular language in a particular community is said to have status different from an official language, or different from a standard language. But being an official language of some sort, or a standard language of some sort, is qualitatively different from being the language of education or the language of religion, at least in the sense that requires the language to perform a number of functions, not just one. Thus, the concept of language status has been used in two different senses: a *weak* sense and a *strong* sense. The weak sense is restricted to one basic language function; the strong sense alludes to a cluster of functions.

It seems convenient for the purpose of facilitating future sociolinguistic analysis to restrict the use of the concept 'language status' in the weak sense to that of 'language function', and clarify the latter. Language status, properly speaking, is not equivalent to language function, as I shall try to show. The concept of status is most frequently used as indicating what I have called the 'strong sense' of language status. Thus it also seems necessary to clarify the concept of language status in the strong sense.

When it is said that the status of a given language or language variety is that of the language of education, the language of religion, and the like, what is being alluded to is the fact that such language has a certain *communicative status*. It is proper here to distinguish language function with regard to the *private intent* of an individual from function as the *communicative status* that a speech act is recognized to have in a sociolinguistic context (Ervin-Tripp 1972). Only the latter is relevant to our purposes. A language is vested with a certain communicative status by virtue of the conventional rules of language use.[5]

A brief semantic analysis may help to reveal some differences between language function and language status and also some of the difficulties entailed by such concepts. To say that a language L has a given function is to say that *language L serves, at least minimally, as a vehicle of communication between a transmitter and a receiver in a specific sociolinguistic context.* This preliminary definition reflects, first of all, that language function is context-dependent. We may also say that a language function is *satisfied* (and functions in general are satisfied in some way, or else they would not be functions) if a *basic communicative need obtains,* and this can only happen in a concrete situation, i.e. in a speech community, in a sociocultural linguistic context. Basic communicative needs are those that cannot be broken down into more elementary needs. Thus basic communicative needs may not be those satisfied by a language functioning as a standard language of some sort; for such needs could be broken down into functions such as serving for supraregional communication, serving as a normative frame of reference or a norm for correctness, and the like. To say that language is a vehicle of communication is tantamount to saying that language establishes a correspondence between at least a transmitter and a receiver. The usual requirement is stronger: namely, correspondence must be established among any members of the speech community who may need to use L for such a function. And here one of the first difficulties emerges. We cannot regard the language functions as having a *modus operandi* similar to that of the formal functions of mathematics and logic. The latter functions establish a certain kind of correspondence between ordered sets, one of which is the value or argument of the function, the other being the range of the function. Such functions are uniquely determined. But the functions of language are not. For the speech acts on which language functions are structured can be ambiguous, particularly if taken in isolation from the social context (Dittmar 1976: 167). Besides, even if we take the set of transmitters to be the values or arguments of language function and the set of receivers to be the range of the function, we must realize that such sets are not ordered; they are rather clusters of individuals, not abstract entities. Thus, there is more to the language function than the establishment of abstract correspondences as in the case of the formal functions. What a basic communicative need is varies from one speech community to another, and our definition of the latter also depends on the former. I believe, it will clarify sociolinguistic analysis to treat the language functions as I have suggested here, i.e. as a vehicle of basic communication between transmitters and receivers in a given sociocultural context. Such functions can be empirically analyzed or specified. Such specification is usually conditioned by our theoretical and explanatory needs. The 'differentiation between various possible sociolinguistic functions can be made as refined as the descriptive goals warrant' (Stewart 1968: 540). The specification of language functions will consist of a description, on the one hand, of the communicative needs satisfied by such function(s) and, on the other hand, the way in which such function(s) differ(s) from other function(s) by virtue of sociolinguistic rules.

It is important to note now that the functions of language may be differentiated by virtue of certain function indicators such as variable rules (Labov 1969), alternation rules, sequencing rules (Erwin-Tripp 1969), and other sociolinguistic rules, and by registers (Halliday, McIntosh and Stevens 1964). Both registers and sociolinguistic rules are conventions that shape up language functions. Our knowledge of such rules is still limited. Sociolinguistic rules can account for language changes that have occurred *spontaneously* as part of the natural process of language change. However, there are conventions of a higher order associated with changes or reallocations of the language functions themselves. These conventions are not spontaneous; they are usually the result of *planned* or *concerted* action. Very often these conventions are forced by specific legislation or executive decisions. Numerous examples can be found in recent legislation in both the U.S.A. and Canada pertaining to the use of languages other than English for purposes of instruction. These changes in conventions as to what functions a language is to have are an integral part of language-status planning.

The language functions may, in a given context, stand either in a *noncompetitive* or in a *competitive* relation. In multilingual communities the relation is often competitive. For instance, a vernacular language and a standard variety may be in a competitive situation at a certain level of the educational process as a language of instruction; or a certain language or language variety may be in a competitive situation with another as the regional official language, e.g. Spanish and English in New Mexico at the turn of the century. Two different languages may even be used by the same speech community. If such is the case and the languages perform different functions (one may be, for instance, the official language and the other the language of religion) there need not be a competitive relation between them and, thus, no language conflict arises. Language conflicts may thus arise if the relation between language functions is competitive and such competition is unresolved; but they most often result from concerted action to change or reallocate the functions of a language. The adoption of Kiswahili by Uganda as a national official language in October 1973 is a clear example of the latter situation; it involved not only the swift introduction of Kiswahili into schools but also the exodus of Asian and other expatriate teachers, not to speak of the harassment of the British. In fact the difficulty in recruiting enough teachers from Tanzania and Kenya, among other things, made Idi Amin dubious about the possibility of short-term implementation of his language policy, and he declared that English was to be considered the official language until a degree of national usage of Kiswahili developed.

We may now perhaps begin to see more clearly the point I have tried to make, namely that the *status* of a language is not to be identified only with the *actual* functions fulfilled by such a language in a speech community. Language status is a concept that is relative to language functions, i.e. in order to know what the status of a language is, we must know what language functions it performs. Furthermore, language status is also relative to other languages and their suitability of eligibility to perform certain functions in a given speech community. Thus, it refers to the relative standing of a language *vis-à-vis* its functions, *vis-à-vis* other eligible languages or language varieties. To put it differently, language status has been used to refer (1) to the actual decisions to allocate or reallocate language functions, whether these are *actual* functions or *potential, simple* or *complex* functions; and (2) to the accepted conventions that permit certain functions to remain roughly as they are. The first aspect corresponds to the *dynamics* of the language status. It is in this sphere that language status relates closely to language change. The second aspect corresponds to the *statics* of language status. It is in this sphere that language status relates to language maintenance.

The *dynamics* of language status seems to be the crux of the matter, and it seems to be the aspect of language status that authors like Kloss and Haugen are more concerned with. Haugen, for instance, is very clear about the need for distinguishing the process of selecting a norm from the process of implementing a norm. He calls 'allocation of norms' what I have been calling 'allocation of language functions' (see Haugen's essay in this book). A language or language variety may first gain a certain status; then a certain degree of additional planning is needed for implementing the function that such a language or language variety has been called upon to perform. The examples may include cases that vary from the adoption of entirely new functions to be performed by a given language, such as the adoption of Kiswahili as the language of education and religion in Uganda, to the adoption of a language variety, such as the adoption of the metric system — a technical or functional variety, *vis-à-vis* other competitive norms as discussed by Haugen in this volume.

Language status proper, in the weak sense or in the strong sense, has to be distinguished from yet another related and important concept, which I will call 'ethoglossia', or communicative character, of a language or variety. Ethoglossia consists partially of a profile of the functional distribution of a given language, containing the actual functions in a given context, in a given speech community, in addition to a description of the clustering, ordering, or ranking of such functions. The ethoglossia of a language or variety is the *expressive power* of the language, i.e. the *communicative strength*, determined by the number of functions a given language performs and the quality of such functions relative to the social structure of the speech community.

It should be noted that the language functions are not totally independent. Certain functions may produce, or motivate, or eventually force, the adoption of other functions. For instance, the use of a language for political and administrative purposes may lead to the officialization of such a language and eventually to the adoption of such a language for instructional purposes, as has been the case with the use of Kiswahili in Uganda. Neither are all language functions of the same rank, category, or degree of social entrenchment.

There is a correlation between language functions and soical structure. However, to determine how this correlation works is one of the most formidable philosophical problems posed by contemporary sociolinguistics.

There seem to be four main views that account for such a correlation between language functions and social structure (Grimshaw 1971). They are as follows: (1) that according to which language determines social behavior, a position that is in the tradition of some interpretations of Whorf's views and, more recently, views presented by Basil Bernstein (1960, 1961a, 1961b, 1962, 1971); (2) that according to which social structure determines language functions and speech behavior. Gumperz (1964) among others, has advocated such a view and stated that 'social restraints on language choice . . . are also a part of social structure'. He also believes that by means of certain relational variables we can 'treat linguistic behavior as a form of social behavior, and linguistic change as a special case of social change'; (3) that according to which there is a codetermination and coocurrence of both social structure and language behavior and language functions. Such a position has been maintained by Grimshaw (1971: 97); (4) that according to which both social structure and language functions are seen as determined by a third element, be it the nature of the human condition, the organization of the human mind (a position which may be consistent with some interpretations of Chomsky's views), or other.

The third position looks most appealing, for it seems to be in agreement with our intuitions that speech behavior and social environment are dialectically somewhat interrelated. However, there is no empirical research available to show how this interaction works. It certainly does not seem to work automatically. And yet one may see the interaction, the clustering of language functions and the way they are prioritized and ranked within a speech community, as responding to economic forces, degree of technological advancement, and deep basic ideological principles, which shape up differences in social organization and structure as well, to name just a few of the extra-linguistic factors that may influence allocations of language functions.

It is difficult to decide which of the preceeding positions to take. However, there is little doubt that language functions are somehow correlated with the social structure, and that ethoglossia will be so correlated as well. Now, one of the interesting aspects of the concept of ethoglossia is that it permits comparison of the ethoglossia of one speech community with that of another, in either a monolingual or a multilingual context, and thus encourages hypotheses that will afford a number of explanations about the nature of language conflicts. The comparison of the ethoglossia of different languages or varieties becomes somewhat of an etiology of language conflicts.

It is important to note that the comparison mentioned does not necessarily have to reveal language conflicts, although it may, and in most instances it will. But it may also reveal the simple coexistence of languages or varieties that actually satisfy different clusters of functions.

The description of the ethoglossia of a language or variety provides, on the one hand, a listing of the functions that a language or variety satisfies. In this sense, it resembles a sociolinguistic profile that may even eventually be reduced to formulas, according to some linguists (Ferguson 1966). However, the comparison of formulas of this kind 'hardly offers enough information to be of real value . . . since so little information is given about the type and function of the respective languages' (Ferguson 1966: 311). We should remember, though, that most sociolinguistic profiles, e.g. Stewart (1968) or Ferguson's profile formulas (1966), are attempts at describing multilingual repertoires of nations, or coexistence of different languages within the boundaries of a given country, whereas the description of the ethoglossia of one language or variety consists of the description of the specific functions of such a language, regardless, in principle, of whether the community of users is monolingual or multilingual. But, on the other hand, the description of the ethoglossia should also include a description of the *entrenchment* of the functions satisfied by a given language, and, in this sense, it can no longer be regarded as a cut-and-dried sociolinguistic profile.

The *entrenchment* of a language function depends upon a number of factors, such as its ratio of speakers *vis-a-vis* another language or variety. The importance of the ratio of speakers was pointed out by both Kloss and Stewart, as indicated in the previous section. I agree with Kloss, Stewart, and Ferguson on the importance of the ratio of speakers and on the fact that extremely low and extremely high percentages are telling. However, I do not find setting up categorical differences on the basis of arbitrary percentages equally informative. I believe that differences in the ratio of speakers become more telling in conjunction with other factors. An important one is obviously the geographic distribution of the speakers. Lower percentages become more significant when there is a high concentration of speakers in one particular region. This suggests that a description of the ethoglossia presupposes an ethnography of communication of the language functions under consideration, detailing both relative percentage and concentration of speakers. The entrenchment of a language function will also depend upon how many of its speakers have used it as a mother tongue. Furthermore, the historicity of functions satisfied by a given language may be used as an additional criterion. To these basic criteria two more can be added. One is to determine whether or not the function is part of a minimally sufficient set of functions which will make the speech community self-sufficient regarding its communicative needs. The other is to determine whether the speakers of a given language will choose to use it as a means of ethnic identity. In other words, the speakers' attitudes toward using the language for specific functions also relate to the level of entrenchment of the language, although the attitudes can be evaluated from different perspectives and with respect to different language functions. An example may help here. Let's take the case of the Albanian Greeks. The large majority of villages in the immediate vicinity of Athens are, and were, Albanian and speak an Albanian variety. Albanians have lived in the area since the eleventh century. They are mostly rural people, not recent urban immigrants, mostly concentrated in the areas of Attica and Biotia and totaling about 140,000 speakers. The language was maintained for centuries and satisfied most of the communicative needs of the Albanian Greek community. However, a wave of hellenization began right after the War of Independence and became stronger in this century after the Greek Civil War ending in 1949.

The end result of the hellenization process is that basically 'the main identifying characteristic of the Albanian Greeks is their language' (Trudgill and Tzavaras 1977: 173). The Albanian language spoken presently in Greece is a language variety known as Arvanitika. What is important for our purposes is to note that the language functions satisfied by Arvanitika are few indeed, basically only those of intergroup and family communication. First, it is not a language of education, since there are no Albanian schools in Greece. Albanian Greeks are not literate in Albanian. It is not the language of religion, either. Albanians as well as Greeks are Greek Orthodox, and the ethnic differences have been downplayed by clergy, who hold services mostly in Greek. These and other changes in the allocation of functions of Arvanitika show that the functions presently satisfied by it do not form a set of functions minimally sufficient to make this community self-sufficient regarding its communicative needs.

In addition, younger speakers seem to be less motivated toward maintaining and using the language than middle-age and older speakers, as the survey conducted by Trudgill and Tzavaras (1977) showed. In the opinion of these authors 'Arvanitika, in all probability, is a dying language, in that younger Arvanites are increasingly shifting to Greek' (1977: 173). Thus, as fewer speakers choose to use the language for purposes of ethnic identity, the entrenchment of the language weakens and a language shift is predictable. It is beyond the scope of this paper to speculate on how many hypotheses can be formulated on the basis of similar situations. The example illustrates a language variety in which last two criteria presented to determine the entrenchment of language functions are not me. Although there may be other factors affecting what I have called the entrenchment of the language functions, such as the economic power and social organization of the speech community, for example, it is not my intention here to offer a complete analysis of such a complex concept.

Let us now turn back to the comparison of the ethoglossia of languages or varieties. It is important to note that such a comparison need not necessarily contain an exhaustive description of all the functions satisfied by the languages under consideration, but only of those needed to show a particular source of language conflict or foreseeable change, if such is the task. Thus, if we choose to compare the current ethoglossia of French and Creole in Haiti, we will find, on the one hand, that French is the official language; it is also the language of education and there are few religious services conducted in it. French has hardly any other recognizable function. Creole, on the other hand, is the vernacular and the national language of the majority of the population, and most communicative needs are satisfied by it. Creole is the language of most radio broadcasts. Folk culture and social rituals take place in Creole. With regard to the comparative entrenchment, there is little doubt that Creole is far better entrenched than French. The percentage of Creole speakers is close to 100%, and it is used with slight variation, all over the country, whereas French is spoken by less than 15% of the population, basically concentrated in the Port-au-Prince area. There also seems to be little doubt that the last two criteria of entrenchment are clearly met by the Creole language, not by French. The historicity of both languages presents a special problem due to the difficulty of establishing the origin of Creole. Although this problem has been the subject of some discussion in the literature (Hymes 1971; Valdman 1977), it is not crucial to our argument here.

The point is that French, which enjoys official status (for which there may be many reasons), and which is also regarded by many as a language of greater 'prestige', has a much weaker entrenchment than Creole. This seems to indicate that it is the ethoglossia and its entrenchment, stronger in Creole than in French, rather than the 'prestige', which accounts for the maintenance of

Creole and its possible spread and elaboration. Thus it is conceivable that new functions will be allocated to Creole, as apparently indicated by the fact that legislation exists since 1979 making Creole a language of instruction up to the third grade, although the legislation has not yet been fully implemented. It is also conceivable that language elaboration will start and a standardized variety be developed.

Now, there is little argument about the fact that French, in and out of Haiti, is a language of greater prestige than Creole. However, it seems clear that a language may have high prestige but weak entrenchment and weak ethoglossia relative to a given speech community. Many have believed, though, that a language of high prestige displaces a less-prestigious language and that, in general, communities do not learn or maintain substandard varieties. This view, held by Hall (1952), among others, has been justifiably criticized by Fishman (1971b) on account of the numerous counterexamples. The maintenance of Creole may be added to the list.

This issue discredits the concept of prestige and its explanatory power. Weinreich (1953: 79) indicated that the term 'prestige' is quite often used indiscriminately and that unless its meaning is restricted it is better to 'dispense with it altogether as too imprecise'. The concept of ethoglossia seems to do a much better job. It also seems to do a better job than the concept of status. Both status and ethoglossia are far more useful and precise than the concept of prestige. The basic difference between status and ethoglossia has already been mentioned: status in the weak or strong sense refers basically to a language function, ethoglossia picks up all the language functions implemented within a speech community, including their interrelation (clustering) and their entrenchment. In other words, the ethoglossia gives the most global account possible of the status of a language in a given context. It also gives a description of the important issue of societal language dominance and thus integrates some important sociolinguistic concepts, such as diglossia, with or without bilingualism, and linguistic repertoire, in a meaningful way.

The concept of diglossia, introduced by Ferguson (1959) and accepted widely by socially minded linguists, is, among other things, a status distinction of two functionally different linguistic varieties of the same language: the L (low) variety, and a superposed H (high) variety. The idea of H being 'superposed' as a variety learned in a more formal setting than L is crucial to the distinction. H and L are distinguished on the basis of the functions they encompass. H includes all the language functions of formal discourse, whereas L includes the functions of informal discourse. Diglossia is, thus, a dichotomous code distinction. And although 'there are always extensive differences between the grammatical structures of H and L' they stand in a noncompetitive complementary relationship. However, H is considered 'as superior to L in a number of respects' by the members of the speech community.

Fishman (1971) combines diglossia + bilingualism

The concept of diglossia has many virtues: it is simple and elegant. However, there are numerous instances in which the speech community under consideration is not homogeneous and the differentiation between H and L may also reflect linguistic and ideological conflict. The concept of diglossia, described by Ferguson, was not geared toward analyzing language in contact situations. It is Fishman (1971b) who combined the concepts of diglossia and bilingualism and offered a fourfold taxonomy which allows classifications of bilingual communities and expands the concept of diglossia at the societal or national level.

The concept of diglossia in Fishman's sense is not restricted to the distinction of two varieties of the same language; it refers to differences between linguistic varieties related in some way to class-governed social functions: 'diglossia is a characterization of the social allocation of functions to different languages or varieties' (1971b: 295).

Fishman's taxonomy is well articulated and makes it possible to differentiate distinct forms of societal bilingualism: stable and unstable (transitional) (Fishman 1972: 91-106).

The concept of language status reappears in Fishman's taxonomy associated with the diglossic distinction between H and L. But it is important to understand that Ferguson's H variety and Fishman's are different in some important respect. Thus, whereas in the former H is a variety 'superposed' onto L as part of a learning process of the formal discourse of the same language used by a given speech community, H is not necessarily superposed in the latter. In Fishman's sense, H is a different language with or without a corresponding nexus with L, which in turn may be another language used by a linguistically different community. Qualitatively, thus, the communities using an H variety are different in each case. In Fishman's sense each of the two varieties has a different ethoglossia. In Ferguson's sense each of the two varieties is a subset of language functions with a different degree of entrenchment but both are part of the same ethoglossia. The speaker's attitudes toward the H and L varieties will be quite different in each situation. If H and L are two languages, it seems clear that one of them will be dominant. Thus, one of the virtues of Fishman's taxonomy is the fact that it provides a framework for explaining the problems of societal linguistic dominance in language in contact situations. However, more may be required in order for such an explanation to meet criteria of adequacy. A description of the degree of entrenchment of the language functions may be needed. This seems to be even more necessary in dealing with complex communities that may satisfy the same quadrant of the typology differently. For example, a community may fall in the quadrant of bilingualism and diglossia either at a local level or at a nationwide level, by including a subcommunity of speakers either concentrated in a given geographic location or province or spread over the nation.

reread important

I personally feel that such understandable pitfalls are not a weakness of the taxonomy itself but rather an indication of the complexity of reality. Perhaps the concept of ethoglossia can satisfy some additional expectations, although, if it does, the price is an increase in conceptual complexity.

THE ROLE OF LANGUAGE PLANNERS

Let us now turn to the role of language planners, i.e. the individuals or agencies that are responsible for the decisions that affect language use and language change. Little has been said about the role of language planners in the language-planning literature. In other planning areas, such as social and economic planning, the role of the planner is mostly conceived of as that of a bureaucrat, a technocrat, or an expert in some technical matter, who serves the interest of a politician or power structure (Beckman 1964 [1973]). An alternative view suggests that the planner, properly speaking, is the individual in a position to make decisions, capable of shouldering the responsibility for what he decides (Minett 1971; Amos 1972). In this sense the planner becomes the politician himself or a body making fundamental policy decisions which in turn may require expert advice in order to have the decisions implemented. Still another view has been proposed by Faludi (1973a), who believes that planning decisions do not necessarily have to be made by individuals, and that 'organizations are even superior to individuals in decision-making' (1973a: 60). In this view, the configuration of organizations provides communication channels not available to individuals, thus making the decisions more 'creative'. Although Faludi's view has its good points for specific types of organizations involved in decision making, whenever such a situation obtains, it is not so relevant to our discussion here, since the organizations he has in mind, I believe, are quite different from the organizations involved in language planning. Language-planning decisions have, by and large, mostly been made by individuals. The situation closest to organizational decision making in the area of language planning has been carried out by language academies, although most of the work of the academies has been devoted to corpus planning, following status-planning decisions made by individuals. The second alternative seems perhaps the most relevant for our purposes here. Kloss's distinction (1969) itself seems to confirm this view. In his opinion, corpus planning 'cannot be done without the help of some specialists, chiefly linguists and writers, who are called upon to form an Academy, Commission or some other official or semi-official body'. 'No such separate set up as a rule can take place for status planning. This is done by statesmen . . . mostly with some legal but very little sociolinguistic background' (1969: 81). This view on the different individuals involved with language corpus and status planning goes back a long way. It is well known that when Antonio de Nebrija finished the first grammar of any European language, he presented his *Gramatica de la lengua Castellana* (1492) to Queen Isabella and dedicated it to her. The bewildered Queen asked what the book was for, and the Bishop of Avila answered swiftly: 'Your Majesty, language is the perfect instrument of the Empire'. This anecdote illustrates Kloss's view that the language planning process involves two different groups of individuals: those like Nebrija, more concerned with the corpus of the language, and those like the Bishop of Avila, more concerned with the status of the language. The decisions made by these two groups of individuals are at least equally important. However, the prevailing view is that language planning is mostly done by language academies.

The first language academy was the *Accademia della Crusca*, founded in 1582 and devoted to eliminating the 'impurities' of the language varieties that were not modeled after the Truscan dialect. The task was commissioned by individuals who considered the Truscan dialect to be 'good' Italian. Purity has been one of the most recognizable concerns of language academies. Purity has often been thought of as an important ingredient of language entrenchment, and language policy. It undertakes the contrasting of native or indigenous language items with borrowings considered foreign to the language, or may also require contrasting archaic language items with new items, or prefer borrowings from one source over another. Most of the 'purification' efforts have been related to lexical elaboration.

Cardinal Richelieu took the *Accademia della Crusca* as a model in the foundation of the French academy in 1635. However, he went a step further and provided statutes for the newly formed academy. He asked its members 'to labor with all the care and dilligence possible to give exact rules to our language and to render it capable of treating the arts and sciences (Robertson 1910). This charge shows a concern for language modernization not noticeable in the *Accademia della Crusca*. Obviously there are differences in the ideological motivation of the French academy. The foundation of the academy was at the time an instrument of political centralization in France, among other things.

Numerous cases of language planning can be cited to show the linkage of language decision making to ideological principles.

Language reform in Turkey was seen as both a modernization effort and a purification of unwanted loans. Kemal Ataturk formed in 1932 a linguistic society, to which he appointed party members and educators and charged them with the task of language reform. Script reform was one of the priorities of the Turkish Republic. Ataturk abolished Persian script in favor of Roman. Script reform was followed by language reform, a 'Turkization' of the language in order to get rid of unwanted foreign elements, mostly Arabic and

Persian loan words (Hazai 1970). However, it is interesting to note that no objections were raised regarding numerous French loan words. As I indicated before, purity may amount, among other things, to a selection of a preferred foreign source and the rejection of another, if that seems to be convenient to the decision maker. Purity may also involve the preservation of classical or archaic language items over new ones. Three Arab academies can be cited as an example, the Syrian (established 1918-1919), the Egyptian (1932), and the Iraqi (1947). 'All regard, among their primary objectives, the preservation and renovation of classical Arabic as an effective and unified language for all Arabic speaking people (Altoma 1970 [1974]: 302). The difficulty with placing such strong emphasis on Arabization has been that the academies only made relative progress in the area of language modernization. Altoma comments on this issue. 'The major problem which none of the academies has been able to resolve is how to make Classical Arabic effective in meeting the needs of modern life'.

Certainly purism and modernization have not been the only ideological goals that have kept language academies busy. Vernacularization has also been an important force in many instances. A good example of vernacularization in language policy can be found in the Philippines. President Quenzon, in his message to the First National Assemby, stated that

The Constitution provides that the National Assembly take steps toward the development and adoption of a common national language based on one of the existing dialects. This mandate of the Constitution recognizes the fact that there is no common native language spoken by the Filipino people and that it is very necessary and highly desirable that there be one (Cf. Sibayan 1974: 223).

He recommends 'the creation of an institute of national language which will study the Philippine dialects in general for the purpose of developing and adopting a common national language based on one of them'. According to Sibayan (1974: 223) this language policy is the expression of the aspirations of a people and its search for identity. In 1937, one year after Quenzon's message, the National Language Institute recommended Tagalog as the basic language on which a common national language could be developed. Pilipino, the language resulting from this development, is being taught today in school at all levels, although three out of four Filipinos are nonnative speakers of Tagalog (Pilipino) (Sibayan 1978). Now, although the development of Pilipino from Tagalog is a good example of vernacularization, this should not be taken as the sole feature of the language policy in the Philippines. The country's policy is commitment to linguistic pluralism. While there are more than 80 languages and varieties (with some estimates as high as 150), 86% of the population speak one of the eight major languages as their mother tongue.

This leaves roughly 14% of the population speaking a minor language. The recognition and preservation of widely used vernaculars is a characteristic of the language policies of the Philippines, but this policy is complemented by the adoption of several languages for official purposes, communication across language boundaries, and education, particularly higher education. There are three official languages in the Philippines: Pilipino, English, and Spanish. The reasons for adopting each one of them are different. The use of local language was not allowed in schools, at least until 1938. While only roughly 2% of the population speak Spanish, the extensive language in contact situation with it for 377 years of Spanish occupation has affected most of the vernaculars more deeply than has English. English, on the other hand, is a convenient vehicle of language modernization and internationalization, and most of the official publications are in English, with occasional translations into Pilipino, in spite of the fact that any of the official languages may be used in official publications. Thus, a country may endorse a relatively complex and articulated language ideology.

Other interesting cases of multilingual language policy can be found in some of the African states, where different languages may satisfy different functions. While in Europe it is not uncommon to find three or four languages coexisting within the same country, more than a hundred languages can be found in some of the African states. Whiteley (1971 [1974] : 548) points out that 'all the countries of Africa are multilingual communities, their different languages performing different functions within the social life of the community, and being accorded different statuses by different groups of people'. Many of the independent African states have emerged from ethnically diverse preconditions, many of them containing linguistically different tribal or communal groups, creating in their emergence as states complex communication problems. Many of these states have also inherited one, two, or more colonial languages producing at times a conflict between attitudes of rejection associated with an oppressive past, on the one hand, and the need to adopt some such language for purposes of international communication, on the other. There is the need for intragroup and intergroup communication, the need for an official language for the intranational conduct of the business of government, and the need for international communication with other African countries and with the international community and with organizations that many of them have joined; there is also the need for a language of education as close to the vernacular as possible in the early stages, and the need for a language that will permit the communication and production of new knowledge, and the need for a language that will reflect certain cultural values and symbolize a specific ethnic reality. These needs are satisfied, or not, differently by different countries in a spectrum of decisions that may go from almost complete adherence to one or more colonial languages, to almost complete rejection of them and adoption of vernacular languages. The solution of language conflicts has not been easy.

Ghana, for instance, inherited English, and a substantial number of English speakers accepted this inheritance, and English kept its previous official status. French is also widely used and its study is encouraged. Although French has no official status, it may at some time become official. The situation in Ghana is completely different concerning the major local languages, some of which are used in broadcasting and newspapers and may even be studied as a subject at school. However, a requirement that the Akan language be taught in all schools of Ghana was easily defeated in the National Assembly, although it has been recognized that the vernacular is a medium of expression.

The situation is different in Tanzania, where an African language, Kiswahili, has been chosen as official language.

Kiswahili is widely used in the administration, the Party, the Trade Unions, the lower courts and on the radio. It is the language of the National Assembly and of Town Councils. It is used as a medium of education throughout the primary school and is taken as a subject at the school certificate level (after twelve years of schooling). Since 1964 it may be taken as a subject for a B.A. degree at the University College, Dar es Salaam. There are many newspapers in the language and a growing body of modern literature (Whiteley 1971 [1974]:185)

The Tanzanian language policy was clearly stated by the Second Vice-President in 1967, who advised that the unnecessary use of English, or any other foreign language, should cease, and that Kiswahili should be used for all official business and whenever possible.

These examples show at least two important aspects of status planning: first, that it is basically done by politicians, statesmen, or a policy-making body; second, that status planning decisions conform to ideologies of the power eltie or respond to conflicting ideologies between those upheld by the power elite and those of other constituent groups.

It is also important to be clear about the modus operandi of these two aspects of status planning in regard to their ethical ramifications. The first involves individuals responsible for status decisions. The second a preferred mode of treatment regarding different language groups affected by status decisions. Individuals who bear ethical responsibility may comprise one main agent or several. Thus, Kamal Ataturk and President Quenzon are examples of one main agent or decision maker. In many states, however, the responsibility is not conncentrated in one individual. It includes decision makers at the federal, state, and local levels, as is the case in Canada or the U.S.A., where the need for popular support in regard to the possible imple-

mentation of language policies is very strong. When such is the case, language
policy decisions have to conform to language ideologies believed to be upheld
by representative groups. Thus, in Canada,

> The policies which were agree to by large majorities of the English speakers
> were also agreed to by even larger majorities of those speaking French, but
> not vice versa . . . There was substantial English-French consensus on at least
> some set of policies, including: a) that all citizens of Canada should be able
> to deal with the federal government in either English or French, whichever
> they choose; b) that English-speaking and French-speaking children should be
> taught French and English, respectively, in school; and c) that all Canadians
> should (ideally) be able to speak both English and French (Pool 1973: 60)

So much for the agreement, but majority seems to rule also in matters of
language policy, and disagreements may rise. Thus, 'the most divisive issues
were over proposed policies that would force English speakers to use (more
than to learn) French (Pool 1973: p. 62). Jonathan Pool also sees a correlation between status policy decisions and ideological matters pertaining to
allocation of language functions, although the concept of 'language policy
repertoire' which he develops (1973: 60) needs, in my view, more elaboration.
But, although the relation of status policy decisions to ideological matters is
so pervasive, it seems difficult to offer a satisfactory model or taxonomy of
language-policy ideologies that will explain and/or predict how a particular
type of ideology affects language change. Language ideologies reflect a mode
of treatment of one language group with respect to another and ordinarily
involve judgements as to what is right or wrong. Also, ideologies involve
frames of reference pertaining to an ideal social group that will evolve, at
some future time, from the segment of reality to which the ideology is being
applied. The ideological aspect related to language-status planning is perhaps
the most neglected area of language planning, in spite of the fact that ideologies underlie all forms of status planning. It is because ideologies involve
value judgements and direct a certain mode of treatment that status decisions
raise ethical issues. Some typical language ideologies, though by no means an
exhaustive taxonomy, are

1. linguistic assimilation;
2. linguistic pluralism;
3. vernacularization;
4. internationalism.

1. The basic tenet of linguistic assimilation is that all speakers of languages other than the dominant language should be able to speak and function in the dominant language, regardless of their origin. It attaches linguistic

superiority to the dominant language and does not grant, in principle, equal rights to linguistic minorities.

Examples are too numerous and it is also important to recognize that there are different types of linguistic assimilation depending upon procedures used in other forms of sociopolitical assimilation. The latter can be achieved differently, for example through colonization, annexation, immigration, and migration. Instances of linguistic assimilation through colonization can be found in Guam, the Philippines under American rule, the areas of Colorado California occupied by American troops in 1846, New Mexico, and to some degree Puerto Rico prior to the 1952 Constitution. In Guam, for example, the system of self-administration was terminated after 1898, a Navy officer was appointed governor of the island, elections were abolished, and the native police force was replaced by U.S. police. Chamorro, the language of the island, which had been the language of religion and community affairs, was denied official status and was not permitted as a language of instruction, not even as a mere subject. Official documents, including Guam's congressional records, were kept in English only. This situation lasted until 1973 when the Guam legislature amended the Government Code to decide that English and Chamorro would be the two official languages of Guam (Kloss 1977: 153). Since 1972, Chamorro has been taught and used, at least in one school, under a grant from Title VII of the ESEA. But such support may not be available in the immediate future if the new policies proposed by the Reagan administration with reference to Title VII funding are implemented.

In the Philippines under American rule, English became the only language of instruction in the public school system. Vernacular languages were not allowed. Although this seems to be, according to Kloss (1977: 242), the only case where the U.S.A. deprived a large indigenous group of instruction in its mother tongue from the beginning, the situation was not corrected until 1940 (Sibayan 1974: 224). Finally, the Filipinos were definitely vindicated with the granting of their independence in 1946.

Examples of assimilation by annexation are, among others, Hawaii, Alaska, Texas, and Louisiana. It is important to distinguish here voluntary annexation, as in the cases of Hawaii and Texas, from annexation through purchasing, as in the cases of Louisiana and Alaska.

Hawaii, for example, was annexed in 1900 by voluntary incorporation, like Texas, and became a territory. It was not in need of federal support but rather contributed to the federal government and became a state in 1959. At the beginning, the Island laws were printed in English and Hawaiian as a result more of habit than of regulation. By 1924 English was the only language used for this purpose. At the time of annexation, Hawaiians had given up any cultivation of their own language.

The situation of Alaska is somewhat different. At the time of purchase from Russia (1867), the largest majority of the inhabitants spoke native languages, which included Eskimo, some Indian languages (mainly Athapaskan and Tlingit), and Russian. A group of Creoles, originating from mixed marriages between Russians and Eskimos or Indians, spoke some of the native languages for community purposes but used Russian as a religious language. The history of public instruction in Alaska is surrounded with language tensions.

I will not discuss examples of assimilation through immigration and migration, which may be more familiar to the reader. The point is that 'assimilation' is not a simple category that can be used without qualification.

2. Linguistic pluralism is also a complex category. Roughly speaking, pluralism involves coexistence of different language groups and their right to maintain and cultivate their languages on an equitable basis. Under pluralism each language is viewed as having an autonomous entrenchment deserving as much respect as any coexistent language. Several forms of pluralism can also be distinguished, depending for instance on whether linguistic coexistence is merely tolerated, whereby the language may be used for some important though restricted function such as religious rituals, education, or both, or whether official support is extended to the language. The strongest and most significant use of the term 'pluralism' is obviously the latter.

Throughout some periods of American history there are examples that come very close to a supportive form of pluralism: the official bilingual status granted to Louisiana during the period prior to its statehood; the official bilingual status of New Mexico from 1852, when it was granted territorial status, until it was awarded statehood, in 1912 (the use of Spanish and English for a number of official functions was extended until 1949); the status of American Samoa, which represents a unique case under American ruling of 'protection' of a non-English language as established in the 1966 Constitution:

It shall be the policy of the Government of American Samoa to portect persons of Samoan ancestry against alienation of their lands and the destruction of the Samoan way of life and language, contráy to their best interests. (Article 1, Section 3, cited in Kloss 1977: 256)

The enactment of bilingual instruction in the U.S.A. in 1968, contrary to what many people think, is not, strictly speaking, a step into pluralism, for most of the programs supported under the Act are of a transitional nature and the use of the student's language is discontinued in favor of an all-English system of instruction as early as possible. It is true that transitional bilingualism leans toward pluralism, in contrast to a school language policy that actually prohibited, with minor exceptions, the use of vernaculars other than

English in the classroom or sometimes for communication among students. The Bilingual Act, permitting the use of a student's vernacular as a language of instruction, allows the languages served under the Act to expand their allocation of one important language function and even supports that function with funds, but the ultimate goal does not seem to be truly pluralistic, i.e. it is not the granting of continued official status, not even for education purposes only, to the languages served. In any event, it is not my goal here to discuss the intricacies of bilingual education but rather to show that pluralism is a complex category and that there is a continuum between weakened forms of assimilationism and weakened forms of pluralism. Strong pluralism normally involves the granting of official status to coexisting languages. There are dozens of communities where two or more languages are used officially, from Afghanistan (Pushtu and Dari) and Belgium (French, Flemish, and German) to Sri Lanka (Sinhalese and Tamil), Swaziland (English and SiSwazi), and Switzerland (French, German, Italian, and Romansh).

3. Vernacularization involves the restoration and/or elaboration of an indigenous language and its adoption as an official language. There are also several processes of vernacularization which include the revival of a dead language (Hebrew in Israel), the restoration of a classical language (the Arabization process in Syria, Egypt, and Morocco), the promotion of an indigenous language to official status and its eventual standardization (Tagalog in the Philippines and Quechua in Peru).

4. Internationalization involves the adoption of a nonindigenous language of wider communication either as an official language or as a language of instruction at some level of the educational process. Thus it is also possible to distinguish degrees of internationalization. A language of wider communication like English may be granted semi-official status for purposes of external communication, as in India, where it holds a 'window on the world' function, as stated by Nehru. Also, a language may be adopted as official for both external and internal communication when the official indigenous languages are not sufficiently developed to carry out all the functions of the state. Such may seem the case of English in the Philippines and Tanzania. Yet a language of wider communication may not be granted official status at all, but may be studied and used as a language of instruction at some level of the educational process, particularly when the official language is not a language of wider communication (such as the use of English in some of the Scandinavian countries), in order to promote the possibility of communicating with the international academic world.

Let us now turn to some of the ethical ramifications of status planning.

presupposition

STATUS PLANNING, ETHICAL PROBLEMS, AND LANGUAGE RIGHTS

The ethical implications of language planning, and more specifically of status planning, fall under political ethics. Yet little attention has been given to them in spite of the fact that substantial academic progress has been achieved both in new areas of ethics and in the sociology of language. Political ethics itself has occupied a good deal of attention in political science and ethics, yet discussion of language-related issues has been only marginal. The allocation of language functions, status planning, generates language rights associated with each language function within the social structure of a state. The origin of language rights should not be confused with the individuals empowered to make decisions about language function allocations. There are at least three important insights on the origin of rights given by Hobbes, Rousseau, and Locke. Hobbes and Rousseau hold that the state originates by a social contract and trace the origin of rights both to the state and to a contract. There are, of course, important differences between them. Hobbes stresses the state over the contract, Rousseau the contract over the state. The social-contract theory of the state differs from the natural theory, which goes back at least to Aristotle and Plato, who maintained that the state (the word they use is *polis* for lack of a word like 'state') is a natural society. Plato derives the state from economic needs, which are natural needs (*Republic*, Book II, 369). Aristotle derives the state from the family (*Politics*, Book I, Chapter 2, 1252[a] 24 to 1253[a] 18). The family is, according to him, the most elementary form of society. In several generations the family becomes a clan, then a tribe, then, even more articulated, a village community, and then a state.

A combination of the natural and contractual origin of the state is to be found in Locke, who believes that there are natural laws conferring natural rights, but that a political society can only begin to exist by the social contract. In his view, we are impelled to make a contract by the demands of our own nature. In his *Second Treatise of Civil Government* (Chapter 8, 95, 99) he says:

Men being, as has been said, by nature all free, equal, and independent, no one can be put out of this state and subject to the political power of another without his own consent. The only way whereby any one divests himself of his natural liberty, and puts on the bonds of civil society, is by agreeing with other men to join and unite into a community for their confortable, safe, and peaceable living one amongst another . . . . And thus that which begins and actually constitutes any political society is nothing but the consent of any number of freemen capable of a majority to unite and incorporate into such a society. And this is that, and that only, which did or could give beginning to any lawful government in the world.

Locke's views, which form the pillars of our political system, are deeply ingrained in the minds of many lawmakers and the citizenry at large, in matters pertaining to the role of the individual and the state. However, they do not reflect existing widespread biases toward linguistic diversity and linguistic inequality. The drive for linguistic homogeneity has been so strong and lasted for so long that it still blinds many sensible individuals to linguistic diversity. The linguistic-assimilation forces have at times been so encompassing that the very thought of inequality in lingustic matters still sounds odd to many ears, though inequality prevails.

Certainly, Locke's assumption that all men are equal and can only be subjected to political power by their own consent runs contrary to our linguistic reality. Black English, Spanish, Navajo, French Creole, Zuni, Appalachian English, Pennsylvania Dutch are but a few components of our linguistic makeup which provide strong examples of different linguistic inequalities. Thus, although Locke's views seem to capture some of our basic democratic beliefs, they fall short of describing our linguistic situation. However, Locke's views are crucial to understanding, as I will suggest, the complexity of language rights.

Locke's conception of the social contract differs from that of his predecessors, particularly Hobbes and Rousseau, in some significant respects. Thus, whereas the former believes, contrary to Locke, that men are not naturally social, the latter believes, contrary to Locke, that men are not equal, neither physically nor politically. Without attempting a thorough philosophical exegesis, let me briefly clarify some points of disagreement between Hobbes and Locke, on the one hand, and between Rousseau and Locke, on the other, that seem somewhat more consistent with the linguistic reality.

Hobbes maintains that before people organized themselves into political communities there was no law and therefore no injustice. Hobbes refers to the situation prior to social organization as a 'state of nature'. In such a state no one has any responsibilities toward others; but he has no rights either. Each individual must be his/her own guard. Life in a state of nature is in Hobbes's own words 'nasty, brutish, and short'. In Chapter 13 of the *Leviathan* he says:

To this war of every man against every man, this also is consequent: *that nothing can be unjust.* The notions of right and wrong, justice and injustice, have there no place. Where there is no common power, there is no law; where no law, no injustice.

Although Hobbes's views cannot be gathered from one quotation, he hints at his conception of rights in Chapter 15:

Where no covenant hath preceded, there hath no right been transferred, and every man has a right to everything and consequently, no action can be unjust.

Thus, according to Hobbes, all true rights come from the state. In a state of nature every individual has every right. But the situation in a state of nature is intolerable; that is the reason why individuals, who are by nature antisocial, agree to hand over their liberties to the state; the social contract is the remedy. Thus, within each nation, there is a certain amount of security and protection — there are laws and a degree of law enforcement. The state undertakes tasks that would be impossible for private individuals. However, we know that not all governments are alike. Some are mismanaged, or corrupt, or led by unworthy individuals; some restrict individual liberties unnecessarily, and still others provide less protection than necessary. The upshot is that even a bad government is preferable to no-government. One of the interesting points about Hobbes's views is that, although the state of nature does not obtain within nations, it does at the international level between nations. Leaving aside Hobbes's pessimistic outlook on man's antisocial nature, the linguistic situation at the international level is still very much in a state of nature. Political independence does not always imply linguistic independence as well, as may be illustrated by the situation in many new nations. Political frontiers hardly coincide with linguistic frontiers. Attempts at developing artificial languages for international consumption, known at least since the creation of Volapuk in 1880 and Esperanto in 1887, have been less successful than the attempts at developing an international political body such as the United Nations, with little power other than airing grievances but not necessarily solving them. Language spread transcends the mechanisms that maintain international equilibrium (Fishman et al. 1977). Language-status planning in many new nations responds to at least two distinct forces: language nationalism, on the one hand, and the urge to develop the linguistic resources needed for modernization, at least in the domains of education, administration, science, and technology, on the other hand. The languages more likely to satisfy the latter need are what some authors have called 'strong languages' (Mackey 1976: 19). Thus, such languages are likely to coexist with and/or eventually displace languages that are well entrenched but not equipped to perform all the language functions needed by a modern state. In such a situation languages will come in contact and conflicts are likely to emerge.

Now, if Hobbes's views clarify at least partially the situation at the international level, Rousseau's views help to clarify the situation within nations. There are important points of agreement between the two. Thus in the *Social Contract* (Book I, Chapter 4) Rousseau says:

The social order is a sacred right which serves as a foundation for all others.

This right, however, does not come from nature. It is therefore based on conventions . . . . The passage from the state of nature to the civil state produces in man a very remarkable change, by substituting in his conduct justice for instinct, and by giving his actions the moral quality they previously lacked.

The similarity with Hobbes is clear. However, the social contract is stressed as the foundation of all rights, rather than the state. Rousseau's understanding of the kind of convention implied in the social contract becomes more illuminating in his work *Discourse on the Origin and Foundations of Inequality Among Men.* In the second Discourse, for example, he says:

I conceive of two sorts of inequality in the human species; one, which I call natural or physical, because is it established by nature . . . ; the other, which may be called moral or political inequality, because it depends upon a sort of convention and is established, or at least authorized, by the consent of men. The latter consists in the different privileges that some men enjoy to the prejudice of others.

This view contrasts sharply with Locke's assumption that men are by nature all free and equal. Certainly the linguistic reality within many countries, including possibly ours, is much closer to Rousseau's than to Locke's description.

There is a correlation between the political inequalities and the linguistic inequalities parallel to the correlation described in the second section between language and social structure. Actually, the former may be conceived of as a special case of the latter. Rousseau is clear in pointing out that political inequalities correspond to different privileges that certain groups possess, and he recognizes that these groups also differ in the degree of power they enjoy. Such differences in power also account for linguistic differences and privileges. These differences are reflected, among other things, in the official attitudes toward linguistic minorities, which may vary from almost complete neglect in many instances, as may be the case with regard to a large number of native American languages in Canada, the U.S.A., Mexico, and Latin America, particularly uncommon vernaculars (Acoma, Tarascan, Zoque, Zuni, Papayo, Cree, Micmac, to name but a few), to the official recognition and support of bilingual districts within the structure of the state. Concerning the latter, compare how different countries, such as Canada and Finland, define bilingual districts. In Canada, the borderlines of bilingual districts are established by a Commission every 10 years at the federal level. In Finland, bilingual districts are defined at the municipal level depending upon the concentration of speakers per language per district. In Finland a district that contains at least 10% of speakers of a given language other than the dominant language is defined as bilingual, whereas in Canada, 10% is a necessary but not sufficient condition for a district to be recognized as bilingual, for the decision is made at the federal level based upon recommendations made by the Commission. The statutes for official recognition of bilingual districts in Finland are municipal and local statutes. In Canada, the districts declared bilingual are more or less permanent, the 10% rule being only a minimal condition, whereas in Finland, if the bilingual concentration in a district drops below 8% it loses its official bilingual status. The 10% rule is not applied if the concentration of speakers is at least 3000, in which case the district becomes bilingual no matter what the percentage is. (Miemois 1980: 3ff).

The issue of the official attitudes toward linguistic minorities has not been stressed sufficiently in the literature. It is not only important to our understanding of the nature of language rights but also shows how language-status planning issues are related to political issues. Official attitudes are important not only because of the possible granting of official status to a given language but because of the effect that official attitudes have upon the clustering and entrenchment of diverse language functions. Think, for example, of the effects of the relexification of Nahuatl and its potential death in the area of Tlaxcala (Hill and Hill 1977). Samples of written Nahuatl date back to the sixteenth century. For a long time, Nahuatl was used as an official language during the administration of the Spanish empire in Mexico; then its official status was progressively lost (Heath 1972). Although the position of the Mexican government has fluctuated, there are Nahuatl-speaking communities, as in Tlaxcala, where primary instruction and local official business have always been conducted in Spanish. Many Nahuatl speakers have developed an attitude of rejection toward their vernacular, while others even refuse to use it although they understand it. The number of Hispanisms in Tlaxcalan Nahuatl is appreciably high. The relexification contributes progressively to language death, and the language seems to be, in some communities, in its last generation of speakers. The situation of Nahuatl in many communities in Mexico contrasts with the recent officialization of Quechua in Peru, although it seems premature to anticipate the effects of such a decision as yet. Official attitudes are good indicators for the analysis of linguistic inequalities insofar as they relate closely to opportunities for language-function allocation and language use. Although it is not my intention to offer an exhaustive taxonomy of official attitudes toward minority languages, the following can be distinguished:

1. attempting to kill a language;
2. letting a language die;
3. unsupported coexistence;
4. partial support of specific language functions; *R. in present Kaz (1993)*
5. adoption as an official language.

Attempts to kill a language are infrequent and for the most part unsuccessful. An example is Franco's attempt to kill the Basque language. Franco attempted to suppress the use of the Basque language in the Basque Provinces in spite of the fact that Basque had become the official language of an autonomous Basque state (1936-1939). This type of decision involves banning the language officially in public life, but the banning can hardly reach the privacy of the family and other communal uses. It imposes a tremendous restriction on the status of the language, but brutally forced assimilation hardly ever succeeds if the threatened language is well entrenched, unless the official policy is extended throughout several generations.

Letting a language die is a more frequent attitude toward minority languages. It does not involve an agresive attempt at eliminating the language, as in the previous case, but rather official neglect. Good examples are easy to find in the situation of many of the native American languages. The results of a survey conducted by Wallace Chafe (1962) indicate that 206 different languages and varieties are used by contemporary American Indians. However, 49 of these languages are spoken by only 10 or fewer individuals, all of whom are over 50 years of age. The foreseeable extinction of these languages is clear, and it is the result in some important sense of official neglect, although other contributing factors, such as low degree of awareness on the part of the community concerning its language rights, should be considered.

Unsupported coexistence means that the official attitude is one of indifferent tolerance. The language(s) in question are tolerated and used at the community level but no support, financial or other, is extended for the use and maintenance of such languages. Language maintenance is entirely in the hands of the community and associated with whatever functions the language is used for within communal life. Many of the native American languages in Chafe's report fall into this category. Still, a large number of languages receive community support and are used in some restricted ways as the language of religion and/or as a subject or even eventually as a medium of instruction (Lewis 1977; Fishman 1979) in the Ethnic Community Mother Tongue Schools.

Partial support of specific language functions involves some kind of official institutional and/or financial support. This kind of support is usually associated with specific legislation granting specific support. A typical example is the federal support of transitional bilingual education in the U.S.A. This should not be confused with the granting of official status to a language, although it increases the language functions in an important sense.

Strictly speaking, adoption of a language as an official language implies that the language in question will be used for formal education. But the fact that a language is being so used does not imply official status in the regular sense (Fishman 1971b: 288). In order for a language to be regarded as official, it has to be used for purposes of government, including use in governmental documents, publication of laws, governmental assemblies, record keeping, and the like. The concept of official status has not been made entirely clear in the literature. In general, it involves official adoption of the language in the sense I have just described. But it is also important to recognize that there may be different levels of officialization. For example, a language may enjoy official status at the municipal or regional level but not at the federal level, such as Ibo in eastern Nigeria or French in Quebec. And yet at the federal level a language may be the only official language or it may be a joint official language, coofficial with at least one other language. In many instances where the latter situation obtains, one of the official languages is mostly for intranational use, whereas another is used for international communication. Official attitudes and, in general, official or legal status are crucial to our understanding of the nature of language rights and of the eventual consequences of using language as a means of social control. Leibowitz (1974, 1976) has shown how language allocation, for example in the U.S.A., has been 'almost always coupled with restrictions on the use of other languages; it has also been coupled with discriminatory legislation and practices in other fields, including private indignities of various kinds which make clear that the issue was a broader one' (1976: 450).

The nature of language rights is in serious need of clarification. Elucidation has been partially obscured by the fact that all language rights have been treated as a homogeneous block. Thus, one of the few explicit references to language rights in the United Nations Charter places language rights in the same category as sex and race, as if they were all basically natural rights (McDougal et al. 1976). But many authors (Leibowitz 1976) have treated language rights as legal and/or moral rights. The distinction between natural rights and legal or conventional rights goes back at least to Hobbes and Rousseau, and the first author who attempted to combine the two, as we have seen, was Locke. I believe the distinction to be illuminating to an understanding of the nature of language rights. Although Locke never addressed the problem of the nature of language rights specifically, I think he would have felt as he did about rights in general, that there are natural language rights and conventional language rights, and that it is wrong to class them as exclusively one or the other. The distinction between natural rights and conventional rights has also been endorsed by a number of contemporary authors (Hart 1953: 16 ff.). The distinction is not without its problems, and in fact defining 'natural rights' is a particularly trying philosophical exercise. Natural rights have also been referred to as inalienable and innate, although these terms are not necessarily coextensive, or interchangeable. For instance, parents may be said to have a natural right to rear their children, but they may have, on occasion, to be deprived of this right because they are incompetent or cruel. Thus, such rights are only inalienable if there is no conflict with other rights, such as the children's right to be well cared for. Other natural rights may include the fulfillment of vital human needs. Kant, for instance, recognizes only one innate right and says in *The Metaphysics of Morals* (Part I):

There is only one innate right. Freedom (independence from the constrain of another's will), insofar as it is compatible with the freedom of everyone else in accordance with a universal law, is the one and sole original right that belongs to every human being by virtue of his humanity.

This is compatible with our Constitutional conception of freedom. The freedom of language choice in community life and in private may very well be viewed as part of our natural freedom. As Locke said, 'men can only divest themselves of their natural liberties by their own consent', and in this sense there are language functions that seem to be part of our natural liberties, whatever this may mean. The distinction is also compatible with a well-known fact, namely that every speech community finds itself in interaction with a larger social context. Such interaction forces allocation of language functions in such a way that the community at large enjoys language rights the smaller community does not. Let me refer to the latter as a 'captive community' and to the larger as a 'dominant community'.[6] Both communities obviously have natural language rights. The dominant community, however, not only has different conventional rights but usually has quantitatively more rights and qualitatively different rights from the capitve community. The dominant community is autonomous: it gives itself conventional rights, as part of the social contract by which it emerges as a community. It can also modify its own rights. In contradistinction, the captive community possesses only those conventional rights the dominant community has willingly granted it or those it has gained by clamoring, protesting, litigating, and claiming rights which otherwise would not be granted. Such a community is not autonomous. The history of bilingual education in the U.S.A. and in many other countries provides numerous examples. The Lau remedies constitute rights emerging from a claim to a right: the right to a meaningful education, the right to learn, the right to use the student's native language at least when no other language could be used meaningfully as a medium of instruction.

The distinctions used so far allow two generalizations related to linguistic inequalities: first, that no state, or nation, is empowered to control all language functions, since captive communities retain at least natural language rights; second, that every state, or nation, is empowered to control some language functions. The first supports the idea that some language rights are inalienable or natural, the second that obviously not all language rights are natural. If these two generalizations are true, the distinction of two kinds of language rights makes sense.

It is worth noting that not all captive communities are the same. At least two different kinds can be distinguished. One is a captive society that has historical precedence over the dominant community. The second is a community founded by immigrants. Kloss makes a similar distinction in his 1971 paper and calls the first 'indigenous' and the second 'immigrant'. The language rights of these two communities are, *prima facie*, different. However, the end result may not be so different. There seems to be widespread agreement that indigenous communities have the right to maintain their own language. However, as they are taken over by the dominant community and the needs for language reallocation and possibly language elaboration grow and become more dramatic, since the captive community cannot ordinarily satisfy minimum standards for linguistic integration with full participation, the gap of linguistic inequality grows even larger. This type of situation opens a number of ethical questions pertaining to the responsibility of the dominant community. However, I will not deal with such issues here.

Kloss (1971) has dealt effectively with the issue of the language rights of immigrants. After examining briefly some typical arguments used against language rights for immigrants, he distinguishes between toleration-oriented and promotion-oriented language rights. Toleration-oriented rights give immigrants leeway to use their language within the domain of their own community and even to use the language for functions such as the printing of periodicals and books, the running of community-sponsored schools and libraries, and eventually in local business over the phone and in the streets. Althoug Kloss uses the concept of toleration-oriented language rights only in regard to immigrant groups, they may be extended to indigenous groups as well. Obviously, different levels of tolerance can be distinguished, but most of them correspond to what I have called here unsupported coexistence. The levels of tolerance are partially determined by the forces of interaction between the immigrant and the dominant communities. Thus, in many instances even ample tolerance may lead to social isolation, social stagnation, ghettoization, and even rebellion. This is more likely to happen if the captive community is expected or required to contribute to the sustenance of the state in the form of taxation, for example, or to support the state in affairs that do not contribute directly to the welfare of the captive community, such as being drafted and going to war. These are forms of taxation without proper representation, and it is more likely that situations like these will produce claims for secession rather than the equalitarian granting of rights. Frictions between captive and dominant society may take several forms (Eisenstadt 1954):

1.   The captive society may be apathetic to the main values and cultural symbols of the dominant society and is not disposed to maintain any significant communication with the bearers and transmitters of such values. The consequence is 'enclosure', isolation or ghettoization. This is the case with many native American Indian communities or others such as the Amish.

2.   The captive community adopts a rebellious attitude toward the dominant group because it feels it has been treated unfairly and does not accept claims to loyalty. The result of this is ordinarily a tense relationship. Some Hispanic communities in the U.S.A. perceive their standing this way.

3.   The captive community accepts the premises of the dominant group and acts accordingly. However, if discriminatory practices persist and are employed against the captive group, inequality is likely to stand in the way of their realizing their aspirations. This is conducive to increasing disorganization, particularly in the second and third generation.

Obviously, tolerance will not produce the same results in each of these patterns. As far as language rights are concerned, each one of the patterns just described (and of course there may be more) corresponds to different ways in which each group perceives its ethoglossia and the strategies it develops.

In contrast to toleration-oriented rights, promotion-oriented rights, as described by Kloss (1971), involve the use of a language by public authorities at either the national, provincial, or municipal level. This may include the use of a nondominant language in the publication of laws and statute books, as well as the use and/or teaching of the language in the public schools and on street signs etc., for information and use by the members of the captive community; or it may involve the actual use of the language for legislating disputes where the meaning of a controversy is resolved by appealing to the version of the text in that language and the text is considered authentic. Only in the latter case should we say that the language is an 'official' language. The former indicates only what I have previously called partial support. Kloss in fact includes both under promotion-oriented rights. The distinctive feature of this type of rights is that the captive community is not blocked from expanding its ethoglossia and, in general, is not denied participation in spheres of linguistic interaction with the dominant group using its own language in the communication process. The road to an authentic pluralism, insofar as linguistic pluralism is concerned, is through at least partial support of specific language functions, or officialization. Such is the road as well to an authentic and lasting linguistic equality. The paradox of American linguistic ideology can be stated as follows: linguistic pluralism regarding natural language rights for each community according to its strength and entrenchment, linguistic assimilationism regarding conventional or contractual rights in any other event whenever possible. In other words, the linguistic ideology is a combination of restricted factual pluralism and contractually legalized assimilationism.

From the above considerations, it should be clear that language rights and claims to rights are not the same. A captive community may be given some rights by the dominant group as a response to a claim, but conventional rights cannot be retained by the captive community unless such rights are protected by legislation; otherwise, existing rights can be removed. For example,

In Louisiana and New Mexico, the languages of the two indigenous groups, French and Spanish, were for some time considered co-equal with English; their use in the legislature was permitted and for many decades public schools conducted wholly in French or Spanish were permitted by law. (Kloss 1971, p. 263)

Adequate legislation is the only protection captive communities have in order not to be treated, with regard to their language, as a 'means', to use a Kantian motto, as instruments of the state without equality.

Linguistic inequality can be monitored by comparing the ethoglossia of both the captive and the dominant communities, describing the language functions and their entrenchment. A diachronic comparison like this may also reveal progressive assimilation, as in the case of Tlaxcalan Nahuatl already mentioned. The linguistic inequality I have been alluding to should not necessarily be equated with multilingual contexts alone. In fact, Berstein (1961a, 1962, 1971) has shown that allocation of linguistic resources and resulting language functions, or, as he calls them, 'codes', is somehow class related. He distinguishes 'restricted' from 'elaborated' codes. Speech codes are a function of a system of social relations. Berstein's prolific production cannot be fairly dealt with here but his ideas certainly permit us to see how a verbal deficit is preconditioned by constraints in the socialization process. It is certainly possible to extend his ideas to a multilingual context. Berstein's theoretical edifice has also been criticized and charged with circularity (Dittmar 1976: 10) in view of the fact that he defines speech codes as functions of a system of social relations, and a system of social relations as a function of a speech code. Whether or not Berstein is committed to such circularity will not be decided here.

The concept of ethoglossia as presented earlier can avoid some of the pitfalls in the analysis of linguistic inequalities.

Describing the ethoglossia of a language reveals what language rights the community using it has, whether they are natural rights or conventional, whether the degree of entrenchment indicates that the language is threatened or will grow stronger. What the description of the ethoglossia will not do, nor will the identification of restricted and elaborated codes, is reveal and counterbalance ideological or political mechanisms affecting the allocation of language functions, more specifically, the granting of conventional language rights to captive communities.

Legislative decisions granting such rights respond normally, but not always, to rationally understandable criteria. I say 'not always' because many legislative decisions are influenced by political pressure and political interest. Think of the economic plan approved in the spring of 1981 by the House with the votes of numerous representatives of both political parties who had never actually seen or read the plan. And I say this not to pick on this particular decision, which could have been based on informed consent, but to show that many decisions are made the same way, particularly less informed ones pertaining to officialization of minority languages or decisions supporting specific language functions which are often obscurely associated with disruptive forces. But, assuming that decisions respond to rationally understandable criteria, let us briefly examine some of them. These criteria may also be considered evaluative criteria of status decisions, and in that sense they belong to the area of evaluation of language status.

The two most widely discussed ethical criteria are the Kantian and the utilitarian. According to Kant (*Foundations of the Metaphysics of Morals*), ethical decisions are universalizable and reversible. In other words, decisions are ethical if the rules by which we arrive at such decisions are universalizable. Thus, breaking promises, for example, is not right, moral, or ethical (I will use these terms interchangeably here) because it is not universalizable. If it were, others would be as entitled to break their promises to us as we are to break ours to them. But persons usually want others to act morally toward them, even though they do not want to act morally toward others. People, and governments, often rationalize, justifying their breach of promise to make them look right. We often hear the argument, for example, that an occupied territory whose return was promised should not be so returned because the circumstances have changed, and strategic or national security reasons are alluded to in this kind of argument. But such rationalizations are not right, according to Kant. No one is to take oneself as an exception. The application of the rule is equal for all: it is universal.

Reversibility is a complementary criterion to universalizability. Employers, for example, would not usually mind universalizing certain antilabor practices and laws. However, were they not in a provileged position, they might not choose to universalize such practices. The idea is that right decisions are not only those that are universalizable but those that all agents would choose to universalize regardless of whether they are at the giving or at the receiving end of the action or decision. Thus, employers would not choose to universalize antilabor practices and decisions if they placed themselves at the receiving end of the action, i.e. if the roles were reversed.

The implications of the Kantian criteria for the study of linguistic inequalities are tremendous. These criteria are a safeguard of equality. But they are also hard to meet, as there are, in fact, many individuals in privileged positions, political or otherwise, that would not picture themselves except at the giving end of the decision, seldom at the receiving one. Many legislators are in fact more loyal to their political affiliations and fears than they are to strictly rational principles. Even assuming that the criteria can be met, and on occasion they may be, still it remains to be seen whether there would be general agreement as to what specific rules every agent would agree to universalize. In other words, there are specific rules, such as telling a lie to save a life, which individuals may not agree to universalize, regardless of what their own position is. A thorough discussion of the Kantian criteria and their implications is beyond the scope of this paper. However, regarding language-rights issues, as presented earlier, Kantian criteria offer a straightforward though ideal answer.

The utilitarian criteria are not that simple to state. First, what goes under the name utilitarianism' does not always refer to the same theory, neither do all the utilitarian authors maintain the same kind of utilitarianism. For the sake of clarity, two basic forms of utilitarianism have been distinguished: actutilitarianism and ruleutilitarianism. According to the first, the righteousness of decisions is measured by their consequences, or the concrete total amount of good (or happiness, as most utilitarians say) brought about by the decisions. General rules like 'keep promises' are considered mere rules of thumb which are used as convenient devices to avoid estimating the worthiness of the consequences in every instance. But they are not regarded, like Kant's, as unbreakable and without exceptions. Thus, promises should be kept only if, in a concrete situation, keeping the promise is what will have the best consequences. What counts for the actutilitarian is the net value of goodness produced. Although there is no room here for an extensive philosophical evaluation of this view, it should be easy to see that perhaps one of its greatest difficulties lies in the problem of assessing the worthiness of the consequences. Thus, this theory is not equipped to deal with the insuperable task of calculating the utility of the consequences of our decisions in the real world.

Ruleutilitarianism is a more modest form of utilitarianism. According to it, each decision falls under a rule, and rules that have ethical value are more than rules of thumb. Whether a rule is to be considered acceptable is to be decided by the consequences of adopting the rule, or, in other words, the consequences of its universalization. Thus, a situation like that in Tennessee Williams's play *Suddenly Last Summer*, where a wealthy widow will leave her money to a needy hospital on the condition that a sane patient be turned insane and a lobotomy performed so that embarrasing facts about the widow will never be revealed, becomes immoral even though many lives could be saved by a better-equipped hospital. Even if the lobotomy were to be kept a secret, still it would be immoral. The problem is that the 'practice' is not generalizable. It is the total result which is bad, regardless of whether the result of a single action is good or bad.

Discriminatory practices toward linguistic minorities, allocation of language functions for educational opportunities, and other familiar concerns that plague our society can be looked at in the light of the latter utilitarian criteria. Obviously those practices will not pass the test. But it so happens that bad practices still persist regarding linguistic inequality. This is the problem.

Both Kant's and ruleutilitarian criteria rest heavily upon the assumption that rational decisions are universalizable. But legislators often follow their political inclinations or heed persuasive information and biases rather than the dictates of their own reason. The relationship between morality and rationality needs to be clarified. Language-status decisions, like many others, may be

1. moral and rational;
2. moral and irrational;
3. immoral and rational;
4. immoral and irrational.

An example of the first kind is the granting of rights to use vernacular languages as media of instruction in the public shcools and provide equal education opportunities through federal funding under Title VII of the E.S.E.A. Decisions were based upon the recognition that equality of opportunity in education cannot be viewed as simply a matter of offering the student the same staff, the same building, and the same lunch menu, but rather as a matter of providing the students with an opportunity to learn in their vernacular, at least until they were able to learn in the dominant language. Assimilationist in the final analysis, this practice is rational and generalizable with respect to specific language functions, although it may not be the best of all possible alternatives, which would include a more egalitarian approach to the overall ethoglossia of the language.

Examples of the second kind are rather infrequent since they include decisions that end up being immoral for the wrong reasons, or by chance. The so called 'doctrine of the double effect' is illuminating here. The doctrine is based upon a distinction between what the decision maker *foresees* or *intends* as the result of a voluntary decision and the *actual* consequences. For instance, increasing the educational level of a community may also increase its suicide rate, and yet we should not regard the furthering of education (intent) as tantamount to driving people to kill themselves, although this happens as part of the *actual* consequences. But the opposite is also possible, although less frequent. Thus, the cohesiveness and self-awareness of a linguistic group may result from discriminatory practices intended to assimilate or eliminate the group. Some of the effects of attempting to kill a language may be, ultimately, by chance, beneficial to the community. But this is a rather odd situation and not entirely relevant to our analysis here.

Examples of immoral and rational decisions concerning language status can be found in numerous cases of linguistic assimilation. Language has been used carefully as a means of social control. The systematic denial of official designation of language varieties (Leibowitz 1974, 1976) has created social polarization and ghettoization. Certainly these practices are not universalizable, although they still prevail.

Examples of immoral and irrational decisions are also frequent. The history of education, including language education, provides ample evidence of instances where the use of vernacular languages was prohibited in public schools, with no apparent acceptable reason. The case of *Meyer* v. *Nebraska* (1923), *Yu Con Eng* v. *Trinidad* (1925), and others may illustrate this case.

Linguistic inequalities are not so different from other forms of inequalities, but they are harder to see and even harder to change. Even if we assume that language status decisions are made with the best of intentions, are rational and moral, still ethical criteria depend upon the ideologies of the dominant group. The very definition of equality responds to certain ideological principles. Think, for a moment, how long has it taken for many to come to the realization that equality of persons and equality of opportunity (Williams 1962 [1970] : 168) are different and should be treated differently. But the road toward equality and the test criteria for equality are clear, though not always easy to apply. Linguistic minorities should not be treated as a means by the state or by the dominant groups but rather as ends in themselves. Support of language functions and eventual officialization of minority languages, at least commensurable to their contribution to the state, is just, and it is also the best alternative to a harmonious coexistence of linguistic groups. Contractual pluralism is better than natural pluralism, natural pluralism is better than assimilationism. Language-status planning will continue to be contingent upon drifting ideologies.

NOTES

1. Cf., for example, the 'Postcript' to J.Rubin's article in this volume.
2. Many of the variables used by Kloss in 1968 were used in his 1966 paper.
3. Spanish had official status in New Mexico during the territorial legislature, and the session records were kept in both languages. During 1860s Spanish was still the lan-

guage of the deliberations, and English appeared only in written documents. Legislation passed in 1874 and 1889 ensured that laws were to govern in the language in which they had been passed whether Spanish or English, and that persons holding office who keep written records should be proficient in either English or Spanish (not necessarily in both), depending upon the language used for record keeping. The Constitution of 1912 ensured the publication of Spanish versions of the laws for the first 20 years of statehood. This limit was extended by 10 years each in 1931 and 1943. The last annual Spanish edition of the state laws appeared in 1949. However, a letter from the New Mexico Legislation Council of August 14, 1975, states that 'although certain election materials and notices are required to be printed in Spanish and we do have a bilingual education provision, New Mexico is not officially bilingual'. This clarifies somewhat the difference between a language with official status and a language which is officially promoted. Many people think they are the same. (I am indebted to H. Kloss in this footnote).

4. Much of the material presented by Stewart in his 1968 paper is contained in his 1962 paper.
5. It is beyond the scope of this paper to deal with the concept of 'convention' and 'conventional rule'. An account of this topic can be found in Lewis 1969.
6. I have dealt with the concept of 'captive community' and the issue of rights elsewhere (cf. J. Cobarrubias and M. Cobarrubias, 1978).

REFERENCES

Altoma, Salih J. (1970 [1974]) 'Language education in Arab countries and the role of the academies', *Current Trends in Linguistics* 6: 690-720. (Also reprinted in *Advance in Language Planning*, ed. by J.A. Fishman, The Hague, Mouton, 1974).
Amos, F.J.C. (1972), 'Management of new local authorities: problems and opportunities', *Journal of the Town Planning Institute* 58: 341-343.
Beckman, Norman (1964 [1973]) 'The planner as a bureaucrat', *Journal of the American Institute of Planners* 30 (Nov. 1964). (Also in *A Reader in Planning Theory*, ed. by A. Faludi. Oxford, Pergamon, 1973).
Berstein, Basil (1960), 'Language and social class', *British Journal of Sociology* 11: 271-276.
_____(1961a), 'Social structure, language and learning', *Educational Research* 3: 167-176.
_____(1961b), 'Aspects of language learning in the genesis of the social process', *Journal of Child Psychology and Psychiatry* 1: 313-324.
_____(1962), 'Social class, linguistic code and grammatical elements', *Language and Speech* 5: 221-240.
_____(1971), 'Social class, language and socialization', in *Current Trends in Linguistics* 12, ed. by A.S. Abramson et al. The Hague, Mouton.
Bright, William, editor (1966), *Sociolinguistics.* The Hague, Mouton.
Chafe, Wallace (1962), 'Estimates regarding the present speakers of North American Indian languages', *International Journal of Applied Linguistics* 28: 162-171.
Cobarrubias, J., and M. Cobarrubias (1978), 'The rights of prisoners and moral reformation', in *Bioethics and Human Rights*, ed. by E.L. Bandman and B. Bandman. Boston, Little, Brown.
Dittmar, Norbert (1976), *A Critical Survey of Sociolinguistics, Theory and Application.*

New York, St. Martin.

Eisenstadt, S.N. (1954), *The Absorption of Migrants*. London, Routledge.

Ervin-Tripp, Susan M. (1972), 'On sociolinguistic rules: alternation and co-occurrence', in *Directions in Sociolinguistics*, ed. by J.J. Gumperz and D. Hymes. New York, Holt, Rinehart and Winston.

Faludi, Andreas (1973a), *Planning Theory*. Oxford, Pergamon.

_____ , editor (1973b), *A Reader in Planning Theory*. Oxford, Pergamon.

Ferguson, Charles A. (1959), 'Diglossia', *Word* 15: 325-340. (Also in *Language and Social Context*, ed. by Pier Paolo Giglioli. Harmondsworth; Penguin, 1972.

_____ (1966), 'National sociolinguistic profile formulas', in *Sociolinguistics*, ed. by William Bright. The Hague, Mouton.

Fishman, J.A., editor (1971a), *Advances in the Sociology of Language*. The Hague, Mouton.

_____ (1971b), 'The sociology of language: an interdisciplinary social science approach to language in society', in *Advances in the Sociology of Language*, ed. by J.A. Fishman. The Hague, Mouton.

_____ (1972), *The Sociology of Language*. Rowley, Mass., Newbury House.

_____ editor (1974), *Advances in Language Planning*. The Hague, Mouton.

_____ (1979), 'The significance of the ethnic community mother tongue school: introduction to a study'. Paper presented at the Bilingual Higher Education Summer Institute, Seton Hall University, N.J.

Fishman J.A., R. Cooper, and A.W. Conrad (1977), *The Spread of English*. Rowley Mass., Newbury House.

_____ , C.A. Ferguson, and J. Das Gupta, editors (1968), *Language Problems in Developing Nations*. New York, Wiley.

Grimshaw, Allen D. (1971), 'Sociolinguistics', in *Advances in the Sociology of Language*, ed. by J.A. Fishman. The Hague, Mouton.

Gumperz, John J., and D. Hymes (1972), *Directions in Sociolinguistics*. New York, Holt, Rinehart and Winston.

Gumperz, John J. (1964), 'Linguistic and social interaction in two communities', in *The Ethnography of Communications*, ed. by J.J. Gumperz and D. Hymes, special publication of *American Anthropologist* 66, Part 2, 137-153.

Hall, Robert A., Jr. (1952), 'Bilingualism and applied linguistics', *Zeitschrift fur Phonetik und allgemeine Sprachwissenschaft* 6: 13-30.

Halliday, M.A.K., A. McIntosh and P. Strevens (1964), *The Linguistic Sciences and Language Teaching*. London, Longmans.

Hart, H.L.A. (1953), *Definition and Theory in Jurisprudence*. Oxford, Clarendon.

Haugen, Einar (1966), 'Linguistics and language planning', in *Sociolinguistics*, ed. by William Bright. The Hague, Mouton.

Hazai, Georg (1970 [1974]) 'Linguistics and language issues in Turkey', in *Current Trends in Linguistics* 6, ed. by Thomas Sebeok: 183. The Hague, Mouton. (Also reprinted in *Advances in Language Planning*, ed. by Joshna A. Fishman. The Hague, Mouton, 1974.

Heath, Shirley Brice (1972), *Telling Tongues: Language Policy in Mexico*. New York, Teachers College Press.

Hill, Jane, and Kenneth Hill (1977), 'Language death and relexification in Tlaxcalan Nahuatl', *International Journal of the Sociology of Language* 12: 33-69.

Hymes, Dell, editor (1971), *Pidginization and Creolization of Languages*. Cambridge, Cambridge University Press.

Kloss, Heinz (1966), 'Types of multilingual communities: a discussion of ten variables',

Sociological Inquiry 36: 135-145.

—————(1968), Notes concerning a language-nation typology. in *Language Problems in Developing Nations*, ed. by J.A. Fishman, C.A. Ferguson, and J. Das Gupta. New York, Wiley.

—————(1969), *Research Possibilities on Group Bilingualism: A Report*, Quebec, International Center for Research on Bilingualism.

—————(1971), 'Language rights of immigrant groups', *International Migration Review* 5 (2): 250-268.

—————(1977), *The American Bilingual Tradition*. Rowley, Mass., Newbury House.

Leibowitz, Arnold H. (1974), 'Language as a means of social control: the United States experience'. Educational Resources Information Center (ERIC), ED 093168.

————— (1976), 'Language and the law: the exercise of political power through official designation of language', in *Language and Politics*, ed. by W. O'Barr and J.F. O'Barr, 449-466. The Hague, Mouton.

Lewis, David K. (1969), *Convention*. Cambridge, Mass., Harvard University Press.

Lewis, Glyn E. (1977), 'Bilingualism and bilingual education: the ancient world to the Renaissance', in *Frontiers of Bilingual Education*, ed. by B. Spolsky and R. Cooper. Rowley, Mass., Newbury House.

Mackey, William F. (1976), *Bilinguisme et Contact des Langues*. Paris, Editions Klincksieck.

McDougal, M., H. Laswell, and L. Chen (1976), 'Freedom from discrimination in choice of language and international human rights', *Southern Illinois University Journal* 1: 151-174.

Miemois, Karl Johan (1980), *The Minority Client's View of Public Administration in a Bilingual Society*, University of Helsinki.

Minett, M.J. (1971), 'Is planning a profession?', *Journal of the Town Planning Insitute* 57: 231.

Pool, Jonathan (1973), 'Mass opinion on language policy: the case of Canada', in *Language Planning: Current Issues and Research*, ed. by Joan Rubin and Roger Shuy. Washington D.C., Georgetown University Press.

Robertson, D.M. (1910), *A History of the French Academy*. New York. (Cited in Haugen 1966).

Sibayan, Bonifacio P. (1974), 'Language policy, language engineering and literacy in the Philippines',*Current Trends in Linguistics* 8: 1038-1062. (Reprinted in *Advances in Language Planning*, ed. by Joshua A. Fishman. The Hague, Mouton, 1974).

—————(1978), 'Bilingual education in the Philippines: strategy and structure', in *International Dimensions of Bilingual Education*, ed. by James Alatis. Washington D.C., Georgetown University Press.

Stewart, William A. (1962), 'An outline of linguistic typology for describing multilingualism', in *Study of the Role of Second Languages in Asia, Africa and Latin America*, ed. by F.A. Rice, 15-25. Washington, D.C. CAL-MLA.

————— (1968), 'A sociolinguistic typology for describing national multilingualism', in *Readings in the Sociology of Language*, ed. by J.A. Fishman. The Hague, Mouton.

Trudgill, P., and G.A. Tzavaras (1977), 'Why Albanian-Greeks are not Albanians: lanfuage shift in Attica and Biotia', in *Language, Ethnicity and Intergroup Relations*, ed. by H. Giles. New York, Academic Press.

Valdman, Albert, editor (1977), *Pidgin and Creole Linguistics*. Bloomington, Indiana University Press.

Whiteley, Wilfred H. (1971 [1974]) 'Language policies of independent African states', *Current Trends in Linguistics* 7: 548-558. (Reprinted in *Advances in Language Plan-*

ning, ed. by J.A. Fishman. The Hague, Mouton, 1974.
Williams, Bernard (1962 [1970]), 'The idea of equality', in *Moral Concepts,* ed. by J. Feinberg. Oxford, Oxford University Press.

*note—article good to explain rise of monolingual
sentiment in U.S., esp. 101-102 describes well what
happened, but not satisfactorily why?*

SHIRLEY BRICE HEATH and FREDERICK MANDABACH

Language Status Decisions and the Law in the United States*

Within the first decade after passage of the Bilingual Education Act of 1968, 'national language policy' became a topic of debate for the U.S. public. Congress, in assessing the results of a decade of federal funding of bilingual education, was asked to consider bilingual education as part of a general policy of accommodation to bilingualism in legal, medical, and other social-service settings. The Presidential Commission on Foreign Languages and International Studies, formed in 1978, repeatedly heard the public urge that it recommend a comprehensive language policy for legislative consideration. The 1978 Executive Order on Plain English set clear writing as a governmental goal. However, federal agency rulings and state legislation designed to make public information available in cohesive, clear, and concise prose were difficult to implement in the absence of a comprehensive official policy on how to judge and accomplish 'plain English'. In each of these three cases, a response to piecemeal efforts to choose and change the oral and written language has led some citizens to call for an official national language policy, one which would decide the status of English *vis-à-vis* other languages and provide citizens with standards for their public language.

Those who think seriously about enactment, implementation, interpretation, and enforcement of the law or laws necessary to achieve such a policy must, however, consider the history of how language status decisions have been made in the United States. The legal history of legislative and judicial decisions related to language in the United States is reviewed here in an effort to answer the question of what has happened in the past when language issues reached the federal level of decision making. A majority of current efforts to obtain a national language policy are based on the belief that it will diminish discrimination based on language; it is therefore important to know whether or not there have been past legal efforts either to sanction or to promote linguistic discrimination. It is also critical for those considering a

*The research upon which this paper is based was supported by a grant (NIE-G-78-0192) from the National Institute of Education, and was completed while the first author was a Visiting Scholar in the Department of Linguistics, Stanford University, 1978-1979.

national language policy today to have a historical perspective on the intentions and principles reflected in any laws which may have attempted to control the language behavior of U.S. citizens, and to be able to place these laws in the context of events at the time of their passage.

The philosophical and legal heritage from England's history helped influence language decisions in the colonial and national history of the United States. Thus, for the origins of legal considerations of language in the United States, one must go back many centuries. The story of language-status achievement for English since the time of the Norman Conquest is not a simple one, and there are many reasons for the complexities of this history. Initially, there is the problem of determining the situation in which to define the terms 'status' and 'English'. Each of these has different definitions, depending on the level of interaction at which it is being viewed. For example, 'status determination' in the language-planning literature is usually taken to mean decisions related to choice of official language for the nation's government and public affairs. However, in the history of English, there have been occasions when debates have centered on the status of English as a language to be spread to other nations, as well as within a single nation in competition with other languages, such as French, Welsh, or German. Status decisions have also been debated both for and at local, regional, and national levels on the choice of language to be used in business, educational, legal, and religious institutions. Distinctions have sometimes been made at the international, national, regional, and local levels between the spread of English in both the written and the spoken channel or in only one of these channels. To further complicate the determination of status, there have been different conceptions of the term 'English'. For some decision makers, English has meant a generalized language form, without regard to its varieties. For other decision-makers, English has meant only a standardized, codified norm, legitimated through its literary forms.

THE BRITISH BACKGROUND

This paper is an attempt to examine these different approaches to determining the status of English in the United States and England, but most particularly in the United States. Heath (1976a), in a review of the language-status achievement of English in the British colonies of America, pointed out that both decision-making institutions and decision-making processes were conceived in the Old World but born and nurtured in the New World. It is necessary, therefore, to look briefly at ways in which English became the mother tongue of Great Britain after 1066, the time of the Norman Conquest. After 1066, Norman French became the standard language of Parliament and the courts and the medium of common daily communication for the upper classes and polite society. Latin was the language of scholarship and legal writings. English, initially reputed to have been relatively unknown among the rulers, continued as the popular tongue of the people. The absence of any official status for English helped provoke King Henry III's English Proclamation issued in 1258. The proclamation railed against monoglot French speakers but achieved nothing in giving English an improved status. However, status promotion through increased use came about as poets, preachers, and some officials of the law quietly used English in their writings and argued for the practicality of their deed. In 1300, a poet justified translating his work into English by noting

I have normally read French verses everywhere here; it is mostly done for the Frenchmen — What is there for him who knows no French? As for the nation of England, it is an Englishman who is usually there. It ought to be necessary to speak mostly the speech that one can best get on with. Seldom has the English tongue by any chance been praised in France; if we give everyone their own language, it seems to me we are doing them no injury. I am speaking to the English layman . . . . (translated from *Cursor Mundi* in Cottle 1969: 17).

By the end of the twelfth century, a large portion of the upper classes had acquired English as well as French; bilingualism was common in this group. By the mid-thirteenth century, English had spread to an increasing variety of uses across classes. By the end of the fourteenth century, an increasing number of legal and quasi-legal documents were written in English, though as yet it had no official status for oral use in the courts. English had become the mother tongue of Englishmen, the general mother tongue of all classes. French was the language of artistic display, an evidence of learning and proper social contacts. By the end of the Middle English period (1100-1500), English was the dominant language of Parliament, English grammar was taught in schools, and Chaucer's *Tales* had widely publicized, if not entirely legitimated, English as a literary language. Few among the nobility knew French, and Anglo-Norman literature had been superseded by English writings. Except for higher education and the law, English had achieved recognition as the norm; in literary art, schools, daily communication in the business world, and social exchanges across classes, English had gained a secure status.

Only in the universities and the courts was little or no status given to English. Latin was the medium of universities. In the courts, the status of English for oral and written legal matters varied at different levels of legal action across the Middle and early Modern English periods. By the end of the thirteenth century, Law French (sometimes call Norman-French or French-

Norman) was the undisputed oral language of the courts as well as the code of legal literature. Throughout the Middle English period, French predominated as the language of the law. In the late thirteenth century, the practice of law became a profession, and lawyers over the next centuries consistently attempted to protect the language of their profession — Law French — from changes or threats imposed from outside. However, by 1356, English was allowed as the language of oral court proceedings at local levels. In 1362, the Statute of Pleading declared that if the oral language of the court remained French, the people of the King's court had 'no knowledge or understanding of that which is said for them or against them' (36 Edward III, st. I c.15, cited in Holdsworth 1923: II, 477). Parliament's growing influence and its use of English spread the notion of English as a language of legal-like situations, and by the end of the fifteenth century, an increasing portion of the oral language of courts was English. Nevertheless, pleadings (formal writings) remained in French, but arguments at the bar could be carried out in English. By the sixteenth century, written pleadings in the common-law courts were written in English. The Chancery law, or law of the Church, was in English, though specialized terms from Law French were plentiful. In 1650, Parliament passed *An Act turning the Books of the Law and all Process and Proceedings in Courts of Justice, into English.* However, struggles ensuing from the Act were bitter: lawyers resisted, the statute was alternately validated and killed in shifts of political power during the seventeenth century, Latin and French each made intermittent gains in either specialized acts of the court or the written law. In 1731, an English-for-lawyers law was passed which called for all proceedings in courts in Great Britain to be 'in the English tongue and language only, and not in Latin or French, or any other tongue or language whatsoever . . . . ' (cited from *Records in English*, 1731, 4 Geo. II, c. 26, in Mellinkoff 1963: 133-134). Major resistance to the shift to English came from those who felt it made lawyers 'illiterate' and did not help the knowledge of the public on matters of law. The law was so weakened in revisions made before its enactment that its original intent was all but lost.

However, by the end of the eighteenth century, English was the accepted language of the law, though codified with a heavy retention of terms and styles both Latin and Law French. English was the language of Parliament, and though there were many diverse dialects throughout England, the tongue of Englishmen was clearly English. The same was not clearly the case for other parts of Great Britain. Subjects in Wales and Ireland were still to be convinced that English was the language of Great Britain. In the early sixteenth century, Henry VIII began an attack on Irish customs, religion, laws, and language. Agreements drawn up between individual Irishmen and the English government during this period charged Irishmen to change their names, to speak English, and to adopt 'English habits and manner'. The same efforts were directed against Wales: all legal proceedings were to be in English and offices filled by those who spoke English (Heath 1976a; Nichols 1977).

In England, once English seemed established, reformers turned their efforts toward setting a standard norm of English. Schools characterized grammar as a set of analytical procedures and promoted grammatical categories as logical or quasi-logical (Michael 1970). In the Middle English period, the close connections between grammar and language in use were not obscured; the teaching of grammar was related to reading, explanation, and criticism. However, by the seventeenth century, grammars of English emphasized correctness of usage and pronunciation in an idealized norm. By the eighteenth century, a seeming fascination with language, grammatical correctness, and changes in language was reflected in the popular media. Magazines condemned 'the poverty of language' said to circumscribe thought and to promote improper behaviors and prejudices. Language was a popular topic, and the pages of fashionable magazines covered topics ranging from chemical nomenclature to dialects and foreignisms in English (cf. Hanes 1940).

In connection with this popular support urging propriety in language on discerning people of all Great Britain, there was a strong effort to institutionalize the standards of speaking. An academy for regulating speech was proposed consistently and enthusiastically between 1712 and 1800 by many leaders of English society and politics, including Lord Chesterfield, Thomas Sheridan, Lord Monboddo, and Dean Swift (Read 1938). Samuel Johnson's dictionary became the instrument, if not the institution, which 'fixed' the language during this period. It did so without support from a national language academy, though publication and promotion of such a dictionary were viewed as major tasks of any proposed academy. However, had official publication of a dictionary come about, such a work was not to be judged as dictation of choice to Englishmen. One proponent of the academy made this point very clear:

. . . lest you should think that I would indeavor to force Men by Law to write with Propriety and Correctness of Style, I must declare, that I mean only to force them to spell with Uniformity . . . . and I can not but esteem the English Language to be of such Consequence to Englishmen in general that a proper Act, for the Improvement and Preservation of it, would do Honor to an English Parliament. (*Observations upon the English Language* . . . , 1752, cited in Read 1938: 145-146).

This comment highlights two critical factors which characterize language-status achievement in England. The first is the view that Englishmen must not be forced by law in their language choices; the second is the conviction that discerning citizens will, of their own volition, make proper decisions about language in order to do honor to their identity. In England, Englishmen had to come to a choice of English and use of proper English through their individual efforts to improve themselves. Exposure to good models, study of manuals of speaking, and diligent attention to prescribed grammar rules were behaviors which gave evidence of good character, taste, and judgment. Rejection of a national academy underscored the view that achievement of status for the English language was not a matter for Parliamentary statutes, but rather one of individual choice for socially-minded individuals. Those born into classes or geographic environments which did not offer exposure to the standard norms of language were to expose themselves to proper speakers, and they had to decide as individuals to adopt the prestige dialect. Failure to make this choice left them open to charges of defaming or downgrading the nation and showing evidence of an absence of self-control, failure to use logic and reason, and lack of diligence in pursuit of good. Today, in spite of numerous efforts to make the status of English 'official' in England and to prescribe officially the variety of English which is the national norm, only two statutes survive. One of these requires Crown writs and incidental papers to be in English; the other requires sailors on British ships to have a knowledge of English (*Crown Writs to be in English,* 1868, 31 & 32 Vict., c. 101, s. 90, and *Prohibition of Engagement of Seamen* . . . , 1906, cited in Mellinkoff 1963: 4-5).

THE UNITED STATES LEGACY

The achievement of the status of English in England came about not through statute, but through cultural and societal forces. Englishmen did not see language as a suitable overt instrument of control to be wielded by the state over its citizens. In England, in the years following the Norman Conquest, official rulings and statutes did not establish English; English became established through the choices of the population, and in large part through its use by the literary elite. Even within the law, mandates did not succeed entirely in removing Latin and Law French from legal usage, either oral or written. The law profession worked to maintain the specialized language of its profession, because it served certain needs and was appropriate for its institutions of learning and practice. There was no doubt, however, that Englishmen viewed English as the language which *should* be chosen by discerning citizens, and that the English modeled by the upper classes and prescribed as correct in grammar books *should* be used by English speakers. Those who did not choose either English or the proper form of English left themselves open to criticism and social exclusion.

The United States inherited the English reluctance to mandate language choice or to regulate language through political decisions. England extended this reluctance to legislate choices for its own citizens to the indigenous of its New World colonies (Heath 1976a). Unlike leaders of the Castilian empire in the New World, England's colonial administrators consistently failed to consider language as the instrument of forced assimilation. Language was viewed as something changed through exposure of speakers to appropriate learning environments and models, not through imposition of political force. In short, for Englishmen, the English language and its culture were the great avenue by which people could, if they so chose, arrive at valuable knowledge, logical reasoning, acceptable ways of conducting one's life, and an advancement in social status.

In England, those born to wealth acquired the prestigious form of the language through the company they kept. In the United States colonies, those who obtained land and became planters, or those who became wealthy through business opportunities, could not count on exposure to ensure proper language choice for their sons. Some sent them to England or the Continent to be educated; those who provided tutoring for their sons here insisted they use English textbooks and study the pronunciation manuals most frequently used in England. Throughout the Revolutionary period and in the early national history, an 'English education' was stressed, and recalcitrant students of grammar were reminded that language was a mark of 'breeding' (cf. Farish 1957: xvii). The lower classes had no such exposure or opportunities on an extended basis, since schools were relatively scarce until well into the nineteenth century. They were forced to seek out proper books and company, using conversational partners as models. Women, though formally excluded or neglected in institutional educational opportunities, were often judged especially adept at studying English lessons and effectively putting these into practice in conversation and debate (Heath 1976b).

Within the United States, therefore, the status of English was achieved as it had been in England, without official declaration and without the help of an official academy. Books, models, and circumstances were the status builders for English in its standard variety. In spite of U.S. efforts to establish an academy of language, well-placed officials rejected the idea, and no such academy at the national level developed (Read 1936, Heath 1976c). Instead, Noah Webster's speller, grammars, and dictionary, and copious writings in the public media promoted the idea of an English for America. Often sold in a triplet package containing the Bible, the blue-backed speller, and a grammar, Webster's books filled a need for information on language desired across regions and classes. American periodicals in diverse fields also included articles, brief notes, and comments on language; the problem of achieving a characteristic norm without an internationally recognized literature was an issue of recurrent concern (cf. Free 1968: 172).

Amont the issues debated in these periodicals was the relative standing of

English with respect to the classical languages and modern foreign languages. Bilingualism and even multilingualism were praised and seen as desirable goals of education and association. Though there was a general tolerance for other languages and a recognition that they provided access to information not available in English, the push for an English education, often defined primarily in terms of its being offered in English and including heavy doses of spelling, grammar, and literature, was consistent and firm. English was recognized as 'mandated' by general usage across vocations and workaday situations in the public world. Yet myths have survived which suggest that either French or German almost became the national language.

One myth has promoted the idea that only one vote kept German from being the national language in the late eighteenth-century legislature. The accurate history of this incident, known as the 'Muhlenberg legend', is that a group of Virginia Germans requested that some laws of the United States be issued in German as well as English. A congressional committee favored the proposal, but when the issue came to a House vote, it was rejected 42 to 41. Frederick August Muhlenberg, a German-speaking Pennsylvanian, may have cast the deciding vote, but congressional records do not allow precise determination of this (Heath 1977). Other legends, current at both the time of the Revolution and in the mid-nineteenth century, suggested that French would become the language of the United States. Sir Herbert Croft, a British etymologist, reported in a letter of 1797 that Americans had once considered 'revenging themselves on England by rejecting its language and adopting that of France' (Croft 1797). American and British journalists in the mid-nineteenth century, a period of extreme cultural insecurity for Americans, picked up stories of the uncertainty of Americans about the dominance of their tongue over French or German (cf. Bristed 1855). However, in spite of these myths portraying French, German, or Latin as the national tongue, there was never serious doubt about the issue, and there was never any official declaration of the status of English.

How then did English achieve its status? In the colonial and early national periods, the question of the status of English resolved itself at local community levels, as individuals chose the language most necessary to economic survival and their own religious and social goals. Institutions provided choices; universities and colleges initially emphasized the classical languages as subjects of study but provided the majority of instruction in English. In the first half of the nineteenth century, English grammars and other writings on language stressed language uses (rhetoric, conversation) and were not nearly so vehement on prescribing correctness as were similar types of material after mid-century (Drake 1977). Webster, though today associated with prescriptivism in the public mind, urged the descriptive approach to grammar which was reflected in numerous grammars of the early nineteenth century:

. . . grammar is built solely on the *structure of language* . . . . Grammars are made to show the student what a language *is* — not, how it *ought to be*. They are compiled for boys, in schools, rather than for men of science, who ought to quit grammars which are the *streams,* and mount to the *source* of knowledge, the genuine construction of the language itself [italics in the original]. (Webster 1978: 6)

The choice of English over other languages and a preferred norm of English usage were matters of faith in the prevailing good judgment among the U.S. citizenry. There were, with the exception of American Indian policies, few efforts to restrict uses of other languages; instead, they were recognized as resources. In addition, diversity in language structures and uses was seen as a valuable asset (Heath 1977). In cities such as St. Louis, Cleveland, and New York, people who were reluctant to take their children out of work to place them in schools were offered bilingual education or instruction in their mother tongue as an incentive to school attendance (Kluwin, forthcoming; Tyack 1974). Private schools taught in the language of those groups which supported them (Kloss 1977: 6-167). Authors of folk literature of the period almost flaunted the dialect variation of the United States. By midcentury, however, these views were starting to shift. The United States began to look for ways of restricting variety, of cutting back on the resources of language varieties in the United States; the drive for uniformity and conformity in speech which reached its peak in the late nineteenth century had begun.

Numerous historical events related to language helped fuel the drive. Webster's dictionary was now being widely and noisily distributed by the Merriam Webster company. Publicity for the dictionary (and news coverage of questions surrounding authorship, rights, and editions) put the book fully in the public eye (e.g. Anonymous 1854a, 1854b). The common school was becoming an expected institution across the country; compulsory attendance laws were being debated in state legislatures. Urbanization and industrialization were bringing the different groups of America, many of which had earlier settled in rural areas and made their living in independent ventures, together for economic reward in urban industries.

By the end of the Civil War, the immigration of groups whose looks and speech were very different from the idealized norm of 'American' prompted widespread efforts, legal and social, to achieve linguistic uniformity and conformity. Composition and grammar books increasingly stressed learning to speak English correctly and leaving aside all other varieties. In a seeming 'search for order' (Weibe 1967) which prevailed at the end of the century and into the next, state laws controlling the teaching of foreign languages and the use of particular languages in teaching proliferated (Kloss 1977: 68 ff.). Literacy rulings became more and more stringent, eliminating more and more voters of different language backgrounds and competencies from the ballot box (Heath, forthcoming a). For all the power of precedent from England and habit established during the first century of nationhood, Americans began to legislate language in both the states and the territories. The history of relations with Puerto Rico, Hawaii, the Philippines, and the other territories of the United States from the late nineteenth century tells the story of a U.S. government intent on implanting English and diminishing the status of other languages as quickly as possible.[1] Contrary to the British mold and the seemingly established American way, forces at the federal level wanted to mandate language status and choice for the territories. State and local levels wanted to mandate language status and choice for their communities. Social institutions changed to reflect the new conservatism. Educational institutions made it clear that language use was a mark of character, taste, intelligence, and reason. In a society suddenly fearing its diversities might be too great to control, there were greater and greater needs for being able to predict the behavior and thoughts of one's neighbor. The choice of English and adherence to norms of corretness became marks openly stressed as those of good citizens, good Americans, and predictable rational neighbors (Piché 1977; Heath, forthcoming b). Legal statutes and cases, grammar texts, and records of school boards and superintendents confirm this shift in society by the last decades of the nineteenth century. The findings may generally be

1.   Until the mid-nineteenth century, very few stipulated restrictions on the teaching or use of languages other than English existed. The language used in instruction was determined not through political judgments, but in accord with the desires of parents and the economic resources of state and local school boards.

2.   Increasingly, throughout the latter half of the nineteenth century, English grammar and composition books and the popular press promoted the value of a standard English, and the use of English by all citizens. These skills were promoted as marks of 'good American citizens'.

3.   Nevertheless, the foreign-language press, local organizations, and private schools continued use of languages other than English. Private and parochial schools in numerous states taught in different languages, and some public school systems offered bilingual instruction across the curriculum.

4.   The policy of publishing state laws in languages other than English was continued in numerous states. The practice of distribution of laws in the language of diverse groups of the population had been initiated by the Constitutional Convention, which published its proceedings in English, German, and French. In states which did not wish to pay for publication of laws in other languages, state legislators often reminded their fellow congressmen that the foreign language press would take on this task and spare the states the expense.

5. Before 1890, only three states (Connecticut, Massachusetts, and Rhode Island) required that English be the language of instruction in the schools. In 1890, New York and seven midwestern states mandated instruction in English in private schools. In Wisconsin, opponents to the rule were able to have the act repealed.

6. In contradistinction to laws prohibiting the use of languages other than English for instruction in schools, laws were also passed which prohibited the teaching of other languages as subjects. In the 1870s, some midwestern states argued the economic basis of laws prohibiting the teaching of foreign languages; state educational funds should go to more important tasks. During World War I, foreign languages as subjects of instruction were forbidden on other grounds: knowledge of a foreign language was believed to be 'clearly harmful'.

It is somewhat ironic that in discussions of language status achievement, points (5) and (6) above have received the greatest attention. In particular, treatment of the *Lau* vs. *Nichols* case[2] (e.g. Teitelbaum and Hiller 1977) and the numerous considerations of its effect on the rights of linguistic minorities have made much of these earlier laws restricting language rights. What has often been lost in the mass of commentaries regarding these laws and the court cases they provoked is that three Supreme Court cases overturned *all* the low-court rulings upholding the restriction of the use of foreign languages.

In Nebraska the Siman Law of 1919 prohibited the teaching of foreign languages to children below the ninth grade. The purpose of the statute was that 'the English language should be and become the mother tongue' of children of immigrants and all other children reared in Nebraska.[3] Robert Meyer, a parochial school teacher, appealed his conviction for teaching German to a child who had not yet passed the eighth grade. The U.S. Supreme Court ruled in 1923 that the statute violated the Fourteenth Amendment. The court declared that the right of a teacher to teach a foreign language and the right of parents to have their child so instructed were rights protected by the Constitution.[4]

Iowa and Ohio passed legislation similar to the Siman Law. The Iowa law required that English be the medium of instruction in the schools.[5] Ohio also passed a law requiring that English be the language of instruction, and went even further by declaring English the official language of the State.[6] Nebraska reworked the Siman Law in an effort to avoid constitutional conflicts.[7] Once again the U.S. Supreme Court in 1923 ruled that these laws violated rights guaranteed by the Fourteenth Amendment.[8]

A 1922 Oregon law provided that all children aged eight through 15 had to attend public schools.[9] One effect of this act was to deny instruction in languages other than English, since instruction in other languages had been available in private schools. However, in 1925, the U.S. Supreme Court struck down the law on the grounds that the State had no general power 'to standardize its children by forcing them to accept instruction from public teachers only'.[10] The State's method of forcing assimilation was found in violation of the Foruteenth Amendment.

In 1920, the foreign-language schools of Hawaii, established primarily by Asians and conducted in Chinese, Korean, or Japanese, were the subject of restrictive legislation.[11] The act imposed fees and limited hours and restricted the required teacher's permit to those who possessed a good knowledge of English. In 1927, the U.S. Supreme Court, noting that the law would probably destroy the schools, ruled that the law violated the due-process-of-law protections of the Constitution. Since Hawaii was a territory rather than a state, the ruling made clear that the rights of parents and students were protected from acts by the Federal government as well as by the states. On the face of it, the U.S. Supreme Court in these decisions moved to maintain a legacy of restraint on imposing English as an overt instrument of control, as a tool of forced assimilation.

If law has not created and maintained the status of English, what has? More specifically, what forces have created and maintained the public belief that throughout our past, English has had an official or quasi-official status somehow linked to the national good, and institutions have been and are, therefore, bound to promote the use and teaching of good English in speaking, reading, and writing? Edwin Newman attacks the logic, reason, and loyalty of citizens who do not speak 'a civil tongue'. The general citizenry is fearful of bilingual education as a new divisive force in the society, one which has never before appeared, because prior foreign-language speakers acquiesced in the use of English. The use of languages other than English and the failure of students to acquire adequate skills in reading, writing, and speaking English are held up as new problems, problems citizens resent having to deal with in a period in which they see all problems as public problems to be solved through increased expenditures. In short, the socialization of those who cry out against these problems has led them to believe that the current language situation is an aberration running counter to the past. What forces, intellectual and sociocultural, have prompted these beliefs?

Two such forces of the past half century are suggested here. The first of these is the role society determined that English should play in the curriculum and in the judgment of individuals; the second is the degree of intensity of legal activities related to abridging the freedom of speech. In many ways, the second may be said to be influenced by the first, but the second was also fostered during the period from 1919 through the 1950s by a fear of 'the foreign element', based primarily on the belief that it did indeed threaten the nation.

During the period between 1860 and 1920, American society regarded the public school as the institution to create a unified conforming citizenry. To support the school in its efforts to organize the linguistic and cultural knowledge and behavior of U.S. citizens, an expanding network of training institutions, publishing houses, and professional organizations developed. Acquisition of the use and appreciation of a standard English became a primary goal for young Americans in the education system. The 'right' language was both a fundamental instrument and a necessary symbol of knowledge and character. There is no scholarly study of the intellectual and social history of the teaching of English in the United States. Such a history does exist for England (Mathieson 1975), and its pages tell a story of powerful socialization of and by teachers of English similar to that of the U.S. As 'preachers of culture', English teachers have been and are trained to pass on their subject and its related skills with a strong sense of moral purpose. Texts and training programs have emphasized that learning English well prepares one for life and for exhibiting all manner of positive characteristics. The goodness of the speech gives evidence of the goodness of the speaker. English teachers have claimed that ethics and esthetics are transmitted through the 'laws of the language', and correct grammar has close connections with 'correct thinking' (Heath forthcoming b). Guarding one's use of language helps one guard the opinions expressed. Proper language was identified in the American mind as a semi-patriotic symbol. Since the late nineteenth century, these views have been perpetuated; the present generation of Americans has been trained in these views, as were their teachers and their teachers before them.

The second contributing factor to a general climate of opinion more restrictive in its approach to language than our national laws has been the free-speech litigation of the past 50 years. Prior to 1919, there were, for all intents and purposes, no First Amendment cases in the U.S. courts. However, during the very period (1919-1925) in which states scrambled to pass laws demanding English only in their schools, at the ballot box, and as a requirement for employment, courts sentenced over 1,000 people to jail for subversive speech. In these cases, prosecution and conviction were based on the notion of 'inchoate crime', i.e. words were said which made people fear something would happen, although no action ensured. The speech people used made them socially dangerous. The thousands of cases which went to trial in the period between World War I and the late 1950s had the support of a general prevailing belief in the causal relationship between speech and behavior. Justice Holmes attempted to objectify this view of the link between mental phenomena and behavior by proposing the 'clear and present danger' doctrine. Judicial decisions of the 1920s having to do with speech critical of national policies emphasized the power of the State to restrain free speech because of its concern with the risk of crimes and disorder ensuing from speech (Gunther

1976: Chapters 6 and 7). Decisions throughout the period were based on the view that language is a predictor, or at least an indicator, of behavior. Increasingly during this period, the phrase 'radical' came to be 'alien radical', and alien language was seen as especially likely to foretell radical behavior.

These First Amendment cases peaked at the same time as the nation experienced massive fear of the foreign, the alien. Until the late 1960s, a majority of those tried on subversive-speech charges were either aliens or individuals linked with 'alien elements' of the society. Relatively few First Amendment cases went to court in the Viet Nam protests of the late 1960s; protesters were children of the establishment, not foreigners. They were seen as individuals who had gone astray, but who could (and probably would) move back into the mainstream of American culture. Unlike the defendants of earlier cases, their speech was not that of foreigners, seen as inherently suspect in terms of absorption into the American culture. Detailed arguments related to the legal doctrine of free-speech cases and the relation of this doctrine to language concerns in general are reviewed elsewhere (Heath and Mandabach forthcoming). Most important for our purposes here is emphasis of the fact that the current trend in legal doctrine is to take certain political risks in order to ensure freedom of speech, i.e. to move away from the past willingness of the courts to try inchoate-crime free-speech cases. Arguments supporting this view maintain that freedom of speech should have a preferred position among freedoms because freedom of speech is a fundamental liberty, one necessary to ensure individual self-expression and the development of individual potential. Legal doctrine since the McCarthy era has moved toward making a firm distinction between belief/opinion and forms of conduct, between expression or communication of ideas and action. In educational litigation, the same trend was reflected in *Tinker* vs. *Des Moines Independent School Dist.* 393 U.S. 503 (1969), in which the majority decision stated that 'state-operated schools may not be enclaves of totalitarianism. School officials do not possess absolute authority over their students'. The Court specifically pointed out diversity as a way of enhancing the educational process:

The Nation's future depends upon leaders trained through wide exposure to that robust exchange of ideas which discovers truth 'out of a multitude of tongues, rather than through any kind of authoritarian selection'. (*Tinker, supra,* at 512, quoting the court's earlier statement in *Keyishian* vs. *Board of Regents,* 385 U.S. 589, 603 [1967])

The *Tinker* case and others make it evident that in terms of achieving educational aims, the court is moving toward placing greater stress on the process of education than on its contents (Berkman 1970), and these aims are being interpreted broadly to provide what Justice Brandeis termed the final end of the state: 'to make men free to develop their faculties . . .' (*Whitney* vs. *California* 274 U.S. 357, at 375 [1927]). These trends and aims seem to be in keeping with those espoused by current proponents of bilingual-bicultural education. Does this shift in legal doctrine then bode well for a return to an appreciation and tolerance of language diversity?

The answer is no. In law, doctrine is illuminated by history. A historical review of the social and cultural context of cases having to do with language in the broadest sense, ranging from free speech to literacy laws and the uses and purposes of language in education makes us aware that it is simplistic to define the status of English today in terms of only the few laws and cases related to language minorities per se which exist. Moreover, history helps us recognize the power of social and economic circumstances which forced the drastic shifts in attitude which occurred in the late nineteenth century and first half of the twentieth. Fear of a 'foreign threat' was fed by racism, intense competition for economic survival and mobility, and two world wars. To unify and conform seemed logical answers, and to do so through control by force of law became a strategy of state and local policy makers. At the federal level, these strategies to restrict foreign languages were rejected; however, their philosophical assumptions of the links between language and behavior were supported in the free-speech cases, particularly those of the World War I period. Currently, legal doctrine is questioning the bases of decision in these cases. The view that law should control or restrict language in order to control behavior currently has little legal support. Repression of languages other than English and abridgment of freedom of speech have little legal sanction.

Yet many linguistic minorities, and some educators and social scientists, argue that there is repression. The legal history, however, does not show that this repression has a basis in law as, for example, denial of the civil rights of blacks did before the landmark cases of the 1950s. It has not been the law which has repressed language diversity, but society. Therefore, the current shift in legal doctrine cannot be expected to be of much help in promoting bilingual-bicultural aims in the society. Observers of American society since Toqueville have noted the American tendency to conformity, to ask the question, 'What is expected of us?' Institutions have tended to move further than the law and to maintain that what is expected is promotion and maintenance of English. Restrictions on the use of languages other than English have been imposed through the unwritten laws of institutions. *Laws* perceived as violating basic national values, i.e. restricting basic freedoms, can be contested as unconstitutional; to contest unwritten laws or *norms of behavior* is much more difficult. We are left then with the historical fact that where there has been no policy, society has created an unwritten 'policy' which is the legacy of English history. One observer has assessed the U.S. failure to enact a specific language policy as 'one of history's little ironies' and suggested 'no polyglot empire of the old world has dared to be as ruthless in imposing a single language upon its whole population as was the liberal republic dedicated to the proposition that all men are created equal' (Johnson 1949: 118-119). The absence of compulsion has been an indirect compulsion for learning English. Haugen (1966) termed the driving force behind language shift 'individual enterprise': if individuals or groups rejected English (or its standard variety), they handicapped themselves, because they limited their chances for socioeconomic mobility and valuation as good citizens. And they have not had even 'the inner consolation of feeling that they defied tyrannous authority' (Johnson 1949: 119).

In its early period, the U.S. valued diversity of language and maintained the English legal custom of not regulating language officially or denying personal liberties in language. However, the late nineteenth century gave rise to promotion of a monolingual tradition and emphasis on standard English as the mark of reason, ethics, and esthetics; the tolerance of diversity which had characterized the early national history declined sharply. An English-only, standard-English-preferred policy was institutionalized though not legalized. Thus the status of English in the U.S. today is based not only on the British custom of no legal restrictions on language, but also on an intolerance to linguistic diversity akin to that which has been prevalent throughout British history. A recent study of language attitudes in Westernized nations of the world concluded that only the British still use accent to judge an individual's standing in the community (cf. Fowler 1965). The British maintain a chauvinistic and exclusionist pride in their language and its standard norm. In America, a society which has historically disclaimed class distinctions, linguistic snobbishness is perhaps more subtly transmitted than it is in England, but it persists nevertheless, and it persists as the major foundation of the status of English here. If the status of English had been achieved through law, methods of changing that status would be clear-cut. But the vision of English so widespread today is the result of our *past*, not our *history*.

J.H. Plumb, the British historian, has suggested a distinction between history and the past (1970). History is a discovery made through historians' attempts to learn the human story in its own terms and not for the sustennace of institutions, societies, or national images. As distinguished from history, the past is a creation keenly linked in human consciousness with a sense of the future, with a sense of destiny. In this dynamic fashion, the past is created and recreated in the service of religion, morality, or the sanctity of institutions. Our language past — as opposed to our language history — has been used to provide moral lessons, to support current images of cultural needs, and to characterize the national past in terms of a homogeneity in values, goals, and experiences. That past is still being used to dictate both how speech communities should speak and what they should believe about what their speech can do.

That *past* is also being invoked to support a national language policy without consideration of the *history* of the treatment of language in federal law. Any proposal for a national language policy must be recognized as a decision to create laws to control an area of behavior never before under federal control. It is difficult to predict public response either to such a law or to the expenses involved in implementing and enforcing the shifts in structure and practices of institutions which will be necessary for conformity to such laws. Societal resistance could take the form of a severe backlash against ethnic and linguistic diversities. We know little about the differences between responses to federal antidiscrimination laws which are reversals or alternations of earlier laws (e.g. the civil rights legislation of the 1960s) and responses to laws newly created to control an area of behavior hitherto not covered in federal law. To be sure, responses will differ in accordance with the clarity of definitions of the categories of the discriminated, i.e. race, sex, age, nationality. Laws prohibiting discrimination on these bases have not had to deal extensively with issues of definition. In the case of language as a basis of discrimination, however, neither it nor its standards can be clearly specified. Dialect differences merge into language differences, and the standards of clarity in language vary greatly from situation to situation.

It will be a difficult task to substitute historical fact for the created past as the basis of decision making in language planning today. History makes us 'see things as they actually were, and from this study to formulate processes of social change acceptable on historical grounds . . .' (Plumb 1970: 137) – a challenge in our current assessment of the status of English in the United States.

NOTES

1. A comprehensive history of language policies for the territories has not yet been written; for many areas, the history is scattered in sources available only in the territories (or former territories) themselves. For a brief summary of language policies in Puerto Rico and the Phillipines and comments on sources for language policies in these areas, see Zentella (1980) and Beebe and Beebe (1980).
2. *Lau* vs. *Nichols*, 413 U.S. 563 (1974).
3. *Meyer* vs. *State*, 107 Neb 657, N.W. 100, at 102 (1922).
4. *Meyer* vs. *Nebraska*, 262 U.S. 390 (1923).
5. 'An Act Requiring the Use of the English Language as the Medium of Instruction in All Secular Subjects in All Schools Within the State of Iowa', Chapter 198, § 1 (1919).
6. An Act to Supplement .§ 7762 of the General Code . . . and to Repeal § 7729, Concerning Elementary, Private and Parochial Schools and Proving that Instruc-

tion Shall be in the English Language', Chapter 614 (1919).

7. An Act to Declare the English Language the Official Language of This State, and to Require All Official Proceedings, Records and Publications to be in Such Language and All School Branches to be Taught in Said Language in Public, Private, Denominational and Parochial Schools; to Prohibit Discrimination Against the Use of the English Language by Social, Religious or Commercial Organizations; to Provide a Penalty for a Violation Thereof; to Repeal Chapter 249 of the Session Laws of Nebraska for 1919, Entitled "An Act Relating to the Teaching of Foreign Languages in the State of Nebraska" and to Declare an Emergency', Chapter 61 (1921).

8. *Bartels* vs. *Iowa*, 262 U.S. 404 (1923).

9. Compulsory Education Act (1922).

10. *Pierce* vs. *Society of Sisters*, 268 U.S. 510, at 535 (1925).

11. An Act Relating to Foreign Language Schools and Teachers Thereof', Act 30, Special Session (1920), *as Amended* by Act 171 of 1923 and Act 152 of 1925.

REFERENCES

Anonymous (1854a), *A Gross Literary Fraud Exposed; Related to the Publication of Worcester's Dictionary in London*. Boston.

_____(1854b), 'Have we a national standard of English lexicography?' (pamphlet). Springfield, Mass., Merriam.

Beebe, Maria, and James Beebe (1980), 'The Filipinos: a special case', in *Language in the USA*, ed. by C.A. Ferguson and S.B. Heath. New York and London, Cambridge University Press.

Berkman, Richard L. (1970), 'Students in court: free speech and the function of schooling in America', *Harvard Educational Review* 40: 567-595.

Bristed, Charles Astor (1855), 'The English Language in America', in *Cambridge Essays* 57-58. London, Parker.

Cottle, Basil (1969), *The Triumph of English 1350-1400*. New York, Barnes and Noble.

Croft, Herbert (1797), *A Letter, from Germany, to the Royal Princess of England: On the English and German Languages*. London.

Drake, Glendon (1977), 'American linguistic prescriptivism: its decline and revival in the 19th century', *Language in Society* 6: 323-340.

Farish, Hunter Dickinson, editor (1957), *The Journal and Letters of Philip Vickers Fithian: A Plantation Tutor of the Old Dominion 1773-1774*. Williamsburg, Va. Colonial Williamsburg, Inc.

Ferguson, Charles A., and Shirley Brice Heath, editors (1980), *Language in the USA*. New York and London: Cambridge University Press.

Fowler, Roger (1965), 'Popular attitudes to the use of English', *Studia Neophilologica* 37: 374-381.

Free, William J. (1968), *The Columbian Magazine and American Literary Nationalism*. The Hague, Mouton.

Gunther, Gerald (1976), *Cases and Materials on Individual Rights in Constitutional Law* (second edition). Mineola, N.Y. Foundation Press.

Hanes, Virginia Lee (1940), 'The British attitude toward American English 1775-1860'. Unpublished master's thesis, Duke University.

Hauger, Einar (1966), *Language Conflict and Language Planning: The Case of Modern*

Norwegian. Cambridge, Harvard University Press.

Heath, Shirley Brice (1976a), 'Colonial language status achievement: Mexico, Peru, and the United States', in *Language in Sociology*, ed. by Albert Verdoodt and Rolf Kjolseth, Louvain, Peeters.

_____ (1976b), 'Early American attitudes toward variation in speech: a view from social history and sociolinguistics'. Unpublished Forum lecture, LSA Institute.

_____ (1976c), 'A national language academy? Debate in the New Nation', *International Journal of the Sociology of Language* 11: 9-43.

_____ (1977), 'Our language heritage: a historical perspective', in *The Language Connection: From the Classroom to the World*, ed. by June K. Phillips. Skokie, Ill., National Textbook Co.

_____ (forthcoming a), 'Toward an ethnohistory of writing in American education'. To appear in *Variation in Writing: Functional and Linguistic-Cultural Differences*, ed. by Marcia Whiteman. Baltimore, Erlbaum Associates.

_____ (forthcoming b), 'The rise of prescriptivism in American English'. To appear in *Standards and Dialects in English*, ed. by Timothy Shopen and Peg Griffin. Arlington, Va., Center for Applied Linguistics and Winthrop Publishers.

_____ , and Frederick Mandabach (forthcoming), *Language and the Law: Judicial and Legislative Decisions on Foreign Language, Literacy, and Free Speech*.

Holdsworth, W.S. (1923), *A History of English Law*, two volumes (third edition). London, Methuen.

Johnson, Gerald W. (1949), *Our English Heritage*. Philadelphia, J.P. Lippincott.

Kloss, Heinz (1977), *The American Bilingual Tradition*. Rowley, Mass., Newbury House.

Kluwin, Mary Bridget (forthcoming), 'Coping with language and cultural diversity: a study of changing language instruction policy from 1860 to 1930 in three American cities'. Unpublished Ph.D. dissertation, Stanford University.

Mathieson, Margaret (1975), *The Preachers of Culture: A Study of English and Its Teachers*. Totowa, N.J., Rowman and Littlefield.

Mellinkoff, David (1963), *The Language of the Law*. Boston, Little, Brown.

Michael, Ian (1970), *English Grammatical Categories and the Tradition to 1800*. London, Cambridge University Press.

Nichols, Patricia C. (1977), 'Ethnic consciousness in the British Isles: questions for language planning', *Language Problems and Language Planning* 1: 10-31.

Piche, Gene L. (1977), *Class and Culture in the Development of the High School English Curriculum, 1880-1900*, volume two- *Research in the Teaching of English*, pp. 17-27.

Plumb, J.H. (1970), *The Death of the Past*. Boston, Houghton Mifflin.

Read, Allen Walker (1936), 'American projects for an academy to regulate speech', *Publications of the Modern Language Association* 51: 1,141-1,179.

_____ (1938), 'Suggestions for an academy in England in the latter half of the eighteenth century', *Modern Philology* 36: 145-156.

Teitelbaum, H., and R.J. Hiller (1977), *The Legal Perspective*, volume three: *Bilingual Education: Current Perspectives*. Arlington, Va., Center for Applied Linguistics.

Tyack, David B. (1974), *The One Best System: A History of American Urban Education*. Cambridge, Mass., Harvard University Press.

Webster, Noah (1798), 'A letter to the governors, instructors and trustees of the universities . . . on the errors of English grammar'. New York.

Weibe, Robert (1967), *The Search for Order, 1977-1920*. New York, Hill & Wang.

Zentella, Ana Celia (1980), 'Language variety among Puerto Ricans', in *Language in the USA*, ed. by C.A. Ferguson and S.B. Heath. New York and London, Cambridge University Press.

JOSHUA A. FISHMAN

Modeling Rationales in Corpus Planning: Modernity and Tradition in Images of the Good Corpus

THE WORM TURNS

Within the course of a decade a fundamental change has transpired within the ranks of students of linguistics *vis-à-vis* the very idea of corpus planning. In the late 1960s, when I and a small number of colleagues were enabled to spend a year at the East-West Center planning the *International Study of Language Planning Processes* (Rubin et al. 1978), the most common reaction to our efforts on the part of linguists and linguists-in-training was 'It can't be done!' Corpus planning was viewed as akin to lashing the seas or chaining the winds at best, and to unsavory meddling in 'natural processes' at worst. The Hallian dictum 'leave your language alone' (Hall 1950) still held sway and it reinforced as well as expressed the predominantly descriptivist bias of Western linguistics in general and of American linguistics in particular. Even those who were alarmed as to the continued decay of the English language – a constant matter of concern for the past century or more of English teachers and stylists – were far from believing that mere man either could or should intercede on an organized, centralized basis, to tamper with its fate or its form (see e.g. Newman 1974, Graves and Hodge 1979).

That view, and all of the metaphors and alarms that it involves, is still with us, of course, and perhaps more so in the U.S.A. than in many other countries. I encounter it during visits to Israel among teachers who are fed up with the Academy's attempts to foster its brand of excessively proper, stilted, artificial Hebrew (*Ivrit shel shabat* [sabbath Hebrew], the opponents call it disapprovingly), *even now* when the language has been fully nativized and when its 'natural juices' appear to be fully activated and *self*-directive. I encounter it among anglophone linguists in Canada, convinced that the Office de la Langue Francaise is not only riding the wicked crest of Quebecois nationalism toward 'francization' but that it is arrogantly trying to change, improve, and modernize the French language even above and beyond Parisian splendor. I encounter it in the world of Yiddishists as well, whenever untraumatized youngsters (e.g. in the student journal *Yugntruf*) and unbowed oldsters (e.g. in the language-planning journal of the Yivo Institute for Jewish

Research, *Yidishe shprakh*), employ neologisms that were clearly unknown to the critics' proverbial 'grandmother in [pre-World War II] Riga'. Nevertheless, the above opposition to corpus planning is clearly passé. It is fixated on local excesses (about which I will have more to say later), but these are the *excesses of success*. The continuing opposition to corpus planning, such as it is, can no longer successfully pretend that corpus planning cannot be done nor that it is impossible to do it well. It is, instead, ever more drawn into discussions of *who* should do it, of *when* it should be done, and of *how* it should be done, rather than of whether it *can* or *should* be done at all.

Indeed, if a formerly biased notion (that corpus planning was inherently impossible or undersirable) is clearly waning — particularly among young linguists — the current danger seems to be from an equally biased but opposite view that considers it to be merely a rather simple, technical, linguistic exercise. One of my students at a recent linguistic institute put it in terms that seem to express the current (younger generation's?) relaxed view of the matter quite succinctly: 'It's nothing more than an exercise in lexical innovation or lexical substitution'. How the worm has turned in one decade! Unfortunately, however erroneous the predominant late-1960s view was, the waxing late-1970s view incorporates a triple error of its own.

A TRIPLE ERROR

The tendency to view 'corpus planning' as nothing special, as just one more technical skill that a linguist should be able to pull out of his bag of tricks, is triply mistaken. It reveals a misunderstanding of lexicons per se, of corpus planning as a whole, and of the societal nexus of language planning more generally. Let me say a few words about each of these misunderstandings.

The snickering view that corpus planning is 'nothing more than lexical innovation or lexical substitution' reveals a profound downgrading of lexicons. This view, one which young linguists have probably taken over from their elders, implies that lexicons represent a somehow dispensable, trivial, and entirely uninteresting and expendable facet of the total language process. But lexicons are not that at all. They are not endless laundry lists, without rhyme or reason, without systematic links to each other and to all other facets of language. Lexicons are not interchangeable, dry, and dreary 'nuts and bolts'. Indeed, not only are they functionally indispensable and conceptually integrated aspects of the language process, but their successful planning involves tremendously complicated socio-cultural-political sensitivities that most linguists neither possess nor imagine. Actually, the current, more relaxed view (that corpus planning involves 'nothing more than lexical innovation') reveals ignorance not only of language planning and language behavior but of linguistics itself. However, for our immediate purposes here, suffice it to say that its downgrading of lexicons masks a downgrading of language/corpus planning by many of its purported friends and willing practitioners. The latter (corpus planning) is considered to be trivial because the former (lexicon) is consider-ed to be trivial. Success with trivia is not considered to be success but, rather, to be trivia (as my Yiddish-speaking grandmother — not from Riga but from Soroke on the Dniester — used to say, 'May God protect me from such friends'. Her great-grandchildren today, when speaking English, topicalize this sentiment and render it, 'Friends like *that* we *don't* need!').

However, a more serious error than the foregoing downgrading of lexicons is the failure to recognize that corpus planning deals with far more than lexicons alone. Corpus planning has been extended to the development of entire stylistic varieties (e.g. nontechnical Somali prose), to number systems (e.g. converting a 'nine-and-thirty' system to a 'thirty-nine' system in Norwe-gian), to pronoun systems (e.g. the selections of nonhonorific second-person singulars in Japanese and Javanese), the simplification of verbal and phonolo-gical patterns (e.g. dropping feminine plural imperatives and complicated pointing/unpointing alternatives in modern Hebrew), etc. Thus, while the lion's share of corpus planning is certainly terminological (and all of my future examples here are unabashedly of this sort), there is, in principle, no reason why corpus-planning efforts should be denied (nore have they been) the 'tighter' linguistic systems that linguists and anthropologists are so proud of (for examples galore on other-than-lexical corpus planning, note several of the papers in this volume [e.g., Ferguson, Milán], as well as in Fodor and Hagege, i.p.).

Most serious of all, however, is the lack of recognition revealed by the 'merely lexicon' view of (1) the delicate and complex social context that commonly surrounds corpus planning, and of (2) the need for professional expertise with respect to *that* context if corpus planning is to succeed. It is a devastating mistake to assume that corpus planning merely requires the inter-play and coordination of linguistic expertise and technological expertise, devastating certainly if one's goal is not merely to do corpus planning (i.e. not merely to *create* a nomenclature in chemistry, for example, or in some other modern technological area) but to have it *accepted* (i.e. to have it liked, learned, and used). If the *latter* is our goal (and anything less strikes me as a travesty), then cultural expertise in all of its ramifications is called for as well. Corpus planning, even when it is concerned with the elaboration and codifi-cation of nomenclatures, requires political/ideological/philosophical/religious sensitivity and expertise, particularly if the acceptance and implementation of corpus planning are not to be heavy-handed *ex post facto* impositions upon corpus planning but part and parcel of its ongoing activity from the very outset.

MODERNIZATION IS NOT PURSUED IN A VACUUM

Every corpus-planning venture is conducted in a particular sociocultural context and that context is denied or ignored at the peril of the corpus planners, for it is that context that defines the parameters of acceptance, implementation, and diffusion. In this sense, modernization is both more than and less than modernization alone, for it constantly requires an amalgam of the old and the new in which the *proportions* of each and the *interpretations* of each must be frequently readjusted. Modernization, if it is to be broadly effective, rather than merely elitist and restricted or continually imposed from above, ultimately comes face to face with massive needs for sociocultural phenomenological continuity, stability, and legitimacy, regardless of how much econo-technical change occurs. The many examples of twentieth-cnetury corpus planning in 'developing countries' reveal most clearly the dialectic between the modern and the traditional, the imported and the indigenous, but even corpus planning in the modernized Western world is by no means free of this dialectic (Berger 1979; Connell 1978).

Basically, modernization alone is just not enough to satisfy the cultural and philosophical needs of human populations (and, indeed, at times it is abhorent to them). As a result, the language technician, the econo-technical technician, and the 'executive arm of power' in concert are also not enough to guarantee the success of corpus planning, particularly where at least a pretense of political and cultural independence and authenticity is maintained. Everyone wants a chemistry terminology of his own nowadays, at least for lower- and middle-level chemistry pursuits, but the generally want it to be *both* 'adequate for chemistry' *and* 'acceptable as their own'. Accordingly, many Israelis want 'theirs' to be faithful to the 'genuine oriental nature' of the Hebrew language. Many Hindi advocates want 'theirs' to reflect the perfection of classical Sanscrit. Filipino planners want 'their' chemistry terminology to be transparent, i.e. to utilize morphs that the young and the common man will understand. Nynorsk advocates want 'theirs' to derive from the uncontaminated Norse well. Katarevusa planners owe(d) allegiance to the pure Greek genius from which the entire world's democratic ethos has purportedly been derived. Many Arabic planners and teachers want to recognize Koranic exquisiteness in their chemistry terminology. Yiddish adherents want(ed) to avoid Germanisms, Anglicisms, Russianisms, or any other massive dependency on outside languages (Fishman, 1981). Of late, French authorities are, if anything, even more alarmed along these lines.

'Chemistry is chemistry; chemistry is universal', but chemistry terminologies are pulled in particularistic directions — by elites who seek to form, to lead, and to follow their masses, and by masses who are ever prone to return to deeply implanted local preferences when their revolutionary fugures and flirtations subside. Everywhere the planner encounters particularistic directions into which and through which 'universal modernization' must be channeled. The amount of pull will vary. The pullers and the pulled will vary. The interpretation of what is 'ours' and what is 'theirs' will vary. The general point, however, remains valid: modernization drives, goals, needs, and processes alone are not enough for corpus planning to succeed. Modernization repeatedly needs to be particularistically digested, legitimated, and domesticated or disguised (Nash, et al. 1976).

BUT THE TRADITION IS NOT ENOUGH EITHER

If modernization has its limits (not to speak of its limitations), so, obviously does the local tradition. The tradition can rarely satisfy the linguistic needs of corpus planning if for no other reason than the fact that it cannot satisfy the compelling econo-technical needs of modernization. The tradition is inadequate both socioculturally and intellectually-conceptually. It lacks the paradigms, the theoretical parsimony, the conceptual systems that are both the resultants of and the contributors to modern expertise. Thus, the tradition can often provide no more than a vague outer limit, a rhetoric, an indigenous guidling principle, and, above all, a stabilizing identity to the process of modernization and to its corpus-planning counterpart. Like modernization, the tradition is both a comforter and a taskmaster. Like modernization it waxes and wanes in its power to constrain and to guide. Like modernization, it is constantly subject to varying interpretations (from interpreter$_1$ to interpreter$_2$ and from time$_1$ to time$_2$). Like modernization it tends to bite off more than it can chew, to claim more than it can deliver, to stake out more than it can control. The corpus planner needs help in order to gauge it accurately, to appreciate its hold and its significance, and to realize that its instability implies that *his* task is never done. The tradition also changes and develops, as does modernity, and the two interpenetrate and are at times interpreted as hostile, and at times as indifferent, and at times as harmonious with respect to each other.

Of course, all of the foregoing applies to the *sociopolitical auspices of modernization as a whole,* as well as to the status-planning context in which corpus planning is conducted. Even nationalistic modernization is far from being a genuine revitalization effort (Fishman 1972). It is at least bimodal in outlook. Indigenous depth and historical legitimization are constantly used for *unprecedented purposes* and in *unprecedented ways* by nationalist movements. The old and the new may appear to the outsider to be odd bedfellows but they cohabit constantly. In each and every modernization experience we love them both and we despair of them both. We want to be in control of them both and wind up being controlled by them both. Corpus planning cannot long escape from their bipolarity. It must struggle to recognize and to integrate them both, and, like every other social pursuit, it is only indifferently successful in doing so for any length of time. For these very same reasons successful corpus planning is no simple thing.

RATIONALE AND RATIONALIZATIONS

Corpus planning is faced by a dilemma — but yet it proceeds: chemistry terminologies continue to be prepared. They are launched under a variety of rationales and rationalizations. These are indispensable. The corpus planner needs to set out guiding principles for himself so that he will know what is 'good' and what is 'bad', what to seek and what to avoid. Even more crucial: the public or target audience also needs to be told why what is being offered to it is desirable, admirable, and exemplary. Critics too need to rationalize their opposition, qualms, or reluctance. For all of these reasons, therefore, models of the good and of the bad are formulated and expounded upon. In addition to extreme or polar solutions or positions, a number of compromise positions are also commonly advanced. They all seek to grapple with the old and the new, to combine them, and to differentiate between them, to find the one in the other or to minimize or otherwise manipulate the gap between them.

Unabashed and undiluted rationalism *a la* Tauli (1968, 1974) (the 'good' is 'short', 'regular', 'simple', 'euphonious'), the unabashed and limitless importation of unabashed foreignisms, and the pursuit of neologisms on a completely *de novo* basis (i.e. via morphs without pedigrees) are also all resorted to on occasion and for special purposes, but these are rarely if ever rationalized as such or as national policy. Complete rationality is, after all, no more than a game played by intellectuals (and even then, only by intellectuals completely innocent of political aspirations or opportunities). To some extent the need to compromise with rationality is due to the limitations inherent in these solutions as solutions; to some extent it is due to their limitations as *approaches to solutions*. Thus, two equally rational principles often conflict (short terms are not necessarily euphonious, euphonious terms are not necessarily simple, simple terms are not necessarily short, etc.). Ultimately, even rationality is not an open-and-shut, completely objective matter and is subject to fairly substantial social and societal interpreation. As a result, even when rationality *is* appealed to it is commonly buttressed by or imbedded in other stated arguments or unstated assumptions.

The following examples (as are the others below) are from the journal *Yidishe shprakh,* published by the Yivo Institute for Jewish Research in New

York (currently the only authoritative corpus-planning agency in the world of Yiddish). This journal (now in its 37th year; a somewhat similar journal entitled *Yidish far ale* was published by the Yivo for several years prior to World War II in Vilne [Wilno, Vilnius]), not only publishes lengthy terminologies, but also publishes replies to inquiries from readers (almost all of them American) who lack a word or expression for some aspect of modernity.

Example 1: 'handout' (as at a scholarly conference or meeting). The anonymous *YS* spokesmen recommends *tseteyl-bletl* and supports his recommendation as follows: 'Although it is a neologism, its composite structure, verb plus noun, is so productive and common that it sounds like a well-established term' (1973, 32 [1-3] : 32).

Note that the rationality of regularity (the structure is much employed and, therefore, has innumerable precedents) is clinched (rendered popularly irresistible) by assuring us that such a term sounds traditional rather than new. A neologism seems to require some sort of passport or apology. If it is new, it should at least *sound* old. It is clear that the recommender would rather have an old term to begin with wherever possible.

Example 2: 'pot roast'. The spokesman recommends *top-gebrotns* and explains why. 'This is not a made-up word. We find this word as far back as the writings of Mendele Moikher Sforim [1836-1917]' (1949, 9: 61).

The recommender clearly recognizes the weaknesses of 'made-up' words. The fact that a word was used by a 'classicist of modern Yiddish literature' clearly establishes its legitimacy in his eyes, above and beyond that of the most rational neologism.

COMPROMISES, COMPROMISES, COMPROMISES

Untempered rationality and undiluted traditionalism are extreme positions insofar as modeling rationales are concerned. More commonly, mixed rationales are employed. One such is to cite supporting usage among ordinary folk, speakers who cannot be suspected of partiality toward the corpus planner's recommendation. At times, this approach derives from serious ethnographic research in which large numbers of folk terms are collected and rescued from oblivion by being resurrected in a closely or metaphorically related meaning. This is a rationale that is not without its difficulties, however. Not all ordinary speakers, nor all widespread usages, are equally acceptable as precedents by corpus planners. Many man-in-the-street usages, indeed, are clearly unacceptable as barbarisms, vulgarisms, slang, archaisms, unjustified borrowings, etc. In modern Yiddish corpus planning, (New High) German influences (post-eighteenth century) are taboo, even if they have been popularly accepted (Schaechter 1969). Thus, the appeal to popular currency normally involves an explicit or implicit set of assumptions as to *which* speech networks (often rural rather than urban, but often also from one region rather than from another), at which time in history, (precontact, preinvasion, preoccupation, pre-floodtide-of-influence) are regarded favorably. A few examples may help:

Example 3: 'matching grant'. The authority recommends *akegngelt* and buttresses his recommendation as follows. 'We have noted *akegnshteln* for "to match" from Dr. Y. Gottesman, a countryman of ours from Sered, Southern Bukovina [Rumania during the Inter-War period; now in the USSR]; from Lifshe Shekter-Vidmanm from Zvinyetchke, Northern Bukovina, we have "the inlaws [actually: *mekhatonim*, i.e. the kinship of in-laws *vis-à-vis* each other] give *akegngelt*" ' (1972, 31 [2] : 56).

Example 4: 'poetry reading'. The authority recommends *poezye-ovnt* [= poetry evening], even if the reading is during the day, since 'Polish Jews greet each other with *gutn-ovnt* [good evening] from mid-day on' (1975, 34 [1-3] : 78).

Note how approved individual speakers (perhaps because they come from the same region as the authority or are well known to him to be of un-blemished speech) or even an approved region are cited. In both cases the usage referred to is pre-American and, in that sense, more authentic, uncon-taminated. Thus the function is new but the word is old. The new is old; the old is new.

Another compromise solution is to find (whether through translation loans or through internationalisms) that 'theirs is ours'. Obviously this line of reasoning must also involve substantial flexibility and eclecticism, and care must be exercised that it not be carried to an unacceptable extreme. Ata-turk's 'Great Sun Theory' is a well known example of this approach. After the expulsion of foreign Arabisms and Persianisms it rationalized the import-ation of numerous Frenchisms/internationalisms on the ground that since all European languages were (purportedly) derived from Turkish, all borrowed Europeanisms were merely long-lost Turkish words returning to the fold, to their original home. Some less extreme exampels of the 'theirs is ours' type are the following:

Example 5: What definite article should be used with the word '*loto*'; *der*, *di*, or *dos*? The authority replies, 'Certainly *not di lotto*. There is an unfortu-nate tendency here [in the USA] always to use *di* with a foreign word . . . due to the influence of English *the* which is closer to *di* than to *der* or *dos*. [However] if *loto* were to be phonetically assimilated and if it were to change to *lóte* then, in such a case, it would certainly be *di lóte*' (1950, 10 [2] : 63).

Seemingly, even a foreign borrowing becomes somewhat naturalized if an article is used with it that does not again reveal foreign influence. However, a subsequent stage of indigenization is reached with phonetic assimilation. At that point the term is fully 'ours' and therefore the usual grammatical paradigm then applies with respect to its article. Words ending in unaccented *a* are mostly feminine in Yiddish (some obvious exceptions: *der tate, der zeyde*) and, therefore, at that point the article would change from *der/dos loto* to *di lote*.

Example 6: Are words such as stimulate, formulate, emulate, etc., acceptable internationalisms? The authority replies, 'Just because an English word has a Latin root that doesn't necessarily make it an internationalism. That very word must occur in at least a few other major languages ('*kulturshprakhn*') for us to admit it into our language with a clear conscience. Each individual word needs to be considered separately. [*Stimulirn, formulirn* are quite acceptable internationalisms but] Why do you need *emulirn* when you can simply say *nokhmakhn*?' (1963, 23 [2] : 63).

Note that a purported internationalism is acceptable as such if creditable others have already acted and accepted it as such. At that point it belongs to everyone (or to no one in particular) and, therefore, also to us. Prior to that point, it is a foreignism. However, even if it is an internationalism there may still be a 'simple' indigenous term that would obviously be preferable. Internationalisms are potential citizens but they are comparable to naturalized citizens. They are still not as authentic as the native-born variety.

OVERDOING IT

Corpus planners attempt to predict and to put into effect 'models of goodness' that target populations will like, learn, and use. However, the corpus planners are not themselves a random sample, either of 'the public' or of any of the more narrowly defined target populations at which corpus planners aim their corpus-planning products. They are commonly more ideologized than 'the public' in the sense of being more likely to reify the model that they are trying to implement. They are certainly more language-conscious (perhaps 'language-centered' is the term to use) relative to most target populations with which they have to deal. Other populations generally view language, at best, as only part of the pie, as only one aspect of the total social reality with which they are seeking to cope. Language planners as a whole, and corpus planners even more so, tend to overstress language as causal (Fishman 1980), as crucial, as special, particularly so if their training is narrowly linguistic rather than broadly sociolinguistic. As a result, there is substantial risk that corpus planners will lose contact with the public and will not really have their fingers on the pulse of how the public is reacting to them, to their products, and to their once-valid model of the ever-changing and delicate balance between 'old' and 'new', between 'theirs' and 'ours', between neologistic and traditionalistic, that publics find acceptable. Because corpus *planners are* (or view themselves as) gatekeepers and custodians of the language, they tend to become overzealous defenders of their model of the good language. Their relative homogeneity in age, training, and background also contributes to the risk of being 'out of touch' at any particular time with what any particular target population will accept. 'Once-believers' of the same generation and 'nonbelievers' of a subsequent generation often view corpus planners as thick-skinned pachyderms at best, or as outlandish and outmoded remnants of an earlier age at worst. When corpus planners continue to do what they have always done, 'the public' (by then no longer the same in attitudes, interests, and needs as it formerly was) begins to consider them, the corpus planners, to be *over*doing it. Narrow-gauged corpus planners often become the butts of humor, sarcasm, and ridicule, unappreciated at best and vilified at worst.

'NOTORIOUS' FAILURES

In such cases of credibility gap, of out-of-phaseness between corpus planners and their publics, anecdotes, jokes, and songs often appear whose goal is to tease, taunt, and otherwise deride the 'excesses' of corpus-planning products. The young native-born Israelis, tired of having old, diaspora-born 'authorities' tell them what proper Hebrew is, laugh endlessly at radio, television, and records that poke fun at the Academy (*Eych korim hatshuptshik al hakumkum?*). Francophone Quebecers gnash their teeth (and Anglophones slap their sides in exaggerated mirth) over the *stop* vs. *arret* 'scandale' in the government's 'francization' program. Yiddish speakers who have been none too observant of the Yivo's spelling strictures ridicule the gallons of ink (or is it blood?) spilled over whether the Yivo's own spelling rules require *fundestvegn* [nevertheless] to be spelled as one word or as three. Corpus planning that continues along its own mirthless path, oblivious of public sentiment and changes in the public model of 'the good language' (which must be internally differentiated for a variety of functions), is likely to find that its mirthlessness is increasingly the object of public mirth and merriment (not to speak of disdain and disregard). Many of the 'scandals' that come to public attention due to out-of-phaseness between corpus planners and target populations become 'fossilized' and continue to be cited for decades after the out-of-phaseness has been corrected.

[margin handwritten notes:] do not be overzealous (this is a cause, not the cause) C.S. Lewis / don't be in-grown — other LP's of same age

A CORPUS PLANNER'S LIFE IS NOT AN EASY ONE (CHORUS: EASY ONE)
CONCLUSIONS

Corpus planning is often conducted within a tension system of changing and conflicted loyalties, convictions, interests, values, and outlooks. On the one hand, authentification/indigenization of the new is admired and courted, but, on the other hand, it is often too limiting in reality and too rural/old-fashioned in image to serve or to be acceptable if uncompromisingly pursued. Successful corpus planning, then, is a delicate balancing act, exposed to tensions and ongoing change. All of this makes the corpus planner all the more dependent on disciplined social and societal sensitivity, theoretical and applied, in order to fully understand the drifts and pressures to which he must react. This is particularly true in newly modernizing contexts. It is also true in postmodern ones — whether they be democratic or totalitarian in nature. Totalitarian regimes may have more clout in the entire culture-planning area, but they too may run out of steam, particularly when it comes to influencing the spoken language, unless rapport is maintained with public sentiments and images of 'the good language', so that these can be either followed or shaped via massive institutions. Thus, it behooves corpus planning to engage in constant research and in ongoing evaluation, and this can only be done if social-research skills are either acquired or hired. A corpus planner's life is not an easy one (chorus: easy one), but then whose is?

[handwritten margin note: delicate balancing act]

REFERENCES

Berger, Peter L. (1979), *Facing Up To Modernity: Excursions in Society, Politics and Religion*. New York, Basic Books.

Connell, John (1978), *The End of Tradition: Country Life in Central Surrey*. London, Routledge and Kegan Paul.

Fishman, Joshua A. (1972), *Language and Nationalism*. Rowley, Mass., Newbury House.

_____ (1980), 'The Whorfian hypothesis: varieties of valuation, confirmation and disconfirmation', *International Journal of the Sociology of Language*. 26, 25-40.

_____ (1981) ed., *Never Say Die! A Thousand Years of Yiddish in Jewish Life and Letters*. The Hague, Mouton.

Foder, Istvan, and Claude Hagege (i.p.) eds., *Language Reform and Modernization* (tentative title).

Graves, Robert, and Alan Hodge (1979), *The Reader Over Your Shoulder: A Handbook for Writers of English Prose*. New York, Random House.

Hall, Robert A., Jr. (1950), *Leave Your Language Alone!* Ithaca. (Reprinted 1960 as *Linguistics and Your Language*. New York, Doubleday-Anchor).

Nash, June, Jorge Dandler, and Nicholas S. Hopkins, editors (1976), *Popular Participation in Social Change*. The Hague, Mouton.

Newman, Edwin (1974), *Strictly Speaking: Will America Be the Death of English?* Indianapolis, Bobbs-Merrill.

Rubin, Joan, Bjorn Jernudd, Jyoti Das Gupta, et al. (1978), *Language Planning Processes.* The Hague, Mouton.

Schaechter, Modkhe (1969), 'The "hidden standard": a study of competing influences in standardization', in *Field of Yiddish III*, ed. by Marvin Herzog et al., 289-304. The Hague, Mouton. Also in Fishman 1981, pp. 671-698.

Tauli, Valter (1968), *Introduction to a Theory of Language Planning.* Uppsala, University of Uppsala Press.

_____(1974), 'The theory of language planning', in *Advances in Language Planning*, ed. by Joshua Fishman, 48-67. The Hague, Mouton.

PART TWO

Codification in Language Planning

WILLIAM G. MILÁN

Contemporary Models of Standardized New World Spanish: Origin, Development, and Use [1]

Language codification has traditionally been considered the work of philosophers, grammarians, and literary scholars. With the rise of the sociology of language, the planning of a linguistic corpus has ceased to be a purely academic endeavor and become a multidimensional sociological issue (Fishman 1972, 1974, 1977). This broader perspective is well advised. After all, language codifications are the results of social processess, are social phenomena in themselves, and have the potential either to help maintain or to change social processes and structures. The present study will be devoted to an illustration of these aspects of language codification. The codification of the Spanish language in the New World will serve as a case in point. Although 487 years can hardly be considered a long period of time when we talk about language history, a full-scale investigation that would cover all forms of language codification, in both North and South America, would exceed the proposed length of this paper. Consequently, our limitations will be many.

We will confine ourselves to language codification in Spanish America. In order to facilitate the illustration and analysis of the sociological circumstances of language codification, only structural codifications of historical significance will be considered. Frequent allusions to lexical codifications will be made, but only as points of reference. The structural codifications under study will meet the following criteria:

1. They must be complete. Each one of them individually must provide sufficient information on Spanish structures to serve as a primary source for a language standard. Partial codifications of various elements of the Spanish language will be excluded.

2. They must address the Spanish language in standardized terms. Dialectological codifications of regional or colloquial forms and structures are not part of our discussion.

3. They must be original and innovative. Regardless of whose linguistic leadership the codifiers may wish to acknowledge, their work must represent a departure from tradition, both in conceptual framework and in structural configuration.

4. They must have had impact. Each codification must have had some

kind of noticeable effects. These may include the extent to which they influenced written expression (e.g. literature), their impact on education, the extent to which they have been officially recognized, and their impact on language codification itself.

This study will address language and its sociohistorical context. Our approach, however, will be essentially philological. We will be looking at codified language, not at language as spoken in social situations. We will be studying written records, not samples of discourse. It would therefore be more accurate to call this a sociophilological inquiry rather than a sociolinguistic one. Since the discovery of the new world coincides with the beginning of language codification in Spain, our historical considerations will begin there. Then we will study the internal and external development of language codification in Spanish America. The study of their external development will consist of a review of the political, ideological, and literary trends and events that influenced language codification; and of the effects that these codifications had in subsequent political, ideological, and literary phenomena. In the study of their internal development, we will review the codification models themselves, highlighting some of their generic characteristics (e.g. conceptual frameworks, morphological configurations, sentence structure theory). Finally we will look at how standardized models are used. Given the broad scope of the topic, and the limitations of this inquiry, our conclusions will be rather conservative, and our recommendations will be very modest.

ORIGIN

> Ala mui alta y assi esclarecida princesa
> Doña Isabel, la Tercera Deste Nombre,
> Reina y Sēnora Natural de España y las
> Islas de Nuestro Mar. Comiença la
> Gramática que nueva mente hizo el
> Maestro Antonio de Lebriẍa sobre la
> Lengua Castellana. Y pone primero el
> Prologo. Lee lo en buen Ora.
>
> De Nebrija, 1492

With these words filled will reverence and devotion, the first planner of the Spanish language dedicates his work to Isabella III, queen of Spain in 1492. Nebrija's *Gramática* is much more than a mere codification of structural rules. It is a complete and comprehensive plan intended to fulfill the language policy needs of the Spanish empire at the peak of its glory. In addition to being a learned man of letters, Nebrija also had a keen sense of history and of the relationship that exists between language and power. In his prologue he discusses the rise and fall of the great ancient civilizations: Hebrew, Greek, and Roman; and talks about the concurrent rise and fall of their languages. In the late fifteenth century, Spain was the greatest empire. The Arabs had been expelled. The peninsula was territorially unified through the convenient marriage of the Catholic monarchs. Columbus had discovered a new world. The international leadership of the Spanish rulers was second only to that of the Pope. And together with this unprecedented surge of power, there came also an equally unprecedented surge of intellectual prosperity (Ugarte 1965). Spain was rapidly becoming the primary center for learning, literature, and the arts. The time was right for a codification of the Spanish language. As a matter of fact, the historical reality of Spain made such a codification more than just desirable; it made it necessary. This was Spain's oppotunity to become the bastion of political power; the Spanish language had to rise to the occasion.

The Nebrija plan

Nebrija's plan had four explicit goals (De Nebrija 1926):
    1.   In order to ensure the longevity of Spain's literary production, Nebrija sought to reduce variations in the written language, by establishing a finite, limited code for the use of writers. A uniform adherence to this code would make it possible for readers in centuries to come to understand and appreciate the works of his contemporaries.
    2.   Since one of the distinctive characteristics of learned men was mastery of the Latin language, Nebrija codified the Spanish language in accordance with the classical model, creating structural parallels between Spanish and Latin. This would give Spaniards the advantage of being able to learn Latin much more easily that the speakers of other languages.
    3.   Because of Spain's powerful position, both its neighboring friends and its neighboring adversaries would need to learn Spanish in order to maintain and improve their relations with the empire. The *Gramática* would facilitate the acquisition of Spanish by speakers of other languages.
    4.   As a mighty nation, Spain had both the right and the obligation to fulfill the historical role of the great empires: to conquer other nations. For Spain this meant more than just taking over someone else's land, or bringing others under its rule. After having waged a furious war against Islam for 800 years, after the experience of the Crusades, and with the rise of the Inquisition, Spain had embraced the apostolate of the sword with fanatic missionary zeal. Therefore, the propagation of the Catholic faith became one of the major goals of the Spanish conquest. The dobious ethics of conquest gave the

conquerors the right to impose their language on the people they conquer. However, history tells us that political and economic subjugation are usually viewed as the primary goals, and that linguistic assimilation is usually sought only to the extent that it will facilitate these goals. In the case of Spain, however, linguistic assimilation was very important. In order for Spain to be able to impose the Catholic faith on its newly acquired subjects, a uniform medium of oral and written communication was necessary. Nebrija's *Gramática* would facilitate the teaching of Spanish; and through this common linguistic bond, both the conqueror and the conquered would be united under one crown and under faith.

Nebrija's ambitious goals are followed by an equally ambitious codification. The *Gramática* consists of five books. The first four are intended to fulfill his first two goals. They are directed to an audience of writers and scholars; and they adhere scrupulously to classical doctrine. The first book is devoted to Orthography, the art of correct writing. The second book is devoted to Prosody, the art of poetic composition. The third book is devoted to Etymology, the study of the origin of words. It should be noted that in Nebrija's times, the main thrust of lexicography was diachronic. Consequently, lexical codifications were primarily of an etymological nature. The fourth book is devoted to Syntax, the proper organization of words into concepts. The *Gramática's* fifth book is intended to fulfill Nebrija's third and fourth goals. It is addressed to speakers of other languages who either wish to or have to learn Spanish. Its thrust is explicitly pedagogical. It is in fact the first curriculum for the teaching of Spanish as a second language ever written.

Antonio de Nebrija is seldom given credit for the full extent of his contribution. His work was scorned and criticized by his contemporaries for no better reason than his Andalucian origin. And today, it is no more than one of those classics that everyone references, but hardly anyone reads. But its impact is undeniable. Nebrija's *Gramática* kicks off the Golden Age of Spanish literature. The works of the great Spanish poets and novelists of the Reinassance and the popular *comedias* of the Spanish Baroque, all have their roots in Nebrija's codification.

La Real Academia 'Española'

History repeats itself. Upon the death of the last Hapsburg king in 1700, Spain's true imperial identity is abolished (Ugarte 1965). The throne falls into the hands of the Bourbons, who seek to make Spain and all its overseas colonies mere satellites of the French empire. This decline in political power is paralleled by a linguistic and literary decline. Although Spanish continues to be the official language, literary masterpieces such as the ones produced during the 200-year span that followed Nebrija's *Gramática* are sorely missing during the eighteenth-century neoclassical period. The French influence, of course, was overwhelming. The Bourbon dynasty set up its own French-style court in Madrid and naturally implemented an imperial policy which was designed to serve France's best interest. The French language was widely used in official and intellectual circles. Spanish ideological and literary production was judged by French standards.

It is during this period of drought in Spanish civilization that the Spanish Royal Academy of the Language was founded in 1713 by Philip V, a Borubon king; following the model established by the Royal Academy of the French Language, which was founded 100 years earlier. Its royal motto synthetizes the goals of its founder: *Limpia, Fija y da Esplendor* [to cleanse, to norm, and to give splendor]. These three functions of the Academia were meant to serve both intellectual and political interests. The 'cleansing' was necessary in order to eradicate the linguistic excesses of the Baroque. The 'norming' was also needed in order to update, increase, and 'improve' codification. This meant a neoclassical codification with an explicit prescriptive intent. The model was to be designed in such a way that it not only could serve as a guide for written expression, but also would serve as a tool to combat certain literary and ideological movements. As for 'giving splendor', this meant to take an active role in ensuring that the Spanish language, especially when written, would meet the standards of the French *bon goût*. The Academia produced two major codifications: a lexical codification, *Diccionario de Autoridades*, in 1730; and a structural codification, *Gramática de la Lengua Castellana*, in 1771. The dictionary was designed as a documented lexicon of the Spanish language. Each entry was legitimized with documented evidence of its use by an accepted literary authority. The *Gramática* makes good use of Nebrija's material, but its structure is characterized by deliberate neoclassical tightness. Even to this day, both the *Gramática* produced by the Spanish Royal Academy (Real Acdemia Española 1924), and the *Grammaire* produced by the French Royal Academy — now part of the Institut de France- (Institut de France 1933) reflect the prescriptive approach of the eighteenth century.

EXTERNAL DEVELOPMENT: LITERARY, IDEOLOGICAL, AND POLITICAL TRENDS AND THEIR RELATIONSHIP TO LANGUAGE CODIFICATION

From the fifteenth century to the War of Independence

Although the Spanish conqueror arrived in the New World with a complete language plan, we have no way of measuring the extent to which it was im-plemented. We can at least assume that effective communication could not have been maintained throughout such an extensive territory by the colonies among themselves, or by the colonies with their foster country, without a codified model of written expression. We have no reliable way of assessing how well Nebrija's curriculum was used to teach Spanish to the conquered population. As a matter of fact, we have reason to believe that it was not widely used on a mass scale, at least not to facilitate the spread of Catholic-ism. Both Charles V and Phillip II favored religious instruction in the native language for the sake of expediency. This policy made the acquisition of the Amerindian languages by Spanish missionaries a priority. The teaching of Spanish to the conquered population became secondary. The Jesuits under-took the task of studying, learning, and even codifying these languages (Fernández-Moreno 1972). However, we do have evidence of Nebrija's effects on the New World through the writings of early Spanish-American authors. Indeed, the Spanish language takes root and bears fruit in American soil immediately upon its arrival. Some of the best authors of the Spanish Golden Age were from the New World. Some of them rivaled and even surpassed their peninsular contemporaries. Even more important, some of them were of Amerindian origin. We may not be able to determine the extent to which Nebrija's *Gramática* may have been responsible for the relatively fast and easy spread of the Spanish language in the New World, but at least we know that a fairly uniform code of written expression was being used by Spanish speakers on both sides of the Atlantic from the very beginning.

The work of the Spanish Royal Academy during the first century of its existance serves to maintain and increase this commonality in linguistic codification. During the second half of the eighteenth century the Academy's codifications are widely used in the New World. With the expulsion of the Jesuits in 1767, the Church's efforts in the area of native-language religious instruction diminish, and the imposition of Spanish on the conquered popu-lation becomes a necessity for both the State and the Church. In 1769 Don Francisco Antonio de Lorenzana, Archbishop of Mexico, complained to Emperor Charles III about the shortage of bilingual priests who could minister to the target populations in their native languages, and about the various administrative difficulties this situation presented. In response to the Archbishop's plight, Charles III ordered the extinction of the Amerindian languages and the imposition of Spanish by royal decree in 1770 (Vázquez 1978). The release of the Academia's *Gramática* in 1771 was no coincidence. The effects of the Academy's works are also noticeable in the writings of Spanish-American authors during the first quarter of the nineteenth century.

Nationalism; political, intellectual and linguistic (1824-1870)

The Spanish Royal Academy became one of the many casualties of the war, and after independence was won in 1824 it ceased to have its once-recognized authority in the New World. But although relations with the crown's Academy might not have been friendly, the interest in language codification was ever present. This is evidenced by various movements intended either to assign the functions of the Academy to local institutions, such as the literary Society of Buenos Aires in 1823, or to create Academy-like institutions to take over these functions. As a matter of fact, the creation of an Academy of the Latin American Language was proposed in Colombia as early as 1825. These and other attempts to institutionalize language codification in the New World met with little success (Guitarte and Torres-Quintero 1974). The first American codification of the Spanish language was to be the work not of an Academy, but of an individual language planner, Andrés Bello.

Born in Caracas, Venezuela, in 1781, Andrés Bello combined all the desirable qualities of the scholar, the statesman, and the ideological leader. He was educated to the marrow. Classical literature, philosophy, medicine, and jurisprudence were among his fields of inquiry. He lived in London for 19 years, where he served as secretary to the legations of Chile and Colombia in England. In 1829, he accepted the post of Minister of Foreign Affairs for the Republic of Chile. A codifier by vocation, he was mainly responsible for the Chilean Code of Law, which was widely adopted and followed throughout the New World. In Chile he had a brilliant political and literary career until his death in 1865. Two prominent figures of the times had a definite impact on Bello. One of them was his student and friend Simón Bolívar, the leader of the Spanish-American revolution. The other was the German naturalist Alexander Von Humbolt, through whose friendship Bello developed an interest in geography (Encyclopaedia Britannica 1975).

In matters of language, Bello was considered a moderate nationalist. He sympathized with avant gard groups such as the Orthographic Reform Movement, which advocated changes in the spelling of the Spanish language that reflected the New-World pronounciation. However, when the movement reached its peak in 1842 under the leadership of the Argentinian scholar and stateman Domingo Faustino Sarmiento, Bello tried to serve as a conciliatory mediator and eventually recommended that the idea of an orthographic reform be abandoned (Guitarte and Torres-Quintero 1974). Such sensible moderation, on the other hand, in no way meant that Bello was satisfied with the state of the art in Spanish language codification. In 1847, Bello published his *Gramática de la Lengua Castella Destinada al Uso de los Americanos*. With this work, Bello introduces the concept of a 'national grammar' addressed exclusively to the free Spanish speakers of the New World. He also introduces the concept of language as a live organism whose vitality depends not on the constant identity of its components, but on the uniform regularity of their *functions* (Bello 1884b). Bello also breaks away from forced cross-linguistic codification. He rejects the classical model as being irrelevant. With Bello, Spanish grammar no longer has to parallel Latin structures nor observe the rubrics of the French *bon goût*. Bello holds the position that languages are perfectly capable of describing themselves. Thus in one single codification, Bello produces not only the first New-World autonomous grammar, but also the first model of the Spanish language which can be called organic, functional, and metalinguistic. To this day, Bello's individual accomplishment has yet to be surpassed by *any* Academia.

One would imagine that, being such a staunch separatist, Bello would encourage or even advocate a total linguistic autonomy from Spain. His goals, however, were more pedagogical than political. He defined grammar as the art of speaking a language correctly according to the good usage of people who were well educated. His work was intended to provide a linguistic standard by which Spanish Americans could measure correctness, not to promote the political success of any state, nor to abolish or impose any particular style. There is a certain irony in Bello's *Gramática.* He addresses his work to Spanish Americans only, because he believes that the linguistic leadership of the Hispanic world still belongs in the hands of the Academia. Yet his codification differs decidedly from the one promoted by the latter.

Bello's *Gramática* was well received on both sides of the Atlantic. The Academia praised its many virtues and rewarded Bello by appointing him honorary member in 1851, and associate member in 1861. In the New World, Bello's *Gramática* was officially adopted for the purposes of education throughout Central and South American and the Hispanic Caribbean. His following in linguistic and pedagogical circles was overwhelming. The extent to which Bello restored respect for language codification in the New World is such that many have viewed the effects of his work as a triumph for the Academic spirit (Guitarte and Torres-Quintero 1974). Unfortunately, Bello's *Gramática* comes at a time of such political, ideological, and literary turmoil that it is difficult to pinpoint those effects. One thing we know for sure, the publication of Bello's *Gramática* is followed by a rapid surge in Spanish-American letters. This of course may be attributed to the rise of two literary movements during this period: Romanticism and Realism, both of which capitalized rather heavily on local nationalistic themes and defended the freedom and authenticity of written expression. Furthermore, both of these movements had substantial theoretical support in the works of the German linguist August Schleicher. Schleicher's application of the Hegelian theory of historical determinism and Darwinian principles of natural selection to a scientific theory of language, known as *Stamm baum theorie* (Encyclopaedia

Britanica 1975), made it possible to accept environmentally determined linguistic fragmentation and differential development as perfectly *natural* phenomena. Thus the success of the national literatures, coupled with Schleicher's popularity in the New World, prevented a full restoration of Academic supremacy.

It is important to note, however, that Bello's standard of 'educated' correctness were observed rather consistently by Spanish-American authors of this period. The New-World literati wrote with confidence. They wrote as Americans, and for Americans, without seeking peninsular approval. The intellectual independence of the New World was no longer an issue for discussion.

The Neoacademic Movement; rise, fall, and renewal (1870- ?)

By 1870, the Spanish Royal Academy becomes aware of America's intellectual independence and makes an effort to bring the lost sheep back into the flock by authorizing the creation of associate Academies throughout the New World. The move was very politically motivated. It encouraged the formation of several analogous Academies in the various Spanish-American countries. These Academies would be recognized by the mother Academy in Madrid and would work cooperatively with it to ensure linguistic uniformity. It discouraged the formation of a single autonomous center for linguistic and literary leadership in the New World. This was hardly the time for the Academia to try to assume an international leadership role. The overwhelming triumph of theRomanticist movement in Spain conclusively demonstrated the Academia's inability to control written expression even within its own territorial boundaries. Therefore, the idea of a network of satellite Academies throughout the New World was less than enthusiastically received. Nevertheless, during this period, several national Academies were established: in Colombia (1871), in Mexico and Ecuador (1875), in El Salvador (1880), in Venezuuela (1881), in Chile (1886), in Peru (1887), and in Guatemala (1888). Most of these were individual efforts undertaken by a select group of Spanish-American scholars with little or no financial support (Guitarte and Torres-Quintero 1974).

The unquestionable leaders of this neoacademic movement were two prominent literary and political figures from Colombia: Miguel Antonio Caro and Rufino Jose Cuervo. The first used his presidency of the Republic of Colombia to promote the development of mass education and literary growth. The second has been acclaimed as Spanish America's first and foremost linguist and philologist. In the midst of the linguistic nationalism of the times, only Caro and Cuervo were politically and intellectually secure enough to speak out in favor of prescriptive codification (Caro 1928; Cuervo 1955). Cuervo himself attempted the ultimate lexical codification of the Spanish language in his *Diccionario de Construcción y Régimen*, of which he was only able to complete and finance the publication of the first two volumes (Guitarte and Torres-Quintero 1974).

While the contributions of the neoacademic movement cannot be denied, its efforts failed to bring written expression under tight control. The resistance against linguistic prescriptivism was strong, particularly if it was to be ultimately sanctioned by the Spanish Academy. Madrid was no longer viewed as the primary source for Spanish America's linguistic and literary growth. New-World scholars were flocking to Paris, London, and Rome in search of new and broader horizons. The most salient of them was the Nicaraguan poet, Ruben Darío, who, after sharing for a while the bohemian lifestyle of the Parnassian and Symbolistic schools of nineteenth-century France, launched a stylistic revolution in the New World with the publication of his book *Azul* in 1888. Darío founded the Modernistic movement, a totally antiacademic approach to free and creative linguistic expression. His works and those of his followers are characterized by a total and deliberate defiance of prescriptivism. Modernism is more than just another stylistic current. It is Spanish America's first literary movement of universal significance. As a matter of fact, Dario's most enthusiastic followers were the Spaniards themselves. For the first time in history, the New World was leading and Europe was following. Spain's linguisitc and literary supremacy was completely annulled.

Toward the end of the nineteenth century, we witness the fall of the neoacademic movement. Even Rufino José Cuervo, its foremost leader, embraced Schleicher's naturalistic theories and joined the ranks of linguistic and literary nationalism (Solé 1970). Cuervo's new position was presented in a letter addressed to his friend, the Argentinian poet Don Francisco Soto y Calvo. In his letter Cuervo praises the work of Spanish-American writers and enthusiastically proclaims America's intellectual independence. He also bemoans the state of Spanish letters and concludes that Americans had little to gain from studying Spanish authors and that the need to turn to other sources in other languages in order to keep up with the times was ever increasing. As he looks toward the future, he sees a centrifugal evolution of the Spanish language in the New World analogous to that of Latin after the fall of the empire. Cuervo's letter appears as the prologue to a poem by Soto y Calvo entitled *Nastasio*, published in Chartres in 1899 (Cuervo 1974a). Needless to say, Cuervo's reassessment of the status and future of the Spanish language in the New World caused a great deal of concern in Spain's academic circles. Cuervo had to be contested. The polemic was inevitable. Juan Valera, the learned diplomat, critic, and novelist became the peninsular champion. He responded to Cuervo with two newspaper articles published in 1900: one in *El Imparcial* of Madrid, (Valera 1947c), and one in *La Nación* of Buenos Aires (Valera 1947a). Valera challenges Cuervo's historico-naturalistic views and discards the possibilities of a Latin-like centrifugal evolution of the Spanish language in the New World, citing differences in historical circumstances. Although Valera was as highly respected as Cuervo, both as a scholar and as a political figure, when it came to a philological debate, he was no match for the latter. Cuervo's rebuttal, published in *Bulletin Hispanique* in 1901 (Cuervo 1947b), practically ended the debate before it had a chance to start. Two more articles followed, one published by Valera in *La Tribuna* of Mexico in 1902 (Valera 1947b), and another by Cuervo in *Bulletin Hispanique* in 1903 (Cuervo 1947c). But by then, the polemic had ceased to be intellectual and had become personal, even emotional. During the decade that followed the Valera-Cuervo debate, a spirit of antiprescriptivism reigned in the New World. The neoacademic generation was extinct, and many of the associate national Academies disintegrated. It was not until the second decade of the twentieth century that affiliate New-World Academies began to appear again (Guitarte and Torres-Quintero 1974), and that Spanish academicians were able to contest Guervo's arguments with modest success (Menéndez-Pidal 1918).

This renewal of the neoacademic spirit, and the restoration and augmentation of Academic bonds between the New World and Spain, fell far short of a recognition of the latter's linguistic leadership; for the next prominent figure in New-World Spanish codification departed from the traditional norm even more drastically than Bello. Rodolfo Lenz was a German-born philologist residing in Chile. His command of and knowledge about the Spanish language were extraordinary. He was professor of Spanish grammar at the University of Chile and considered himself a devout follower of Bello's doctrine. In 1916 he published his rather novel structural codification of the Spanish language, *La Oración y Sus Partes.* His work was well received throughout the New World and highly respected in Spain. A subsequent edition of his work was endorsed with a preface by Spain's foremost academician, Don Ramon Menendez Pidal (Lenz 1925). Lenz made good use of his multilingual ability to keep up with the latest scientific developments throughout the world. A dedicated student of human behavior, he was strongly influenced by the works of the German scientist Wilhelm Wundt, the father of experimental psychology. In his prologue, Lenz gives credit to Wundt's *Ethnic Psychology* as one of the major sources for his psychological perspective (Lenz 1925). His vast knowledge of Amerindian and other exotic languages comes across through the various references he makes to their structures as he discusses the elements of his Spanish codification. In the final analysis, Lenz presents a model that is more critical than descriptive. The boldness of his approach and the magnitude of his work should have earned him a solid following. His work, however, although widely respected, was not viewed as being applicable to all of Spanish America, because of its strong Chilean orientation. He presented the Spanish language as taught in Chile, illustrated with samples of the local norm. Furthermore, his psychological approach to language, although widely acclaimed, was not viewed at the time as something genuinely Spanish-American. It was more of a phenomenom that could only occur given Lenz's unique multilingual/multidisciplinary background. But while Lenz may not have caused the same kind of impact as Nebrija, the Academia, or Bello, he showed that language codification was still an open field, and that nobody had said the final word yet.

After Lenz, the study, criticism, and application of linguistic codification became popular. Some Spanish-American grammarians prepared structural codifications for pedagogical purposes (Lemos-Ramírez 1937; Alonso and Henríquez-Ureña 1928; Moner-Sans 1943). Others entertained novel approaches to the scientific study of language (Castañeda-Calderón 1944). In spite of the fact that Academic bonds had been restored with Madrid, there seemed to be no need for peninsular leadership. As a matter of fact, criticism against the Academia was open, and at times abrasive. Some of the major concerns of Spanish Americans during this period were the lack of effective communication between the mother Academy and its affiliates, and the assumptions made by the mother Academy about the Spanish language as spoken in America without adequate empirical validation (Amunatequi y Reyes 1943). Some of the works published by the Academia became rather unpopular, especially the *Diccionario* (Ezeyza Gallo 1942). Even an alternative to the existing system of associate Academies was proposed: the incorporation of representatives from Spanish America into the mother Academy itself, so that the governing body of the Spanish language would be representative of its speakers (Álvarez 1943).

In 1951, President Miguel Alemán of Mexico convened the first International Congress of the Academies of the Spanish Language. The Congress was held in Mexico City and was financed by the Alemán administration. Alemán's goals were very praiseworthy. In a world in which international power was best exercised in political blocks, nations that shared common interests and historical bonds would make better allies. Therefore, Alemán sought to promote close cooperation among the institutions responsible for the Spanish language in the various nations that spoke it. The Congress succeeded in establishing the Association of Academies of the Spanish Language and creating its Permanent Commission. The latter now has representatives from Spain and other Spanish-American countries and has its permanent headquarters in Madrid. The Permanent Commission is officially recognized by several governments of Spanish-speaking countries. Its functions are to implement the resolutions adopted by the Association and to serve as a consultative body to the Spanish Royal Academy. Under the new structure, the roles and functions of the Academies themselves have not been altered. The Spanish Royal Academy provides leadership and guidance; the Spanish-American Academies act as consultants. The Association has extensive and impressive plans for the production of collective works in language codification (Guitarte and Torres-Quintero 1974).

INTERNAL DEVELOPMENT: SAMPLE MODELS OF NEW-WORLD SPANISH

There are three widely recognized structural codifications of the Spanish language in the new world: Bello's *Gramática*, the Spanish Royal Academy's *Gramática*, and Lenz's *La Oración y Sus Partes*. This review will provide some general remarks about their salient features. Nebrija's *Gramática* also warrants some consideration because of its historical significance, and because its classical authenticity makes it a good point of reference. A comparative analysis of these models is far beyond the limits of the present study. Instead we will look at some of their generic characteristics, such as conceptual frameworks and morphosyntactic interpretations. Although no label is ever totally accurate, for the purposes of this review, we can safely classify Nebrija's model as classical, the Academia's model as neoclassical, Bello's model as functional, and Lenz's model as critical (see Table 1).

Classical codification

Nebrija defines grammar in the classical tradition, as the art of letters. As the Greeks divide grammar into historical and methodical, Nebrija divides it into declarative and doctrinal. Historical or declarative grammar is that which presents and studies language through its literature. Methodical or doctrinal grammar is that which presents and studies the precepts of the art of letters. He describes the Spanish language in Latin-like terms. He declines the noun into three declensions: those that end in '*a*' (first declension), those that end in '*o*' (second declension), those that end in other letters (third declension). The morphology of the verb is also very classical. He recognizes five verbal modes: indicative, imperative, subjunctive, infinitive, and optative (modern Spanish: imperfect subjunctive ending in '*-se*'). Nebrija's syntax presents a sentence with ten possible parts: noun, pronoun, article, verb, participle, gerund, infinite participial noun, preposition, adverb, and conjunction (Nebrija 1926). The forced classical parallelisms are obvious. Even in Nebrija's times, parts such as the gerund and the infinite participal noun were not truly functional.

Table 1. *Internal development: model conceptual framework and structural configuration*

Models → / Characteristics ↓	Nebrija (classical)	Academia (neoclassical)	Bello (functional)	Lenz (critical)
Conceptual framework (definition)	Grammar is the art of letters. Historical/declarative grammar studies language through its literature. Methodical/doctrinal grammar presents and studies the precepts of the art of letters.	Grammar is the art of speaking and writing correctly (i.e. '*bon goût*').	Grammar is the art of speaking a language correctly in accordance with the good usage of people who are 'educated'.	A sentence is the phonetic expression of the intentional breakdown of a total representation into its logically related elements.
Morphology (sample)	The noun has three declensions: first '*a*'; second, '*o*'; third, ending in other letters. The verb has six modes: indicative, imperative, subjunctive, infinitive, and optative.	The noun has five cases: nominative, genitive, accusative, dative, ablative; and six genders: masculine, feminine, neuter, epicene, common, ambiguous. The verb has four modes: indicative, imperative, subjunctive, and conditional.	The noun has two genders: masculine and feminine, which are interpreted both semantically and inflectionally. The verb has three modes: indicative, subjunctive, and imperative.	The verb has three modifications: objective (voices), subjective (modes), relative (tenses). There are five verb modes: infinitive, subjunctive, optative, imperative, and dubitative.
Syntax (parts of the sentence)	Parts of the sentence (10): noun, pronoun, article, verb, participle, gerund, infinite participial noun, preposition, adverb, and conjunction.	Parts of the sentence (9): five variable parts (noun, adjective, pronoun, article, and verb); four invariable parts (adverb, preposition, conjunction, and interjection).	Parts of the sentence (7): substantive, adjective, verb, adverd, preposition, conjunction, and interjection.	Parts of the sentence (6): substantive, adjective, verb, preposition, and conjunction.

Neoclassical codification

The Spanish Royal Academy defines grammar as the art of speaking and writing correctly. In 1713, this meant avoiding linguistic excesses of both form and content. The model boasts of an elaborate (but totally fictitious) Spanish case system: nominative, genitive, accusative, dative, ablative; and of a six-gendered noun morphology: masculine, feminine, neuter, epicene, common, and ambiguous. Verb morphology, on the other hand, has been simplified. The infinitive is not treated as a mode. Four modes are recognized: indicative, imperative, subjunctive and conditional (Spanish: *potencial*). Like its counterpart, the French *Grammaire* (Institut de France 1933), it divides and treats the parts of the sentence in two groups: the variable or inflectionable forms, and the invariable forms. According to the Academia's model, Spanish has five variable forms: noun, adjective, pronoun, article, and verb; and four invariable forms: adverb, preposition, conjunction, and interjection (Real Academia Española 1924).

Functional codification

Bello defines grammar as the art of speaking a language correctly in accordance with the good usage of people who are educated. His prescriptive intent is obvious. However, Bello's standards of 'educated' correctness do not come from predetermined models. Instead he proposes to let the Spanish language describe itself. Although he does not pretend to challenge the Academia, he departs rather drastically from traditional codification. His noun morphology is simple when compared with its two predecessors. Bello identifies two major genders for the noun: masculine and feminine; and disposes of grammatical exceptions by treating generization in terms of both meaning and structional marking. In this way, he avoids establishing rules exclusively under either set of criteria. Verb morphology is further simplified. The modes are only three: indicative, subjunctive, and imperative. His classification of the parts of the sentence is strictly along functional lines. There are only seven: substantive (noun), adjective, verb, adverb, preposition, conjunction, and interjection (Bello 1884b).

Critical codification

Lenz is rather noncommital in his definition of grammar. Although his work is a true codification, he focuses on the sentence and its structure, rather than taking a broad view of the language as a whole. Lenz's conceptual framework comes from Wundt. It presents human experience as having two components: the subject that makes the experience, and the objective content of the experience. The elements of the first are the simple sentiments, while sensations are the elements of the latter. The products of psychic phenomena can be classified depending on the components from which they draw their elements. They are called emotions if the elements are simple sentiments. If the elements are sensations, they are called representations. For Lenz, a sentence is the phonetic expression of the intentional breakdown of a total representation into its logically related elements (Lenz 1925). Lenz's psychological approach yields numerous and hair-splitting classifications for the various types of sentences, constructions, and forms. His verb morphology is a good example. He recognizes three possible modifications of the verb: the objective modification, voices; the subjective modification, modes; and the relative modifications, tenses. He classifies verb modes according to their 'logical value': infinitive, subjunctive, optative, imperative, and dubitative. The latter is actually the conditional bearing a psychologically oriented label. Lenz's 'sentence' has six possible parts: substantive, adjective, adverb, verb, preposition, and conjunction (Lenz 1925).

USE

There are few cases of comprehensive language policies in the New World. Paraguay, of course, is an exception, due to its unusual historical and sociological circumstances (Rubin 1968). Outside of Guarani in Paraguay, and Quechua in Peru, no other language besides Spanish enjoys official national status in any Latin American country. The thrust of language policy in the New World is pedagogical. This is to be expected because of two very important sociological factors. Fist, illiteracy is still a major problem even among the Spanish-descent and mestizo populations. Second, there is still a large Amerindian population that does not speak Spanish. The task of teaching Spanish to the conquered population still continues. There are other uses of a language standard which can be called nonpedagogical, such as the official nature of orthography and various government decrees promoting standardized usage.

Pedagogical applications

Two models are widely used for pedagogical purposes: Bello's and the Academia's. Bello's *Gramática* is of course the more popular of the two. This is a fulfillment of the author's own goals, as he intended his work to be used primarily in education. As matter of fact, Bello himself wrote textbooks for language instruction based on his model (Bello 1884a). In general, Bello's standards of 'educated' correctness are still the most common norm in Spanish-American education. Even the more innovative applications of language codification for pedagogical purposes, which seek to incorporate twentieth-century linguistic theory into the teaching of Spanish, use Bello as the primary source (Alonso and Henríquez-Ureña 1938). Applications of a modified Academic model are not uncommon (Lemos-Ramírez 1937; Moner-Sans 1943). And certainly, these are expected to become more popular through the work of the Academies. The Academies can also be expected to address issues of dialectal morphology for the purposes of eventual codification (Guitarte and Torres-Quintero 1974). There is also a noticeable trend toward integrating elements of various models, particularly in higher education. The University of Puerto Rico's *Manual de Nociones y Ejercicios Gramaticales* incorporates elements from Bello, the Academia, Lenz, and other codifiers (Universidad de Puerto Rico 1978). As the study of other languages in Spanish America progresses, we can anticipate an increased utilization of other models. For example, the most respected work on Spanish/English contrastive analysis is of North American origin and applies a generative model (Stockwell et al. 1965).

Nonpedagogical applications

Traditionally, Spanish orthography has been a battleground for etymologists and phoneticians on both sides of the Atlantic. In Spanish America, where most Spanish-American countries share pronunication characteristics which in turn are different from those of Spain, the outcry for a phonetically oriented orthographic reform was great in the latter part of the nineteenth century. Such reforms have been proposed and even attempted. However, the Academia's Orthography is still considered the official norm for public documents.

Much of the credit for the application of a language standard to various aspects of daily life must be given to the national Academies. Nicaragua has a law requiring proper usage in official documents and announcements intended for widespread public dissemination. More far-reaching legislation in Colombia not only regulates the use of the Spanish language in official documents and other public concerns and services, but it regulates the use of other languages as well. By legal decree, the Colombian Academy also serves as a consultative body to the government in matters related to language (Guitarte and Torres-Quintero 1974). As the work of the Academies progresses, more standard-oriented language policies are expected.

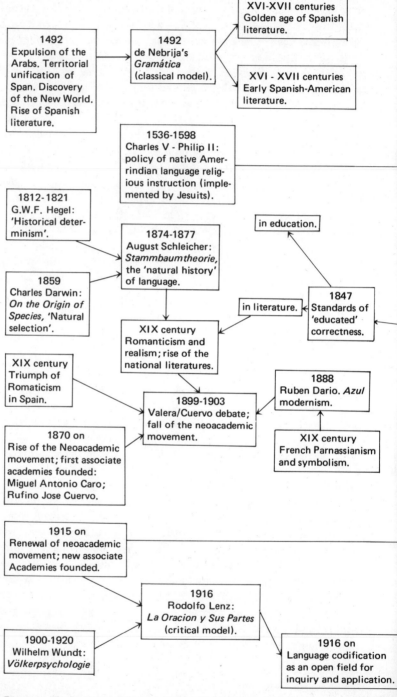

Figure 1. *The historical dynamics of language codification*

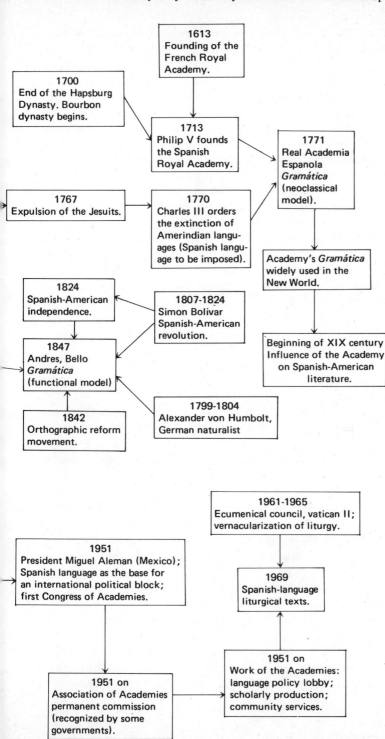

Another institution that should be recognized as promoting a standardized model of Spanish is the Roman Catholic church. The vernacularization of the liturgy which occurred after Vatican II required the development and adoption of official Spanish-language liturgical texts to be used throughout the Hispanic New World. These tasks were accomplished with the assistance of the Academies (Guitarte and Torres-Quintero 1974). Although the Church's work in this area may not be as intense and as deliberate as that of governments or learned institutions, it is likely to reach a larger segment of the population, particularly the uneducated poor.

Written expression in twentieth-century Spanish-American literature is not readily qualifiable in terms of its observance of a particular standard norm. Spanish America's literary production in the twentieth century is not only large but also varied and often eclectic in both themes and styles. Prose fiction presents an interesting situation in which the author's writing style may be laced with the colloquial speech of the characters. However, the universal acceptance of the contemporary Spanish-American novel is indicative of the fact that a major breakdown of literary language standards has not occurred. On the other hand, the lack of a stylistic uniformity such as the one observed at the beginning of the nineteenth century would tend to indicate the absence of an absolute standard of written expression.

CONCLUSIONS

There are a few lessons which can be learned from this brief overview of structural codification in the New World. Language codifications are historical phenomena. As such, their occurrence, conception, and success are affected by the historical trends and events that preceed them and surround them (See Figure 1). There might never have been a Spanish Royal Academy of the Language without a Bourbon king. It is unlikely that Bello's 'national grammar' would ever have seen the light without a war of independence. Lenz would never have produced a psychologically oriented critical model without the influence of Wundt. On the other hand, Nebrija's plan might have been widely implemented in the New World, if Queen Isabella's successors had not adopted a policy in favor of native Amerindian language religious instruction. As historical phenomena, language codifications also have an effect on the historical trends and events that surround them and follow them. For example, the impact of the Academy's *Gramática* on literary production toward the end of the eighteenth century and at the beginning of the nineteenth century is rather noticeable. Likewise, the impact of Bello's *Gramática* on the subsequent development of Spanish-American letters and formal education is undeniable. Let us also consider the relationship that exists between the success of a codification and the credibility of the codifier. Surely Bello's *Gramática* is far superior to that of the Academia. However, how much of its success can be attributed to its quality, and how much of it must be attributed to Bello's prominence? Who else could have displaced the Academia, but a national hero?

There exists a relationship between the conceptual framework that supports a codification and the structural configuration of the latter. Nebrija's model, for example, is almost as classical as its sources. Bello's organic conceptualization of language, however, results in a functional codification. Lenz's psychological perspective yields a critical grammar.

Cooperation and communication between language codifiers and language policy makers are lacking for the most part throughout Spanish America. This may be due to the fact that, outside of the essential linguistic protocols, most Spanish-American governments do not view language planning and standardization as a policy-making area. The existance and function of language is simply assumed. Language is not viewed as a national resource whose usefulness depends on the effectiveness with which it is managed. Outside of providing basic language policy for officialdom and education, most Spanish-American governments neglect to address language-policy issues.

RECOMMENDATIONS

If language planning is to be a comprehensive endeavor, the codification of a language should take into consideration the presence of other languages in the society where the standardized norm is to be applied. The effect that contact languages may have on the status and/or evolution of a given language should not be ignored (Di Pietro 1970; Gumperz and Wilson 1971; Milán 1976). Lenz's extreme application of a multilingual perspective is not necessary. However, the extent to wich a codification may promote or hinder multilingualism should be considered. Could languages in multilingual nations be codified following a contrastive approach that would facilitate mutual second-language acquisition by both marked and unmarked groups? How are the codification efforts and resources to be distributed among the various languages? Should minority groups be provided with the resources so that they can codify their *own* languages? How will language codification affect the social status and use of the individual languages? These are only some of the questions that need to be asked.

Language codification and language planning are not the same thing. It is possible for a grammarian to prepare a codification without any specific social purpose in mind. However, language codifications which are intended for the social generalization of a standardized norm should be prepared under a plan. Language planning should not be based on language codification. Instead, codification should follow planning. In the same way that a spoken language is only as vital as the community that uses it, a language codification is only as effective as the policy that supports it. The dialogue between those involved in codification and those that make policies about language must be improved. Token endorsements of the Academies and their occasional involvement in language-related government endeavors fall far short of the kind of cooperative effort that is needed. The original Spanish Royal Academy was founded as an agency of the court. Accordingly, it received substantial political and financial support from the crown. This is hardly the situation of the Academies in the New World. Once the governments are persuaded that language goals must be established and planned for, then the institutions and individuals that work in language codification will be in a better position to make a substantive and lasting contribution.

The historical significance of language codification places some serious responsibilities on language planners. A codification should be designed in such a way as to provide a link between the current status and the future stages of language evolution. Such a link would have two functions: to promote and maintain a standardized norm over time, and to provide a point of reference for the future study of language change. Models used for structural codification should be based on sound theoretical foundations from the various language sciences. These models, however, should be as neutral as possible. They should also be flexible enough so that changes needed to keep pace with advances in language research may easily be effected.

Finally, sooner or later, we are going to have to deal with the most delicate and controversial aspect of language codification, prescriptivism. The prescriptive nature of a codification is a double-edged sword. This normative perspective is used in order to bring about a reduction of linguistic variation and the generalization of a standard. On the other hand, it is also responsible for a codification's resistance to inevitable or even consummated linguistic change. This problem warrants serious consideration. Contemporary linguistic theory and even advanced technology should provide some solutions. Linguistic codification should not be tantamount to linguistic fossilization. In spite of their many contributions, all the codifications discussed in this study are unfortunate examples of this reality.

NOTE

1. The author wishes to express his special recognition for three very significant sources which provided much of the information refered to in various parts of this study, important leads for the identification and examination of other sources, and

considerable intellectual perspective for the interpretation of the findings presented herein. Of all the sources referenced in this study, these three are the most highly recommended: Encyclopaedia Britanica (1975), *Britanica III: Micropadeia*. Chicago, Encyclopaedia Britanica; Guitarte, Guillermo L, and Rafael Torres-Quintero (1974), 'Linguistic correctness and the role of the academies in Latin America', in *Advances in Language Planning*, ed. by J.A. Fishman. The Hague, Mouton; and Solé, Carlos A. (1970), *Bibliografía Sobre el Espanol de America (1920-1967)*. Washington. Georgetown University Press. Much gratitude is also owed to professor Juan Cobarrubias for his assistance in the final revision of this manuscript.

REFERENCES

Alonso, Amado, and Pedro Henríquez-Urena (1938), *Gramática Castellana*. Buenos Aires, Argentina.

Álvarez, Juan (1943), *¿A quién corresponde el gobierno de nuestro idioma?* Buenos Airés, Argentina, Academia Argentina de Letras.

Amunatequi y Reyes, Miguel Luis (1943), *La Real Academia Española y Sus Relaciones con Sus Hijas de América*. Santiago, Chile.

Bello, Andrés (1884a), 'Compendio de Gramática Castellana, escrito para el uso de las escuelas primarias', in *Obras Completas*, volume four. Santiafo, Chile, Consejo de Instruccion Publica.

_____ (1884b), 'Gramática de la Lengua Castella, destinada al uso de los americanos', in *Obras Completas*, volume four. Santiago, Chile, Consejo de Instruccion Publica.

Caro, Miguel Antonio (1928), 'Del Uso en Sus Relaciones con el Lenguaje', in *Obras Completas*, volume five. Bogota, Colombia, Imprenta Nacional.

Castañeda-Calderón, Hector Neri (1944), *Al Margen de la Gramática Tradicional*. San José, Costa Rica.

Cuervo, Rufino José (1947a), 'Carta a Don Francisco Soto y Calvo', in *El Castellano en América*, ed. by Luis Alfonso. Buenos Aires, Librería y Editorial 'El Ateneo'.

_____ (1947b), 'El Castellano en America I', in *El Castellano en América*, ed. by Luis Alfonso. Buenos Aires, Librería y Editorial 'El Ateneo'.

_____ (1947c), 'El Castellano en America II', in *El Castellano en América*, ed. by Luis Alfonso. Buenos Aries, Librería y Editorial 'El Ateneo'.

_____ (1955), *Apuntaciones Críticas Sobre el Lenguaje Bogotano*. Bogota, Colombia, Instituto Caro y Cuervo.

De Nebrija, Elio Antonio (1926), *Gramática Castellana*, ed. by Ignacio Gonzalez-Llubera. London, Oxford University Press.

Di Pietro, Robert J. (1970), 'The Discovery of Universals in Multilingualism', in *Bilingualism and Language Contact*, ed. by J.A. Alatis. Washington, D.C., Georgetown University Press.

Encyclopanedia Britanica (1975), *Britanica III: Micropaidia*. Chicago, Encyclopaedia Britanica.

Ezeyza-Gallo, Arnaldo (1942), *Lápiz Rojo a la Academia*. Buenos Aires, Argentian, Juan Castagnola.

Fernandez-Moreno, César (1972), *América Latina en su Literatura*. Mexico, Siglo Veintiuno.

Fishman, Joshua A. (1972), *The Sociology of Language*. Rowley, Mass., Newbury House.

——————, editor (1974), *Advances in Language Planning*. The Hague, Mouton.

——————(1977), *Bilingual Education; Current Perspectives: Social Science*. Arlington, Va., Center for Applied Linguistics.

Guitarte, Guillermo L., and Rafael Torres-Quintero (1974), 'Linguistic correctness and the role of the academies in Latin America', in *Advances in Language Planning*, ed. by J.A. Fishman. The Hague, Mouton.

Gumperz, John, and Robert Wilson (1971), 'Convergence and Creolizations: a case from the Indo-Aryan/Dravidian border', in *Pidginization and Creolization of Languages*, ed. by D. Hymes. Cambridge, Cambridge University Press.

Institut de France (1933), *Grammaire de l'Académie Française*. Paris, Firmin-Didot.

Lemos-Ramírez, Gustavo (1937), *Gramática Española*. Quito, Eduado, Talleres Graficos de Educacion.

Lenz, Rodolfo (1925), *La Oración y Sus Partes*. Madrid, Centro de Estudios Históricos.

Menéndez-Pidal, Ramon (1918), 'La Lengua Espanola, su Unidad', *Hispania* 1.

Milán, William G. (1976), *New York City Spanish; Myths, Structure, and Status*. New York, Institute for Urban and Minority Education Report Series No. 1.

Moner-Sans, R. (1943), *Gramática Castellana*. Buenos Aries, Argentina, Estrada y Cia.

Real Academia Espanola (1924), *Gramática de la Lengua Española*. Madrid.

Rubin, Joan (1968), *National Bilingualism in Paraguay*. The Hague, Mouton.

Solé, Carlos A. (1970), *Bibliografía Sobre el Espanõl en América (1920-1967)*. Washington, D.C., Georgetown University Press.

Stockwell, Robert P., J. Donald Bowen, and John W. Martin (1965), *The Grammatical Structures of English and Spanish*. Chicago, University of Chicago Press.

Ugarte, Francisco (1965), *España y su Civilización*. New York, Odyssey Press.

Universidad de Puerto Rico (1978), *Manual de Nociones de Ejercicios Gramaticales*. San Juan, Editorial Universitaria.

Valera, Juan (1947a), 'Carta a *La Nación*', in *El Castellano en América*, ed. by Luis Alfonso. Buenos Aires, Librería y Editorial 'El Ateneo'.

——————(1947b), 'Carta a *La Tribuna*', in *El Castellano en América*, ed. by Luis Alfonso. Buenos Aires, Librería y Editorial 'El Ateneo.

——————(1947c), 'Sobre la Duración del Habla Castellana', in *El Castellano en América*, ed. by Luis Alfonso. Buenos Aires, Librería y Editorial 'El Ateneo'.

Vasquez, José A. (1978), *El Español, Eslabón Cultural*. New York, Las Americas.

BRAJ B. KACHRU

Models for New Englishes*

In discussing the concept 'model', a distinction has to be made between the use of this term in theory construction − for example, a *model* for linguistic description (see, e.g., Revzin 1962 [1966]) − and its use in pedagogical literature, where *model* is sometimes interrelated with *method* (see, e.g. Brooks 1960; Christophersen 1973; Cochran 1954; Finnocchiaro 1964; Gauntlett 1957; Halliday et al. 1964; Lado 1964; and Stevick 1957). In pedagogical literature the term 'model' is used in two senses: first, in the sense of acceptability, generally by the native speakers of a language; second, in the sense of fulfilling codified prerequisites according to a given 'standard' or 'norm' at various linguistic levels. In this sense, then, we may say that a model provides a *proficiency scale*. This scale may be used to ascertain if a learner has attained proficiency according to a given norm. The term 'norm' is again used in two senses: in one sense it entails prescriptivism, and in another sense it entails conformity with the usage of the majority of native speakers, defined statistically (for a detailed discussion, see Lara 1976).

1.0.   MOTIVATIONS FOR A MODEL

The question of a model for English has acquired immense pedagogical importance, mainly for two reasons. First, non-native varieties of English have emerged in areas such as South Asia (Kachru 1969 and later), Southeast Asia (Crewe 1977; Richards and Tay 1980), Africa (Spencer 1971a), the Philippines (Llamzon 1969), and the West Indies (Craig 1978; Haynes 1978). Second, in those areas where English is a native language, as in North America and Scotland, this question of a model has aften been raised with reference to bidialectism.

*I am grateful to several agencies for their support of my research on this and related topics on non-native varieties of English, specifically to the Research Board of the Graduate College and the Center for International Comparative Studies, both of the University of Illinois at Urbana Champaign.

The identification of specific 'nonstandard' dialects leads to questions: which dialect should be taught for what function? and what should be the role of bidialectism in the school system? These and related questions are being debated in educational and linguistic circles (see, e.g., Bailey 1970; Bernstein 1964; Burling 1970; Ellis 1967; Labov 1966, 1969; Riley 1978; Shuy 1971; Sledd 1969; Stewart 1970; and Wolfram 1970). Educators and linguists are also concerned about maintaining national and international intelligibility in various varieties of English (see, e.g., Christophersen 1960; Kachru 1976a; and Prater 1968).

We may discuss 'model' either as a general concept or as a language-specific concept. In language-specific terms, for example, as in the case of English, one has to discuss it in the context of sociocultural, educational, and political motivations for the spread of English. The term 'spread' is used here to refer to 'an increase, over time, in the proportion of a communications network that adopts a given language variety for a given communicative function' (Cooper 1979: 23).

The question of a 'model' is then also related to the question of language spread. In the case of the spread of English, one might ask, does English have an organized agency which undertakes the job of providing direction toward a *standardized* model, and toward controlling *language change* — as is the case, for example, with French? Such attempts to control innovations or deviations from a 'standard' in English through an Academy were not taken very seriously in Britain or in North America. The first such proposals by Jonathan Swift in Britain (around 1712) and by John Adams (in 1821; see Heath 1977) in America were not received with enthusiasm. One must then ask, in spite of the nonexistence of an organized Academy, what factors have determined linguistic 'etiquette' in English, and what models of acquisition have been suggested?

The documented models of English have no authority of codification from a government or a body of scholars, as is the case, for example, with Spanish (see Bolinger 1975: 569) or French. The sanctity of models of English stems more from social and attitudinal factors than from reasons of authority. These models, more widely violated than followed, stand more for elitism than for authority — and in that sense they have a disadvantage. The native models of English were documented partly for pragmatic and pedagogical reasons. There was a demand from the non-native learners of English for materials on learning and teaching pronunciation, for standards of usage and correctness, and for linguistic 'table manners' for identifying with native speakers.

Some native speakers also wanted 'authoritative' or normative codes for 'proper' linguistic behavior. Of course, there have always been linguistic entrepreneurs who have catered to such demands from consumers. In 1589

Puttenham recommended that the model should be the 'usual speech of the court, and that of London and the shires lying about London within 60 miles and not much above'. Cooper (1987) went a step further and provided such a book for 'gentlemen, ladies, merchants, tradesmen, schools and strangers', with the enticing title *The English Teacher, or The Discovery of the Art of Teaching and Learning the English Tongue.*

This nonauthoritarian elitist prescriptivism is also found in several manuals and books on usage. A typical title, following this tradition, is *The Grammarian; or The Writer and Speaker's Assistant; Comprising Shall and Will Made Easy to Foreigners, with Instances of Their Misuse on the Part of the Natives of England.* This book by J. Beattie appeared in 1838. The often-quoted work on *Modern English Usage* by Fowler (1926) also belongs to this tradition (see also, e.g., Alford 1869; Baker 1770 [1779]; also relevant to this discussion are Hill 1954; Leonard 1929; Whitten and Whitaker 1939).

In English when one talks of a model, the reference is usually to two well-documented models, namely Received Pronunciation (RP), and General American (GA). Non-native speakers of English, even at the risk of sounding affected, often aim at a close approximation of these models. The works of Daniel Jones and John S. Kenyon encouraged such attempts. What Jones's *Outline of English Phonetics* (1918 [1956]) or *English Pronouncing Dictionary* (1956) did for RP, Kenyon's *American Pronunciation* (1924) did for GA in a restricted sense.

What type of 'standard' do these pronunciation norms provide? RP as a model is about 100 years old, and it is closely associated with the English public schools. Abercrombie, in his excellent paper, considers it unique 'because the public schools are themselves unique' (1951: 12). Because it is acquired unconsciously, says Abercrombie, 'there is no question of deliberately teaching it'. The status of RP is based on social judgement, and has no official authority. The advent of broadcasting played an important role in making RP widely known. It was therefore indentified with the British Broadcasting Corporation (BBC) and also termed 'BBC English' (see Gimson 1962: 83; Ward 1929: Chapters 1 and 2). In the changed British context, Abercrombie makes three points. First, the concept of a standard pronunciation such as RP is 'a bad rather than a good thing. It is an anachronism in present-day democratic society' (1951: 14). Second, it provides an 'accent bar' which does not reflect the social reality of England. 'The accent-bar is a little like the colour-bar — to many people, on the right side of the bar, it appears eminently reasonable' (1951: 15). Finally, RP does not necessarily represent 'educated English', for while 'those who talk RP can justly consider themselves educated, they are outnumbered these days by the undoubtedly educated people who do not talk RP' (1951: 15).

The term 'General American' refers to the variety of English spoken by about 90 million people in the central and western United States and in most of Canada (see Krapp 1919; Kenyon 1924: vii, 14). In describing GA, Kenyon was not presenting a model in the same sense in which Jones had earlier presented his. Rather, Kenyon suggests linguistic tolerance toward various American varieties of English. He is conscious of the harm done by the elitist, prescriptivist manuals for pronunciation and therefore is concerned that 'we accept rules of pronunciation as authoritative without inquiry into either the validity of the rules or the fitness of their authors to promulgate them' (1924: 3). The cause for such easy 'judgment' or quick 'advice' on matters connected with pronunciation is that people are 'influenced by certain types of teaching in the schools, by the undiscriminating use of textbooks on grammar and rhetoric, by unintelligent use of the dictionary, by manuals of "correct English", each with its favorite (and different) shibboleth' (1924: 3).

Kenyon's distaste for linguistic homogeneity is clear when he says, 'Probably no intelligent person actually expects cultivated people in the South, the East, and the West to pronounce alike. Yet much criticism, or politely silent contempt, of the pronunciations of cultivated people in other localities than our own is common' (1924: 5). In his view the remedy for this intolerance is the study of phonetics. A student of phonetics 'soon learns not only to refrain from criticizing pronunciations that differ from his own, but to expect them and listen for them with respectful, intelligent interest'.

Now, despite the arbitrariness of the above two models, one is usually asked the questions, what is a standard (or model) for English?[1] and, what model should be accepted? The first question is easy, and Ward (1929: 1) has given the answer in crisp words: 'No one can adequately define it, because such a thing does not exist'. And, in the case of English, as Strevens (1980) says, ' "standard" here does *not* imply "imposed", nor yet "of the majority". One interesting aspect of standard English is that in every English-using community those who habitually use *only* standard English are in a minority'.

2.0.   MODEL AND THE NORM

It has generally been claimed (see, e.g., Bloomfield 1933: 56) that being bilingual entails having 'native-like' proficiency in a language. A rigid application of this rather elusive yardstick is evident in the fast-increasing literature and growing number of texts for the teaching of English as L2. It is more evident in the structural method which followed the tenets of structural linguistics in America. Consider for example the following, which is typical of such an attitude:

Authentic models: Teachers can now provide authentic pronunciation models easily for their students by means of a tape recorder or a phonograph. Visitors and professional speakers can be recorded for the benefit of students, thus bringing to the class a variety of good native speakers even when the teacher does not happen to be a native speaker of the target language. (Lado 1964: 89)

In purely pedagogical methods, with no underlying serious theoretical framework, such as the structural method developed at the Institute of Education, London,[2] the same ideal goal for pronunciation was propounded.

One cannot disagree that the criterion of 'native-like' control is appropriate for *most* language-learning situations. But then, one must pause and reconsider whether such a goal for performance can be applied to the case of English in *all* situations. The case of English is unique because of its global spread in various linguistically and culturally pluralistic societies; its differing roles in language planning in each English-using country; and the special historical factors involved in the introduction and diffusion of English in each English-speaking country. Therefore it is rather difficult to define the concept 'norm' for various speakers of Englishes.

3.0.   ORIGIN OF NON-NATIVE MODELS

The origin of non-native models therefore must be related to what is termed 'the context of situation' — the historical context, and the educational setting. Furthermore, it should be emphasized that the question of a 'model' for English did not originally arise with reference to a model for 'non-native' users of English. This issue has a rather interesting history, essentially with reference to the transplanted *native* varieties of English. The attitude of American English users provides a fascinating and illuminating controversy on this topic, which eventually turned into a national debate (see Heath 1977; Kahane and Kahane 1977).[3] This national debate provides a good case study of the relationship of political emancipation to language and the identification of language with nationalism. The controversy of the *American* identity of the English language has received more attention and is therefore better known, for which credit must be given to Mencken (1919). But in Britain itself there is the case of Scottish identity, and on a far-off continent, Australia, murmurs for such identity have been heard in an occasional publication.

In the case of *non-native* varieties, the situation is much different. There has never been a Mencken, or a Webster. The local identity for English was never related to political emancipation or national pride. On the contrary, the general idea was that, with the end of the Raj, The English language would be replaced by a native language or languages. The demand was not for an identity with English, but for abolition of English; not for nativization of English, but for its replacement. In recnet years, however, the concept has been discussed primarily with reference to non-native Englishes. What do we understand by that term? The distinction between *native* and *non-native* varieties of English (Kachru 1981) is crucial for understanding the formal and functional characteristics of English.

In the international context, it is more realistic to consider a spectrum of Englishes which vary widely, ranging from standard native varieties to standard non-native varieties (see Kachru 1976a, 1981, forthcoming a; and Quirk et al. 1972: 12-32). The situation of English is historically and linguistically interesting and complex for several reasons. First, the number of non-native speakers of English is significant; if the current trend continues, there will soon be more non-native than native speakers of English. At present there are 266 million native speakers and 115 million non-native speakers. That is, 34.4% of English speakers are non-native users. This figure, which includes only those who are enrolled in schools, therefore does not provide the total picture. Consider the following statement of distribution (see Gage and Ohannessian 1977):

Native varieties (in millions)

British	American	Australian	Canadian	New Zealand
55	182	13	13	3

Non-native varieties (in millions)

Asia (excl. USSR)	Africa	West and Central Europe	Soviet Union	Western hemisphere
60	20	15	10	10

The spread of English is unique in another respect. Because the language is used in geographically, linguistically, and culturally diverse areas, its use cuts across political boundaries (Fishman et al. 1977; Smith 1981). The large range of varieties of English cannot be discussed from any one point of view. There are several, mutually *non*exclusive ways to discuss their form and function. One might, for example, consider them in *acquisitional* terms, in *sociocultural* terms, in *motivational* terms, and in *functional* terms. These may further be divided as follows:

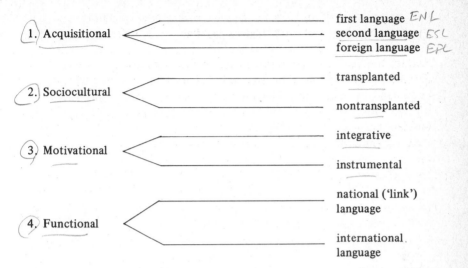

1. Acquisitional

- first language ENL
- second language ESL
- foreign language EFL

2. Sociocultural

- transplanted
- nontransplanted

3. Motivational

- integrative
- instrumental

4. Functional

- national ('link') language
- international language

A further distinction is necessary between English as a second language and English as a *foreign* language (see Christophersen 1973: 30-31; Quirk et al. 1972: 3-4). The second-language varieties of English are essentially institutionalized varieties, as in, for example, South Asia and West Africa. The foreign-language varieties are primarily performance varieties, as in Iran, Japan, etc. This distinction is also important with reference to the role and functions of English in the educational, administrative, and sociocultural context of a country in which English is used as a non-native language. The distinction between a transplanted variety (e.g. American English, Indian English) and a nontransplanted variety is important for the understanding of the acculturation and 'nativization' of the transplanted varieties (for specific case studies see, e.g., Abdulaziz 1978; Bokamba 1979; Craig 1978; Haynes 1978; Kachru 1981, forthcoming a; Kandiah 1978; Richards and Tay 1980; Wong 1980; and Zuengler 1979).

In the literature, two types of motivations have been suggested for second-language acquisition: integrative and instrumental. The distinction is essentially based on what function the L2 learner envisions for the acquired language. If the learner's motivation is integrative, then the desire is 'to identify with the members of the other linguistic cultural group and be willing to take on very subtle aspects of their language *or even their style of speech*' (Prator 1968: 474; emphasis in original). On the other hand, the instrumental approach has been defined as basically 'utilitarian'; a language is acquired as a linguistic tool, not as an instrument for cultural integration. Terms such as 'library language', 'auxiliary language', 'link language', or 'language for special purposes' (LSP) are essentially utilitarian concepts, in which language is seen as a 'restricted' code for a specific goal. In such contexts, acquiring a second culture is not the main motivation for learning the language (see also Christophersen 1973).

If we look at the global spectrum of English as a *non-native* language, we can clearly divide, as stated earlier, the non-native uses of English into two broad categories, namely, the performance varieties and the institutionalized varieties. This distinction is extremely useful and is directly related to the question of a model.

The performance varieties *(EFL)*

Performance varieties include essentially those varieties which are used as *foreign* languages. Identificational modifiers, such as *Japanese* English or *Iranian* English, are indicative of geographical or national performance characteristics. These do not indicate an institutionalized status. The performance varieties of English have a highly restricted functional range in specific contexts; for example, those of tourism, commerce, and other international transactions.

Institutionalized varieties

It is the institutionalized varieties which have some ontological status. The main characteristics of such varieties are that (1) they have an extended range of uses in the sociolinguistic context of a nation; (2) they have an extended register and style range; (3) a process of *nativization* of the registers and styles has taken place, both in formal and in contextual terms; and (4) a body of nativized English literature has developed which has formal and contextual characteristics which mark it *localized*. On the other hand, such a body of writing is considered a part of the larger body of writing labeled English literature.

An institutionalized variety always starts as a performance variety, with various characteristics slowly giving it a different status. The main characteristics of an institutionalized variety seem to be (1) the length of time in use; (2) the extension of use; (3) the emotional attachment of L2 users with the variety; (4) functional importance; and (5) sociolinguistic status. In the development of non-native models, two processes seem to work simultaneously; the *attitudinal* process, and the *linguistic* process.

A non-native model may be treated as a competitive model for teaching English as L2 if it fulfills certain conditions. In attitudinal terms, a majority of L2 speakers should identify themselves with the modifying label which marks the non-nativeness of a model: for example, *Indian* English speakers, *Lankan* English speakers, *Ghanaian* English speakers. A person may be a user of *Indian* English in his linguistic behavior, but may not consider it the 'norm' for his linguistic performance. There is thus a confusion between linguistic norm and linguistic behavior.

In linguistic terms, a viable model should describe the formal characteristics of a *generally acceptable* variety. If English is used in a culturally and linguistically pluralistic context, the norm for the model should cut across linguistic and cultural boundaries. It is natural that in such a variety a part of the lexicon will have been nativized in two ways. On the one hand, native items will be used in localized registers and styles to contextualize the language. On the other hand, English lexical items may have acquired extended or restricted semantic markers. This process then extends to other levels of language, as has been shown in several studies (see, e.g., Kachru 1981, forthcoming a).

4.0. DEVELOPMENT OF NON-NATIVE MODELS

The term 'development' is used here not in the Darwinian sense, but in essentially a historical sense. I shall attempt to discuss it with reference to changing attitudes toward a model, in terms of a scale of acceptance. A variety may exist, but unless it is *recognized* and *accepted* as a model it does not acquire a status. A large majority of the non-native speakers of institutionalized varieties of English use a local variety of English, but when told so, they are hesitant to accept the fact.

The non-native institutionalized varieties of English seem to pass through several phases which are not mutually exclusive. At the initial stage there is a *nonrecognition* of the local variety and a conscious identification with the native speakers. In South Asian terms, it may be called the 'brown sahib' attitude. A 'brown sahib' is more English than the Englishman; he identifies with the 'white sahib' in manners, speech, and attitude, and feels that his brown or black color is a burden. At this stage an 'imitation model' is elitist, powerful, and perhaps politically advantageous, since it identifies a person with the rulers. This is also the stage when English is associated with the colonizer, and therefore may be a symbol of antinationalism.

The second stage is related to extensive diffusion of bilingualism in English, which slowly leads to the development of varieties *within* a variety. The tendency then is to claim that the *other* person is using the 'Indianized', 'Ghanaianized', or 'Lankanized' English. The local model is still low on the attitudinal scale, though it may be widely used in various functions. South Asia provides an excellent example of this attitude. In India, for example, the norm for English was unrealistic and (worse) unavailable – the British variety. In actual performance, typical 'Indian' English was used. But to have one's English labeled 'Indian' was an ego-cracking linguistic insult.

The third stage starts when the non-native variety is slowly accepted as the norm, and the division between the linguistic norm and behavior is reduced. (3) The final stage seems to be that of *recognition*. This recognition may manifest itself in two ways; first in attitudinal terms, when one does not necessarily show a division between linguistic norm and linguistic behavior. This indicates linguistic realism and attitudinal identification with the variety. Only during the last 20 years or so do we find this attitude developing among the users of non-native varieties of English. Second, the teaching materials are *contextualized* in the native sociocultural milieu. One then begins to recognize the national uses (and importance) of English and to consider its international uses only marginal.

The literature provides enough evidence that the institutionalized varieties of English have passed through one or more of these stages in Africa, South Asia, the West Indies, or the Philippines. I shall not elaborate on this point here.

5.0.   FUNCTIONAL USES OF NON-NATIVE ENGLISHES

I have earlier used the term 'context of situation' without explaining it in the context of the English L2 situation. There is a relationship between the *context of situation*, the sociolinguistic profile, and the pedagogical model. Before claiming universality for a model, one must understand that what is linguistic medicine for one geographic area may prove linguistic poison for another area.

A sociolinguistic profile should consider the type of information suggested in Catford (1959: 141-142) and in Ferguson (1966: 309-315). The linguistically relevant information is as important as are the political, geographical, and economic factors. In addition, the attitudinal reactions toward an *external* or an *internal* model cannot be neglected. I shall return to that point in the two following sections.

The context of situation will then provide a cline ('a graded series') both in terms of *proficiency* in English, and in its *functional* uses. The English-using community must be seen in a new framework, in which a linguistic activity is under analysis within a specific sociocultural context. Within the framework of user and uses, one has to take into consideration (cline of participants, cline of roles, and cline of intelligibility.)

Without the perspective of this relationship it is difficult for native speakers of English to understand the uses of non-native Englishes. This type of approach has been used and recommended in several studies (see especially Candlin 1980; Kachru 1965, 1966, 1981, forthcoming a and b; Richards and Tay 1981).

The institutionalized varieties of non-native English may be arranged along a lectal continuum. This continuum is not necessarily developmental but may be functional. All subvarieties within a variety (for example, basilects, mesolects, and acrolects) have functional values and may stand as clues to code diversity as well as to code development. These are, however, not mutually exclusive.

Let me now briefly elaborate on the functional aspects of a cline. One can claim that, for example, in South Asia, English is used in four functions: the instrumental, the regulative, the interpersonal, and the imaginative/innovative.[4] In each function we have a cline in performance which varies from what may be termed an 'educated' or 'standard' variety to a pidginized or 'broken' variety. The varieties *within* a variety also seem to perform their functions, as they do in any native variety of English (for details see Brook 1973; Kachru 1981, especially subsection on 'The cline of varieties'; and Quirk et al. 1972: 13-32).

A discussion on the non-native uses of English in 'un-English' contexts will entail presenting several sociolinguistic profiles relevant to a number of institutionalized varieties of English. Since in this paper I have not set that as my goal, I will merely provide a general view of the possible functional range of non-native varieties of English.

In the case of some varieties, the English language is used in all four functions mentioned earlier. The instrumental function is performed by English as a medium of learning at various stages in the educational system of the country. The regulative function entails use of English in those contexts in which language is used to regulate conduct; for example, the legal system and administration. The interpersonal function is performed in two senses: first a *link* language between speakers of various (often mutually unintelligible) languages and dialects in linguistically and culturally pluralistic societies; and second, by providing a code which symbolizes modernization and elitism (see Sridhar 1978). The imaginative/innovative function refers to the use of English in various literary genres. In this function, the non-native users of English have shown great creativity in using the English language in 'un-English' contexts. This aspect of non-native Englishes has unfortunately not attracted much attention from linguists but has now been taken seriously by literary scholars[5] (see Kachru forthcoming b).

The 'range' and 'depth' of functional uses

The functional uses of the non-native varieties extend in two senses. The term 'range' means the extension of English into various cultural, social, educational, and commercial contexts. The wider the range, the greater the variety of uses. By 'depth' we mean the penetration of English-knowing bilingualism to various societal levels. One has to consider, for example, whether bilingualism in English is restricted to the urban upper and middle classes, or whether it has penetrated to other societal levels, too. What are the implications of these functions, and their range and depth, for a model?

The degrees of nativization of a variety of English are related to two factors: the range and depth of the functions of English in a non-native context, and the period for which the society has been exposed to bilingualism in English. The greater the number of functions and the longer the period, the more nativized is the variety. The nativization has two manifestations, cultural and linguistic, with 'cultural' here referring to the acculturation of English. The result is that, both culturally and formally, the English language comes closer to the sociocultural context of what may be termed the *adopted* 'context of situation'. This new, changed 'context of situation' contributes to the deviations from what originally might have been a linguistic 'norm' or 'model'.

6.0.   ATTITUDE OF NATIVE AND NON-NATIVE USERS TOWARD NON-NATIVE VARIETIES

In view of the unique developments and functions of the institutionalized non-native varieties of English, one might ask, what has been the attitude of native speakers and native users of English toward such non-native Englishes? The native speakers' attitude toward the development and the nativization of institutionalized varieties has traditionally not been one of acceptance or ontological recognition. Because of the linguistic manifestation of the nativization, these varieties have been considered *deficient* models of language acquisition. This attitude has not been restricted to speech performance but extends to lexical and collocational items which are determined by the new sociocultural context in which the English language is used in Africa or Asia. It seems that the contextual dislocation (or transplantation) of English has not been recognized as a valid reason for 'deviations' and innovations. Thus, the parameters for making judgments on the formal and functional uses of English continue to be culturally and linguistically ethnocentric, though the pragmatic context for such Englishes is 'un-English' and 'non-native' (see Kachru 1981, forthcoming a). Over a decade ago, I mentioned with some elation (Kachru 1969) that with World War II a new attitude of 'linguistic tolerance' had developed, which was reflected in proclamations such as 'hands off pidgins' (Hall 1955), and 'status for colonial Englishes'. Now, over a decade later, this statement warrants a postscript with reference to colonial Englishes. One has to qualify the earlier statement and say that this attitude was restricted to two circles. First, a body of literary scholars slowly started to recognize and accept the Commonwealth literature in English written by non-native users of the language as a noteworthy linguistic and literary activity. Britain was somewhat earlier in this recognition. Second, few British linguists, notably Firth (1957: 97), Halliday et al. (1964), Strevens (1977: 140), and Quirk et al. (1972: 26), accept the linguistic and functional distinctiveness of the institutionalized non-native varieties. It seems that even in America that linguistic fringe has been rather slow in providing such recognition and looking at these varieties in a pragmatic perspective (for a detailed discussion, see Kachru 1976a, 1981, forthcoming a and b).

The non-native speakers themselves have not yet been able to accept what may be termed the 'ecological validity' of their nativized or local Englishes. One would have expected such acceptance, given the acculturation and linguistic nativization of the new varieties. On the other hand, the *non*-native models of English (such as RP or GA) are not accepted without reservations. There is thus a case of linguistic schizophrenia, the underlying causes of which have yet to be studied. Consider, for example, Tables 1, 2, and 3 (for details see Kachru 1976a).

What does such an attitude imply? In Ghana, for example, *educated* Ghanaian English is acceptable; but as Sey (1973: 1) warns us, it does not entail competence in speaking RP since in Ghana ' . . . the type that strives too obviously to approximate to RP is frowned upon as distasteful and pedantic'. In Nigeria the situation is not different from Ghana or India (see Kachru 1976a). Bamgboṣe (1971: 41) emphasizes that ' . . . the aim is not to produce speakers of British Received Pronunciation (even if this were feasi-

Table 1. *Graduate students' attitude toward various models of English and ranking of models according to preference*

Model	Preference		
	I	II	III
American English	5.17	13.19	21.08
British English	67.60	9.65	1.08
Indian English	22.72	17.82	10.74
I don't care		5.03	
'Good' English		1.08	

Table 2. *Faculty preference for models of English for instruction*

	Preference		
Model	I	II	III
American English	3.07	14.35	25.64
British English	66.66	13.33	1.53
Indian English	26.66	25.64	11.79
I don't know		5.12	

Table 3. *Graduate students' 'self-labeling' of the variety of their English*

Identity marker	Percentage
Anerican English	2.58
British English	29.11
Indian English	55.64
'Mixture' of all three	2.99
I don't know	8.97
'Good' English	.27

ble!). . . Many Nigerians will consider as affected or even snobbish any Nigerian who speaks like a native speaker of English'. In another English-using country, the Philippines, the model for 'standard Filipino English' is ' . . . *the type of English which educated Filipinos speak, and which is acceptable in educated Filipino circles'* (Llamzon 1969: 15, original emphasis). There seems to be some agreement that an *external* model does not suit the linguistic and sociolinguistic ecology of most of Africa, the Philippines, or South Asia.

7.0.   DEVIATION, MISTAKE, AND THE NORM

I have used the term 'deviation' in this study and earlier (Kachru 1965: 396-398) with reference to the linguistic and contextual 'nativeness' in the non-native varieties of English. This term needs further elucidation since it is crucial to our understanding of the question of the model. The inevitable questions concerning the linguistic and contextual deviation are, what is the distinction between a 'deviation' and a 'mistake'? and, how much deviation from the norm is acceptable pedagogically, linguistically, and above all with reference to intelligibility?

We shall make a distinction between the terms 'mistake' and 'deviation' on linguistic and contextual levels. A 'mistake' by a native speaker may be acceptable since it does not belong to the linguistic 'norm' of the English language; it cannot be justified with reference to the sociocultural context of a non-native variety; and it is not the result of the productive processes used in an institutionalized non-native variety of English. On other other hand, a 'deviation' has the following characteristics: it is different from the norm in the sense that it is the result of the new 'un-English' linguistic and cultural setting in which the English language is used; it is the result of a productive process which marks the typical variety-specific features; and it is systemic within a variety, and not idiosyncratic.

There is thus an explanation for each deviation within the context of situation. It can be shown that a large number of deviations 'deviate' only with reference to an idealized norm. A number of 'deviations' labeled as 'mistakes' are· present in native varieties of English but are not accepted when used by a non-native speaker.

In earlier studies on the non-native Englishes by educators, specialists in the teaching of English, and native speakers in general, the deviations in such varieties of English have been treated essentially as 'deficiencies' in foreign-language learning (e.g. Goffin 1934 and Smith-Pearse 1934 for South Asian English; Hocking 1974 for African English). It seems to me that a crucial distinction is warranted between a deficient variety and a different variety. Deficiency refers to acquisitional and/or performance deficiency within the context in which English functions as L2. On the other hand, a different model refers to the *identificational* features which mark an educated variety of language distinct from another educated variety. The exponents of 'difference' may be at one or more linguistic levels. The following example from South Asian English illustrates identificational features.

1. Phonetics/Phonology
    (a) Series substitution involves substitution of the retroflex consonant series for the English alveolar series.
    (b) Systemic membership substitution involves the substitution of members in a system with members of another class; for example, the use of stops in place of fricative   and   , or substitution of 'clear l' for 'dark l'.
    (c) Rhythmic interference entails the use of syllable-timed rhythm in place of the stress-timed rhythm of English (see Abercrombie 1951; Kachru 1969: 643).

2. Grammar. I shall list some characteristics discussed earlier in Kachru (1965, 1969, 1976b). A discussion on African varieties of English is available in Bokamba (1979), Bamgboṣe (1979), Sey (1973), and Zuengler (1979).
    (a)   There is tendency to use complex sentences.
    (b)   Selection restrictions are 'violated' in 'be' + '-ing' constructions (e.g. use of 'hear' and 'see' in 'I am hearing', 'I am seeing').

(c)   A 'deviant' pattern appears in the use of articles.

(d)   Reduplication is common (e.g. 'small small things', 'hot hot tea').

(e)   Interrogatives are formed without changing the position of subject and auxilliary items (e.g. 'What you would like to eat?')

3. Lexis. The productive processes used in lexis have been discuased, for example, in Sey (1973), Kachru (1965, 1975, 1981) and Llamzon (1969). The term 'lexis' includes here what may be termed non-native collocations (Kachru 1965: 403-405). Consider, for example, 'turmeric ceremony', 'dung-wash', 'caste mark', 'police wala', and 'lathi charge' from Indian English, 'chewing-sponge', 'cover-shoulder', 'knocking fee', 'dunno drums', and 'bodom head' from Ghanaian English.

4. Cohesiveness. Discussion of phonology, grammar, and lexis present only one part of the total picture of the difference between 'deficient' and 'different' in a non-native variety. It is equally important to account for the following:

(a)   the cohesive characteristics of the text which mark it distinct, for example, in terms of its Nigerianness, Kenyanness, Indianness, or Caribbeanness;

(b)   the lexical and grammatical features which mark the register type and the style type;

(c)   the features which separate the literary genres of one non-native variety from those of another non-native variety.

The focus is then on setting up a relationship between the communication domains or contexts and their formal manifestations.

A non-native variety is 'deviant' not only in having specific phonetic, lexical, or grammatical characteristics, but it is also 'deviant' as a *communicative unit,* if we compare it with other native or non-native communicative units. It is therefore necessary to establish what Firth terms a 'renewal of connection' (see Firth 1956: 99, 1957: 175) between the 'interpretive context' ('the context of situation'), which gives the text a meaning, and its formal characteristics. The 'differences' in each institutionalized non-native variety may thus be viewed in a larger context, which incorporates the 'context of situation', and not purely from the view of language deficiency. Consider Figure 1.

If one adopts a functional view of the institutionalized varieties, it might help to abandon earlier views about two very important questions concerning intelligibility and the applicability of a monomodel approach to all the non-native varieties of English. I shall now discuss these briefly.

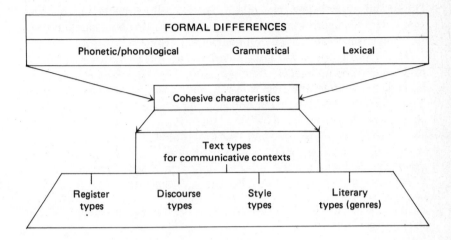

Figure 1. *Context of situation which provides interpretive context for each institutionalized variety*

8.0.   MODEL VS. INTELLIGIBILITY

In the prescriptive literature on second-language acquisition, the concepts 'norm' or 'model' seem to play a pivotal role, primarily with regard to the non-native speaker's being 'intelligible' to native speakers of English. The concept of 'intelligibility' is the least researched and least understood in linguistic or pedagogical literature (see Kachru 1981: Nelson 1978). The difficulty is that intelligibility seems to have a number of variables, and when used with reference to English it becomes more elusive. Therefore we must use the term in a specific sense. The questions one has to ask are, what is meant by intelligibility with reference to each linguistic level? Who is the judge for determining intelligibility in various varieties of English – the users of the varieties themselves, or the idealized native speakers? What parameters should be used to distinguish intelligibility between those varieties of English which are essentially regional or national (e.g. Indian English), and those varieties within a variety which have exclusively *international* functions? What role does a native speaker of English (and what type of native speaker) play concerning the judgment about the non-native varieties? What is the relationship between intelligibility of formal (linguistic) exponents and that of contextual exponents?

'Intelligibility' has been interpreted in a rather narrow sense in earlier studies. Such studies have focused primarily on decoding a phonetic/phonological signal at the lexical level. Earlier studies, especially those of Catford

(1950) and Voegelin and Harris (1951), mentioned the importance of 'situation' and 'effectiveness' in intelligibility. Nelson (1978) attempts to provide the parameters of intelligibility for non-native Englishes.

The intelligibility of the institutionalized non-native varieties of English forms a cline. Some speakers are more intelligible than are others, the variables being education, role, region, etc. The situation in the non-native varieties is not different from that in Britain or the U.S.A. The situation in Britain has been succinctly presented by Ward (1929: 5):

It is obvious that in a country the size of the British Isles, any one speaker should be capable of understanding any other when he is talking English. At the present moment, such is not the case: a Cockney speaker would not be understood by a dialect speaker of Edinburgh or Leeds or Truro, and dialect speakers of much nearer districts than these would have difficulty in understanding each other.

In the well known cone-shaped diagram (see Ward 1929: 5), Daniel Jones has graphically represented the situation: 'as we near the apex, the divergencies which still exist have become so small as to be noticed only by a finely trained ear' (Ward 1929: 6). Ward also rightly presents the argument of 'convenience or expediency' (1929: 7), observing that 'the regional dialect may suffice for those people who have no need to move from their own districts'.

The case seems to be identical to that of non-native varieties of English. Intelligibility then has to be defined in regional, national, and international terms.

9.0.   MONOMODEL VS. POLYMODEL APPROACH

In view of the special characteristics of the English speech community in various parts of the world, the pragmatic question is: Is it possible to suggest a monomodel approach, as opposed to a polymodel approach (Kachru 1977)? A monomodel approach presupposes that there is a homogeneous English L2 speech community and that the functional roles assigned to English in each area are more or less identical. More important, it assumes that the goals for the study of English in various parts of the world are more or less similar. Such a position presupposes that the 'context of situation' for the use of English in all the English-speaking areas is identical. It has already been demonstrated that such is not the case (see, e.g., Kachru 1976, 1981; Strevens 1977).

The assumptions underlying a polymodel approach are diametrically op-

posed to the monomodel approach. A polymodel approach is based upon
pragmatism and functional realism. It presupposes three types of variability
in teaching English for cross-cultural communications; namely, variability ①
related to acquisition, variability related to function, and variability related ②
to the context of situation. We may then have to recognize a cline in terms ③
of the formal characteristics of an L2 variety of English; of functional diversity in each English-speaking area; and of diversity in proficiency.

The concept of 'cline of bilingualism' (Kachru 1965: 393-396) may, therefore, be recognized as fundamental for the discussion of a model for English.
The cline applies not only to the proficiency at the phonetic/phonological
levels; it must also be interpreted in a broader sense, including the overall
sociolinguistic context.

10.0. CONCLUSION

And now, in conclusion, let us face reality. The truth is that the non-native
Englishes — institutionalized or noninstitutionalized — are linguistic orphans
in search of their parents. Several native and non-native users of English do
not understand that they are adding insult to injury by calling these varieties
'deficient Englishes'. The development of such varieties is not unique to
English; in a lesser degree Hindi, Persian, French, and Spanish have also
developed such transplanted varieties.

The problem is that even when the non-native models of English are linguistically identifiable, geographically definable, and functionally valuable,
they are still not necessarily attitudinally acceptable. There is an 'accent bar'
which continues to segregate the non-native users. The acceptance of a model
depends on its users: the users must demonstrate a solidarity, identity, and
loyalty toward a language variety. In the past, the Americans demonstrated it
(though not unanimously), and the result is a vigorous and dynamic 'American' English. But then, when it comes to recognizing and accepting the varieties within American English, or accepting other non-native Englishes, Americans have shown reluctance, condescension, or indifference. The users of non-
native varieties also seem to pass through linguistic schizophrenia, and cannot
decide whether to accept a mythical non-native model or to recognize the
local model instead.

I must also mention the unique international position of English, which is
perhaps unparalleled in the history of the world. For the first time a natural
language has attained the status of an international (universal) language,
essentially for cross-cultural communication. Whatever the reasons for the
earlier spread of English, we should now consider it a positive development
in the twentieth-century world context. We should realize that this new role

164   *Braj B. Kachru*

of English puts a burden on those who use it as their *first* language, as well as on those who use it as their *second* language. This responsibility demands what may be termed 'attitudinal readjustment'. I have elsewhere discussed 'the seven attitudinal sins' (Kachru 1976a: 223-229) which the native speakers are committing in their attitude toward the non-native varieties; a classic case is presented in Prator (1968).

The non-native users' attitudinal readjustment toward English entails the following acts, among others:

First, non-native users must now dissociate English from the colonial past and not treat it as a colonizer's linguistic tool.

Second, they must avoid regarding English as an evil influence which necessarily leads to Westernization. In South Asia and Africa the role of English in developing nationalism and mobilizing the intelligentsia at large for struggles toward freedom cannot be overemphasized. Although it is true that such use of English has resulted in a linguistic elitism, that has also been true in the past of Sanskrit and Persian, and recently of Hindi.

Third, non-native users should accept the large body of English literature written by local creative writers as part of the native literary tradition. Indian English literature, West African English literature, and Caribbean English literature not only have pan-national reading publics, but have also become part of a larger body of world writing in English. These literatures not only interpret the national traditions and aspirations to readers across linguistically and culturally pluralistic areas; in addition, these literatures also have an international reading public (see, e.g., for Indian English literature, Kachru 1976b: 168-173, 1978a, 1978b, forthcoming b; Lal 1969: i-xliv; for other literatures in English see Bailey and Görlach forthcoming).

Fourth, it is important to distinguish between the national and the international uses of English. It is primarily the *national* uses of the institutionalized varieties which contributed toward the nativization of these varieties.

Fifth, non-native users ought to develop an identity with the local model of English without feeling that it is a 'deficient' model. The local (non-native) models of English are functionally as much a part of the linguistic repertoire of people as are the native (non-Western) languages. After all, in Asia or Africa it is not unusual to find that the number of users of English exceeds the number of speakers of several of what the Indian constitution terms 'scheduled languages' (or nationally recognized languages). In India, the number of English-using bilinguals is about 3% of the total population; the numbers of speakers of six scheduled languages are close to or even much less than this figure, i.e. Assamese (1.63%), Kannada (3.96%), Kashmiri (0.45%), Malayalam (4%), Oriya (3.62%), and Punjabi (3%).

The international profile of the functions of English is encouraging: we may at last have a universal language as an offshoot of the colonial period. In this context, two questions may be asked: first, is there a coordinating agency which has a realistic view of the international and national functions of English? Second, do the non-native users of English feel that any significant theoretical and methodological leadership is being provided by those British or U.S. agencies which are involved in the teaching or diffusion of English? The answers to these questions, while not relevant to this paper, are closely related to our concern for studying English in the world context.

NOTES

1. I should mention that other models, such as Scottish (English) or Australian, have been suggested in the literature. But the main viable models in the past have been RP and GA.
2. The term 'structural' in this method is not related to structural linguistics as understood in North America or in Britain.
3. Also see Jones (1965) for a survey of the 'triumph' of English and 'a history of ideas concerning the English tongue – its nature, use, and improvement – during the period 1476-1660'.
4. My view of these four terms is somewhat different from that of Basil Bernstein, who originally used them. The functional model proposed in Halliday (1973) extends the model to nine language functions: instrumental, regulatory, interactional, personal, heuristic, imaginative, representative or informative, ludic, and ritual.
5. This fast-growing body of writing provides impressive evidence for linguistic and contextual nativization of the English language. The result is the development of English literatures with areal modifiers, such as *West African* English literature, *Indian* English literature, *Caribbean* English literature, and so on. These modifiers convey not only the geographical variation, but the cultural and sociolinguistic attitudes, too. These literatures are one manifestation of the national literatures in multilingual and multicultural non-Western English-using nations. In India, for example, one can claim that there are only three languages in which pan-Indian literature is produced with an *all-India* reading public, English, Sanskrit, and Hindi' (Kachru 1981). For a detailed bibliography on commonwealth literature in English, specifically in Africa, India, and the West Indies, see Narasimhaiah 1976.

REFERENCES

Abdulaziz, M. (1978), 'Influence of English on Swahili: a case study of language development'. Paper presented at the Conference on English in Non-Native Contexts, University of Illinois, Urbana.

Abercrombie, D. (1951), 'R.P. and local accent', *The Listener,* 6 September. (Reprinted in *Studies in Phonetics and Linguistics*, ed. by D. Abercrombie. London, Oxford University Press).

Alatis, J., editor (1969), *Georgetown Monograph on Language and Linguistics.* Washington D.C., Georgetown University Press.

_____, editor (1978), *International Dimensions of Bilingual Education. George-town University roundtable on languages and linguistics.* Washington, D.C., George-town University Press.

_____, and G. Richard Tucker, editors (1979), *Language in Public Life. George-town University roundtable on languages and linguistics.* Washington, D.C. George-town University Press.

Alford, H. (1869), *A plea for the Queen's English.* London, Strahan.

Avis, W.S. (1967), *A Dictionary of Canadianisms on Historical Principles.* Toronto.

Bailey, B.L. (1970), 'Some arguments against the use of dialect readers in the teaching of initial reading', *Florida FL Reporter* 3: 47.

Bailey, R.W., and M. Görlach (forthcoming), *English as a World Language.*

Baker, R. (1770 [1779]), *Remarks on the English Language,* second edition. London, Bell. (First edition entitled *Reflections on the English Language*).

Bamgboṣe, A. (1971), 'The English language in Nigeria', in *The English Language in West Africa,* ed. by J. Spencer. London, Longmans.

_____(1979), 'Issues in the investigation of a standard Nigerian English'. un-published manuscript.

Beattie, J. (1838), *The Grammarian; or, the Writer and Speaker's Assistant; Comprising Shall and Will Made Easy to Foreigners, with Instances of Their Misuse on the Part of the Natives of England.* London.

Bernstein, B. (1964), 'Elaborated and restricted codes: their social origins and some consequences', *American Anthropologist* 66: 55-69.

Bloomfield, L. (1933), *Language.* New York, Holt, Rinehart and Winston.

Bokamba, E. (1979), 'The Africanization of English'. Unpublished manuscript.

Bolinger, D. (1975), *Aspects of Language,* second edition. New York, Harcourt Brace Jovanovich.

Bright, W., editor (1966), *Sociolinguistics: Proceedings of the UCLA Sociolinguistics Conference, 1964.* The Hague, Mouton.

Brook, G.L. (1973), *Varieties of English.* London, Macmillan.

Brooks, N. (1960), *Language and Language Learning: Theory and Practice.* New York, Harcourt, Brace and World.

Burling, R. (1970), 'Colloquial and standard written English: some implications for teaching literacy to non-standard speakers', *Florida FL Reporter* 3: 9-15, 47.

Candlin, C. (1981), 'Discoursal patterning and the equalising of interpretive opportuni-ty', in *English for Cross-Cultural Communication,* ed. by L. Smith. London, Mac-millan.

Catford, J.C. (1950), 'Intelligibility', *English Language Teaching* 1: 7-15.

_____(1959), 'The teaching of English as a foreign language', in *The Teaching of English,* ed. by R. Quirk and A.H. Smith, London, Secker and Warburg.

Christophersen, P. (1960), 'Toward a standard of international English', *English Lan-guage Teaching* 14: 127-138.

_____(1973), *Second-Language Learning: Myth and Reality.* Baltimore, Penguin.

Cochran, A. (1954), *Modern Methods of Teaching English as a Foreign Language. A Guide to Modern Material with Particular Reference to the Far East.* Washington, D.C., Educational Services.

Cooper, R.L. (1979), 'Language planning, language spread, and language change', in *Language and Public Life,* ed. by J. Alatis and G. Richard Tucker. *Georgetown University roundtable on languages and linguistics.* Washington, D.C. Georgetown University Press.

Craig, D.R. (1978), 'Aspects of Caribbean English'. Paper presented at the Conference on

English in Non-Native Contexts, University of Illinois, Urbana.

Crewe, W.J., editor (1977), *The English Language in Singapore*. Singapore, Eastern Universities Press.

Ellis, D.S. (1967), 'Speech and social status in America'. *Social Forces* 45: 431-437.

Ferguson, C.A. (1966), 'National sociolinguistic profile formulas', in *Sociolinguistics: Proceedings of the UCLA Sociolinguistics Conference, 1964*, ed. by W. Bright. The Hague, Mouton.

Finnocchiaro, M. (1964), *English as a Second Language from Theory to Practice*. New York, Regents.

Firth, J.R. (1956), 'Descriptive linguistics and the study of English', in *Selected Papers of J.R. Firth 1952-59*, ed. by F.R. Palmer. London, Longmans.

_____ (1957), A synopsis of linguistic theory 1930-55, in *Selected Papers of J.R. Firth 1952-59*, ed. by F.R. Palmer. London, Longmans.

Fishman, J., R.L. Cooper, and A.W. Conrad (1977), *The Spread of English*. Rowley, Mass., Newbury House.

_____ , et. al., editors (1968), *Language Problems in Developing Nations*. New York, Wiley.

Fowler, H.W. (1926), *A Dictionary of Modern English Usage*. London, Oxford University Press.

Gage, W.W., and S. Ohannessian (1977), 'ESOL enrollments throughout the world', *Linguistic Reporter*, November, (Reprinted in *English Teaching Forum*, July, 1977).

Gauntlett, J.O. (1957), *Teaching English as a Foreign Language*. London, Macmillan.

Gimson, A.C. (1962), *An Introduction to the Pronunciation of English*. London, Arnold.

Goffin, R.C. (1934), *Some Notes on Indian English*. S.P.E. tract no. 41. Oxford.

Hall, R.A. (1955), *Hands Off Pidgin English!* Sydney, Pacific.

Halliday, M.A.K. (1973), *Explorations in the Functions of Language*. London, Arnold.

_____ , A. McIntosh, and P. Strevens (1964), *The Linguistic Sciences and Language Teaching*. London, Longmans.

Haynes, L. (1978), 'Caribbean English: formal and functional aspects'. Paper presented at the Conference on English in Non-Native Contexts, University of Illinois, Urbana.

Heath, S.B. (1977), 'A national language academy? Debate in the nation', *Linguistics: An International Review* 189: 9-43.

Hill, A.A. (1954), 'Prescriptivism and linguistics in English teaching', *College English*, April. (Reprinted in *Readings in Applied English Linguistics*, ed. by Allen. New York, Appleton-Century, 1958).

Hocking, B.D.W. (1974), *All What I was Taught and Other Mistakes. A Handbook of Common Errors in English*. Nairobi, Oxford University Press.

Jones, D. (1918 [1956]), *An Outline of English Phonetics*. Cambridge, Heffer.

_____ (1956), *Everyman's English Pronouncing Dictionary*. London, Dent.

Jones, R.F. (1965), *The Triumph of the English Language*. Stanford, Stanford University Press.

Kachru, B.B. (1965), 'The *Indianness* in Indian English', *Word* 21: 391-410.

_____ (1966), *Indian English: A Study in Contextualization*, in *In Memory of J.R. Firth*, ed. by C.E. Bazell et al. London, Longmans.

_____ (1969), 'English in South Asia', in *Current Trends in Linguistics*, volume five, ed. by T. Sebeok. The Hague, Mouton.

_____ (1973), 'Toward a lexicon of Indian English'. in *Issues in Linguistics: Papers in Honor of Henry and Renée Kahane*, ed. by B. Kachru et al. Urbana, University of Illinois Press.

_____ (1975), 'Lexical innovations in South Asian English', *International Journal of the Sociology of Language* 4: 55-94.

_____(1976a), 'Models of English for the third world: white man's linguistic burden or language pragmatics?' *TESOL Quarterley* 10 (2): 221-239.

_____(1976b), 'Indian English: a sociolinguistic profile of a transplanted language', in *Dimensions of Bilingualism: Theory and Case Studies*, ed. by B. Kachru. Special issue of *Studies in Language Learning*, Urbana, Unit for Foreign Language Study and Research, University of Illinois.

_____(1977), 'The new Englishes and old models', *English Language Forum*, July.

_____(1978a), 'Toward structuring code-mixing: an Indian perspective', in *Aspects of Sociolinguistics in South Asia*, ed. by B. Kachru and S.N. Sridhar. Special issue of *International Journal of the Sociology of Language* 16.

_____(1978 b), 'Code-mixing as a communicative strategy in India', in *International Dimensions of Bilingual Education*, ed. by J. Alatis. *Georgetown University roundtable on languages and linguistics*. Washington, D.C., Georgetown University Press.

_____(1979), 'The Englishization of Hindi: language rivalry and language change', in *Linguistic Method: Essays in Honor of Herbert Penzl*, ed. by I. Rauch and G. Carr. The Hague, Mouton.

_____(1981), 'The pragmatics of non-native varieties of English', in *English for Corss-Cultural Communication*, ed. by L. Smith. London, Macmillan.

_____(forthcoming a), The Indianization of English: The English Language in India. New Delhi: Oxford University Press.

_____(forthcoming b), 'South Asian English', in *English as a World Language*, ed. by R.W. Bailey and M. Görlach.

_____, et al., editors (1973), *Issues in Linguistics: Papers in Honor of Henry and Renée Kahane*. Urbana, University of Illinois Press.

Kahane, H., and R. Kahane (1977), 'Virtues and vices in the American language: a history of attitudes', *TESOL Quarterley* 11: 2.

Kandiah, R. (1978), 'Disinherited Englishes: the case of Lankan English'. Paper presented at the Conference on English in Non-Native Contexts, University of Illinois, Urbana.

Kenyon, J.S. (1924), *American Pronunciation*. Ann Arbor, George Wahr.

_____, and T.A. Knott (1953), *A Pronouncing Dictionary of American English*. Springfield, Mass., Merriam.

Krapp, G.P. (1919), *Pronunciation of Standard English in America*. New York, Oxford University Press.

Labov, W. (1966), 'Some sources of reading problems for Negro speakers of non-standard English'. NCTE Spring Institute on New Directions in Elementary English (mimeographed): 1-38.

_____(1969), 'The logic of nonstandard English', in *Georgetown Monograph on Language and Linguistics*, ed. by J. Alatis. Washington, D.C., Georgetown University Press.

Lado, R. (1964), *Language Teaching: A Scientific Approach*. New York, McGraw Hill.

Lal, P. (1969), *Modern Indian Poetry in English: An Anthology and a Credo*. Calcutta, Writers Workshop.

Lara, L.F. (1976), *El concepto de norma en linguistica*. Mexico, D.F., El Colegio de Mexico.

Leonard, S.A. (1929), *The Doctrine of Correctness in English Usage, 1700-1800. University of Wisconsin studies in language and literature no. 25.*

Llamzon, T.A. (1969), *Standard Filipino English*. Manila, Anteneo University Press.

Mencken, H.L. (1919), *The American Language*. New York, Knopf.

Narasimhaiah, C.D. (1976), *Commonwealth Literature: A Handbook of Select Reading Lists*. Delhi, Oxford University Press.

Nelson, C.L. (1978), 'Intelligibility in non-native varieties of English'. Paper presented at the Conference on English in Non-Native Contexts, University of Illinois, Urbana.

Palmer, F.R., editor (1968), *Selected Papers of J.R. Firth 1952-59*. London, Longmans.

Pickering, J. (1816 [1931]), 'A vocabulary or collection of words and phrases which have been supposed to be peculiar to the United States of America', in *The Beginnings of American English; Essays and Comments*. Chicago, University of Chicago Press.

Platt, J.T. (1975), 'The Singapore English speech continuum and basilect "singlish" as a "creoloid" ', *Anthropological Linguistics* 17: 7.

——————(1977), 'The sub-varieties of Singapore English: their sociolectal and functional status', in *The English Language in Singapore*, ed. by W.J. Crewe. Singapore, Eastern Universities Press.

Prator, C.H. (1968), 'The British heresy in TESL', in *Language Problems in Developing Nations*, ed. by J. Fishman et al. New York, Wiley.

Puttenham, G. (1589), *Arte of English Poesie*. London.

Quirk, R., and A.H. Smith (1959), *The Teaching of English*. London Secker and Warburg. (Reprinted in *Language and language learning series* 1964. London, Oxford University Press).

——————, et al. (1972), *A Grammar of Contemporary English*. London, Longmans.

Revzin, I.I. (1962 [1966]), *Models of Language*. London, Methuen. (Originally published in Russian).

Richards, J., and M.W.J. Tay (1981), 'Norm and variability in language use', in *English for Cross-Cultural Communication*, ed. by L. Smith. London, Macmillan.

Riley, R.D. (1978), 'Should we teach urban black students standard English?', *Lektos: Interdisciplinary Working Papers in Language Sciences* 3 (1): 93-119.

Sebeok, T., editor (1971), *Current Trends in Linguistics*, volume seven. The Hague, Mouton.

Sey, K.A. (1973), *Ghanian English: An Exploratory Survey*. London and Basingstoke, Macmillan.

Shuy, R.W. (1971), 'Social dialects and second language learning: a case of territorial overlap', *TESOL Newsletter* September-December.

Sledd, J. (1969), 'Bi-dialectalism: the linguistics of white supremacy', *English Journal* 58: 1,307-1,315, 1,329.

Smith, L., editor (1981), *English for Cross-Cultural Communication*. London, Macmillan.

Smith-Pearse, T.L.N. (1934), *English Errors in Indian Schools*. Bombay, Oxford University Press.

Spencer, J., editor (1963), *Language in Africa*. London, Cambridge University Press.

——————(1971a), *The English Language in West Africa*. London, Longmans.

——————(1971b), 'Colonial language policies and their legacies', in *Current Trends in Linguistics*, volume seven, ed. by T. Sebeok. The Hague, Mouton.

Sridhar, K.K. (1978), 'English in an urban context: a South Indian case study'. Paper presented at the Conference on English in Non-Native Contexts, University of Illinois, Urbana.

Stevick, E.W. (1957), *Helping People Learn English: A Manual for Teachers of English as a Second Language*. New York, Abingden.

Stewart, W. (1970), 'Current issues in the use of Negro dialect in the beginning reading texts', *Florida FL Reporter* 3-6.

Strevens, P. (1977), *New Orientations in the Teaching of English.* London, Oxford University Press.

——————(1981), 'Forms of English: an analysis of the variables', in *English for Cross-Cultural Communication*, ed. by L. Smith. London, Macmillan.

Voegelin, C., and Z. Harris (1951), 'Determining intelligibility among dialects', *Proceedings of the American Philological Society* 95 (3): 322-329.

Ward, I.C. (1929), *The Phonetics of English.* Cambridge, Heffer.

Whitten, W., and F. Whitaker (1939), *Good and Bad English.* London, Newnes.

Wolfram, W. (1970), 'Sociolinguistic implications for educational sequencing', in *Teaching Standard English in the Inner City*, ed. by R. Fasold and R. Shuy. Washington, D.C., Center for Applied Linguistics.

Wong, I.F.H. (1981), 'English in Malaysia', in *English for Cross-Cultural Communication*, ed. by L. Smith. London, Macmillan.

Zuengler, J.E. (1979), 'Kenyan English'. Unpublished manuscript.

PART THREE

Language Planning in North America

WILLIAM F. MACKEY

U.S. Language Status Policy and the Canadian Experience

Applying one country's solutions to another country's problems is valid only insofar as the problems are the same. A country's successful solution for flood control, for example, is of little use to an area permanently devoid of water. It would be futile — and indeed presumptuous — to elaborate general or universal theories based on Canada's experience in the making of language policy. It might be useful, however, to explain why certain types of policies were possible in Canada, why others were not, why some promising policies failed, and why others succeeded.

Such explanations, it must be repeated, are useful to other countries only insofar as their language situations are similar. Now, if there is any country in the world which resembles Canada, it is certainly the United States — so much so that one theory on the impossibility of developing a unique Canadian culture explains that Canadians have been far too busy trying to prove to the Americans that they are not British and to the British that they are not Americans. So in answering the question that has been assigned to me I should limit its scope to read, to what extent is the Canadian experience applicable to language-status planning within the United States?

It has often been stated that the parallel settlement histories of Canada and the United States have left both counties with similar language patterns, not only the dominant North American variety of English, which ignores the international boundary, but also in the type and distribution of language minorities — Amerindian substrata and a superimposition of the same immigrant languages in comparable proportions. All this, coexisting with two great colonial language groups, the French to the north and the Spanish in the south. It would seem, therefore, that the forty-ninth parallel of latitude, which separates Canada and the United States, can in no way be considered as a language boundary.[1] Furthermore, if different political institutions to the north have applied solutions to these comparable language problems, then these solutions should likewise be applicable to the south of the frontier.

Let us examine this proposition insofar as it affects what has here been entitled 'language-status planning'.[2] What does language status involve? We must, of course, first make this clear before we can make plans to modify it.

Status has many faces. But it mainly has to do with people — who they are, how many they are, what they own, where they live, what they do, and even how they look. And all this is associated with how they sound, that is, with the languages they use to communicate with others and among themselves.

The status of a language depends therefore on the number of people using it, their relative wealth, the importance of what they produce and its dependence on language, their social cohesiveness, and the acceptance by others of their right to be different. In other words, the faces of language status are demographic, economic, cultural, social, political, and juridical (Mackey 1973). These are what we have to examine if we are to find answers to our question concerning language-status modification in Canada and the U.S.

DEMOGRAPHIC LANGUAGE-STATUS DETERMINANTS IN CANADA AND THE U.S.

Let us first examine the demographic aspects of language status in Canada as compared with those of the United States. Language demography has to do with the number, proportion, and distribution of people using different languages.

Number is basic. Modification of the status of a language like that of the nomadic Dogrib of the Canadian northland poses different problems than does the status of a language like French or Spanish, which is used by millions of people throughout the world. Both Canada and the United States harbor a number of native Amerindian languages spoken by a couple of thousand or fewer people. Both countries also have concentrations of the same colonial and immigrant languages, numberically among the world's most populous — English, Chinese, Hindi, Spanish, Russian, German, Japanese, Arabic, and French — to name only these. In neither country, however, do the relative concentrations that are found throughout the world correspond to the relative numerical importance of these groups within each country. Chinese, Japanese, Hindi, and Arabic have fewer speakers in Canada and the United States than have Polish, Dutch, Portuguese, and Icelandic. Yet immigrant languages like German, Dutch, Italian, Greek, and Polish do have the same relative demographic importance in Canada as they do in the United States. Numerically, however, it is the two colonial languages, Spanish in the United States and French in Canada, that are the most comparable. Since these are the languages other than English which dominate by far, having greatest claim to official status, they are the languages the comparison of whose status — real and potential — would seem most useful.

In numbers, according to the United States (1970) and Canadian (1971) census figures, there are about as many native speakers of Spanish in the United States as there are speakers of French in Canada. That does not mean, however, that the languages are comparable in demographic status. For one thing, the United States is ten times as populous as Canada, meaning that the proportion of Hispanic citizens to total population is in the order of a twentieth as compared to French in Canada, which is the home language of more than a quarter of the population. To obtain a numberical status comparable to that of French in Canada, the number of United States citizens having Spanish as their home language would have to be in the order of some 60 million.

Such an increase might seem patently impossible — at least in the near future. Yet this is in fact about the proportion we get for Spanish within a decade, if we consider some of the figures available for people not covered by the United States census, particularly the undocumented aliens whose mother tongue is Spanish. If we look at the official estimates, there seem to be as many illegal Spanish-speaking residents of the United States as there are legal ones. According to the United States Immigration and Naturalization Service, there were in 1978 some 8.2 million undocumented aliens in the United States, about 90 percent of whom were Spanish-speaking. These, one might safely assume, would know more Spanish — or Amerindian — than they would English. What is even more encouraging for the future of Spanish in the United States is that the number of Spanish speakers of this category is increasing at the rate of a million a year — even after taking into account the deportation rate of about the same number.

If we look to the future it seems highly probable that this rate of increase will continue for some time, since there were in 1979 some 10 million Spanish speakers on the Mexican side of the border still looking for jobs. And this population is itself increasing at 3.5% annually — one of the world's highest growth rates. Even though in the United States the fertility rate of Spanish speakers is only half as high (1.8% in 1978), it still surpasses the national average sufficiently to enable the people of Hispanic origin within the decade to account for more than a quarter of the population of the United States. It is already approaching the 10% mark. A 1978 estimate of alien and nonalien speakers produced a total of some 19 million Hispanics, whose numbers are now increasing steadily as a result of a high fertility rate coupled with massive undocumented immigration of the order, as we have seen, of a million a year, and of periodic waves of Cuban refugees, including the one in the spring of 1980.

Comparatively speaking, the Government of Quebec, knowing that the birth rate in French Canada has fallen to the lowest in Canada, might feel less concerned about the future of French in America if it could be assured of annual influx from France of a million unilingual Francophones. It might then, however, have to turn most of its attention to the consequent problems of unemployment, labor unrest, and welfare.

This does not imply that the United States would be free from such problems if it were to open its Mexican border to unlimited immigration. It would at least put some 4,000 border guards out of a job in addition to some hundreds of *coyotes* (as the dealers in illegal entry are locally known). For if the people south of the border are hungry for jobs, those north of the border have become thirsty for oil. Some sort of mutually advantageous deal may well be in the cards, even though neither player has been so undiplomatic as to show his hand.

If the two thousand miles of Mexican border were opened to free immigration, one could expect a consequent rise in the demographic status of Spanish in the United States. But any consequent increase in the potential juridical status would depend on where the Spanish-speaking immigrants settled — if at all. If they were to settle in all of the states, the potential status of Spanish would be different than it would if they were to settle in only one of the states, or even in one region.

No state in the Union has a majority of Spanish speakers. In fact, no state has a majority whose mother tongue is a lgnauge other than English. It is this minority situation which makes the potential status of Spanish weaker than that of French in Canada, where the concentration of French speakers constitutes a majority in Quebec, which, a few years ago, elected a party whose policy converted the status of French to that of the only official language.

This remarkable difference in demographic status did not develop by accident. In both Canada and the United States, it was the result of divergent strategies and patterns of settlement which took place at different periods in the colonization of North America.

French settlements in Canada were already well established in the St. Lawrence Valley when in 1759 North America fell under British rule.[3] The new British rulers had no intention of repeating their adventures of a few years earlier, when the Acadian settlement had been dispersed, and most of its population, having refused to submit to Protestant rule, were deported — parts of families ending up as far away as Louisiana. Rather, the British had planned to confine the French within the St. Lawerence Valley through a policy of containment, granting the land to the south and to the north of the French colony to English-speaking landlords and settlers. In fact, the then-Prime Minister of Great Britain, William Pitt, had in mind the establishment of a French state in North America. Although the northern settlements, touching as they did the Precambrian shield, turned out to be more fit for lumbering than for farm settlement, the settlements south of the French colony developed into rich farming communities — especially after the

American revolution, when hundreds of loyal American colonists (United Empire loyalists) came to join their British cousins (Cartwright 1973). Within the enclave so created, the ever-increasing French population eventually became too dense to support an agrarian economy. Unable to occupy the fertile lands to the south, the landless youth either sought work in the growing mill towns of New England or joined the church-inspired new colonies far to the West in the fertile Red River Valley on the Peace River, or in the rugged woodlands of northern Ontario; so that today, their descendants number about a million in New England and a million in Canada outside Quebec. The bulk of the population, however, remained and prospered in the St. Lawrence heartland.

Spanish settlements in the southwest, however, evolved along different lines. Sparsely populated well into the eighteenth century, they remained so until such times as the westerly movement of Anglo-American settlement was to reach the area. It was then that the Mexican government of the day was moved to invite these settlers to come and colonize the then-northern limits of the vast Mexican state of Coahuila. Yet, by the time that part of the southwest had become a United States territory, there were a number of contiguous settlements where Spanish speakers were in the majority, in such a way that it would have been possible at that time to map most of them into a Spanish-speaking state. This, however, would have run counter to the policies of a Congress in which Spanish culture was associated, not with equality, liberty, and individualism, for which the United States had fought, but rather with the feudalism and authoritarian politics which then characterized so many of the regimes in Europe and Latin America.

No part of this vast Spanish territory, therefore, achieved statehood until the use of two different strategies. State boundaries were drawn in such a way as to ensure an English-speaking majority. Or Congress waited until such a majority was created by settlement (see below). Consequently, different parts of the territory became states at different periods: California in 1850; Nevada in 1864; Colorado in 1876; Utah in 1896. Furthermore, some of the state boundaries actually bisected Spanish-speaking settlements. In 1861, for example, a large area was taken to create the Colorado territory, with a new border cutting through the Spanish area of settlement. Since new immigration from Mexico did not go into these older areas of settlement, an English-speaking majority was assured, and five years later, Colorado became a state.

Other territories, like New Mexico proper, before being granted statehood had to wait until the majority, through settlement from the north, had become English-speaking (see below).

State boundaries in the southwest could admittedly be redrawn to create a Spanish-speaking majority; but this state would not include all the Spanish-speaking communities in the country. Geographically, culturally, and ethnically, one would have to create three different states, for the simple reason that there are really three different Spanish-speaking populations in the United States. According to a 1978 estimate there were some 7.2 million Mexican-Americans in the southwest, 1.8 million Puerto Ricans in the northeast, 0.7 million Cubans in the southeast, and 2.4 million Spaniards and South Americans in all three regions. The bulk of the official Spanish-speaking population (7,823,580) is concentrated in only seven states. This gives Spanish in the United States a much higher degree of territoriality that the comparable German-speaking population of 6,093,054, which is the dominant language minority in 26 states, and itself more dispersed than the less numerous Italian population of 4,144,315, which is dominant in five states; or the French population of 2,598,408, which is dominant in seven. The pattern of distribution for the major immigrant languages — German, Italian, Polish, and Yiddish — is quite similar to that in Canada, where none of these ethnic tongues has been able to achieve any sort of exclusive status.

Another reason why no language — immigrant or colonial — has been capable of achieving demographic territoriality in any one state is that each language group has had to share the percentage of the non-English mother-tongue with others. Although half of the states harbor large ethnic populations — ranging from a fifth to a third of the total population of the state — this population of non-English mother tongue invariably includes two or more different ethnic languages. Illinois has four major non-English groups, Pennsylvania five, New York six, and California eight. Although such is also the case in most Canadian provinces, some provinces have non-English populations composed mostly of a single ethnic group; more than a third of the non-English population of New Brunswick, for example, is French, all others combined accounting for less than one-twentieth. Simply by extending the boundaries of Quebec to include the French-speaking part of New Brunswick and part of neighboring Ontario, more than 98% of the entire French-speaking population of Canada could be encompassed within the boundaries of a single province (Cartwright 1976). For the Spanish-speaking population of the United States, such a simple territorial solution is not an option.

If Spanish cannot achieve territoriality in any one area or state, can it do so in the cities? Three United States cities can claim the status of being Spanish-speaking — Los Angeles, Miami, and New York. Each represents one of the three dominant Spanish ethnic groups in the country — Mexicans, Cubans, and Puerto Ricans. Each is the result of a rapid ethnic transformation which has taken place within living memory. A few decades ago (in the 1950s) the mother tongue of 80% of the Angelenos was English; by 1979 it was down to 45% — and declining. Los Angeles during the 1970s had become the largest Mexican city in the world, outside Mexico (1.6 million). Miami (0.2 million) is the second-largest Cuban city after Havana. By the end of the decade, New York and not San Juan was the largest Puerto Rican city in the world (1.3 million), not counting the 70,000 Cubans in neighboring west New York and Union City, N.J. One may be tempted to compare these large bilingual cities to Montreal, which calls itself the second-largest French-speaking city in the world. But there is an important difference. In Montreal, English is the minority language, accounting for less that 39%. It is even less in Quebec City, the capital, counting for less that 3%. While most of Quebec's towns and cities are dominated by French, no large United States city seems to be dominated by any other language than English, although during the 1970s, one did hear a lot of Spanish used as a language of service in public places in Miami (Mackey and Beebe 1977).

Canada's language policy has long been dominated by the historical concept of two founding peoples: the French, who settled mostly in what has become Quebec, and the English, who concentrated in what has become Ontario — in about the same proportion. In fact, populations of British and French origin in Ontario and Quebec are in complementary distribution. As far as the two 'founding races' are concerned, these two large central provinces are in a demographic relation of ethnic complementarity, there being almost as many British (640,045) in Quebec as there are French (737,360) in Ontario, and almost as many French (4,759,360) in Quebec as there are people of British origin (4,576,010) in Ontario, according to the last (1971) census.

What upset the linguistic balance was the influx of millions of immigrants, most of whom were assimilated to the English-speaking population rather than to the French. If these immigrants had learned French instead of English, Canada would today be a French-speaking country. For the majority of its population (56%) is not of British origin, while about a third of its population (almost 29%) is French. Since those of British origin outnumber those of French parentage by only 16% the population of immigrant and native origin, which accounts for a quarter of the total, becomes crucial. Since most of this large ethnic population has assimilated to the English-speaking population of British origin, they are most concentrated in Ontario, which houses almost half (48%) of Canada's half-million Dutch (as against 3% in Quebec), more than half (63%) of the Italians (23% in Quebec) totaling three-quarters of a million, more than a quarter (27%) of the half-million Ukranians (3% in Quebec), more than a third (36%) of the country's million-and-a-quarter Germans (4% in Quebec), and almost half (45%) of Canada's quarter-million Poles (as against 7% in Quebec). Only for Canada's Jewish population of a quarter-million are the figures comparable (45% for Ontario and 39% for Quebec) (Vallee and Devries 1975). Whether in Ontario or in Quebec, most of these ethnic minorities use English as their working language. So do most French-speaking Canadians outside Quebec. Moving westward from Ontario, the same holds true for the vast area lying between the Great Lakes and the Pacific, a land which was settled by European immigrants, British immigrants, and French Canadians. Here the dominance of English has persisted, so that, as the settlements grew, and interlingual contact increased, more and more of the descendants of these settlers, including the French, adopted English as their main language; so much so that by 1971 some 60% of the population of Canada had English as a home language, although only 44% were of British origin, a language gain of some 16%. Contrariwise, although 29% were of French ethnic origin, only 26% maintained French as a home language, a language loss of some 3%. This decline, small though it is, has worried some of the French Canadian elite. But it is easy to explain. While the population of British origin has been maintained through an average birth rate, coupled with steady immigration from the British Isles (12% British-born in 1971), the population of French origin has proportionately declined due to a lower-than-average birth rate and a lower immigration increase (1.8% French-born in 1971). This is contrary to the demographic trend which had so long prevailed in Canada.

For two centuries the superior birth rate of rural French Canadians had been a counterweight to the more intensive British immigration. By the mid-1960s this was no longer the case. Decreasing birth rates and non-French immigration and language contact have combined to lower the percentage of Canadians of French origin whose home language is also French. But not everywhere. While outside Quebec there was indeed more language contact, bilingualism, intermarriage, and proportionately less French, inside Quebec the use of French began a slight but steady rise some time during the 1960s (see below).

It is true that the incidence of bilingualism (almost a third) is higher among people of French origin than it is among people of British origin (about a twentieth). But this is mostly true outside Quebec, where most French speakers must work in English. It is less common inside Quebec where most French speaking are unilingual – and increasingly so. Here two-thirds of the French-speaking job holders work in their home language, as do two-thirds of those of British origin. The other third of both ethnic groups and more than a third of the other minorities work in both English and French, while the remaining two-thirds of the other ethnic minorities work in either of these languages – but twice as many in English, since most have attended school in that language (Carlos 1973). Since the new Quebec language policy of the 1970s directed most of the schooling for these minorities toward French with the intention of reversing these trends, the above trends may change. French colonization of Canada having virtually ceased, French immigration having become sporadic and selective, and the French Canadian birth rate having fallen so low, the future demographic status of French in Canada has understandably become a matter of concern. If these trends continue, what does the future hold in store?

What has happened is that the linguistic distribution of Canada's population has tended toward greater and greater linguistic nucleation. With increased mobility and urbanization, French areas, it seems have become more French, English areas more English, and bilingual areas more bilingual. It an increasing rate, unilingual English workers are moving into unilingual English areas (Caldwell 1974). As a result of the rapid assimilation of French speakers in bilingual areas and the increasing accommodation by the English Canadians as reflected in the federal Official Languages Act, the bilingual belt is becoming more bilingual. French Canadians are moving more into French-speaking areas where there is greater status given to French unilingualism as reflected in Quebec's Official Language Act. In Montreal for example, there have been within a decade (1961-1971) an actual decrease (of 3.5%) in the bilingualism of those whose mother tongue is French, adding to the already large segment of the population (43.2%) who know no English (Vallee and DeVries 1975). Among those whose mother tongue is not French, there has been an increase in (French/English) bilingualism of 8% during the same period, thus reducing the small percentage of the population (18%) who know no French. About 6% of the population of Montreal whose mother tongue is English now have French as their home language, while only 2% of those of French mother tongue have English as the language of the home. Language choice of Montreal's large ethnic population, however, varies according to nationality. Although fully 80% is split evenly between English and French as home languages. Germans and Jews, however, have opted mostly for English, but about 50% but not all the remainder have opted for French, this being the home language of about 10% of the Germans but of only 2% of the Jewish group.

The French unilingual area of Canada has become more concentrated. About 99.2% of Canada's French unilinguals are now concentrated in a contiguous area which includes Quebec and the northeastern areas of New Brunswick and Ontario (Duckworth 1975). It is here where we find French native speakers whose ethnic origin is not French. While 84% of those whose mother tongue is French live in Quebec, about 77% of those whose ethnic origin is French live in that province, whereas in Ontario, these two figures are comparable for the English-speaking population (46% and 47%).

Trends in immigration are also favoring linguistic nucleation. About a third of those immigrating to Quebec now know French; in fact, a fifth know only French. Of the 27,000 people who immigrated to Quebec in 1973, however, 42% know only English and about 27% had no knowledge of either English or French.

If Quebec is becoming more French, the bilingual belt which encompasses it is becoming more bilingual (Vallee and Dufour 1974). In the French-speaking areas of the bilingual belt outside Quebec there has been an increase (between 1961 and 1971) in official bilingualism among both French and non-French populations. In southwest Quebec near the language frontier, bilingualism has increased by 12% during this period (from 23.3% to 35.5%), much of it from people whose ethnic origin is British. English-origin Quebecers (6.7%), however, lose their mother tongue (6.1%) at a slower rate than to the French of Ontario, where the difference between the two figures has been about 3% in a decade. How about retention of other languages?

This seems to correlate with the interlingual distance (or differences) (Mackey 1976; International Center for Research on Bilingualism 1971) between the language and English or French, as the case may be. It was as if Romance languages seemed to act as a buffer for Germanic languages and vice versa. The Dutch have an 18% better chance and the Germans a 10% better chance of preserving their mother tongue in Montreal, where French is the buffer, than they have in Toronto; whereas the Italians have a 4% better chance of keeping their mother tongue in Toronto, where English is the buffer, than they have in Montreal (Vallee and Devries 1975).

West of Toronto the rate of rentention decreases considerably; but here it also depends on the period of immigration. For immigrants born between 1947 and 1951, about 50% of the Poles in Toronto retain their mother tongue, as against 4% in Vancouver; about 50% of the Germans in Montreal as against 25% in Edmonton; and about 45% of the Ukrainians in Montreal as against 8% in Vancouver. In most cases, language retention means bilingualism, if not trilingualism.

Language-wise, Canada's population can be divided into these three categories, and they differ on territorial and ethnic lines. Leading the monolingual group are the British, 94% of whom understand nothing but English; then come the French, 60% understanding no language but French; then the Italians, 16% whom are monolingual in that language; all the other ethnic groups rate 2% monolingualism, or less, in the home language. Leading the bilingual population in official bilingualism are the French, more than 30% of whom understand English; then the British, only 5% of whom understand French; then the others, some 2% of whom know both French and English. Finally there are the trilinguals, which include 20% of the Jews, 10% of the Italians, 5% of the Poles, and a lesser percentage of the other minorities. These ethnic foreign-born populations who have retained their home language are mostly concentrated in the ethnic enclaves of large cities like Montreal, Toronto, Winnipeg, and Vancouver. But they are numerically too small to have any claim to territorial status.

Contrariwise, in the United States, there are non-English enclaves within large cities which are almsot cities in their own right. In the heart of Miani,

Little Havana covers five square miles. Spanish Harlem in New York and the East Los Angeles barrios are equally extensive. Politically, however, these comprise mostly city wards or groups of wards the political jurisdiction of which is quite limited. Yet such limited territoriality can be and has been used to obtain official bilingual status for an ethnic tongue. It was thus than in 1973, Spanish became official in Miami, just as for some time French had been official in parts of Louisiana (Kloss 1971).

The argument for obtaining such status has been that since a substantial percentage of the population is Spanish, French, German, or whatever, then these people should be served in their own language. But what represents a substantial percentage? And once this is agreed upon, how many can be counted as falling with in a particular ethnic category? This is the game of ethnic demography.

The use of ethnic demography in obtaining language status brings to mind the story of the three drunks who were contemplating their last bottle of rare old Scotch. One says, 'Take it easy fellows, it's almost half empty'. 'Come on!' says the other, 'It's more than half full'. 'No wonder', says the third, 'It's obviously been watered down'. Which half you look at may well depend on which side you're on. And this, in turn, will affect your judgment on the authenticity of the contents.

In some countries, like Finland, an official minority as low as 6% is accorded official status (Svenska Finlands Folkting 1976; Laurens 1978). In Canada, also for no apparent reason, the lower limit has been set at 10%. The percentage, of course, is arbitrary. Yet even within a group so designated, it is not always clear who is a percentage of what. A statement like 'More than 37% of the population is Hispanic' (or French, German, or whatever) may mean that 37% of the population (a) understands only Spanish and speaks no other language; (b) speaks only Spanish but understands English; (c) speaks Spanish better than English; (d) speaks English better than Spanish; (e) clains Spanish as the first language learned; (f) has a Spanish name; (g) uses Spanish at home; (h) has some Spanish blood; (i) possesses some combination of the above traits. The latent ambiguity of official ethnic statistics has prompted certain bilingual countries, like Belgium, for example, to discontinue their compilation. In some countries, ethnic activists have been known to quote ethnic-origin figures as if they represented masses of people having no knowledge of any other language but that of their ancestors.

No two countries, it seems, count their speakers of other languages in exactly the same way. That is why it is so difficult to compare language statistics in Canada with those of the United States. In the 1960 federal census of the United States, Spanish surname and place of birth were used in the compilation of the Spanish ethnic figure. In the 1970 census, Hispanic ethnic origin was included. For 1980, ethnic leaders want the Bureau of the

Census people to be even more generous. Language demographers would prefer that they be more accurate.

Such statistical problems, because of their profound implication for language policy in Canada, have led to the addition of census questions designed to obtain more specific information on languages and language usage. Although more improvements could be made, the basic language questions on the Canadian census, now have the following meanings: (1) What language did you first learn as a child and still understand? (This is known as the MT [mother tongue] question). (2) What language do you speak most often at home? (This is the HL [home language] question). (3) What language did your ancestor on your father's side speak when he first came to this continent? (This is the EO [ethnic origin] question). (4) Can you maintain a sustained conversation on everyday topics in French? In English? In both of these languages? (Do not include a language studied only in school). This is the OL (official languages) question (for a brief analysis of the semantic problems involved, see Mackey and Cartwright 1979).

By cross-tabulating answers to one of these questions against answers to the others it is possible to get some idea of the real language status of various elements of the population in different parts of the country. On the basis of answers to these questions in the Canadian census it had become evident that about 89.3% of all Canadians whose mother tongue is French were not fluent in English. This was an indication that something on the order of four million Canadian citizens were capable of dealing with their government only in French. Since such citizens had always been legally schooled in French, and not in English, the government had no juridical alternative other than to accommodate them in the official language of their choice. It was information such as this that was used to justify the passing of the Official Languages Act, whereby services were to be made available by the federal government and its agencies in both French and English in all areas where the demand was justified.

A comparable justification could hardly be argued for all areas in the United States under its present constitution. No language other than English is official throughout the United States, and there is no constitutional provision for the promotion of unilingualism in another language. The need for individual bilingualism, however, can be argued in the area of schooling, since the U.S. constitution grants all children of U.S. citizens equal opportunities for public education, although responsibility for such education is delegated to the states, where all American children must be educated — not only those whose home language is English (for the text of the *Lau* vs. *Nichols* decision, see Andersson and Boyer 1978: Appendix E, 256-263). Likewise in Canada, education is under provincial jurisdiction; but the official bilingualism is not individual, but rather institutional and territorial (see below).

In sum, the Canadian experience seems to demonstrate the importance of territorial unilingualism in achieving language status. Although bilingualism may better the status of the individual, it does not necessarily enhance the status of his languages.

ECONOMIC LANGUAGE-STATUS DETERMINANTS IN CANADA AND THE U.S.

Unilingual territoriality, of course, is not enough to maintain language status. If people within the territory are utterly dependent for their livelihood on outsiders who do not understand their language, the prestige of that language will be so affected. The traditional settlers in Canada's St. Lawerence heartland were largely self-sufficient, living on the land and off the land, which enabled them to raise some of the largest families on the continent. As good land became scarce, however, many of the descendants of these farming families had to find jobs in urban industries operated by people who knew no French. It is true that the largest of these industries were part of Anglo-Canadian or multinational enterprises which operated elsewhere, and exclusively, in English. Yet part of the French-speaking industrial masses continued to operate in French as they had always done. As this segment of the population gained enough power and influence to affect language policy, English began to recede as the usual language of work in some industries. The use of French as a working language eventually spread to all sectors of this basically rich economy, which included agriculture, fisheries, and light and heavy industry which produced everything from aircraft to textiles in sufficient quantities to generate a flourishing international trade. But more important, this French-speaking area contained vast reserves of primary resources in energy (three-fourths of the country's hydroelectric potential), industrial metals and minerals (three-fourths of the world's asbestos), vast iron deposits, and extensive forests. Economic indicators like employment, income, and GNP have admittedly been somewhat lower than in the United States and the English-speaking provinces to the west; but they have been consistently higher than those of the Anglophone provinces to the east. There seems to be little doubt that this measure of economic independence has contributed indirectly to the prestige of French in Canada and directly to the dominance of French in Quebec.

Yet we do not have to go beyond the borders of the United States to study the effects of economic status on language prestige. Simply compare the fate of the smallest of the three Hispanic ethnic enclaves with that of the largest. The fact that the Cuban refugees often did more than pay their own way surely contributed to the ease and rapidity with which their language was accepted in Miami, where Spanish actually obtained official status at the municipal level. At a time when unemployment of Spanish speakers in New York and California was double the national average (5.8% in 1978), Cubans in Florida had started new enterprises which created more than a hundred thousand new jobs generating some two billion dollars in annual income; and they contributed to the transfer to Miami of some 80 international firms employing some 200,000 people. In language status, as in everything else, the gods of the copybook maxims always have the last word: he who pays the piper calls the tune. If there were as many oil barons coming up from Mexico as there are farm laborers, the accents of Pancho Villa might sound more musical to American ears.

Yet the cruel fact remains that, in spite of the lofty rhetoric of union leaders and labor ministers, few citizens in either Canada or the United States are willing to labor at farm work or perform menial tasks when welfare is available for the asking. Differences between what they get for nothing and what they can get by working have not been enough to move them to places where jobs are waiting. In some cities more than a third of the ethnic population is on welfare (35% of Puerto Ricans in New York City in 1978). At the same time only three out of ten offers of farm jobs have any takers, and in some areas even fewer. Last year (1978), for example, to save their crops, farmers in a Texas town (Presidio), with the help fo the Federal Immigration and Naturalization Service, launched a well-publicized campaign offering 4,000 farm jobs at a federally approved wage. As a result they were able to recruit only 300 workers and were forced to bring in the others from Mexico.

It is really not surprising that undocumented aliens — most of them Spanish-speaking — have little difficulty finding work in the United States. It is because they are needed. So much so that workers from outside the country have become an indispensable part of the economy in the United States — and increasingly so in Canada. Without them, thousands of tons of fruit and vegetables would rot on the ground for want of hands to pick them. Since three-quarters of these workers have both federal income tax and social security tax deducted from their wages (according to a 1975 U.S. Department of Labor study) without receiving anything in return, it must be concluded that such people are counted as a net asset to the economy.

Even more of an asset is their availability and mobility. Some have regularly moved from tomatoes in Texas to apples in Oregon. Yet this very mobility waters down the influence which their home language could exert in a settled community. In Canada, mobile French Canadian lumberjacks, for example, did little to increase the status of the language of Voltaire or to Gallicize the areas through which they passed. On the whole, it would seem that migrant workers are less of an asset to the language they speak than to the economy of the people they serve.

The economic status of a language, however, is often confused with that of the bilinguals who speak it. For many years in Canada, Anglo-Canadians went out of their way to discover bilingual French Canadians in the higher levels of business, industry, education, and government. Placed on boards of directors and in public relations posts, French Canadian colonels became almost as ubiquitous as were their counterparts in Kentucky. In both Canada and the United States, much is made of the fact that some people of ethnic origin are now achieving economic status equal to that of the top Anglos; they have become lawyers, doctors, businessmen, and even millionaires. All very well. But what does it prove? It proves that the American system works; all enjoy equal opportunity as individuals. But not as members of any particular ethnic group. These individuals have succeeded, not because they were ethnics, but in spite of it. Yet that has seemed unfair. They should succeed because they are ethnics. So we establish quotas. And we put in the people with ethnic status. Then we are hit by that backlash phenomenon redundantly known as 'reverse discrimination'. So what to do? Abolish quotas and establish standards — the main one being bilingualism, so that all may cash in on their knowledge of both languages. Fine for the minorities. But what about the public? Are they still worried about not getting the best services available? That depends on what they think they know, as this little story will illustrate.

A few years ago in a federal national park in the Canadian west, a French Canadian tourist drowned, and he drowned in French, which was his right under the Official Languages Act. But he also went down within hailing distance of a lifeguard whose duty it was to save him. This got into the papers and the local Francophone community was up in arms, claiming that had the lifeguard understood some French this would not have happened. Here was yet another example of government indifference to the rights of the official French language minority. At the inquest, testifying on his own behalf, the lifeguard was asked whether he understood what the drowing man was yelling. Perfectly well. 'Then why didn't you jump in and save him?' asked the judge. 'No use. I can't even swim'. 'You can't swim? Then how did you get the job in the first place?' 'Well', said the lifeguard 'I was the only guy who qualified as bilingual'.

Even when ethnic quotas are imposed and employers are obliged to offer equal employment opportunity, the fact remains that the minorities will probably have to work in the language of the majority. That is why so much emphasis has been placed in Quebec's language policy on the language of work. That is the language which achieves economic status (Mallea 1971).

SOCIAL LANGUAGE-STATUS DETERMINANTS IN CANADA AND THE U.S.

Another type of status is achieved through organizations which produce a measure of social solidarity. To obtain this, much has been done in the United States by the action of some 150 Hispanic organizations, especially by such umbrella organizations as the National Council of *La Raza*, which can claim to represent large constituencies.

Regional organizations may succeed in exerting control over specific services, as the United Farm Workers under Cesar Chavez have done in California, or the hotel workers in Miami, where most jobs, requiring as they do both English and Spanish, are in the hands of Cubans. In Canada, there have been French Canadian organizations for more than a century: la Societe St-Jean Baptiste, l'Ordre de Jacques Cartier, La Survivance nationale, and hundreds of others, each with some specific or general objective. But in Quebec these organization are rapidly becoming redundant as more and more of their work is taken over by the government. For example, in the field of language planning proper, the work of such old and well-established organizations as the Conseil de la vie francaise en Amerique and the Société du parler francais au Canada, which never had more than a few dozen regular workers, has now been taken over by large government language bureaucracies like the French Language Board (with 325 full-time employees in 1979) and the French Language Council (with some three dozen workers). But these bodies are still relatively small compared to the federal language bureaucracies where language workers may be counted in the thousands (see Bibeau and Mackey 1976).

In no field of social organization, however, is language more decisive than it is in the domain of education. It is through the schools that a language is transformed from a family vernacular to a vehicle for cultural, scientific, and professional advancement. An ethnic group which, in the course of this transformation, must switch to another language reduces to that extent the social status of its mother tongue.

In the United States, especially during the past decade, this switch has been eased through various types of bilingual education. But there have been far too few bilingual teachers to answer the need. In New York City, for example, where 25% of the public school children are Puerto Rican, only about 4% of the teachers are Hispanic (according to the 1978 figures of the New York City Board of Education: 2,333 out of 48,813 in 1978). Similarly in Los Angeles, where only 5.5% of the teachers are Spanish-speaking (2,300 out of some 30,000 in 1978). This may account for the fact that the Chicano dropout rate in California is 42% and that 23% of the Spanish speakers in that state spent less than five years in school. Where the ethnic minority includes a sufficient number of its own teachers this situation can be changed. The

Cuban refugees in Florida crossed over with their own contingent of trained bilingual teachers. As a result, although fully a third of the pupils in the Dade County School System (sixth-largest in the United States) are Hispanic, more than three-fourths of this number go on to college.

The fact that they do go to college, however, does not necessarily advance the status of the Spanish language, since most of the courses are taught and studied in English. Since there are no unilingual Spanish universities, law schools, or medical schools, there is no alternative. At these levels, the English language holds the status. The more an ethnic group is dependent on another language for such education, the less will its own language be able to claim this sort of status.

In Canada, this problem, as far as French is concerned, is known only outside Quebec. For Quebec has always had its own French-language educational institutions. It has six French-language universities, including law schools, medical schools, technology institutes, and other professional schools in which all the learning and teaching are done in French. It is true that many of the textbooks are imported from France and that English texts are widely used as references, as indeed they are in France. Yet in the field of education, Quebec has been almost as linguistically self-sufficient as France itself. And in the past decade, intense and massive cultural and scientific exchange between the two countries has contributed to Quebec's language self-sufficiency in North America.

Outside Quebec, in Ontario, the Maritimes, and the West, education in English has been the rule for all French-speaking minorities. In some areas, however, there has been a certain measure of bilingual schooling. Bilingual education for French Canadians outside Quebec has increased during the past decade, and in areas where bilingual schooling was the rule, the trend has been to education in French. The Maritimes, for example, have their own French-language university (at Moncton) and a French primary and secondary school system. Such developments are the reflection of the increase in the the social status of French in Canada, and especially in Quebec.

CULTURAL LANGUAGE-STATUS DETERMINANTS IN CANADA AND THE U.S.

Closely dependent on education is the cultural status of a language. Here there is a marked difference between Quebec and the rest of Canada. The Francophones in Quebec have become culturally self-sufficient in all fields — newspapers, magazines, cinema, media, library resources, and other cultural services. Outside Quebec, the French-speaking population has been depended for such services on English-language sources. Because of this, the federal goverment as a consequence of its language policy has attempted to equalize the availability of French cultural resources throughout the country. Francophones throughout the country are now served by two French national television and radio networks stretching from the Atlantic to the Pacific, in addition to a number of regional networks.[4]

Although France supplies an abundance of French films, records, books, and magazines, most of the entertainment in Quebec is locally produced. There is a flourishing film and television industry, a lucrative record industry, and several publishing houses. Locally written books of all descriptions are produced, including an average of 100 French Canadian novels a year — permitting students in universities to take bachelor's degrees in Quebec literature. Most Anglo-Canadian universities outside Quebec have now created chairs in Quebec literature, but only after their cousins in Britain where, at the University of Birmingham, such a chair has been maintained for more than a quarter-century. It is an indication of cultural status of a language when outsiders will learn that language in order to enjoy the cultural products of its people.

This does not mean that there has been no cultural influence in the other direction. After long isolation from North American cultural patterns of behavior and life in a rural parochial society dominated by the cultural values of traditional French Catholicism, the French Canadians became an urban people, absorbing many of the Anglo-American cultural patterns of life, behavior, and attitude. This has resulted in both an outer conflict and an inner contradiction, much as the intercultural contact with Anglo-American culture has been creating in the Hispanic south resistance to so-called 'cultural colonization', producing calls for 'linguistic liberation', and the like. What is really quite often at stake, however, is the cultural integrity of the family, with its patriarchal structure, its strong personal morality, its many interpersonal ties, its male-female role allocation, and its relationship to the community. It is not surprising, therefore, that the exogamy rate for Cubans in Miami has been less than 5%.

If the Hispanic family is still intact in America, the traditional French family has collapsed in Quebec, but not through exogamy. In the process, the individual has become more dependent on the state for the solution of his problems — even for the protection of his mother tongue. Part of this change is attributable to the modifications in the role and influence of the Catholic church — especially in the period following Vatican II. In Quebec the state has taken over many of the functions formerly performed by the Church and its para-religious organizations. Welfare is now in the hands of the state, which supplies free education, free medical care, employment insurance, no-fault auto coverage, and even a guaranteed annual income. All this, in addition to linguistic and cultural autonomy. Social guarantees of this order, however, must rest on a certain measure of political autonomy.

POLITICAL LANGUAGE-STATUS DETERMINANTS IN CANADA AND THE U.S.

Though Quebec has long preferred to look after itself, this preference has become more marked since the election of a separatist government committed to political, linguistic, and cultural — if not economic — autonomy. One of the first actions of the new government was indeed linguistic. It passed a revised Official Language Act, making French, not English, the official language.[5]

The linguistic territoriality of Quebec also provides political leverage at the federal level. No single political party is able to control Canada without the support of the Quebec electorate. For almost a century, this special role has been recognized by the dominant Liberal party, in which, for almost a century, as a matter of tradition, every second Prime Minister has been a French-speaking Quebecer: Laurier — St.-Laurent — Trudeau. The same policy of alternation has been applied to the nomination of the native Canadian governors-general (Vanier and Leger are examples) and to an increasing number of cabinet posts.

No language minority in the United States possesses, as yet, this sort of political leverage. The time is not exactly near at hand when every second president of the United States will by custom have to be a Spanish-speaking Hispanic. To begin with, there are proportionately few Hispanic political figures — none in the Cabinet, none in the Senate, and only five in the House. For an ethnic constituency one-tenth the size, there are 22 Jewish Congressmen.

When it comes to political status, voting is the name of the game. The Spanish-speaking population of the United States has yet to learn how to play it to its own advantage. If most Hispanics were citizens and most of them voted in the same way, this would translate into political status. But such is far from being the case. By the end of last year (1978) only 47% of the Cubans had become United States citizens. At the same period only 37% of the seven million Hispanic U.S. citizens eligible to vote had bothered to register — half the national average of 66%. It is not surprising if at the same time only 3.4% of federal jobs were held by Spanish speakers, and all of these below Cabinet level.

The pattern is repeated at the state level. In California, for example, even though Spanish speakers comprise 15.8% of the electorate, they hold only 2% of the elective posts. In Florida too, Spanish speakers have no state or federal representation. When the Spanish-speaking population does get involved in effective politics, it is generally at the more intimate level of the community. In Miami, Cubans held 20% of the city jobs in 1978 and they had even elected a Spanish-speaking mayor, Manuel Ferre — even though he happened to be a Puerto Rican.

Yet, coming from a culture which values character and direct personal leadership so highly and from countries with a tradition of strong centralized regimes, it is not perhaps surprising that Hispanic Americans should harbor some distrust for the abstractions and uncertainties and indirectness of representative politics at the federal and state levels. It is nevertheless at those levels that national status has to be won. The degree of political participation, social organization and conscientization have to reach state and federal levels. Here is a lesson to be learned from Canada's experience in language-status modification: only through active participation in the political process have the French-speaking peoples of Canada been able to obtain official status for their language and culture.

JURIDICAL LANGUAGE-STATUS DETERMINANTS IN CANADA AND THE U.S.

This official status enjoyed by the French-speaking peoples of Canada has been achieved only after two centuries of struggle, based on the foundation of an uninterrupted sequence of legal precedents dating from the Articles of Capitulation of the French forces on the Plains of Abraham in 1759. The English royal proclamation of October, 1763, forbidding the use of French law notwithstanding, the Act of Secession of the same year implied the continued use of French. French law, language, and custom were guaranteed by the Quebec Act of 1774 and confirmed in the Constitution of 1791. Since then, except for a stormy decade between 1839 and 1849 when English traders in upper Canada tried to get the upper hand, French has always been recongnized as having juridical status, not only in the courts, but also in the legislature (Warkentin and Cole 1974). When Canada became a Confederation in 1867 the use of French was explicity guaranteed in the Articles of Confederation and in the BNA Act (Art. 133), and implicitly in education (Art. 93), which fell under provincial jurisdiction. Much of the history of Canada over the past two centuries has been the story of a struggle by the French Canadians to make the Anglo-Canadians respect the terms of these constitutional and treaty obligations.

First there was the fight for the use of French in the courts and in the legislature, then in official documents, then in the currency, then on the stamps — each new concession, no matter how trivial, being the result of long and bitter infighting against a well-entrenched and often bigoted English-speaking bureaucracy. It took ten years of struggle, for example, to change the name of Canada's national airline from the unilingual Trans-Canada Airlines to the bilingual Air Canada.

Here we run into the distinction between symbolic and functional bilingualism which, although rare in the United States, has become widespread in

Canada. American traditional tolerance toward language minorities has always been more pragmatic than legalistic (Kloss 1977). If Spanish safety signs on aircraft might actually save lives, why not install them? Here is an example of functional bilingualism.

Symbolic bilingualism is something else. In Canada, for example, bilingual minorities have been fighting an unending battle for outward signs that their mother tongue is indeed an official language. This symbolic use of bilingualism takes many forms — street signs, advertising, bank notes, and the like — depending on whether the jurisdiction is municipal, provincial, or federal. At the muncipal level, for example, the French Canadian citizens of Winnipeg, although they make up only. 6% of the population, as against 26% for the unofficial minorities, have succeeded, as of April 1979, in winning over a majority of the city council to the idea of bilingual street names. The opposition had argued that since everyone knew English such signs would be useless, in addition to being a waste ($3,000) of the taxpayers' money. Anyway, what help would it give anyone to read 'Avenue Portage Avenue' or 'Place Martin Place' or 'Rue Kennedy St.' where the untranslatable proper name is what one is looking for? But the holdouts finally yielded to the argument: 'If a few thousand bucks will keep a few thousand voters happy, what the hell! We've wasted more money on crazier projects'.

What the well-meaning aldermen failed to understand, however, was the fact that these bilingual signs were no more useless than the flags fluttering over their buildings. The signs were symbols of status, conveying the meaning that French was an official language. That message was what the official minority wanted to see — and also to hear, again and again, like the wife who knows her hunsband loves her, but wants to hear him say it.[6] Had the city fathers spent some time in Quebec they would have had the opportunity of living a minority experience not entirely unlike that of their French-speaking fellow citizens back home. Here only French signs have an official status, though others may be tolerated alone side. Even advertising posters must appear in French. And this sometimes poses certain problems in cities like Montreal, which houses more than half a million English speakers, many of then unilingual. What happens, for example, when an English-language newspaper like the *Montreal Star* wants to tell its lost readership that the strike of many months is finally over? Well, it uses the front page as a picture and explains it in French.

Many years ago when English was dominant, it was the French who promoted bilingualism in Quebec, as they are now increasingly doing in the west, meaning of course more French. In Quebec they are still promoting more French, but also less English, meaning more French unilingualism. In the past, the dominant English population opposed the use of public bilingual signs. Now, after a long struggle by the French, these signs are taken for granted.

Such street signs as 'ARRÊT/STOP' are everywhere to be seen. Except that, for more than a decade, the English half in many areas has persistently been smudged off by language-conscious vandals, anticipating their government's policy of French unilingualism — but this time, in the wrong direction. For according to their policy of making Quebec usage conform to that of France, government language planners would prefer to change traffic signs to what they are in France, where the French sign for stop is 'STOP', and not 'ARRÊT' 'which is a spot for stopping, as in 'bus-stop'. In 1979, authorities began yielding to the use of the unilingual 'ARRÊT' in rural areas.

Could one project similar scenarios for any minority language in the United States? And if so, which one? The most obvious candidate, of course, is Spanish, a colonial language which was official over much of the United States southwest before that area fell under the jurisdiction of an English-speaking population. But what juridical foundations remain to form a basis for obtaining legal status for Spanish as an official language?

We know that Spanish exploration and claims to parts of the southwest go back to the year 1539, with permanent settlements dating back to 1690. Most of the area had become part of Mexico and remained so until ceded in the mid-nineteenth century to the United States, much of it becoming part of the Territory of New Mexico. Nothing in the articles of transfer, however, be it those of the Guadalupe Hidalgo Treaty of 1848 or the Gadsden Purchase of 1853, could be construed as a guarantee for the survival of the Spanish language. Apart from considerations of real estate, it is not the language but the protection of individual rights and the implied abolition of peonage that constitute the main thrust of these articles. Article 9 of the Guadalupe Hidalgo Treaty, for example, promises the people all the political rights of United States citizens in addition to free government 'at the proper time', which is actual fact turned out to be more than half a century later. Even though parts of this vast territory had become states earlier, Arizona, for example, in 1863, it took New Mexico proper 66 years to achieve this status. Even though some 50 petitions had been submitted to the Congress between 1872 and 1900, there were always delays and changing pretexts. The real reason, however, came out at the 1902 Congressional Committee on Conditions in the Territories. It seemed that there was a general reluctance in Congress to create a state in which most people were able to work only in Spanish. The Committee concluded that the majority was Spanish in language and culture and that English was a foreign language in New Mexico. But by 1910, after a decade of intense settlement from the north, the majority was English-speaking, and in 1912 the constitution of the new State of New Mexico was enacted.

Other states in the Spanish-speaking southwest had been anglicized at an earlier date. Some Anglo-Americans, as they called themselves, had actually been living under the Mexican government as settlers in the Mexican state of Coahuila. But they complained of being governed by a faraway 'hostile majority' and in 'an unknown tongue'. Not surprisingly, one of their first legislative acts as part of the new independent state of Texas (1841) was to suspend, by a joint resolution of both houses, the printing of the laws in Spanish. No mention is made in their constitution of any language other than English, except that the Governor might permit the use of other languages for administrative purposes. Although seven foreign languages were permitted in Texas schools in 1896, a by-law of 1905 stipulated that all teaching be done in English, and a law of 1919 excluded from state schools all teaching in languages other than English.

In Arizona, Spanish was excluded from public schools, and Spanish pupils were to be taught in English. In this territory, only the first four territorial legislatures (1864-1867) permitted laws to be published in Spanish. California was more conciliatory to Spanish in its state constitution. It had been ceded to the United States in 1848 and, in spite of the gold rush of 1849, which almost overnight converted the 5,000 Spanish residents to a minority, the state constitution of that year specified that any official document needing wide distribution 'be published in English and Spanish' (Art. 11.21). Nevertheless, the later constitution of 1871 made it clear that English was the only official language (Art. 4). In practice, however, the administrative use of Spanish continued on an 'as needed' basis.

New Mexico, which had waited so long before achieving statehood, voted a constitution designed more for the people than for the survival of the language. Yet there was, at the time, some recognition that both were intimately related. Provisions of the New Mexico Constitution of 1912, still in effect, give all people the right to vote regardless of condition of servitude (Art. 21.5), and require publication of all laws in Spanish and English for a period of 20 years (Art. 20.12). This was later extended 10 more years in 1931, and again in 1943, the final extension ending in 1949. Although Spanish was permitted in the legislature, all state officials were required to have a good knowledge of English. From 1935 on Spanish was no longer considered official in the legislature. That language did, however, persist in the schools. According to the Constitution, all Spanish children should attend public schools (Art. 10.10). Although the language of instruction was to be English (Art. 21.4), the state was required to provide bilingual teachers of English (Art. 12.8) to the Spanish-speaking pupils. Here, as elsewhere in the southwest, the language policy has been one of transitional bilingualism. Despite much tolerance and even promotion of Spanish (and later of Navajo), New Mexico cannot be classed as a bilingual state, as some have suggested. For Spanish is not an official language in the sense that all laws and the work of the legislature are in that language.

Can the federal government change the status of Spanish within the states? How about the federal Bilingual Education Act of 1968 and the precedent setting *Lau* vs. *Nichols* decision of the U.S. Supreme Court (Andersson and Boyer 1978: Appendix E). Both of these initiatives have indeed resulted in some profound changes in the ways the states treat their language minorities, and the full impact of these provisions is still to be felt.

Do such federally induced changes permit us to forsee the development of official status for one or more other languages in the United States? A careful reading of the intent of these documents would lead us to say no. The message in them is not 'save the language' but rather 'save the child' − if necessary through his language, so that he may acquire an equal chance of reaching the main stream. In other words, lead him gradually to an ability to learn through English. Here again we have a policy of transitional bilingualism.

Yet will the prolonged practice of transitional bilingualism tend to convert the United States over the years into a cosmopolitan society − into an continent-wide San Francisco? And out of this, could one or more languages emerge as national tongues? Just as in Canada, French is official from the Atlantic to the Pacific in all matters under federal jurisdiction, is it also conceivable that Spanish or any other language will be so recognized from coast to coast and from the Rio Grande to the Canadian border?

To answer these questions is to ask another. To what extent is it possible for a situation to develop in the United States which would set off a series of events similar to those which led to the present language policies in Canada? To understand this possibility it is necessary to know what these events were and how the language policies consequently evolved.

The series of events in question started in an emotional climate heated by long-smoldering feelings of historical and ethnic injustices to Canada's French-speaking population, which in the space of a few decades had left the restraining and protective frontiers of rural parishes for the anonymous uncertainties of urban life. But it took almost a revolution and a menace of civil war to get the status-planning process under way.

In the early 1960s, when separatist urban guerilla groups like the FLO were being organized for a fight for ethnic justice, the Canadian federal government felt that something was indeed radically wrong. To find out, it appointed in 1963 the first language-policy commission in Canadian history and endowed it with a generous and largely open-ended budget. Its hearings and some of its voluminous research soon became known to every newspaper reader in the country as the B & B Commission (Royal Commission on Bilingualism and Biculturalism). The investigation lasted six years.

In the intervening time, the government, spurred on to action by events and by the alarming preliminary report of the Commission, took a number of stop-gap measures, such as the hiring of more French-speaking civil servants and the language training of the English-speaking ones. Under great pressure from French-speaking minorities it anticipated some of the recommendations of the B & B Commission in developing permanent language legislation. Thus, in 1969, the Official Languages Act was passed by the federal parliament, committing the government and all its administration to a policy of widespread and official bilingualism, putting French on an equal footing with English from the Atlantic to the Pacific. The Act also provided for bilingual districts in areas with a 10% official minority, and it created the post of Commissioner of Official Languages to oversee the implementation of the policy.

The following year, Parliament approved some hundred recommendations of the B & B Report. In 1970 it created within the Department of the Secretary of State a large Language Programs Branch, enabling the federal government to pay for the development of language-status equality in areas outside its jurisdiction. Domains like education and culture were always under provincial jurisdiction. As in the United States, federal funds were used to obtain leverage for the implementation of federal policies. The second official language (English or French as the case may be) was supported by payments of 5% of the per capita cost of local undertakings and 9% of the cost for the language and culture of official language minorities, providing suport for programs in language and bilingual education and for language acquisition research and development, including special language schools and bilingual programs for business and public administration. The outlay for the first five-year period was in the order of 500 million dollars — seemingly enormous, but relatively small, if compared to the billions expended on the unsucessful bilingualization of the public service.

This extensive program began to pick up steam with the publication of the Official Languages Resolutions of 1973, which unleashed a massive bilingualization campaign, the details of which would take hours to recount. They included all sorts and dimensions of training programs, the linguistic classification of some quarter-million jobs, and the elaboration of norms and measures of bilingualism, the application of which kept some 500 people busy (Coulombe Report). The campaign created an enormous tenured language bureaucracy which, every year, absorbed a bigger slice of the federal budget.

In addition to this, in 1977 came the Federal Language Charter in which was proclaimed the right of all Canadians to have their children taught in the official language of their choice.

Changes in these language policies and programs had to be made as a result of internal and external investigations and evaluative reports of which the following are the most important:

The Report of the Royal Commission on Bilingualisma and Biculturalism, which recommended most of the legislative measures (Laurendeau and Duncan 1967-1970).

The Report of the First Bilingual Districts Advisory Board (the Duhamel Report), which recommended on a parity principle a maximum number of bilingual districts, including all of Quebec (Bilingual Districts Advisory Board 1971). This infuriated most Quebecers, and the report was not implemented.

The Report of the Second Bilingual Districts Advisory Board, which rationalized the creation of bilingual districts, rejecting parity and complementarity and thus minimizing the Quebec districts (Bilingual Districts Advisory Board 1975). This annoyed the government and the report was not implemented.

The internal Coulombe Report on bilingualism in the public service, which caused the administration to question its methods (Coulombe 1972-1973).

The external Bibeau Report on the bilingualization of the public service, which demonstrated the extent to which the language policy had failed (Bibeau and Mackey 1976a, 1976b).

The annual progress reports of the Commissioner of Official Languages on the equalization of language status and the implementation of the Official Languages Act (Commissioner of Official Languages 1970-1980).

The intensive Pepin-Roberts report (1979) on the preservation of Canadian unity.

In retrospect, it seems that the great reserve of good will within the country enabled the language-rights aspects of the policy to be respected most of the time (80% of the time, according to the final report of the first Commissioner of Official Languages). On the otherhand, the behavior-modification aspect was largely a failure. It proved impossible to change the working language of thousands of Anglophones, and the bilinguals still operated in English out of necessity or out of habit. This was because most public servants were unilingual in English, a language which the minority who were French-speaking could all understand. To rectify this, unilingual French-language units were created in the federal administration, but in practice nearly all of them ended up in Quebec, where the internal working language had long been French and external services traditionally bilingual. There was little success in making French a working language outside Quebec.

In sum, if we look back over the decade, we can conclude that federal language legislation was unable to modify the basic geolinguistic equation. Here was a government which, in the early 1960s, set out to prevent the country from splitting up into two nations. And it did so by legislating the status of French in Canada to a position equal to that of English, and by placing the implementation of that language policy over all other priorities of the federal jurisdiction. Because of the limits of this jurisdiction, however, the success of the language policy had to depend on whether or not English-speaking provinces would follow suit. None of them did. Bilingual New Brunswick became officially so, and Quebec had always operated more or less bilingually. Here the Anglophone minority had had its own school systems, its own hospitals and councils, operating almost with the status of a nation within a state. But the numerically comparable Francophone minority in Ontario were accorded no educational, linguistic, or cultural status in that province, no more than in other Anglo-Canadian provinces.

These century-long inequities had already caused a not-so-quiet revolution in the early 1960s and the consequent reaction of the federal government with the above-mentioned special language legislation. After waiting for 15 years to see the effects and promises of such language-status planning on the Anglo-Canadian provinces, the Quebec electorate lost patience. In November, 1976, it voted in a separatist government and gave support to its policy of cultural equity, whereby English minorities in Quebec were to be given the same privileges accorded to French minorities in Ontario and the west. This policy became law in the Official Languages Act of the following year.

This elaborate piece of language legislation was the culmination of almost a decade of language-status planning and trial-and-error legislation which attempted successively to approximate the wishes of the French-speaking majority. Disappointed with the long-drawn-out investigations of the federal B & B Commission, the Quebec Government in 1967 launched its independent language investigation, this one into the status of French in Quebec: it became known as the Gendron Commission, after its chairman, Jean-Denis Gendron. The investigation also took years to complete (for a bibliography of public reaction to these and other Canadian and Quebec language commissions, see Mackey 1978: 540-554). In the meantime, in 1979, the Quebec government, pressed by the people to do something about language policy, enacted a measure (Bill 63) providing for official bilingualism with greater emphasis on French. It created a language borad (*Office de la language*) to advise the government on language matters and to hear complaints in this area. The board had no executive power. The policy adopted the principle of freedom of choice for all minorities in matters of education, unwittingly, or at least indirectly, encouraging an increase in Anglophone school population. The bill almost created another revolution and a new policy had to be elaborated over the ensuing four years.

The new policy, enacted in 1974 (Bill 22), ended the century-old tradition of official Quebec bilingualism by making French the official language. English, however, was accorded a *de facto* national status, since the English language institutions (school systems, health services, and the like) were to be maintained. Yet optional bilingual schools were to be allowed for the English; but not for the French, the English being also permitted, and other minorities being compelled, to use the French school system, unless competence in English could be demonstrated. This policy seemed to please no one, and within the ensuing three years, another language policy (Bill 1) had to be elaborated.

Here it must be pointed out that most of the technical parts of the previous bills, those concerning such matters as standardization of the language, terminology, contracts, permits, and professional certification, were left substantially intact. Provisions concerning language agencies were expanded and refined. Even this bill, radical as it seemed to some, was criticized as giving too little relative status to the French language. This was soon to be rectified, however, as a result of subsequent political events.

Before the bill could be enacted, the government was overthrown and a newly elected separatist regime empowered by a large majority of the electorate to do what was necessary. Modifying the status aspect of the bill, the new government enacted it in 1977 (Bill 101) as Quebec's Official languages Act. By it, French became the only official language of Quebec, and English was relegated to the status of other minority and immigrant languages, as indeed French had long been in Ontario and other provinces. All schooling was to be in French. Traditional minority rights, however, based on the school language of the parents, were to be respected. Canadians from other provinces, like the immigrants, were to be schooled in French — this provision being open to bilateral agreement on the reciprocal language treatment of nationals.

Is it conceivable that any state in the United Stages could pass a language law of this sort? Just as in Quebec, the language of official documents is French rather than English, is there any state likely to deny the use of English as an official language? Are we to see the day, for example, when all business deals in Texas and California will be legal only in Spanish — the English language policies, now in force in Canada, do not seem applicable to the United States, perhaps some of the formulas developed in the process may be worthy of study.

Let us consider, for example, the territorial provisions for official minorities in the federal Official Languages Act of 1969. Areas where at least 10% of the population have as their mother tongue an official language (French or English) which is not that of the majority in the area may be designated as federal bilingual districts. Within these districts all official minority speakers have the legal right to be served by federal officials in their mother tongue (Cartwright 1977). After three years of work on the possible application of this provision, we finally saw some of the flaws. The law had been based on an abstract formula, not on the observation of bilingual behavior. It failed to take into consideration the fact that if such a minority had been dealing with its government in the majority language for several generations, as was almost invariably the case, it had already become bilingual, having had to develop a sort of home-office diglossia to deal with the government in a language other than that of the home. Even after a great effort of language promotion and much expense, it was evident that the local population would continue to deal with any bilingualized public service in the same majority language to which they had been accustomed. Local federal officials, having taken a couple of years off to learn French, for example, at government expense, would return home and subsequently have to reply to so little demand for the newly acquired language skill that it would eventually be lost for want of use, especially since local and provincial governments made no change.

It would be a mistake to try to apply such a formula to any language minority in the United States, especially if the initiative came form the top. Instead of creating federally impounded speech areas, it would be more consistent with American practice and tradition to let the people in each area decide for themselves, starting from the local level and working up to the more general levels — from town to county to state to the federal level. This is the political process which has already operated quite successfully in the United States. The federal government follows the lead of the states, the state follows the lead of the counties, and the county follows the municipality. For example, this would in practice work out something like this. In 1973, Miami declared itself to be a bilingual city. If this meant that one could fill out traffic accident reports and the like in Spanish, then the county should permit property deeds and other contracts under its jurisdiction to be made out in that language. When that happened, the state could follow suit by permitting things like driver certification in Spanish. This would justify the federal government to offer its own services in Spanish in the same area, including the possibility to file income tax returns and the like in that language. This seems reasonable, since there is a long tradition of service to the citizen in languages other than English, not as a right, but as a need. For example, the New Mexico Constitution of 1912 states that all amendments must be printed in Spanish in counties having Spanish newspapers (Art. 19.1), a criterion of need which is simple and functional. The principle, however, is not the right of the language to survive, but the right of the citizen to know.

It is of course not impossible that by serving the individual in his own language, teaching his children in that language, and abolishing all restrictions to its use, the United States may in practice be assuring language survival. This, added to massive immigration and language nucleation, could create a chain-reaction demand from the local level for official language recognition, and a counter-action based on a fear of linguistic factionalism such as that which has plagued Belgium, Canada, and Spain.

If indeed another language should become official in the United States, it supposes two things: the right of the citizen to use the language of his choice and the corresponding duty of the official to use that same language. Should the government official fail to comply, the citizen may take the government to court for violating his rights. With more than a quarter-million faceless federal bureaucrats answering the public, someone's language rights are bound to be infringed upon sooner or later. And since the individual, as has been well established, has little chance against a well-entrenched bureaucracy, he needs some one to protect him. Hence, the language ombudsman. This official appears in Canada's Official Languages Act as a Commissioner of Official Languages. He is answerable not to the government or to the bureaucracy but directly to the people through their representatives in Parliament. Each year he publishes a book recounting the many failures of the federal bureaucracy to create the bilingual utopia. The Commissioner has a large staff at his disposal to enable him to handle all the complaints. Though such an ombudsman is not here being suggested as an additional burden to the already overloaded bureaucracy, the reports of the first seven years are recommended reading. For they are undoubtedly the most unconventional and amusing official documents ever penned by a federal bureaucrat. It is as if the story he had to tell was so sad that it needed an awful lot of comic relief.

As might be expected, the language policy of Canada has created a lot of enemies within the country. In some areas, old ethnic settlements predating either English or French were given no consideration. The resulting political backlash whipped up by nonofficial ethnic minorities resulted in the creation of a federal department of multiculturalism, the purpose of which was to encourage such minorities through federal funding to maintain their cultural heritage. Although this provided no more legal rights than they had before, it did offer them a sympathetic ear and a most generous hand. This type of federal promotion is of course nothing new in the United States, where many well-organized ethnic groups have lobbied for more bilingual education, more bilingual government jobs, and more ethnic immigration. But what will these ethnic groups ask for next?

Since the melting pot, to use Einar Haugen's phrase, has never reached the melting point in the United States, the very recognition of this fact, and the changing educational laws this recognition has engendered, seem to have set the United States on the long road toward ethnic bilingualism and even political multinationalism (for a selection of multinational states and a study of their problems, see Mackey and Verdoodt 1975). Countries like Canada and Belgium have traveled this road, and they know all too well where it leads. Perhaps something, after all, can be learned from the Canadian experience. But even more can be learned from the American past. The Constitution of the United States reserves enough power to the states to make possible, if the voters so decide, the creation of a Spanish state, a French state, or another ethnic polity. This possibility may be important for some ethnic groups, and I hope that I am not being in any way subversive in pointing this out. In case I have left such an impression, allow me, in conclusion, to say something which can taken simply as my personal opinion.

One of the maxims I was taught as a child is that the whole is always more important than its parts. After pondering this truism for a half century, I must confess that I no longer agree. The maxim may be correct in mathematics, but to apply it to human life can be morally false. Its application has been used throughout history to justify policies whereby man is made to exist for the state under oppressive regines in which the behavior of the individual must conform to that of the group. That the group should be an ethnic minority does not make conformity any more palatable. It was on the primacy of individual freedom that the United States was founded, and the corresponding freedom of association, applied with equity and justice, has given a great deal of happiness to a great number of people. It would be a shame if, in the name of ethnic justice, this principle were to be abandoned. America has continually striven toward the ideal of the primacy of individual freedom under the rule of justice. It is my hope that this is the road this fortunate land will continue to follow.

NOTES

1. It is true that a number of low-frequency lexical items (like 'chesterfield' and 'sofa') have been identified whose semantic distribution varies along the Canadian-American border (Avis 1954). Like all other varieties of North American, Canadian English has its regionalisms, most of which have been well documented (Avis 1965). Yet the core of phonology, grammar, and lexicon makes it difficult, if not impossible, to distinguish Anglo-Canadians from speakers of General American (which, of course, excludes the Deep South and most of New England).

2. The distinction between 'status' and 'corpus' seems to have been first introduced by Heinz Kloss (1969: 81). Corpus planning includes such things as the making of glossaries and grammars, terminology, and other instruments of standardization. Status planning has to do with the assigning of roles and uses to the languages. For other distinctions in language planning, see the writings of LePage, Rubin, Fishman, Haugen, and Ferguson. My own views are stated in Mackey 1979.

3. There were really two battles for British North America, the decisive military conflict settled in less than a day on the Plains of Abraham in Quebec City, and the long demographic competition which lasted more than two centuries. After 1759, the settlement competition continued. The English had achieved two important advantages as a result of the military victory; they could halt all further immigration from France, and they could promote British settlements both from the British Isles and from their 13 American colonies, the population of which then totaled in the millions. The French, with a population base of 65,000 souls, could expand only from their heartland in the St. Lawrence Valley. They could also outperform

the British in natality. Confined at first to rural areas, the French were able to create larger families than could the more urban British. In a few generations the results became evident in the expanding French-speaking population. The endless baby boom became known as the *revanche des berceaux*, a sort of demographic revenge on the British. In theory, it supplied a long-term option of continued French colonization of North America, despite the British conquest.

4. Similarly for the minority regional English-language radio network in Quebec, which counted 33 stations in 1979, extending from the Ontario border in the west to Labrador City and the Magdalene Islands, where the Anglophone minority numbers less than 800 speakers.

5. Fulfilling an election commitment, this government, by way of referendum, asked the people of Quebec for a mandate to negotiate sovereignty-association with the rest of Canada. In the general referendum of mid-May, 1980, this mandate was refused by 60% of the public after an intensive campaign of confrontation between two coalitions — the autonomists, centered around the party in power (the *Parti québécois*), and the federalists, led by the opposition provincial Liberal party, strongly backed by the federal Liberals, who had been elected in a snap election in mid-December after having brought down the less-centralist minority Conservative government in a no-confidence vote on the budget. In the referendum, in which the vast majority of the eligible voters participated, almost 40% of those who voted did opt for the sovereignty option, while the majority, far from voting for the status quo, really opted for greater autonomy, but within a federal system, as detailed in the 'beige paper' of the provincial Liberals.

6. Before Confederation Manitoba was essentially a French-speaking colony, more than half the population being French Canadian or Francophone *métis*. Section 23 of the Manitoba Act (1870) gave official bilingual status to the area. Although a subsequent language act of 1890 declared English to be the only official language, the legislation was judged in 1892 by the higher courts as being *ultra vires*. But despite a bloody rebellion, this decision was ignored. It was not until 1977 that the law was again challenged, in the form of a test case based on a unilingual all-English parking ticket handed to a Georges Foret, who took the matter as far as the Canadian Supreme Court and on December 13, 1979, won his case. As a consequence, on February 22, 1980, French was officially used in the Manitoba legislature for the first time after a century of prohibition.

REFERENCES

Andersson, Theodore, and Mildred Boyer (1978), *Bilingual Schooling in the United States*. Austin, National Educational Laboratory Publishers.
Avis, Walter (1954), 'Speech differences along the Ontario-United States border', *Canadian Journal of Linguistics* 1: 3-8.
———— ————(1965), *Bibliography of Writings on Canadian English 1875-1965*. Toronto, Gage.
Bibeau, G., and W.F. Mackey (1976a), *Independent Study on Language Training Programmes of the Public Service of Canada*, volume one: *General Report*. Ottawa, Treasury Board.
————————(1976b), *Independent Study on Language Training Programmes of the Public Service of Canada*, volume twelve: *Report of Interviews with Departments*. Ottawa, Treasury Board.

Bilingual Districts Advisory Board (First) (1971), *Recommendations of the Bilingual Districts Advisory Board*. Ottawa, Information Canada.

Caldwell, Gary (1974), *A Demographic Profile of the English-Speaking Population of Quebec 1921-1971*. *CIRB publication B-51*. Quebec, International Center for Research on Bilingualism.

Carlos, Serge (1973), *Utilisation du francais dans le monde du travail. Gendron Commission étude E-3*. Quebec, Editeur officiel.

Cartwright, D.G. (1973), 'French Canadian colonization in eastern Ontario: process and pattern'. Unpublished Ph.D. thesis, University of Western Ontario.

―――――― (1976), *Language Zones in Canada*. Ottawa, Secretary of State.

―――――― (1977), 'The designation of bilingual districts in Canada through linguistic and spatial analysis', *Tijdschrift voor Economische en Sociale Geografie* 68: 1.

Commissioner of Official Languages (1970-1980), *Report of the Commissioner of Official Languages*. Ottawa, Office of the Commissioner of Official Languages.

Coulombe, P.E., editor (1972-1973). *Projects 1-22*, nineteen volumes. Ottawa, Treasury Board.

Duckworth, auth. guery: initials? (1975), 'Appendix', in *Report of the Second Bilingual Districts Advisory Board*. Ottawa, Information Canada.

International Center for Research on Bilingualism (1971), *La distance interlinguistique*. *CIRB publication B-32*. Quebec, International Center for Research on Bilingualism.

Kloss, Heinz (1969), *Research Possibilities on Group Bilingualism. CIRB publication B-18*. Quebec, Internat.onal Center for Research on Bilingualism.

―――――― (1971), *Les droits linguistiques des Franco-Américains aux Etats-Unis. CIRB publication A-2*. Quebec, Presses de l'Université Laval.

―――――― (1977), *The American Bilingual Tradition. CIRB publication C-105*. Rowley, Mass., Newbury House.

Laurén, Christer, editor (1978), *Finlandssvenskan: Fakta och Debatt*. Borgå, Söderströms.

Laurendeau, A., and D. Duncan, chai.men (1967-1970), *Report of the Royal Commission on Bilingualism and Biculturalism*, six volumes. Ottawa, Queen's Printer.

Mackey, William F. (1973), *Three Concepts for Geolinguistics. CIRB publication B-42*. Quebec, International Center for Research on Bilingualism. (Reprinted 1976 in *Heinz Kloss Festchrift, Sprachen und Staaten*, volume two. Hamburg, Stiftung Europa Kolleg).

―――――― (1976), *Bilinguisme et contact des langues*. Paris, Klincksieck.

―――――― (1978), *Le bilinguisme canadien: bibliographie analytique et guide du chercheur. CIRB publication B-75*. Quebec, International Center for Research on Bilingualism.

―――――― (1979), 'Language policy and language planning', *Journal of Communication*, Spring: 70-73.

―――――― , and Von N. Beebe (1977), *Bilingual Schools for a Bicultural Community: Miami's Adaptation to the Cuban Refugees. CIRB publication C-107*. Rowley, Mass., Newbury House.

―――――― , and D.G. Cartwright (1979), 'Geocoding language loss from census data', in *Sociolinguistic Studies in Language Contact*, ed. by W.F. Mackey and J. Ornstein, 69-98. *Trends in linguistics 6*. The Hague, Mouton.

―――――― , and A. Verdoodt, editors (1975), *The Multinational Society*. Rowley, Mass., Newbury House.

Mallea, John R., editor (1971), *Quebec's Language Policies: Background and Response. CIRB publication A-13*. Quebec, Presses de l'Universite Laval.

Pépin, Jean-Luc, John P. Robarts, et al. (1979), *The Task Froce on Canadian Unity: Observations and Recommendations*. Ottawa, Ministry of Supply and Services.

Svenska Finlands Folkting (1976), *Svenskt i Finland*. Borga, Trycheri & Tidnings.

Vallee, Frank G., and John DeVries (1975), *Data Book for a Conference on the Individual, Language and Society*. Ottawa, Carleton University Department of Sociology.

_____, and A. Dufour (1974), 'The bilingual belt: a garotte for the French', *Laurentian University Review* 6:2.

Warkentin, J., and H.R. Cole (1974), *Canada before Confederation*. Toronto, Oxford Univeristy Press.

DENISE DAOUST-BLAIS

Corpus and Status Language Planning In Quebec: A Look at Linguistic Education

In August 1977, less than a year after the election which brought the Parti Quebecois to power, the Québéc government adopted the 'Charter of the French Language', whose aim is to make Quebec an essentially French-speaking society. The bill declares that French is the official language in Quebec, the language of the legislature and the courts as well as of the civil administration. It defines the social contexts in which French is to be used in public utility firms, by professional corporations, and in commerce and business, as well as in the field of education. In addition, the bill identifies the persons and institutions affected and prescribes the mechanisms of implementation.

In this paper, I would like to describe briefly the situation in Quebec which led to the adoption of the Charter as well as the different language-oriented laws which were promulgated before the Charter. I will then describe the most important and innovative aspects of the Charter and discuss a few major points from a 'corpus-status' point of view. We shall see, however, that this typology is not sufficient to account totally for the approach to language planning adopted in Quebec.

1.0. THE QUEBEC LINGUISTIC SITUATION BEFORE 1970

Three major factors must be considered in order to describe the linguistic situation before 1970.[1] The first has to do with the status of English in the economic sphere, while the second deals with the demographic evolution in Quebec and mainly with the anglicization of immigrants. As for the third factor, it is a twofold sociolinguistic one which has to do with the internal linguistic situation of the French language spoken in Quebec, as well as with its social and official status with regard to both European standard French and English.

1.1.   The dominance of English in the economic sphere

This question has been extensively studied in the last 15 years, especially by two commissions, one federal, the other provincial: a federal commission on bilingualism and biculturalism in Canada in the middle 1960s ('Commission royale d'enquête sur le bilinguisme et le biculturalisme', 1963-1967) and a provincial commission in the early 1970s ('Commission d'enquête sur la situation de la langue francaise et sur les droits linguistiques au Québec', 1968-1972). Both commissions have shown that within Québec, English is the language of power, and of upward mobility. At the managerial level of large business firms, the English-speaking population is overwhelmingly superior to that of the French-speaking population, and English is, for all practical purposes, the language of work. This situation has been described by some as one of diglossia in which linguistic affiliation tends to split up according to position in the economy and social ranks.

Although the linguistic situation did — and still does to a certain extent — present certain characteristics of a diglossic situation, it is extremely difficult to describe and explain the linguistic situation which was prevalent in Quebec at that time in such terms, as the usual defitions of diglossia do not, from my own point of view, apply *in extenso* to Quebec.[2] But I will not elaborate on this point here, since diglossia is not the focus of this paper. Suffice it to say that, even though the economic domination of English was apparent at the time, no official action was taken by the government.[3]

I must add, however, that the linguistic pattern described above was not a universal one, since some sectors of the Quebec economy functioned, and still function, in French. These sectors include the civil administration as well as the small and middle-sized French Canadian firms.

All in all, however, we can describe the Quebec situation before 1970 with regard to language use as an example of a 'tacit division of political and economic powers' (McConnell et al. 1979: 5). While French speakers were preponderant on the political scene, the English-speaking population was in control of the main economic institutions. Even though Quebec's French-speaking population totaled about 80% of the population, the late urbanization of the French-speaking population as well as the industrialization of the labor force resulted in a demographically unequal division of the labor force, with the French-speaking population being massively employed at the blue-collar and service levels.

On the linguistic level, this was to be reflected in the anglicization of broad areas of technical and semi-technical vocabulary as well as of the language of work generally. As a result, the French-speaking population of Quebec, at least as far as the French-speaking labor force is concerned, developed a knowledge of English at least as the language of work.[4]

1.2.   The demographic evolution in Quebec

Until the 1960s, Quebec had the highest birth rate in Canada. However, there has been a rapid decline of the birth rate in French Quebec over the last 20 years, so that maintenance and reinforcement of the French language in Quebec have become more and more dependent on the language allegiance of the neo-Quebecers, whose mother tongue is neither English nor French. Naturally, this poses a number of new difficulties related to the maintenance of the French language. In the 1961 Canadian census data, we find that only 30.4% of Quebecers of origins other than British or French have made a language transfer to French, compared to a 52% language transfer toward French in 1931 (Charbonneau and Maheu 1973: 67, 68).[5] An analysis of a question in the 1971 census on knowledge of French and English (independently of the mother tongue) reveals that for those Quebecers born outside Canada and residing in Quebec at the time, 39% knew only English, while 18% knew only French (Joy 1978: 29). However, the 1976 data from the Immigration Department of Quebec reveals that for the same population, 30% know only English, while 29% know only French (Joy 1978: 29).

The demographic situation has been felt as politically alarming, especially in the Montreal area where the strength of attraction of English is much stronger than in the other parts of Quebec. As of 1961, in the metropolitan region of Montreal, language transfers were made toward French in the proportion of 23.2% as compared to 56.6% in the rest of Quebec (Charbonneau and Maheu 1973: 108). Add to this the fact that, in 1971, 80% of the nonfrancophone Quebec labor force was concentrated in the Montreal area (Quebec, Gouvernement du, 1972: 14), and you have all the makings of a major conflict. The source of conflict lies in the demographic distribution of language groups in Montreal. The anglicization of immigrants is seen as a major source of the strengthening of the English-speaking community and of the weakening of the French-speaking group.

Not surprisingly, the 1970s saw the rise of the 'freedom of choice' controversy. The question was whether or not neo-Quebecers should be free to send their children to the school of their choice when most of them were choosing the school system of the English-speaking minority.

On the whole, the demographic projections were alarming, and it was felt that legal intervention was needed in order to maintain the relative importance of the French-speaking group in Quebec (Charbonneau and Maheu 1973: 237).

1.3.   The sociolinguistic situation of English and French in Quebec

1.3.1.   *English as a language of prestige.*

Despite the fact that French is the language spoken by the majority of the Quebec population, English has been the prestige language throughout both the French- and the English-speaking communities, as well as the other linguistic communities.

Until the adoption of the 'Official Language Act' (Bill 22) in 1974, which declared French the official language of Quebec, emphasis was placed on the bilingual character of Quebec society at the institutional and public level. On the other hand, a social class structure has evolved reflecting the economic position of the ethnic groups who make up the population, that is, mainly the French and English groups (Porter 1969: 60).

With the English-speaking group dominating the economic scene, the English-speaking community and the English language acquired prestige among all other groups and languages. On this subject, the findings of a study conducted by Lambert (1967) are most relevant. French- and English-speaking university students were asked to rate the personality characteristics of ten speakers, five of whom spoke English and five French. Actually, five bilingual speakers were used and each speaker spoke twice. Nonetheless, English-speaking students evaluated the English-speaking persons more favorably on most traits: intelligence, job, education, personal traits, etc. But still more interestingly, the French-speaking students not only evaluated the English-speaking persons more favorably than the French-speaking ones, but they also evaluated the French-speaking persons significantly less favorably than the English-speaking students did.

1.3.2.   *The variety of French spoken in Quebec and its relationship to standard European French.*

After the conquest of Canada by England in 1760, Quebec was cut off politically from France. Until quite recently, Quebec French evolved on its own with little contact with European French and French culture and civilization, except for the elite, which had been educated in the classical college tradition (which dates back to the nineteenth century). French Canada in general and Quebec in particular developed a culture of its roots in North America and is characterized by the fact that it evolved alongside what Porter has called the 'English Charter group' (1969: 60) in Canada but also alongisde Canada's all-powerful American neighbor.

As a consequence, the linguistic variety of French spoken in Quebec has retained or developed certain traits — above all phonetical, lexical, and morphological — which differentiate it from European French.[6] On the other hand, there developed in Quebec, among the elite but also among the population in general,[7] a normative conception of language which associated correct speech with standard European French (if ever such a linguistic variety can be circumscribed).

Language matters have always been a great concern in Quebec among the elite. This concern was first expressed through religious, then through cultural and educational movements and later through political channels.

The concepts of religion, language, and nation were three closely-linked concepts used by the Quebec French-speaking elite to promote its social and political ideas. For example, for some of the mid-nineteen-century elite, the concept of 'nation' implied religious and linguistic unity as well as a uniform set of morals, customs, and even education (L.F. Laflèche 1866, quoted in Eid 1978: 233). Above all, unity of language and of religion were considered the most important elements on which a nation was built (Eid 1978: 233). According to Lafleche, unity of language is the 'first constituent of a nation', *ex aequo* with unity of religion which is 'the most powerful support of national unity' (Eid 1978).

Seen from this angle, one could formulate the hypothesis that this generalized concern for linguistic matters in Quebec is actually a by-product of the more fundamental nationalistic ambitions aimed at by Quebec's French-speaking upper class, these nationalistic ambitions being more or less openly encouraged by the Church.

According to d'Anglejan and Tucker (1973: 2), however, this interest in language matters can be explained by the fact that, first, French has played an important role in preserving a distinct French culture in Quebec and preventing the French-speaking population from assimilation by the English population, and, second, that nationalistic movements usually give language matters a position of priority.

As for the fact that the linguistic prestige model proposed was — and still partly is — a European variety of French (actually, a standard model which evolved from the Ile-de-France dialect), one can suppose that this might be due, in part at least, to the fact that in France, and even more so in Quebec, language and religion, as well as language and culture, have always been closely linked. Quebec's French-speaking community, and especially its socio-economic and religious elite, in trying to survive and to maintain its unity, has been forced to emphasize these cultural, linguistic, and religious values. Since France and French culture have enjoyed a considerable prestige throughout the world and especially throughout all other French-speaking nations (Spilka 1970, quoted in d'Anglejan and Tucker 1973: 2), it could easily become a model for the struggling French-speaking community in Quebec. Furthermore, Quebec's French-speaking community having an inferior economic status in Quebec and in Canada, it was all the easier to look upon France and the French language as a model.

Another interesting hypothesis has been put foreward by Spilka (1970, quoted in d'Anglejan and Tucker 1973: 2), who attributes the high status of European French partly to the fact that France already had a long tradition of successful efforts at language standardization through its 'Académie française'.[8] From the point of view of Quebec's French-speaking community, who had to struggle against what was perceived as the 'invasion' of the English language, as well as against what was seen as the danger of linguistic differentiation between Quebec French and European French, it was in fact tempting to adopt the European-French model in the hope that it would help maintain a link with the 'mother country' and that it would stabilize the ongoing 'contamination' of Quebec French and prevent it from assimilation to English.[9]

Whatever the reasons behind the choice of a European-French model,[10] the 'contamination' of French by borrowings from English (mostly as far as vocabulary was concerned) was felt as alarming, and public campaigns were organized to awaken the French-speaking population to the fact that its language was in danger.

This situation led the Quebec government to establish, in 1961, a board called 'l'Office de la langue francaise', which was assigned the task of revitalizing French in Quebec by bringing it closer to standard French.[11] The first publications of this 'Office' (1965, 1969; Valin 1970) marked the triumph of normative principles and the rejection of any differentiation between Quebec French and European French. In its very first official publication, entitled *Norme du français écrit et parlé au Québec* (1965), the 'Office' states that if the French language in Quebec is to survive the pressures of an English-speaking North American milieu, it must adhere to the same norms which prevail in other francophone countries and especially in France. No variation in morphology or syntax can be tolerated; phonetic and lexical variation should be reduced to an absolute minimum.

Attitudes such as those account for the importance in Quebec given to corpus planning from a cultivation point of view, either through cultural and educational movements or through political action, as we shall see later on.

Alongside this normative movement, however, there evolved − probably due to the rise of a new nationalistic movement preoccupied more with the development of a positive self-image than with the preservation of traditional and historical values − another movement which gave rise to more positive attitudes toward Quebec French. Actually, this movement tended to favor the recognition of the particularities of Quebec French.

Thus, attitudes toward Quebec French and European standard French have changed, although European standard French still appears to have the upper hand. At the very least, it is still perceived as the basis for comparison and evaluation (which tend to be unfavorable to Quebec French).

As an example of these changing attitudes of the French-speaking population of Quebec, I would like to describe here, briefly, the results of three studies dealing with this subject.

The first study was conducted in 1971 by Sorecom for the 'Gendron Commission' and aimed at describing the attitudes and feelings of the Quebec French-speaking population toward its language, as well as identifying the linguistic model (or models) recognized by the population. The research was carried out by questionnaire on a representative sample of the adult Quebec French-speaking population. The survey consisted in presenting the population with a choice of three linguistic models, each symbolizing one of three speech styles used in Quebec and identified as 'popular', 'familiar', and 'stately', the last one being close to the formal speech style used in state television programs.

This study brings out the fact that, in general, the French-speaking Quebec population wishes to improve its language. Asked to identify their speech to one of the three speech styles presented, 62% of the population admitted to speaking a 'familiar type' of speech, 25% a 'popular type', and 11% a 'stately type' of French.

When they were asked to identify the linguistic model to which they aspire, nearly two-thirds of the subjects aspired to acquire a 'stately' type of speech, while only 29% wished to conform their speech style to the 'familiar' type.

When asked if they wished to identify themselves with standard European French, 45% of the respondants said that they would like to conform to standard European French as far as vocabulary is concerned and 35% of them answered that they would like to adopt the standard European French pronunciation.

In spite of this last data, the authors of the study conclude that the choice of the linguistic models presented indicates that the French-speaking population of Quebec aspires to better its language but wishes to speak what we might call a standard Quebec French.

Without going into further details of this study, I would like to point out that the 'stately' speech style presented to the subjects of the study and chosen by the majority appears, to me, very ambiguous as to the values it carries. This variety of French, even though it is spoken in Quebec, may well be interpreted as a choice for standard European French. If this is true, one might conclude that attitudes toward Quebec French were still ambiguous in the early 1970s. As we shall see later on, this ambiguity between the preference for European French or Quebec French underlies the official texts dealing with recent corpus planning.

A second study, conducted by d'Anglejan and Tucker (1973) on a sample consisting of a population of 280 students and professors at the secondary level as well as workers from three geographic locations in Quebec[12] showed that all groups reported being moderately, but not entirely, satisfied with their own speech style. It also revealed that the French spoken by Radio-Canada speakers (the state television station), a variety close to standard European French, represents the 'best' form of Quebec French for subjects from all areas. Among those who do not agree that Radio-Canada represents the prestige model, there is no consensus concerning an alternative, although the subjects in Montreal frequently proposed private radio and television stations, whose announcers tend to speak what we might call a Quebec-style French (d'Anglejan and Tucker 1973: 11-12).

When asked to indicate how their own speech style differs from the best form of French in Quebec, all groups rated vocabulary and pronunciation as the most important sources of difference (d'Anglejan and Tucker 1973: 13). Note that the subjects in the Sorecom sample (1971) expressed the same opinions toward standard European French. This leads me to think that the difference between these two varieties (standard European French and what we might call standard Quebec French) may not be very clearly felt by Quebec's French-speaking population, which seems to react to these two varieties in much the same way.

Furthermore, the d'Anglejan and Tucker study reveals that there is a consensus to the effect that all groups agree that the French spoken in Quebec needs improvement.[13]

Finally, although the subjects refused to accept the clichés that Quebec French 'is not so nice as European French' and that 'Parisian French is the best French' (d'Anglejan and Tucker 1973: 13), another part of the study revealed a consistent pattern of downgrading both the 'upper French-Canadian speech' and the 'lower French-Canadian speech' in favor of a standard European-French style (d'Anglejan and Tucker 1973: 24). Thus, the authors conclude that standard European French is the recognized prestige form of the language.

However, in an ongoing survey by Madeleine Levesque (personal communication) in the Sherbrooke region, it seems that there is a now-perceptible change in the attitudes of the French-speaking student population in favor of Quebec French. The preliminary analysis of part of the secondary-school students' sample seems to reveal that Quebec French is perceived more favorably and that the group studied feels less need to fall into line with standard European French. Unfortunately, all the data has not yet been analyzed, and although we cannot draw any final conclusions, it is tempting to suppose that this apparent change in attitudes is an indication of a trend toward an improved self-image.

On the other hand, the same study reveals another very important aspect of the linguistic preoccupations of the population in that it shows that the English language is seen as extremely important in Quebec. Knowledge of

English is felt to be an essential asset by the majority of the subjects, who feel that English is still essential in the work field in Quebec.

If the preliminary analysis holds, this will mean that, at the same time that French is officially declared the language of work in Quebec, English is still considered the most important language in the work field by at least part of the French-speaking population.

2.0.   LANGUAGE LEGISLATION IN QUEBEC BEFORE THE 'CHARTER OF THE FRENCH LANGUAGE'

It is against this background that the different pieces of legislation dealing with language in Quebec came into existence. As we have seen, the source of discontent of the French-speaking population of Quebec was manyfold. First, the socioeconomic situation and the resulting domains of use of the French language were a target of protest;[14] second, the assimilation of the immigrants to the English-speaking population was a source of concern; third, the prestige of both English and standard European French, as well as the negative perception by Quebecers of Quebec French, opened the way to a type of language planning which took into consideration both aspects of language planning, that is, corpus planning and status planning.[15]

2.1.   Corpus planning before legislation

As already mentioned, the year 1968 marked the beginning of a series of language bills which were to lead to the present 'Charter of the French Language'. Before that, even though no official language planning of any significance had been undertaken, an unofficial language-planning process had been initiated through religious, cultural, and social movements whose aim was the improvement and enrichment of Quebec French. This 'mission' had been entrusted to the 'Office de la langue francaise', the language board established by the same 1961 law which created the Ministère des Affaires culturelles. Since its role consisted mainly in keeping watch over the quality of French, its language-planning efforts were confined to the corpus-planning aspect from a cultivation[16] point of view. Thus, it regularly disseminated normative bulletins to educational institutions, businesses, and the media, drawing attention to the specific differences between Quebec French and standard European French and providing appropriate standard-French vocabulary lists to replace certain terms in common use. Anglicization of Quebec French was a major concern.

Nonetheless, it is important to note that the mandate assigned to this

'first' 'Office de la langue francaise' was very broad and potentially encompassed the whole future development of language legislation. This 'Office'
even had the power to propose certain French place-names and to urge
business firms to use French.·

However, perhaps because of an almost total lack of means, this first
language board's program was restricted to two fields of activity, both from
a corpus-planning point of view. First, it was concerned with questions of
correctness of Quebec French in general. Second, it undertook work on
scientific and technical terms. Terminological inventories made it possible to
identify the deficiencies in technical fields and to proceed with the creation
and standardization of appropriate terminology for these fields. It was
through this aspect of corpus planning that the first 'Office' established its
contacts with the business world and thus, in a sense, paved the way for a
formal and official type of language planning from both the corpus and the
status point of view.

2.2.   The advent of legislation and the broadening scope of language planning

If, since 1961 (and the creation of the first 'Office'), priority had been given
to the normative approach from a corpus planning point of view, the advent
of legislation broadened the scope of language planning to include status
planning.

On the whole, and as was pointed out in McConnell et al. (1979), we will
see that the successive pieces of legislation dealing with language are characterized by the following facts:

1.   The 'status' aspect of the language-planning process increases in importance with each piece of legislation.

2.   There is a shift from legislation dealing mainly with the language of
education to that dealing primarily with the language of work.

3.   A similar shift of emphasis can be observed in the underlying principles of the legislation, which start out supporting the 'personality principle'
and gradually evolve toward the 'territorial principle'.

4.   The legislation starts out supporting the bilingualism approach and
ends up establishing French unilingualism.

5.   The implementation mechanisms are gradually emphasized and refined
with each piece of legislation; and finally,

6.   The different pieces of legislation start out as inciting in their formulation and end up imposing coercive measures.

We shall see, also, that each successive piece of legislation is a response by
the different governments to the pressure exerted by the French-language
community, which increasingly saw itself as a territorial majority and exerted

pressure for the political, social, and cultural recognition of its language in all fields of public activity.

2.2.1.   *Bill 85.* Bill 85, presented in 1968 as an amendment to the 'Education Department Act', basically aimed at protecting the language choice of Quebec's linguistic minorities as to the language of education. This bill, although it was never promulgated a law, prepares the way for future legislation on the status of French in the field of education since it proposes provisions to ensure that people coming to reside in Quebec 'may acquire . . . a working knowledge' of French 'and cause their children to be taught in schools recognized (. . .) as being French-language schools' (Section 1). More compelling, however, would have been another section of the bill, which proposes the creation of a linguistic committee in order to see to it that those attending an English-language institution at the elementary and secondary levels have a working knowledge of French.

2.2.2.   *The 'Act to Promote the French Language in Quebec' (Bill 63).* The second bill, the 1969 'Act to Promote the French Language in Quebec' (Bill 63), reinforces the measures set out in Bill 85 to ensure that the English-speaking children of Quebec as well as the immigrants (adults and children) who settle in Quebec acquire a working knowledge of French. But it also confirms the parents' right to choose either French or English as the language of education for their children.

This bill does, however, prepare the way for more coercive future legislation in that it entrusts the already-mentioned language board with special duties to promote the use of French in Quebec. Thus, this language board was not only to pursue its mission in the field of language cultivation (for both the common French language and the technical terms), but received the following instructions:

1.   to advise the government on any measures which might be undertaken in order 'to see to it that French is the working language in public and private undertakings in Quebec' and that French has priority in matters of public posting (Section 14);

2.   to prepare programs with the above-mentioned undertakings which would help all employees of these firms acquire a working knowledge of French; and

3.   to hear any complaints by employees regarding the use of French at work, to conduct inquiries, and to make public recommendations.

Future legislation will refine and consolidate the different measures described in this bill, especially regarding the following: the language of work, the language of education, the population and institutions affected by the different legal measures, the prestige given to French both as a language of use and as a symbolic recognition of the *fait français* in Quebec, and finally, the improvement and enrichment of French.

2.2.3.   *The 'Official Language Act' (Bill 22).* In July 1974, Bill 22, the 'Official Language Act', was assented to under the Liberal government and gave Quebec its basic impetus with regard to French. In many respects, the present 'Charter of the French Language' is not significantly different from Bill 22, which immediately preceeded it.

In fact, it is in this piece of legislation that French is declared the official language of Quebec (Section 1), and thus it is this bill which inaugurates official and legal measures in status planning. Bill 22 even goes so far as to say that the French texts of the statutes of Quebec prevail over the English texts in case of divergence (Section 2).

Although bilingualism is still the rule, special measures are taken to ensure that official texts and documents emanating from the public administration be drawn up in French and that French be the 'ordinary language of communication in the public administration' (Preamble), not only for internal communications but also for official communications with all government agencies, be they provincial or federal.

Special measures are taken to ensure that public utilities and professional bodies offer their services in French and that any official texts be written in french.

A working knowledge of the official language is a prerequisite to employment and promotion in public administration; it is also obligatory in order to obtain a permit from a professional corporation.

It declares that French must be in use at every level of business activity, in firm names, on public signs (along with another language if desired), on products, on menus, and in contracts. It is also specified that the personnel of business firms must, in their work, be able to communicate in French among themselves and with their superiors (Preamble).

To promote the use of French as a language of work, private commercial, financial, and industrial organizations were compelled to develop what has been called a 'francization program' aiming at spreading the use of French at all levels of activities. Such a program was a prerequisite to the acquisition of a certificate attesting that the firms were applying a francization program or that the status of French within these firms met the requirements of such a program (Section 26). This certificate was obligatory for the firms who wished to receive premiums, subsidies, or other benefits from the government or to make contracts with the government (Section 28).

Administrative machinery, the 'Régie de la langue francaise', a French-language board, was created with the purpose of implementing these francization programs, delivering the certificates, and enforcing the law.

In order to help the industries and business firms elaborate such francization programs, the 'Régie' developed and proposed a methodology for the analysis of the linguistic situation of public firms.[17] In the document, entitled 'Le français dans l'entreprise. Guide général d'implantation' (Régie de la langue française 1975), it is said that in order for French to become the language of work in Quebec all the different types of communications, oral or written, must be in French. Special care is taken in identifying all the different possible types of internal and external communications, as well as different possible interlocutors.

A detailed quantitative analysis is proposed for all the different types of communications, and special attention is given to terminology. Each business firm is asked to evaluate its needs 'quantitatively' and 'qualitatively' as far as technical vocabulary is concerned. The proposed analysis requires that these needs be stated in terms of number of technical words used and needed as well as in terms of other particularities.

All the different forms are to be analyzed, as well as all the different types of postings. Also, all personnel must be categorized as far as knowledge of French is concerned.

After this exhaustive analysis, a francization program can be elaborated which not only defines the proposed objective but also enumerates the measures taken to attain it. These measures, as explained in the document, range from language courses aiming at the bilingualization of all non-French-speaking personnel to the translation of technical and nontechnical texts.

However, as far as implementation is concerned, few guidelines are given.

In another domain, Bill 22 introduced provisions intended to influence the stream of immigrants' children into French-language schools. One major provision involved language testing to determine if children whose mother tongue was neither English nor French had a sufficient knowledge of English to attend English-language schools (Section 43). If not, these children had to conform to the norm and receive their instruction in French, since French was declared the language of instruction in the public schools (Sections 40 and 41).

Bill 22 thus marked a spectacular shift toward status planning and French as a language of use. There was also a marked effort to give Quebec a French 'visage'.

Nevertheless, the corpus aspect of language planning was still present, although less emphasized. In this respect, the new board was expected to take over the former language board's functions (that is, those of the first 'Office de la langue française'), not only as to the language-cultivation aspect but also as to the technical aspect of corpus planning. Moreover, its counselling mandate was broadened and it was given an important responsibility for the dissemination of the French language (Section 55).

As far as the technical aspect of corpus planning is concerned, the 'Régie de la langue française' pursued the action undertaken by the terminological center of the first 'Office de la langue française', which had been instituted in 1969.

In the early 1970s, there was no policy as to what type of terminological work was to be undertaken by the first language board. Since French terminology was needed in every industrial and economic sector, the first language board concentrated its efforts on those sectors where the largest number of workers were involved, namely the mining industries and other primary industrial sectors. After the findings of the Gendron Commission had been made public and the different industrial and economic sectors had been inventoried, the language board oriented its terminological research toward those vocabularies which were common to most industrial sectors: that is, the general technical vocabulary as well as the vocabulary relating to general management and administration.

Follwoing Bill 22, terminological work in these two fields was intensified, and this orientation became a matter of public policy since, in 1976, the 'Regie de la langue francaise' published an official document in which it stated that it would assume the terminological research for these two technical areas but that all other terminological work relating to any specific technical areas was to be taken in charge by the industries and business firms concerned.[18]

Furthermore, Bill 22 provided measures to establish terminology committees whose mandate was to make inventories of technical expressions and to draw up lists of proposed terms, which the 'Régie' was to standardize and whose use would be obligatory in public administration and in all texts and documents approved by the Minister of Education (Sections 50, 51, 52, and 53).

As for the cultivation-type approach to corpus planning which had been prevalent up to the adoption of Bill 22, we note a slight evolution in the linguistic orientation in the official texts. Whereas in 1965, the first language borad proclaimed that variation between standard European French and Quebec French should be reduced to a minimum (Office de la langue francaise 1965), it now proclaimed in an official document from the 'Regie de la langue francaise' that the French-speaking Quebecers are equal partners with the French as far as the evolution of the French language is concerned (Corbeil 1974a: 5). A distinction is made between everyday language (*langue commune*), technical language, and official language (Corbeil 1974b: 6).

As far as everyday language is concerned, the official position of the 'Régie de la langue française' is that, from a language-planning perspective, the only objective to be pursued is to provide individuals with the opportunity to become aware of the existence of different speech styles in order to be able to adapt their own speech to the appropriate styles commanded by the circumstances, social, cultural, or other (Corbeil 1974a: 8; 1974b: 7).

As for the technical vocabulary, the objective is to reduce, as much as possible, the differences between the Quebec and French usage, this action being justified by the fact that the scientific and technical domains do not admit linguistic divergences (Corbeil 1974a: 8; 1974b: 8). Thus, only the technical vocabulary of a language should constitute a target in a language-planning strategy.

But it is the 'official' language which should be the main objective of a corpus-planning policy, the 'official' language being defined as the oral and written language of the state as well as the language of the mass media and any written public text (Corbeil 1974a: 9; 1974b: 9). This form of French in Quebec should be 'as close as possible to the French spoken in France. Every single difference should be justified' (Corbeil 1974a: 10; and 1974b: 9-10).

All in all, if the official positions have changed with regard to the 'ordinary' language, which is now considered to be part of what might be called a personal domain where the state does not feel free to legislate, little has changed since 1965 (Office de la langue francaise 1965) as far as the technical and official domains are concerned.

The fact that the official position with regard to 'ordinary' language did change may be indicative of the attitudes of the French-speaking population toward the role of the government regarding language planning. In the study by d'Anglejan and Tucker (1973), the subjects were asked if they believed it was desirable to influence the evolution of Quebec French. Although there was consensus to the effect that the French spoken in Quebec needed to be improved, certain groups doubted that language evolution could or should be externally oriented, and one group felt that it was inappropriate to interfere with language (d'Anglejan and Tucker 1973: 16).

Although this study is not representative of the total population of Quebec, it is certainly indicative of a trend among certain groups, and one might assume that such a trend is partly responsible for the change in official positions.

Nevertheless, since the policy has remained the same with regard to the technical and official domains, one might wonder if the underlying hypothesis behind the proposed corpus planning in these two domains does not consist in the belief that in the event that this type of corpus-planning effort were to succeed, and that the proposed variety of French was to be implemented, the use of this same variety would spread to the 'ordinary' language.

3.0. THE 'CHARTER OF THE FRENCH LANGUAGE' (BILL 101)

As I said at the beginning, the 'Charter of the French Language' which replaced Bill 22 was adopted in August, 1977, less than a year after the election of the new 'Parti Québécois' government. The rapidity with which it was passed is an indication of the importance of language matters in Quebec and of the pressure which was exerted on the newly elected government to take a position on the matter.

When the Charter was adopted, Bill 22 had been in force for nearly two years (up to the Liberal defeat in November, 1976), and noticeable changes had already been carried out, particulary with regard to public signs[19] and to the different dispositions aiming at reinforcing the French (or at least the bilingual) 'visage' of Quebec. As far as the francization of firms was concerned, a few public firms had agreed to participate in an experiment initiated by the 'Regie de la langue francaise' and were proceeding to the analysis of their linguistic situation in order to develop a standard model for future linguistic analysis and francization programs.

As far as the measures taken by Bill 22 to promote French as the language of education were concerned, they had given rise to much controversy from all sectors of the population, anglophones, New Quebecers, and francophones alike.

3.1.   *The innovative aspects of the 'Charter of the French Language'*

Although in many respects the Charter is not significantly different from Bill 22 (the 'Official Language Act'), it does differ on the following three points:

1.   Whereas, like Bill 22, the Charter maintains French as 'the official language of Quebec' (Section 1), it goes a step further in that it states that only the French texts of laws and regulations are official (Section 9). Thus, French is declared the language of legislature and the courts, the language of civil administration as well as the language of public utility firms and professional corporations, with the French version of the documents being the official one. Artificial persons are to address each other in French, but special measures are taken to preserve the rights of natural persons. As for French in commerce and business, the dispositions outlined in Bill 22 are intensified. Instructions on products, catalogues, brochures, toys and games, contracts, job-application forms, order forms, signs, posters, and firm names have to be in French. Only French is to be used on public signs and posters as well as for firm names, although a few exceptions are provided for in this domain as well as in a few others.

2.   Whereas, in Bill 22, only those business firms which wished to receive premiums, subsidies, or other benefits from the public administration, or to obtain contracts with the government, were compelled to proceed to their linguistic analysis and to obtain a 'francization certificate', the Charter decrees that every public utility and business firm employing 50 or more employees is required to obtain a 'francization certificate' attesting that the firm is applying a 'francization program' or that French already enjoys a high-enough status in the firm so that no such program is needed (Sections 135, 136, 138).[20] Furthermore, all of the above firms must hold such a 'francization certificate' by December 31, 1983, at the latest (Section 136).[21]

3.   As for the language of instruction, the Charter decrees that instruction in the public or subsidized kindergarten classes as well as in elementary and secondary schools shall be in French (Section 72). Again, however, special measures are provided for those children who are considered to be exceptions to the rule: children whose parents — at least one of whom — have received their elementary instruction in English, and those (along with their younger brothers and sisters) who were lawfully receiving their instruction in English before the act came into force (Section 73).[22]

As for the machinery needed for the supervision and enforcement of the law, the Charter established three different boards to which were assigned the main functions formerly held by the 'Regie de la langue francaise': (1) the 'Office de la langue francaise', (2) the 'Conseil de la langue francaise', and (3) the 'Commission de surveillance de la langue francaise'.

The 'Office de la langue francaise' still holds the main work mandate in that it sees to it that French becomes 'the language of communication, work, commerce, and business in the civil administration and business firms' (Section 100). It has the authority to direct and approve the francization operation, to issue and suspend francization certificates, and to administer French competency tests to the members of professional corporations. Furthermore, it is responsible for setting up terminology committees and for standardizing and publicizing the terms and expressions it approves. Finally, it is expected to play a role in assisting the civil administration, the public and semipublic firms and agencies, and the population in general to refine and enrich spoken and written French in Quebec (Sections 113-114).

As for the 'Conseil de la langue francaise', its main task is to monitor the progress of language planning from the point of view of both status and corpus planning (Sections 188-189).

Finally, the 'Commission de surveillance de la langue francaise' deals with failure to comply with the law (Section 158)

On the whole, as one can see, whereas Bill 22 was inciting in its provisions for making French the official language of Quebec, the 'Charter of the French Language' uses more coercive measures to attain its objectives.

3.2. *Status language planning in the 'Charter of the French Language'*

On the whole, the status aspect of language planning has been reinforced to the detriment of corpus·planning, although corpus planning is still a preoccupation, as we shall see later on.

The Charter not only sees to it that French is the official language of Quebec, but it puts an end to the bilingual tradition in Quebec by instituting unilingualism, with English remaining a language of use in restricted and specific domains of social activities without official status.

The use of French is presented in the Charter as a fundamental right. Thus, it is said that 'every person has a right to have the civil administration, the health services and social services, the public utility firms, the professional corporations, the associations of employees and all business firms (. . .) communicate with him in French' (Section 2). The same is true for the workers who 'have a right to carry on their activities in French' (Section 3), for the consumers who 'have a right to be informed and served in French' (Section 5), as well as for the persons 'eligible for instruction in Quebec' who have a 'right to receive that instruction in French' (Section 6).

As far as the language of work is concerned, the Charter decrees that all written communications to employees shall be in French and offers of employment or promotion shall also be in French (Section 41). Exclusive knowledge of French or insufficient knowledge of a language other than French cannot be a reason for dismissing, demoting, or transferring a staff member (Section 45). Furthermore, the obtaining of employment dependent upon the knowledge of a language other than French is prohibited. The proof that knowledge of a language other that French is needed is on the employer, and the 'Office de la Langue Francaise' decides any dispute (Section 46). Collective agreements must be drafted in French (Section 43).

Failure to respect these provisions may result in a fine.[23]

As for the francization of business firms, the Charter provides a general guideline concerning the objectives that must be attained through the application of a francization program. This program is intended to generalize the use of French and implies the following:

1.   knowledge of the official language by the management, the members of the professional corporations, and other staff members;

2.   an increase, at all levels, in the number of persons having a good knowledge of French;

3.   the use of French as the language of work and as the language of internal communications in the working documents of the business firms as well as in communications with clients, suppliers, and the public;

4.   the use of French terminology;

5.   the use of French in advertising; and

6. appropriate policies for hiring, promotion, and transfer (Section 141).

A formal procedure for the obtaining of a francization certificate has been devised by the 'Office de la langue francaise' in accordance with the dispositions provided for in the Charter. Four stages have been defined:

1. First of all, the public firms concerned must ask for a temporary francization certificate. This temporary certificate is delivered to business firms on the following conditions: the firm must submit a form by which it acknowledges that it wishes to comply with the law and that it has formed a francization committee as stipulated by law (Section 146).[24]

2. Once the firm has obtained its temporary certificate, it has one year in which to analyse its linguistic situation and to present this analysis to the 'Office', which then determines whether the use of French is generalized enough so that the firm does not have to elaborate and apply a francization program. If this is the case, a permanent francization certificate is delivered. If not, the firm is asked to devise and present a francization program.

3. By the end of the one-year period, the francization program must be examined and approved by the 'Office'. Note that the 'Office' deals directly with each business firm concerned, and all francization programs are negotiated on an individual basis between the 'Office' and each business firm. The elaboration of the francization program is done in constant collaboration with the 'Office', which sees to it that all relevant elements are included in the francization program presented by the firm.

Once the program has been accepted by the 'Office', the firms have 24 months to apply this program, during which time they have to report on their progress every six months.

4. Finally, a permanent francization certificate is delivered, attesting that French has attained the desired status in that firm or that the firm is applying a francization program approved by the 'Office'.

To help the firms establish a francization program, the 'Office' has devised a guide in which it defines the objectives of such a program and the domains that it must cover, and for which it suggests a timetable for the different stages involved.[25]

It should be noted that every agency of the civil administration as well as every public utility firm must also comply with the law and may also have to adopt a francization program if the use of French is not generalized enough.

As for professional corporations, they are required not to issue permits in Quebec except to persons whose knowledge of French is appropriate to the practice of their profession (Section 35).

Proof of such knowledge has to be made to the 'Office', which has devised appropriate language tests.

3.3. 'Labor-market planning' in the 'Charter of the French Language'

The measures mentioned above all aim at giving French an official status in all sectors of activity in Quebec. However, as has been pointed out in a paper by Laporte (1979: 13-14), other aspects of the Charter go beyond that of status planning as such. The measures taken in dealing with the language of education are a case in point.

By restricting attendance to English schools, in the long run the growth of the anglophone primary and secondary school sector will be limited. This, as Laporte points out, is a controversial aspect since it affects not only the newcomers who want to establish themselves on a permanent basis in Quebec, but also the children of those coming to work in Quebec on a temporary basis. As an example, this provision actually concerns highly qualified personnel coming to Quebec on either a permanent or a temporary basis. What seems at stake here is more than language planning as such and can be viewed as a type of 'labor-market planning'. In the long run, business firms may have to change the orientation of their personnel recruitment, since a working knowledge of French should be a prerequisite in future recruiting policies. Thus, both the demographic balance of language groups as well as the long-range balance of power between language groups is at stake (Laporte 1979: 14).

3.4. 'Corpus planning' in the 'Charter of the French Language'

On the other hand, although corpus planning is not emphasized as such in the Charter, specific provisions are made for what has been called 'technical corpus planning',[26] that is, corpus planning concerning scientific and technical terms.

Terminological work has been emphasized in accordance with the orientation given under Bill 22. Fundamental research in terminology has also been emphasized in order not only to fulfill the present terminological needs but also to develop the necessary 'expertise' so that the 'Office de la langue francaise' may act as a counsellor in the normalization process of terminology. Work in neology is also carried out on a larger scale.

As far as the methodology is concerned, the 'Office de la langue francaise' has perfected a technique based on the exhaustive and comparative analysis of all known French and English terminological sources, usually followed by consultation with a committee on which a representative of the business firms concerned is present. However, outside a few endeavors, no preliminary sociolinguistic survey or any study aiming at analyzing or determining actual needs has ever been done before undertaking the actual terminological research. Nor has there been any evaluation made in terms of the success or failure of the technical words proposed.

Furthermore, a 'Commission de terminologie' has been formed and given a mandate to draw up a list of scientific and technical terms whose use may be either suggested by the 'Office' or made compulsory upon publication in the *Gazette officielle du Quebec* (Section 118). This Commission is made up of seven members, three of whom are not staff members of the 'Office de la langue francaise'. It meets at least 10 times a year. The Commission examines either words or lists of words on whose appropriateness a person or an organization has requested an official opinion, or even the whole of a scientific or technical vocabulary pertaining to a specific domain.

The official criteria used in the normalization process are criteria of 'quality' based on coherence of the data presented and the methodology used.[27] No other criteria, be they linguistic, sociolinguistic, or otherwise, are mentioned.

Still in the field of terminology, the 'Banque de terminologie du Quebec' (B.T.Q.), inaugurated in 1974, has as its primary mandate to stock up in a computer all available French-language terminological data. In the near future, terminals directly connected with business firms and other organisms will make this terminological data directly available. Furthermore, through international agreements, the B.T.Q. will provide the 'Office' with the latest available data and will help spread the 'Office''s terminological know-how.

At the same time, the 'Office' has intensified its relations with business firms, with the result that it now initiates the creation of committees through which business firms receive help from the 'Office' in their terminological work.

Business firms are incited to get together to solve their common terminological problems. The 'Office' provides the experts, who work together with the representatives of the different business firms. This measure is intended, hopefully, to cut the cost of the francization of terminology for the firms, while at the same time it aims at promoting the idea that francization of business firms is a feasible task.

Finally, the 'Office' has also generalized one of the services offered by the first language board: the telephone consultation service. Through this service, people in the business field as well as the Quebec population at large can consult the 'Office' on any linguistic problem, technical or otherwise.

This service offered by the 'Office' leads us to speak of another aspect of corpus planning, that is, corpus planning with regard to ordinary speech.

In the 'Office''s 1978-1979 annual report, it is stated that more than half the questions asked the 'Office' through this consultation service during that year dealt with the question of the norm in everyday speech or with questions relating to grammar, orthography, or the like. This is an indication that, even though emphasis is now placed on the status aspect of language planning, the cultivation aspect is still a priority among certain sectors of the Quebec population.

We must note, however, that if the 'Office' does not do any official planning of ordinary language, it does have to make judgments on borderline technical or semitechnical terms, as in the vocabulary of automobiles and the vocabulary relating to food, which must be written in French on menus. This leads the 'Office' to evaluate such terms as 'hamburger', 'hot dog', 'club sandwich', and 'fishburger'.

The sections of the law regarding labels, directions, and publicity in general have also led the 'Office' into making decisions on the appropriateness of common-language words. These decisions often give rise to public debates which reveal the heart of the matter. An example of this is the *'arrêt-stop'* controversy. Although the 'Office' has not yet officially pronounced a judgment as to which of the two words is appropriate on road signs, the media and the general public have been confronted with the problem, which reveals the sociolinguistic problems at stake. In fact, the *'arrêt-stop'* controversy has occupied a great deal of attention in the media. The word *'arrêt'*, which can be translated as 'a stop', is a Quebec French word, while 'stop' is ambiguous in Quebec since it can be viewed as either an English word or the standard French word used on road signs. Symbolically, to choose *'arrêt'*, which is widespread in Quebec, would amount to promoting Quebec French with all its particularities,[28] while the choice of 'stop', even though it can be justified on grounds of international comprehensiveness, can be felt by the French-speaking Quebec population as a rejection of Quebec French and all that it stands for. Historically, Quebec's French-speaking population has always been aware of the threat exerted by English on the French spoken in Quebec. This self-consciousness has led the Quebecers to reject any obvious English influence, or for that matter any word interpreted as such. This explains the fact that 'stop' has never been largely used in Quebec.

Thus, if a word such as 'stop' were to be officially proposed, Quebec's French-speaking population, or at least part of it, would have to face a difficult reality. The choice of the word 'stop' would not only mean, for the majority of the people, the promotion of a European standard-French word which has no intimate connection with the Quebec reality, but it would also mean the promotion of an English word which French-speaking Quebecers have, consciously or not, been trying to banish from their vocabulary. Indeed, as we can see, the debate is not merely a linguistic one, and behind the linguistic arguments lies a deep social, cultural, and political problem.

Even though the 'Office' has not pronounced yet on the variety of French it means to promote, we can expect in the near future that, as soon as French is truly recognized as the official language of Quebec and has attained the desired status, the corpus aspect of language planning will become more and more important and that the 'Office' will have to make judgments as to which variety of French it wishes to promote.

4.0. CONCLUSION

In this paper, we have examined the different pieces of legislation which have led to the adoption of the 'Charter of the French Language'. After a brief analysis of the social, economic, demographic, and linguistic situation in Quebec, we have tried to demonstrate that the present orientation of the Charter was brought about by the social evolution of the French-speaking population of Quebec, which was reflected in its attitudes toward English as well as European French and Quebec French. We have also seen that the first 'Office de la langue francaise' paved the way for the present Charter and contained in a nutshell the future developments of the different pieces of legislation concerned with language in Quebec. Finally, we have tried to show that language planning in Quebec, be it official or unofficial, can be analyzed from the double point of view of corpus language planning and status language planning, although these two aspects have not developed simultaneously and are not present in the same proportion in each language-planning attempt. Also, from the point of view of language planning, we have tried to demonstrate that the Quebec legislation goes further than corpus (both technical and common) and status planning and that it encompasses what has been called 'labor-market planning' (Laporte 1979).

All in all, each piece of Quebec legislation in general, and the Charter in particular, can be seen as an act of political mobilization, at least as far as the French-speaking population is concerned. It can also be seen as an act of self-assertion by this same population. Seen from this point of view, it does not matter if, as some say, the francization of Quebec was already well under way if not irreversible before the adoption of the 'Charter of the French Language'. On the contrary, the Charter may be looked upon as an act which consolidates what has already been acquired or is on the verge of being acquired.

NOTES

1.   These factors have also been discussed in McConnell et al. (1979), as well as in Laporte (1979).
2.   For a discussion of diglossia as applied to the linguistic situation in Quebec see in particular Saint-Pierre (1976), Chantefort (1976), and Martin (1979).

3. Prior to 1968, two pieces of legislation had been promulgated by the Government of Quebec: the 'Lavergne Law' in 1910, which officialized the bilingual character of Quebec by decreeing that the use of both English and French was obligatory in public utility firms, and a bill decreeing the primacy of French in the interpretation of laws and regulations in 1937. This last bill, however, was to be repealed in 1938. See Mallea (1977) for a list of language-oriented laws in Quebec.

4. In the report on language of work in Quebec by the 'Commission d'enquete sur la situation de la langue francaise et sur les droits linguistiques au Quebec', called 'Commission Gendron', it is said that 32% of the francophones (i.e. people whose mother tongue is French) in the labor force used both French and English at work (see Québec, Gouvernement du, 1972: 17). Note, however, that 'bilingual' is defined in the report as meaning 'the use at work of a language other than one's own at different levels of usage' (Québec, Gouvernement du, 1972: 24, note). It does not mean, then, that all of the 32% of the francophones are bilingual in a broader sense, but it does mean that they use English some of the time at work and thus have a working knowledge of English.

5. For a complete picture of linguistic transfers toward English and French for 1931, 1941, 1951, and 1961, see Charbonneau and Maheu 1973: 71.

6. For a discussion of the phonetic aspect of the question, see Gendron (1966); for the lexical aspect, see Guilbert (1976) and for some of the syntactical aspects see Daoust-Blais (1975) and Daoust-Blais and Lemieux-Nieger (1979). See also Boudreault (1973) for a general discussion. As for a discussion of linguistic variables in correlation with social variables, see in particular Kemp (1979), Sankoff and Thibault (1977), and Cedergren and Sankoff (1974).

7. Sociolinguistic studies have shown that there is a social cleavage as to the use of certain linguistic variables and that some of the sociolinguistic variations are recognized by the population in general. Furthermore, Quebec's French-speaking population is preoccupied with, or at least aware of, language differentiation between Quebec French and European French (from France). This clearly shows up in the Sankoff-Cedergren corpus, collected around 1971-1972 and representative of the Montreal French-speaking community, as well as in the different sociolinguistic studies examined in this paper.

8. The Academie Francaise, entrusted with the defense and preservation of the French language, was founded in 1635, and its first dictionary was published in 1644.

9. Valin (1970) even went so far as to say that if Quebec French was left to evolve naturally, it could become unintelligible to speakers of standard French.

10. We have not examined here the role of the upper socioeconomic classes as well as the influence of the Church in the promotion of this model. The importance of these social groups was pointed out to me by William Kemp.

11. This 'Office de la langue francaise' was a board created in 1961 by the bill instituting the Ministère des Affaires culturelles. This 'Office' must not be confused with the present 'Office de la langue francaise', a board created in 1977 by the 'Charter of the French Language' in order to see to it that the law is enforced.

12. The three regions studied were Montreal, Alma, and Quebec city.

13. Note, however, that the Montreal students are relatively less adamant in their belief that Quebec French needs improvement (d'Anglejan and Tucker 1973: 16).

14. In their report on the language of work, the members of the 'Commission Gendron' explicitly recommend that the government legislate on the status and the use of French and English in Quebec (Québec, Gouvernement du, 1972: 186-187).

15. This typology follows Kloss's distinction between 'corpus planning' and 'status planning'. See Fishman (1974: 19) for a definition of these terms. Generally speaking, we can say that 'corpus planning' refers to the technical linguistic aspects of language planning while 'status planning' refers to policy formulation aimed at enforcing the choice of sociolinguistic and linguistic patterns decided upon.

16. I refer here to the typology proposed by Neustupný (1970), who distinguishes two different approaches to language planning: the 'policy' approach, which focuses attention on the language code and covers problems like selection of a national language, standardization, orthography, etc.; and the 'cultivation' approach, which focuses attention on questions of correctness, efficiency, and style.

17. This methodology, at least insofar as technical vocabulary is concerned, was developed partly with the help of a few business firms who agreed that some of the officers of the language board would come and help them analyze their terminological situation and needs. Unfortunately, in none of these experiments was the implementation stage reached and no analysis at a later date was ever done to evaluate the results of these experiments.

18. This document is entitled 'Partage des tâches en matière de travaux terminologiques' and was published by the 'Régie de la langue française'.

19. Section 35 of Bill 22 decreeing that 'public signs must be drawn up in French or in both French and another language' had been in force since July 31, 1974.

20. Special provisions have been made for research centers and head offices.

21. Note that even though public utility and business firms are expected to hold a 'francization certificate' by December, 1983, implementation of the francization program could last much longer.

22. Special provisions have been made for children whose parents are in Quebec on a temporary basis. These provisions, however, have not been found flexible enough by the population concerned.

23. For example, a person who contravenes a provision of the Charter is liable, in addition to costs, for the first offence, to a fine of $25 to $500 for a natural person and of $50 to $1,000 for artificial persons. The fines are more important for any subsequent offence (Section 205).

   A business firm which does not hold a francization certificate by December 31, 1983, will be fined, in addition to costs, $100 to $2,000 for each day during which it carries on its business without a certificate (Section 206).

   As far as public postings are concerned, these can be destroyed if they are found not to be in conformity with the Charter. A special procedure is provided for these cases (see Section 208 fo the Act).

24. Business firms were asked to form, before November 30, 1977, a francization committee composed of at least six persons, a third of whom are to represent officially the body of workers (Sections 146-147).

25. To date, however, very few firms are officially applying a francization program, and no evaluation of the results has yet been made, so that nothing definite can be said either about the success of this enterprise or about the implementation methods used.

26. See McConnell et al. (1979) for the distinction between the 'technical' aspect of language planning and the 'cultivation' aspect of corpus planning.

27. This passage is taken from a 1979 public folder.

28. It has been argued that the use of '*arrêt*' is incorrect in this context, linguistically speaking. The details of this controversy are not important here, since what is at stake is the policy behind the promotion of a linguistic variety, be it Quebec French of European French.

REFERENCES

Boudreault, Marcel (1973), *La qualité de la langue*. Synthesis carried out for the 'Commission d'enquete sur la situation de la langue française et sur les droits linguistiques au Québec, SI'. Québec, Editeur officiel du Quebec.

Canada, Gouvernement du (1963-1967), 'Commission royale d'enquête sur le bilinguisme et le biculturalisme'.

Cedergren, Henrietta, and David (1974), 'Variable rules: performance as a statistical reflection of competence', *Language* 50: 333-355.

Chantefort, Pierre (1976), 'Diglossie au Québec: limites et tendances actuelles', in *La sociolinguistique au Québec,* Cahier de linguistique No. 6, pp. 23-53. Montreal, Presses de l'Université du Québec (P.U.Q.).

Charbonneau, Hubert, and Robert Maheu (1973), *Les aspects démographiques de la question linguistique*. Synthesis carried out for the 'Commission d'enquete sur la situation de la langue française et sur les droits linguistiques au Québec, S3'. Quebec, Editeur officiel du Québec.

Corbeil, Jean-Claude (1974a), *Notes sur les rapports entre le français québécois et le français de France*. Etudes, recherches et documentation No. 1, Regie de la langue francaise. Quebec, Editeur officiel du Quebec.

——————— (1974b), *Description des options linguistiques de l'Office de la langue française*. Etudes, recherches et documentation No. 2, Régie de la langue francaise. Quebec, Editeur officiel du Québec.

D'anglejan, Alison, and Richard G. Tucker (1973), 'Sociolinguistic correlates of speech style in Quebec', in *Language Attitudes: Current Trends and Prospects,* ed. by Roger W. Shuy and Ralph W. Fasold, 1-27. Washington, D.C., Georgetown University Press.

Daoust-Blais, Denise (1975), *L'influence de la négation sur certains indéfinis en français québécois'*. Unpublished Ph.D. dissertation, University of Montreal.

——————— , and Monique Lemieux-Niéger (1979), '/TUT/ en français du Québec', in *Cahiers de linguistique,* volume nine, Montreal, Presses de l'Université du Québéc (P.U.Q.).

Eid, Nadia F. (1978), *Le clergé et le pouvoir politique au Québec*. Cahiers du Québec. Montreal, Hurtubise HMH.

Fishman, Joshua A. (1974), 'Language planning and language planning research: the state of the art', in *Advances in Language Planning,* ed. by Joshua A. Fishman, 15-33. The Hague, Mouton.

Gendron, Jean-Denis (1966), *Tendances phonétiques du français parlé au Canada*. Paris/Quebec, Klincksiek, Presses de l'Université Laval (P.U.L.).

Guilbert, Louis (1976), 'Problématique d'un dictionnaire du français québécois', in *Langue française,* no. 31, pp. 40-54. Paris, Larousse.

Joy, Richard J. (1978), *Les minorités des langues officielles au Canada*. Institut de recherches C.D. Howe. Quebec, Bibliothèque nationale du Québec.

Kemp, William (1979), 'La variation entre les formes en SKE, KES, et KOS dans le français parlé à Montréal: étude d'un cas de changement linguistique en cours'. Unpublished M.A. thesis, Université du Québec a Montréal.

Lambert, Wallace E. (1967), 'A social psychology of bilingualism', *Journal of Social Issues* 23 (2): 91-109.

Laporte, Pierre E. (1979), 'The meaning and consequences of the French Language Charter from the point of view of sociopolitical and linguistic evolution of Quebec'. Paper presented at the Conference at the University of British Columbia, March 23.

Levesque, Madeleine (forthcoming), 'Analyse des attitudes sociolinguistiques et des idéologies qu'elles reflètent auprès d'un groupe d'étudiants du Secondaire face aux différentes variétés de langue utilisées au Québec'. Unpublished Ph.D. thesis, Faculté des Lettres, Université de Sherbrooke.

Mallea, John R., editor (1977), *Quebec's Language Policies: Background and Response*. International Center for Research on Bilingualism. Quebec, Presses de l'Université Laval (P.U.L.).

Martin, André (1979), 'Diglossie, situation linguistique et politique linguistique: le cas du Québec'. Paper presented at the conference on 'Théories et pratiques de la sociolinguistique', Université de Haute-Normandie, Rouen, France. (To appear in 'Cahiers de linguistique sociale de l'Université de Haute-Normandie', Universite de Haute-Normandie, Rouen).

Mcconnell, Grant D., Denise Daoust-Blais, and André Martin (1979), 'Language planning and language treatment in Quebec'. Unpublished manuscript. (To appear in *Language Planning and Language Treatment: Worldwide Case Studies*, ed. by R.E. Wood).

Neustupný, Jiři V. (1970), 'Basic types of treatment of language problems', *Linguistic Communications* (Monash University) 1: 77-98.

Office de la langue française (1965), *Norme du français écrit et parlé au Québec*. Cahiers de l'Office de la langue française 4. Quèbec, Ministere des Affaires culturelles.

_____(1969), *Canadianismes de bon aloi*. Cahiers de l'Office de la langue française 4. Quebec, Ministère des Affaires culturelles.

_____(1978), 'Guide d'élaboration d'un programme de francisation destiné à l'entreprise'. Unpublished manuscript.

Porter, John (1969), *The Vertical Mosaic. An Analysis of Social Class and Power in Canada*. Toronto, University of Toronto Press.

Québec, Gouvernement du (1968-1972), Commission d'enquete sur la situation de la langue française sur les droits linguistiques au Québec (often called 'Commission Gendron').

_____(1972), *Rapport de la Commission d'enquête sur la situation de la langue française et sur les droits linguistiques au Québec* ('Commission Gendron'), Volume one: *La langue de travail. La situation de la langue française au Québec*. Quebec, Éditeur officiel du Québec.

_____(1977), *Projet de loi no. 101: Charte de la langue française*. Assemblée nationale du Québec. Quebec, Éditeur officiel du Québec.

_____(1978), *Charte de la langue française. Réglementation*. Quebec, Éditeur officiel du Québec.

Québec, Ministère de l'Immigration du (1977), *L'immigration au Québec*, volume 4: *Bulletin statistique annuel*. Quebec, Ministère de l'Immigration du Québec.

Régie de la Langue Française (1975), *Le français dans l'entreprise. Guide général d'implantation. Extraits de la Gazette officielle du Québec*. Quebec, Éditeur officiel du Québec.

_____(1976), *La normalisation terminologique*. Quebec, Éditeur officiel du Québec.

_____(1976), *Partage des tâches en matière de travaux terminologiques*. Quebec, Éditeur officiel du Québec.

Saint-Pierre, Madeleine (1976), 'Bilinguisme et diglossie dans la région montréalaise', in *La sociolinguistique au Québec*. Cahier de linguistique no. 6: 179-198. Montreal, Presses de l'Université du Québec (P.U.Q.).

Sankoff, Gillian, and Pierrette Thibault (1977), 'L'alternance entre les auxiliaires *avoir* et *être* en français parlé à Montréal', *Langue française* 34: 81-107.

Sorecom (1971), *Les mass-media, l'attachement à sa langue et les modèles linguistiques au Québec en 1971*. Study carried out for the 'Commission d'enquête sur la situation de la langue française et sur les droits linguistiques au Québec'. Quebec, Éditeur officiel du Québec.

Spilka, Irène Vachon (1970), 'For a study of diglossia in French Canada'. Unpublished manuscript, University of Montréal. (Quoted in d'Anglejan and Tucker 1973).

Valin, Roch (1970), *Quel français devons-nous enseigner?* Cahiers de l'Office de la langue française 7. Quebec, Ministère des Affaires culturelles.

BERNARD SPOLSKY and LORRAINE BOOMER

The Modernization of Navajo*

While we were preparing this paper, Lorraine Boomer discussed it with her mother, who could see very little reason for coining new words in Navajo. When Lorraine suggested the need for a Navajo word for 'plastic', her mother replied that the Navajo language was already perfectly adequate for talking about all the things that one needs to talk about in it. A little while later, a telephone was installed in the house and Lorraine heard her mother complaining in Navajo about the difficulty of making calls, even with the help of an operator. For 'operator', she used the Navajo *saad aháąh deidinili*, (literally, 'one who links conversations together'). Asked where she had heard the term, she replied, 'I made it up'.

With deep respect, we dedicate this paper to all those, named in it or not, who have contributed to the modernization of Navajo.

As languages record the changing culture of their speakers, so modern Navajo is now starting to be able to meet the needs of a people in increasing contact with modern technology and general American life. While anthropologists generally point out that the Navajo people are themselves highly adaptive, linguists writing in the 1940s agreed with Sapir that their language seemed remarkably impervious to borrowing: Navajos remained predominantly monolingual, and their language was seemingly unaffected by centuries of contact with other native American languages and with Spanish. Sapir put it like this:

The Athabaskan languages of American are spoken by peoples that have had astonishingly varied cultural contacts, yet no where do we find that an Athabaskan dialect has borrowed at all freely from a neighboring language. These languages have always found it easier to create new words by compounding afresh elements ready to hand. (Sapir 1921: 196)

Sapir characterizes as the 'psychological attitude' of the language the struc-

*We are grateful to Robert W. Young and Alice Neundorf for comments on an earlier version of this paper.

tural characteristics that affect its ability to accept foreign words. Specifically, he is referring to the importance and nature of the Navajo verb. Navajo verbs consist of a comparatively small stock of verb stems that enter into an extraordinarily complex system of pre- and suffixes, and, with a small set of exceptions, Navajo nouns are themselves derived from verbs. It is not easy, therefore, to fit an alien word into the grammar of Navajo.

The dictionary (Young and Morgan 1943a) and works by Harrington (1945), Liebler (1948), and Reichard (1951), list fewer than 40 words borrowed from Spanish, and Young and Morgan list even fewer loan words from English. In the 30 years since the first edition of the dictionary was published, there would seem to have been quite a marked change. While the language is still basically as before, capable of elaborate coining of new words from native elements, the amount of contact with English has increased tremendously. Large numbers of Navajos served in the armed forces during the Second World War; even more left the Reservation to work in war-related industries. Since then, there has been continually growing contact with the outside world. As late as 1949, fewer than half the Navajo children of school age were actually in school, but by 1955, attendance was close to 90%.

As a result of these increasing contacts with English, there has been a marked increase in borrowing, for, as Dozier (1967) pointed out, sociocultural rather than structural factors explain the likelihood of the acceptance of loan words. In a study of the speech of six-year-old Navajos that we completed in 1971, we discovered the extent of borrowing that did occur (Holm et al. 1973). In a corpus of taped interviews with over 200 children, we found that loan words represented 9% of the different words children used in the corpus and accounted for 3.6% of the total 33,580 words. Admittedly the occurrence of a word in the speech of one child in a taped interview is not evidence that it has been integrated into the vocabulary, but there is good reason to believe that many of the 500 words we found in our limited sample are in fact classifiable as loan words; at least, the children we interviewed were growing up assuming that they were part of Navajo.

Borrowing words from another language is clearly one method of modernization. It has many advantages: it takes place informally at the point of contact with the alien culture and continues to mark the object as borrowed, thus permitting the maintenance of the integrity of the indigenous system. At the same time, it is less likely to be favored when there is consciousness of the process: in conscious modernization (language planning) the process of adding new words to handle new objects or concepts (lexical elaboration) tends to favor seeking out native words for adaptation or coining new words in accordance with the resources of the language. Navajo, with the ease with which it can go from descriptive sentences to nouns, is an ideal language in which to build transparent coinages, and studies in progress by Alice Neundorf (personal communication) suggest that this is in fact the favored manner of dealing with lexical elaboration. However, our focus in this paper is not on linguistic processes so much as on the modernization itself. We wish to trace the various individuals and agencies who have been involved in the work of adapting Navajo to the modern world, and leave to others the study of the manner of their operation and the success of their efforts. Our study is limited to those who have been conscious of the process they have been involved in; we cannot start to explore the complexity of the widespread and unconscious activities illustrated in the story with which we opened this paper.

We will sketch first the changing status of the Navajo language and then describe three interconnected strands of activity: the development of written Navajo, the conscious coinage of new terms, and the development of notions and means of standardization.

THE STATUS OF NAVAJO

An Athabaskan language, Navajo is the language of some 150,000 Navajos living on a reservation the size of West Virginia and overlapping territory from the states of Arizona, New Mexico, Colorado, and Utah. If we accept estimates of a population of 7,000 a century ago, it is clear that the number of speakers has grown more than 20-fold, and in spite of the steady inroads of English referred to above and reported in a number of papers (Spolsky 1970, 1974, 1975), the still-high rate of population growth almost certainly means a continuing increase in the absolute number of native speakers of the language. As we mentioned earlier, the Reservation was more or less left alone until the 1940s; extensive contact began about then, with Navajos leaving the Reservation to enlist or take jobs in industry, and was followed by the postwar development of schools and roads and the effects of the recent importance of mineral and energy resources found on the Reservation.

Under U.S. federal control, the Navajo Reservation has never had a formally established language policy. The policy of the Bureau of Indian Affairs in schools has been to assume that education and English are synonymous, although, as we will note later, on a number of occasions there have been policies accepting the value of transitional bilingual education. Tribal government was built by the Bureau of Indian Affairs, but there has been acceptance of the oral use of Navajo in almost all institutional situations except school. Local chapter meetings and Tribal Council meetings continue to be conducted in Navajo, with interpreters available to facilitate communication between non-English-speaking Navajos and non-Navajo-speaking officials. Similarly, government offices and health services assume the need for interpreters. All official writing, however, is in English: the minutes of Tribal Council meetings, resolutions submitted to it, records of Navajo court hearings, forms used in tribal offices, all are in English. With the exception of a brief period referred to in a later section, the tribal newspaper has been published in English, although there have been a couple of recent attempts by individuals concerned with Navajo literacy to add sections to the newspaper in Navajo. Even the newspaper published by one of the contract schools, Rough Rock Demonstration School, a school with a strong commitment to bilingual education, is published entirely in English. While the written media use English almost exclusively, Navajo is used orally in other media: there are a large number of radio stations around the Reservation that regularly broadcast programs in Navajo, and there are television programs in Navajo. Essentially, then, the situation may be characterized as a special kind of diglossia, with Navajo the preferred and normal language for oral use and English the almost-exclusive language for written use (see Irvine and Spolsky 1980 for a discussion of this).

As far as we know, there has been only one formal resolution of the Navajo Tribal Council dealing with language; that was a decision made by the Excutive Committee of the Council some years ago calling for the word 'Navajo' to be spelled in the Spanish way, with a 'j' rather than, as had become common, with an 'h'. Some of the groups concerned with Navajo literacy, such as DBA, the Navajo Linguistic Society, and the bilingual education section of the Tribal Division of Education, have from time to time suggested a more established status for Navajo, and a group associated with the Division of Education is at the moment discussing a draft resolution to be presented to the Tribal Council that would formally recognize the status of Navajo in both oral and written use. As far as we can tell, the only version of the draft resolution available is in English.

THE DEVELOPMENT OF WRITTEN NAVAJO

The history of written Navajo has been described by Young (1978) and in a doctoral dissertation by Holm (1972). The development of written Navajo falls into four major periods: an early period, during which linguists, ethnologists, and missionaries developed independently their own orthographies for their own uses; a second period from 1936 to 1940, when the government orthography was developed; a period of 10 years or so after that, when the government made various efforts at literacy campaigns; and a more recent period, in the last 10 years or so, of indigenous literacy movements associated generally with bilingual education.

Both Protestant and Catholic missionaries were active in the development of Navajo orthographies. The first Roman Catholic mission was established by the Franciscans in 1898; they immediately developed their own phonetic alphabet and published an ethnological dictionary in 1910 and a vocabulary in 1912. Using a modified transcription, *A Manual of Navajo Grammar* was published by Haile in 1926. After 1930, the transcription was changed again and based on the one developed by the linguist Edward Sapir. Except for a few religious works, such as *A Navajo-English Catechism of Christian Doctrine for the Use of Navajo Children* (Haile 1937) and *Origin Legend of the Navajo Enemy Way* (Haile 1938), most of the material published by the Franciscans was not meant for use by Navajos but was of ethnographic or linguistic interest. Their work was jsutified to higher authorities in the church on the grounds that better knowledge of Navajo customs and language was necessary for effective missionary work. The fathers were quick to adopt writing systems which would enable them to reduce native speech more accurately and efficiently. In more recent times, the mission policy of the Franciscans has changed: fewer are diligent about learning the language and other Roman Catholic groups have become influential.

During the early twentieth century, various Protestant groups developed their own writing systems and published a variety of religious materials, the most important of which, *Dinê Bizãd: a Handbook for Beginners in Navajo,* was written by Fred Mitchell and published in 1910. The first portions of translations of the Bible appeared in that same year (American Bible Society 1910). The basic work in the translation of the Bible began under Fay Edgerton and continued with a group of Wycliffe translators including Faith Hill, Turner Blount, and Helen Blount. Of greatest importance to the standardization of the government orthography (which will be described below) was the fact that the Wycliffe translators and, under their influence, the other Protestant missionaries accepted it and used it in their Bible translation and religious work. Edgerton worked with several native speakers, mainly Geronimo Martin and Mary Lowe, and later with Roger Deal, who taught himself and several others at the Fort Defiance Tuberculosis Sanitarium to read Navajo using the Young and Morgan dictionary (Wallis 1968). Protestant missionaries also made an effort to teach literacy and conducted courses or visited hogans and missions to teach monolingual Navajos to read and write in their own language. Literacy charts, primers, and readers with selections and stories from the Bible were published.

The early anthropologists working with Navajo tended to develop their own writing systems. In the late 1920s, Edward Sapir collected a body of Navajo texts which were later edited by Hoijer and published in 1942. Sapir's orthography was the first to mark tone and has influenced all later systems. Gladys Reichard, a student of Boas, also developed her own individual system for transcribing Navajo and continued to use it in her various books and articles even after the development of the Young and Morgan orthography. She argued that her orthography, which was based on an early version developed by Sapir but not used by him in his own work, was superior because it had been widely used, because it worked well, and because it included items that would be useful in recording historical change. Generally, however, anthropologists and linguists since 1940 have used the Young and Morgan orthography. One notable modification was made by Werner and Begishe for use with a computer.

The story on the development of the government orthography has been described by Young (1978). In the 1930s, under the leadership of Williard Beatty, the Bureau of Indian Affairs decided to teach Navajo children and adults to read and write in both English and Navajo. None of the existing orthographies appeared suitable, so John Harrington was asked to develop a practical alphabet. In 1937, he teamed up with a young graduate student, Robert W. Young, and a Navajo, William Morgan, and, working together, the three of them developed the new orthographic system. A number of primers were published in it. During the early 1940s, Young, Morgan, and others worked on the Navajo literacy staff of the Bureau of Indian Affairs and published primers, teaching materials, a sketch of Navajo grammar, and a bilingual dictionary. In 1943, a monthly Navajo newspaper was started.

For the next decade or so, Navajo publishing flourished. The 1868 Treaty was published bilingually; historical narratives were collected, transcribed, and published first in the Navajo newspaper and later as the *Navajo Historical Series*. Grazing and voting regulations, Congressional bills and acts, and other documents were translated into Navajo and printed. A first supplement to the dictionary was published (Young and Morgan 1951), followed in 1958 by a second, written by William Morgan and Leon Wall. Publication of the newspaper ceased in 1957. During the period between 1940 and 1958, a good deal of material had been published in Navajo and a few thousand people had learned to read the language. However, the movement slowly petered out, perhaps mainly because it remained something imposed from the outside, serving the purposes either of missionaries or of the government.

The newest movement toward Navajo literacy is associated with the recurring interest in bilingual education. Almost all of the new material is produced in association with bilingual programs, either at schools like Rough Rock, Rock Point, Ramah, or Sanostee, or in centers like the Navajo Reading Study, the Native American Materials Development Center, or the bilingual section of the Tribal Division of Education that support these bilingual programs. In 1969 and again in 1976, conferences were held to discuss orthography, and minor modifications in the Young and Morgan orthography were recommended.

In the development of written orthography, the most important two steps

were the development of the Young and Morgan orthography and its acceptance by the Protestant missionaries. Those concerned with Navajo literacy
have therefore been spared the difficult choices faced by many groups that
continue to have competing orthographies even when their literacy movement
is hardly established.

THE DEVELOPMENT OF MODERN TERMINOLOGY

In this section, we will sketch the history of formal conscious attempts to
develop new words in Navajo to handle the many new concepts and objects
introduced through contact with modern life. It is hard at this point to estimate what proportion of new words developed in such formal conscious
attempts, compared to the proportion that developed informally and later
came to be accepted widely enough to be considered as a part of the Navajo
language: this could well form the basis of a study that might look at terms
added to the second edition of the Navajo dictionary (Young and Morgan
1980). The general picture of formal planning efforts reflects closely the
pattern of the development of written Navajo, for, with one significant exception, many of those involved in developing written material in Navajo also
very soon became involved in problems of lexical elaboration. We will describe in order the work of the mssionaries, the work of Young and Morgan
and of other people involved with the government Navajo literacy work, the
activities related to the schools, and, finally, some of the activities of Navajo
linguists. Most of these activities are concerned with written Navajo; the
significant exception is the work of interpreters, and we will describe both
the work of a number of interpreter schools in the mid-1930s and the continuing work of the interpreter of the Tribal Council.

We can find no records of the work of the early missionaries, most of
whom did not themselves speak Navajo but worked through interpreters,
young Navajos previously converted who had learned English at mission
schools. We assume that many of these were involved in developing terminology, at least in the religious domain. The Franciscan fathers working out of
St. Michaels are reported to have developed vocabulary for conveying Roman
Catholic religious concepts in church doctrine. According to a report in the
newspaper in 1947, the fathers met with various respected Navajo leaders
and medicine men and came up with translations like *Diyin Ayói' At'éii* for
'God'. The principal work in developing vocabulary in the religious area was,
however, the work of the Protestant missionaries in connection with the
translation of the Bible.

Two important conferences for interpreters took place in 1934 and
1935. In 1934, under the auspices of the Bureau of Indian Affairs, Gladys

Reichard held two workshops for 13 interpreters at Ganado. There was discussion of orthography and the students printed a small newspaper and two articles on health. Reichard herself was involved at the time in her studies of Navajo religion. She felt it extremely important to have some interpretation of the language, and this school gave her ready access to informants from different parts of the Reservation. Teaching them to read and write made them more effective informants in tasks such as deriving paradigms and etymologies. The Bureau hoped that this group of trained Navajos would eventually be able to carry out adult education in their own communities, where the BIA was at that time planning to open community day schools. Reichard herself gives some account of the workshop in a fictional book, *Dezba*. It is hard to be sure how successful the instruction in literacy was. At least two of the 13 interpreters appear to have gone on to college; one worked in a day school; some worked in the soil erosion control division of the Department of Agriculture as interpreters for implementing a soil rehabilitation plan; another was a judge; and another was an interpreter for the BIA. Some of the students felt that making up and writing down translations for words like 'germ', 'antiseptic', 'trachoma', and 'tuberculosis' would enable them to introduce new concepts, to use the words more uniformly, and to be more effective interpreters. However, other than the two health articles, it is not clear whether there was much discussion of the technical vocabulary needed for fields such as education, soil conservation, law, and health, or whether the terms arrived at were recorded.

The following year, between January 28 and February 28, 1935, an interpreters' institute was conducted at Fort Wingate under the direction of Berard Haile and Albert ('Chick') Sandoval. The purpose of the institute was twofold: to prepare a list of Navajo phrases to be learned by Anglos working with Navajos, and to establish terminology in various technical areas for use by the Navajo interpreters. The areas to be covered included medicine, Parliamentary procedure, modern transportation and communication systems, federal and chapter governments, legal proceedings, and agriculture. Kruis (1975) quotes Robert Young as saying that most of the terms were descriptive translations and were often lengthy and even ungrammatical. Perhaps this evaluation is a little harsh. Many of the terms are still used today. A few have been shortened over time; for instance, the term coined for radio, *nítch'i dahalni'ígíí*, has now been shortened to *nítch'i halné'e*, and the word for telephone, *béésh halne'é*, has become *béésh bee hane'é*. There appears to have been willingness not only to coin new words but to continue to use a borrowed term: the lists include such words as *stéed* [state], *kóngres* [congress], *seneters* [senators], *íínlzhin* [Indian], *kálij* [college], *yuniwérsidii* [university], and *hái skul* [high school]. Most of these terms, which are listed in an unpublished manuscript by Berard Haile held by the University of

Arizona Special Collections Library, have since been replaced by coined terms, such as *bitsi' yishtlizhii* [Indian], *adeii hooghan* [senate], and *adeii dóó ayaii hooghan* [Congress].

The area in which the greatest changes have taken place from the words originally developed is in terms dealing with chapter government. The term suggested for presiding official was *aláájí' bohólníihi* ['the chief boss who decides'] and for a temporary chairman was *ádahsidahi* ['he who sits for someone else']. Today, the first term is not used for either the chairman of the Tribe nor for the president of the chapter organization; rather, the second term is used for both: a chairman sits for the Tribal Council and a chapter president sits for the community. In 1935, tribal government had not yet become a well-organized self-governing body. The farm-chapter concept was introduced by John Hunter in 1927. These chapters provided places where community people could gather to settle disputes, discuss local problems, talk to government officials. However, chapter organization was not integrated into tribal government until the 1950s.

Under the auspices of the Bureau of Indian Affairs, two Navajo medical dictionaries were developed (Bitanny 1941; Bureau of Indian Affairs 1956). Both were intended to list and standardize common medical terms used in interpreting. The first medical dictionary was developed at the Medical Interpreters School held in July, 1940, at Fort Defiance. Adolph Bitanny, who edited the dictionary, writes about the school:

Students were unanimous in their expression of their desire to have an established "clearing house", a bilingual rendezvous as it were, for fostering a common cultural meeting ground. Students became almost over-enthusiastic in having cold medical terms reduced into their language through analysis from English (mostly Latin) into Navajo; the forum took its course automatically along what might be called a popular Navajo democratic discussion. (Bitanny 1941)

Young and Morgan included the terms developed at these conferences and listed in the *Medical Dictionary* edited by Bitanny (1941) in their 1943 and 1951 dictionaries. All three dictionaries, for example, translate 'pneumonia' as *ajéi yilzolii biih yilk'aaz* [literally, 'the chilling of the lung'] rather than the more common term used today, *dikos nitsaaígíí* ['the big cough']. The usefulness of some of the coined terms given in these dictionaries is questionable, for a term like *łóód na'agházhígíí* ['the kind of sore that grows around'] for ulcers presupposes some knowledge of Western medicine.

When he began work on the Navajo medical atlas, Werner selected 110 medical terms from the various dictionaries and sent them to a small group of native speakers for translation, identification, and validation. Forty-seven of the terms were accepted, 28 were rejected, and there was disagreement over the remainder. Young discusses the problems of these early attempts at developing new words:

The invention of terms to be applied to alien concepts is productive only if full understanding of the concept accompanies dissemination of the term. The medical terminology created in the 1930s in the course of the interpreter schools was not very useful because many of them related to concepts that were matters of concern to the medical professional primarily — not to lay-men and not even the interpreters who were trained in medical science. (Kruis 1975: 50)

It appears, however, that many of the other terms were in fact useful and likely to be included in Haile (1950) and in later dictionaries.

The Public Health Service continues to conduct programs to train inter-preters. There is no use of written Navajo in the training, and we are not sure whether any use is made of the extensive atlas of Navajo medical terminology developed by Werner, Begishe, and others.

As has been mentioned already, most of the business of the Navajo Tribal Council has been conducted in Navajo. Interpreters therefore have been needed to make it possible for Bureau of Indian Affairs and other non-Navajo-speaking officials to communicate with the Council. Before the 1930s, the Tribal Council had little importance, for Navajos dealt directly with govern-ment officials, and community groups settled problems with the BIA locally. The change came when the BIA used the Council to implement the stock-reduction program and it was realized that Council decisions could have serious effects on daily life. The Council itself came to see that it was necessary for it to recognize and consult the people affected by its actions. In the mid-1930s, then, a movement developed to make sure that the Council would be representative. In 1938, the Tribal Council was enlarged and reform-ed, its membership elected by a more democratic procedure. Since then, most major decisions affecting the Reservation have been discussed by the Council, which has slowly developed more and more power as the federal government has come to pay increasing attention to community rights. The Tribal Council interpreters have had a key role in creating terms to explain and describe the various concepts presented by BIA officials and other specialists who appear before the Council. According to Young (personal communication), the Council has always insisted that interpreters not use borrowed terms in their translations, so that interpreters have been regularly involved in coinage of new words. By the time an issue has been debated on the floor of the Council, the councilmen at least have probably got quite used to the word. When they return to the local level to report on the new policies, we assume that they explain and make use of the new terms. It would be interesting to study the effectiveness of this method of developing new terminology and to see how effective various interpreters and various council-men have been in the process. (An interesting comparison might be made with a similar process in Tonga, where decisions of the central government are communicated at the village level in regular weekly meetings).

During the period that Young, Morgan, and others were employed by the BIA as Navajo linguists, they were necessarily involved in a good number of projects developing terminology. In the 1940s, Young and Morgan were call-ed on to develop bilingual Navajo-English legal forms to be used in court proceedings such as divorce, civil complaint, subpoena, notice of civil action, and judgment orders. Sometimes, words on the Navajo forms like 'complain-ant', 'judge', 'clerk', and 'officer' appear in English even though they appear in Navajo in other parts of the text. It was probably assumed by the Bureau officials that using Navajo in these written court forms would make the Navajo court system more accessible to Navajos. None of the Navajo judges have law degrees; these forms written in Navajo might well have made it easier for them to conduct legal proceedings, if only they were literate in Navajo. However, as few of the judges, recorders, or court clerks were in fact literate in Navajo, records continued to be kept in English and the forms were not used.

Probably the major activity in terminology development that Young and Morgan were involved in was related to the newspaper, *Ádahooníłigíí*, publish-ed monthly from 1943 until 1947 completely in Navajo and then from 1947 until 1957 bilingually or with an English summary. One of the functions of the newspaper in the first period was to explain the War to the Navajo people and to provide a link with home for the 3,000 Navajos in the armed services and the 10,000 or so who had left the reservation for work in war-related industry. Two interesting books published by Young and Morgan in the early 1940s were an abridged version of *Robinson Crusoe* translated by Alice Willets (Young and Morgan 1944) and a translation of a book called *War With the Axis – Defending our Freedom* (Young and Morgan 1943a).

Some of the principal recent activities in the development of new termino-logy have been associated with the four community schools: Rough Rock Demonstration School, Rock Point Community School, Ramah School, and Borrego Pass School. Since 1968, each of these schools has been involved in developing bilingual programs, and as this has happened, they have faced up to the need of developing new terms for such items as classroom furniture (desks, blackboard, chalk) and for teaching mathematics and science. In con-nection with one of these programs, Martha Austin prepared in 1972 a Nava-jo-English thesaurus organized into semantic headings like 'school' or 'office supplies' or 'time according to the clock'. Under the sponsorship of the Navajo Reading Study and the Sanostee Teacher Training Project, a brief attempt was made by Kruis to encourage contact between the various schools, but generally they have worked quite independently. Since the establishment of the Native American Materials Development Center, funded by the Office of Education and administered by the Ramah Navajo School Board, there has been some formal attempt to control the development terminology. The Center has been working since 1976 on the development of a bilingual-bicultural curriculum. A file of new terminology is being kept. Most of the entries so far deal with first-grade science and the kindergarten curriculum; Neundorf (personal communication) reports that very few new words have been coined, many have been taken from available words, and others are at the moment still descriptive translations which will probably undergo natural modification or change if they are used to any extent. Agreement on terms is arrived at through informal discussions among the staff. The materials developed include a glossary of terms which may be new to either teacher or child. Some attention is given in training sessions to terminology, and teachers are encouraged to make recommendations about changes.

Some significant coining of new terms in the domain of linguistics took place at the summer workshops organized by DBA (the Navajo education association) during the summers of 1973 and 1975. Inspired in large measure by the work of Kenneth Hale, students in the workshops wrote papers on linguistic topics not just in English but also in Navajo; Paul Platero (1972) published an introduction to Navajo syntax for Navajo speakers in Navajo and edited (1973) 19 papers on Navajo phonology syntax and semantics, which include four papers written in Navajo. The paper by Becenti and Chee (Platero 1973) contains a number of newly coined Navajo terms for discussing phonology. In early work such as the unpublished manuscript by Hale and Honie (n.d.), linguistic terms were translated descriptively and explained (e.g. *hadaa' alch'į' át'éego* for 'bilabial'); Bicenti and Chee, however, use radically reduced forms such as *daa'ii* [bilabial], *za'áán* [vowel], *zatł'ah* [consonant]. In coining these words, Becneti and Chee appear to have tried shortcuts with what has in the past been a historical process. Usually, coined terms are descriptive translations, with reduction taking place over time. These terms were coined with the historical rules for reduction taken into account.

In summarizing some of the problems of her attempt to monitor the lexical elaboration going on in 1971-1972, Kruis points out that one of the basic problems was the lack of commitment teachers evidenced to the modernization process itself: 'More important, if they doubted the validity of bilingual education or did not understand much of the rationale behind it, the rationale for modernizing their language for classroom use seemed even less well founded'. Without some clarification of the official position of Navajo, without some clear commitment to universal literacy in Navajo, and without some clear understanding that it is necessary to use Navajo for dealing with fields such as chemistry, physics, and linguistics, all the various terminological development attempts have lacked either official backing or a strong sense of local relevance. The easy acceptance of the kind of diglossia referred to earlier between spoken Navajo and written English seems to have led to an equally easy acceptance of functional and domain differentiation between the two languages; terminology development then becomes important only in those areas where new concepts are clearly integrated. The story with which we opened this paper is an excellent illustration of this principle; objects easily remain alien, but people, even telephone operators working with alien objects, need to be integrated into the language.

PROGRESS TOWARD STANDARD NAVAJO

There have so far been no conclusive studies of Navajo dialectology, and while there is a general assumption of lexical and phonological variation in different parts of the reservation, it appears to be quite difficult to establish. There are, however, a number of well-known shibboleths, such as the word for 'cat' or for 'snow'. There are sufficient cases to create some problems for those developing school books, but not enough to make standardization an urgent need. In looking at formal processes of standardization in Navajo, it seems appropriate to divide our study into three periods: the period before the work of Young and Morgan in fixing the orthography and publishing the dictionary, the work of Young and Morgan and its effect, and the more recent considerations associated with school programs.

We have already described the work of the Catholic and Protestant missionaries in developing two separate orthographies. The Franciscan fathers' ethnologic dictionary, published in 1910, is still used to verify translations, but its orthography has had little effect: their *Catechism* and their *Selection of Holy Gospels for Sundays and Holy Days,* published in 1937 and 1938, used, of course, their current orthography. The Protestant orthography, used in the American Bible Society publication, *God Bi-zā̦d,* included a number of extracts from the New and Old Testaments. The other attempts at standardization have been referred to above and were connected with the schools for interpreters conducted in 1934 and 1935. The Reichard literacy workshops in 1934 were attempts to establish standard use of terminology, as was the 1935 Interpreters' Institute conducted by Berard Haile and Albert Sandoval.

The central work on standardization was the work of Young and Morgan in developing the standard practical orthography and in their publications, including, of course, the three dictionaries referred to earlier. The American Bible Society published in 1948 a trial volume in the new orthography (the

Gospel of St. John); the acceptance of this volume persuaded them to use the new orthography in the complete Bible translation. The 1943 and 1951 dictionaries remain key works and continue to be widely consulted by all concerned with arriving at a correct spelling or correct word.

In recent times, in connection with the school-related literacy developments, there have been two conferences to consider orthography. The first was sponsored by the Center for Applied Linguistics at the request of the Bureau of Indian Affairs in May, 1969 (Ohannessian 1969). The BIA was at the time interested in establishing bilingual kindergartens. An earlier planning conference had recommended a meeting on orthography to make sure that there was no problem with developing competing orthographies. The conference, which was attended by a number of linguists and educators, agreed to accept the Young and Morgan alphabet with just a few of the modifications which had been introduced earlier as a concession to Protestant missionaries (such as eliminating initial glottal stops, writing 'w' for 'gh' before 'o', writing 'y' for 'gh' before '?' and 'e'). Most people writing Navajo today follow the recommendations of the conference. Those who rely heavily on the Young and Morgan dictionary for spelling, including most who are newly literate, still tend to write 'gho' rather than 'wo'. Very few people have followed the Conference's recommendation to use French angular quotation marks instead of English quotation marks.

A second conference was called by the Native American Materials Development Center in 1976. As the Center was planning to have individuals write materials on a contract basis, they needed some guidelines on spelling and stylistic conventions. The conference was attended by 150 people, mainly Navajos. The elimination of diacritics and modification of some of the symbols were discussed, but the issues became so complicated that it was decided to deal with less-complex issues such as changing '*tł*' to 'tl' and '*tł*' to 'tl'' since the '*ł*' was redundant when it appeared with 't'.[1] The discussions became more and more heated and emotional. The language of the confernece switched from English to Navajo, and one woman kept on shouting '*dine bizaad doo lahgo anidadoohdliil da*' ['you will not change the Navajo language'].[2] Even though Wayne Holm in his dissertation (1972) had demonstrated the possibility of simplifying the orthography, it appears that those people who were literate in Navajo had become enamored of the '*ł*' and the diacritics. These were the very elements that seemed especially Navajo. Discussions on word boundaries were calmer and some tentative suggestions were made.

As a result, the Native American Materials Development Center told its writers in an internal style sheet:

The alphabetic writing system that you should use is the one recommended by the Conference on Navajo Orthography held by the Center for Applied Linguistics in 1969 along with the adaptations and additions decided upon at the Second Navajo Orthography Conference in 1976.

In practice, it is not clear that either the style sheet or the recommendations are being followed. William Morgan, who works at the Center, makes final decisions on written Navajo, and he does not always agree with what is on the style sheet.

As mentioned earlier, the revised edition of the Young and Morgan dictionary is virtually ready for publication. It follows essentially the same orthography as the early edition, with the exception that it drops the initial glottal stop.

The second orthography conference proposed the establishment of a Navajo Language Academy. There is a similar proposal in the draft resolution referred to earlier being prepared for the Tribal Council. Should these intiatives be sucessful, there will presumably be a good deal more to report on standardization in the next decade.

MODERN NAVAJO

We have not attempted so far in this paper to draw any lessons for those concerned with understanding the process of modernization and standardization of a vernacular. Essentially, what we seem to have been describing are limited attempts to control the process by which a vernacular language comes into contact with a modern literate technological society. Most of these conscious attempts at what we suppose is called language planning have, until quite recently, come from outside: they have been as alien and as non-Navajo as the concepts and objects they have been meant to deal with. Only in the last few years have there developed some indigenous support for making it possible for Navajo to continue to function in a modern world: the supporters of this notion are few and are working in opposition to what appears to be a widespread acceptance of the notion that modernization necessarily involves Anglicization. Even leading Navajo educators remain unconvinced of the potential of bilingual education: in a situation where even the notion of transitional bilingual education is looked on askance, the formal processes of language modernization that imply maintenance of the language are difficult to justify. We believe, however, that there is evidence from some of the processes we have so far described that Navajo itself is capable, like its speakers, of modernization without giving up its basic spirit.

Feelings of ambivalence about modernizing Navajo can be found among even the staunchest proponents of bilingual education and among those who realize the value of modernizing the language to serve new ends. Acknowledging that new terms have to be developed is a recognition that a part of your most precious possession, your language, is inadequate. The people consciously involved in language planning are also involved, consciously or unconsciously, in the push toward other kinds of social change. Almost all the language-planning activities we have been describing have been associated with a desire to replace what is essentially Navajo with something else. The missionaries wanted to replace traditional Navajo ceremonial practices with Christianity. Even the period of the 1930s, when government policy under Collier was nominally directed toward preservation of Indian culture and language and toward establishment of community control, brought wide, sweeping changes in an opposite direction. Stock reduction and restriction or denial of grazing rights laid the foundation for reliance on outside sources of income and affected especially younger Navajos. Instead of dealing directly with established community chapter organizations, the BIA set up a centralized Tribal Council. Instead of letting local extended-family or clan groups settle disputes, the BIA set up a system of courts to handle litigation. In place of their traditional reliance on medicine men, Navajos were urged to use hospitals and white doctors. All these agents of change used the Navajo language to give their activities some degree of authenticity.

The Navajos who are today involved in language-planning activities are for the most part younger, educated in white schools, and so acculturated and perhaps even marginal to Navajo society. Thus, they are themselves not well equipped to authenticate new developments in language. Few younger Navajos claim to know their language as well as their elders do. When one is working to expand the repertoire of the language as a whole, it is easy to forget that in many domains the language is already well developed. A crucial question being faced by those developing bilingual programs, and working with modern Navajo, is not so much 'How do we modernize Navajo in order to handle the concepts of white education?' but 'How do we cultivate and pass down to our children the rich legacy of the Navajo language and culture?'

NOTES

1. This convention was one used by Werner and Begishe (n.d.) in their orthography for computer use. It was also a convention that Rough Rock had followed in its printed materials.
2. According to one report, she didn't want '*gaad bizaad*' changed; which may be translated 'God's word' and is a pun for the Gospel or God's language.
3. For fuller details of works published in Navajo, see James M. Kari, *A Navajo Reading Bibliography*, Albuquerque, University of New Mexico General Library, 1974.

REFERENCES[3]

American Bible Society (1910), *Moses bi natltsos alsedihigi hidesiz hilyehigi indo yistainilli ba hani. Mark naltsosye Yiki-iscinigi Tohatcidi enisoti dine bizadkyehgo ayila.* New York.

_____(1976), *Diyin God Bizaad.* New York.

Bitanny, Adolph (1941), *Medical Dictionary, English to Navajo.* Window Rock, Ariz., Medical Division, Navajo Service.

Bureau of Indian Affairs (1935), 'The Navajo language and the School for Interpreters', *Indians at Work* 2(11): 28.

_____(1956), *Glossary of Common Medical Terms. English-Navajo.* Window Rock, Ariz.

Dozier, Edward P. (1967), 'Linguistic acculturation studies in the Southwest', in *Studies in Southwestern Ethnolinguistics*, ed. by Dell H. Hymes and William E. Bittle. The Hague, Mouton.

Franciscan Fathers (1910), *An Ethnologic Dictionary of the Navaho Language.* St. Michaels, Ariz.

_____(1912), *A Vocabulary of the Navajo Language*, two volumes. St. Michaels, Ariz.

Haile, Fr. Berard (1926), *A Manual of Navaho Grammar.* St. Michaels, Ariz.

_____(1937), *A Navajo-English Catechism of Christian Doctrine for the Use of Navaho Children.* St. Michaels, Ariz.

_____(1938), *Origin Legend of the Navaho Enemy Way.* New Haven, Yale University Press.

_____(1950), *A Stem Vocabulary of the Navajo Language*, two volumes. St. Michaels, Ariz.

Hale, Kenneth (n.d.), 'Navajo linguistics, Parts I-IV'. Unpublished manuscript, Massachusetts Institute of Technology.

_____, and Lorraine Honie (n.d.), 'An introduction to the sound systems of Navajo'. Unpublished manuscript, Massachusetts Institute of Technology.

Harrington, John (1945), 'Six common Navajo nouns accounted for', *Journal of the Washington Academy of Sciences* 35(12): 373.

Holm, Agnes, Wayne Holm, and Bernard Spolsky (1973), 'English loan words in the speech of young Navajo children', in *Bilingualism in the Southwest*, ed. by Paul R. Turner. Tucson, University of Arizona Press.

Holm, Wayne (1972), 'Some aspects of Navajo orthography'. Unpublished dissertation, University of New Mexico.

Irvine, Patricia, and Bernard Spolsky (1980), 'Sociolinguistic aspects of the acceptance of literacy in the vernacular'. *Proceedings of the 1978 SWALLOW Meeting.*

Kruis, Sally (1975), 'Language planning and Navajo education'. Unpublished Masters thesis, University of New Mexico.

Liebler, H. Baxter (1948), Unpublished 'Christian concepts and Navaho words', *Utah Humanities Review* 2(2): 169-174.

Mitchell, Fred (1910), *Dine Bizad: A Handbook for Beginners in Navajo.* Los Angeles, Commercial Printing House.

Ohannessian, Sirarpi (1969), *Conference on Navajo Orthography.* Washington, D.C. Center for Applied Linguistics.

Platero, Paul (1972), 'An introduction to Navajo syntax for Navajo speakers' (written in Navajo). Navajo Linguistics Workshop.

_____, editor (1973), *Papers on Navajo Linguistics.* Navajo Linguistics Workshop.

Reichard, Gladys (1950), *Navaho Religion.* Pantheon Books.

_____ (1951), *Navaho Grammar.* New York, Augustin.

Sapir, Edward (1921), *Language.* New York, Harcourt Brace.

Spolsky, Bernard (1970), 'Navajo language maintenance: six-year-olds in 1969', *Language Sciences* 13: 19-24.

_____ (1974), 'Speech communities and schools', *TESOL Quarterly* 8(1): 17-26.

_____ (1975), 'Prospects for the survival of the Navajo language', in *Linguistics and Anthropology, In Honor of C.F. Voegelin,* ed. by M. Dale Kinkade, Kenneth L. Hale, and Oswald Werner. Lisse, Peter de Ridder.

Wall, Leon, and William Morgan (1958), *Navaho-English Dictionary.* Bureau of Indian Affairs.

Wallis, Ethel Emily (1968), *God Speaks Navajo.* New York, Harper & Row.

Werner, Oswald, and Kenneth Begishe (n.d.), 'Anatomical atlas of the Navajo'. Unpublished manuscript, Northwestern University.

Young, Robert W. (1978), 'Written Navajo: a brief history', in *Advances in the Development of Writing Systems,* ed. by Joshua A. Fishman. The Hauge, Mouton.

Young, Robert W., and William Morgan (1943a), *Dii k'ad Anaa'igii Baa Hane'.* Phoenix, Ariz.

_____ (1943b), *The Navaho Language.* Phoenix, Ariz., U.S. Indian Service.

_____ (1944), *The ABC of Navaho.* Phoenix, Ariz., Education Division, U.S. Indian Service. (Revised in 1946 to include an abridged version of Robinson Crusoe and a Navaho-English glossary).

_____ (1949), *The Navaho Historical Series,* volume one. Phoenix, Ariz.

_____ (1951), *A Vocabulary of Spoken Navaho.* Phoenix, Ariz., U.S. Indian Service.

_____ (1952a), *The Navajo Historical Series,* volume two. Phoenix, Ariz.

_____ (1952b), *The Navaho Historical Series,* volume three. Phoenix, Ariz.

_____ (1980), *A Sketch of Navajo Grammar and a Dictionary of Colloquial Navajo.* Albuquerque, University of New Mexico Press.

GARY D. KELLER

What Can Language Planners Learn from the Hispanic Experience with Corpus Planning in the United States?

Spanish in the United States has now acquired an official status in certain areas of public life, particularly suffrage and education. In its twentieth-century avatar, as contrasted to Spanish's nineteenth-century official status in legal documents such as the Treaty of Guadalupe Hidalgo, which accorded Spanish-speaking citizens the 'rights and privileges of citizenship', but which was rarely respected, the official status of Spanish is a very recent phenomenon, traceable back to the Voting Rights Act of 1965 and the Bilingual Education Act of 1968. Moreover, it is important to note that the official status that Spanish does enjoy is not specific to the Spanish language, nor does it even relate to a language policy in the first instance. In fact, the United States at present does not have a comprehensive, unified, and explicit policy with respect to language. Nothing in the United States Constitution, its Code of Laws, or its Statutes at Large appears to set such a policy. Instead, the laws contain numerous discrete, specific provisions concerning language. Taken all together, these separate references yield a less than fully coherent picture of 'language policy in the United States'.

However, there exists throughout the laws and practices of this nation a recognizable, although tacit, assumption that English is and should be the official and commonly used language of the United States. One of the few explicit references that can be found with respect to a language policy is instructive: in a court of appeals case (*Fronters* vs. *Sindell*, 522 F.2d 1215), the court states that 'statutes have been enacted which provide exceptions to our nation's policy in favor of the English language. . . but these exceptions do not detract from the policy or deny the interests the various levels of government have in dealing with the citizenry in a common language'. I need to reiterate that the court is referring only to a 'policy' of assumptions here rather than to any statutory provision, yet it seems to me that this assumption ranges wide and deep not only in the judiciary but in the American body politic in general.

What, then, is the official status that Spanish enjoys in the United States based upon? Essentially on a number of 'exceptions', as the appeals court put it, to the assumption of an English language policy, 'exceptions' determined by the overarching requirements of the civil rights of individuals or groups. In short, the official status of Spanish is based on the civil rights of Spanish-speaking persons when these rights have been found to be more compelling or significant than the interests of government or of society in dealing with the citizenry in a common language. Moreover, I expand the point that I alluded to earlier: Spanish per se enjoys no particular or unique status; there is here simply a question of demographics, or minority-group statistics. In theory at least, all other-than-English-language speakers enjoy the same rights; Spanish stands out because there are so many Spanish speakers. Other languages, moreover, have enjoyed and will continue to enjoy a similar status, albeit more moderate in scope, as they are able to pass demographic muster. That language rights are clearly tied to and the result of civil rights law is clear when we examine the fact that there is no U.S. law except for the Guam Bill of Rights which outlaws discrimination based on language. In view of Congressional policy on suffrage and education, there might be good reason to enact a general law that makes discrimination based on language unlawful. However, it might be argued that existing laws against discrimination based on race and/or national origin actually cover language discrimination as well. The federal Civil Rights Commission appears to feel that this is the case; so does the Equal Employment Opportunity Commission, which monitors discrimination in state and local government and in the private sector. Finally, we should realize that both the Voting Rights Act of 1965 and the Bilingual Education Act of 1968 rose out of civil rights issues, as do all of the major cases involved in bilingual education, such as *Lau* vs. *Nichols* in 1974 or *Keyes* vs. *School District No. 1, Denver, Colorado,* in 1975.

It is critical to understand this fact, that Spanish in the United States enjoys a sort of quasi or indirect status, one that is based on the civil rights of Spansih speakers, in contrast, say, to the situation of countries such as Canada, or Switzerland or Belgium in Europe, or Paraguay or Peru in Latin America, where official, constitutional policies have been promulgated with respect to multilingualism. This peculiar status of Spanish in the United States explains much of the uncertainty, conflict, and flux with respect to both the status planning and the corpus planning of United States Spanish. While some of the other countries I have mentioned certainly have their share of political conflict with respect to language planning and policy, the quality of *angst* involved in the planning of United States Spanish, I believe, is uniquely attributable to this lack of a status base.

Let us proceed to enumerate those areas in which Spanish, and often other languages as well, have established an official status:

1.   American citizens are permitted to vote in Spanish, if they are not fluent in English. (This right is guaranteed by the Voting Rights Act of 1965, as amended in 1975).

2.   Children residing in the continental United States (whether citizens or not) can be taught in Spanish, if they are not proficient in English. They are not required to be taught in Spanish (a simple special program of instruction that may include only ESL satisfies the law of the land), but Spanish-language instruction is encouraged, at least for a certain number of years, normally three. This possibility is the result of the amendments of 1968, 1975, and 1978 to the Elementary and Secondary Education Act of 1965, as well as to numerous state laws which have even stronger, mandatory bilingual-education requirements. In addition, classroom-oriented bilingual-education legislation has been extended to other education programs. Among these are the Equal Educational Opportunity Act of 1974; the Emergency School Aid Act of 1972, aimed primarily at ending minority-group segregation and discrimination; the basic education for adults programs; the National Reading Improvement Program of 1974; and the Vocational Education Act of 1963, as amended in 1976.

3.   Spanish has in certain localities been a required language in the broadcasting medium, as a result of the Federal Communications Commission (FCC) policy. The Commission has the authority to grant and suspend the licenses under which radio and television stations operate in the U.S. The law asks the FCC to promote the 'public interest' in the use of the media. The Commission has construed its responsibility to serve the interests and needs of specific communities as a basis for, at times, requiring broadcasting in languages other than English. This situation has arisen from court cases pursued by minority groups which have complained about the lack of broadcasts in languages other than English.

4.   There are numerous provisions in the various civil, criminal, and military courts of the land for the use of interpreters and translators, in Spanish and other languages as required. At present the House Judiciary Committee has before it several bills that consolidate these provisions. It is likely that in the near future Spanish will be officially required in the federal courtroom in the form of a translator or interpreter when called for by a specific case. In this regard, state law, as in New Mexico, is often stricter, requiring the actual conduct of court cases in Spanish.

These, then, are the four civil rights areas in which Spanish has attained a sort of official status: in the voting booth, in the classroom, on the radio waves, and in the courtroom. Not unexpectedly, the logic of Spanish has extended to other domains as well. In the pertinent geographic areas we will find Spanish movies and television shows, books and newspapers and periodicals, signs in subways, busses, and other transportation vehicles, and so on. In addition, some states have extended the logic of civil-rights-protected Spanish to other domains. For example, the California Dymally-Alatorre Bilingual Service Act of 1973 (amended in 1975) declares that every state agency (such as welfare, police, motor vehicles, and so on) must provide bilingual persons in public-contact positions or as interpreters. California also requires the use of languages such as Spanish by certain emergency telephone operators and employees of community colleges and local educational agencies.

Aside from the negative function of prohibiting discrimination, is there an official sanction for Spanish? More generally, are there in U.S. law positive provisions to encourage the learning, propagation, and maintenance of languages other than English in use among linguistic minorities in the United States? Let us discount the National Defense Education Act of 1958, Title VI, as fulfilling this provision. This act provides for the study of languages for national defense purposes; although funds were provided for the study of Spanish, it was only in relation to its existence in Latin America. Nevertheless, there are two laws which fulfill the provision I have cited above, albeit in a very limited fashion. The Ethnic Heritage Program subchapter of the Elementary and Secondary Education Act of 1965 (as amended in 1974) authorizes such activities as the development of curriculum materials relating to language and literature of ethnic groups connected with the American heritage. However, the allocation of funds for Ethnic Heritage has been severely limited and the activities carried out by it have focussed mostly upon teacher training. Finally, there is the American Folklife Preservation Act of 1975 which establishes in the Library of Congress an American Folklife Center to preserve and present American folklife. 'Folklife' is defined to include both language and literature, and part of the law states that 'the history of the U.S. effectively demonstrates that building a strong nation does not require the sacrifice of cultural differences'. Finally, I must mention the existence of an Academy of the Spanish Language in the United States, ostensibly modeled on academies in the other Latin American countries, which correspond with the *Real Academia de la Lengua* in Madrid. At this time the Academy is a self-appointed, self-annointed group of philologically oriented entrepreneurs who seem to be interested in naught but dressing up in tails and having themselves photographed in certain Spanish nightclubs in Manhattan accustomed to proferring clicking castanets and Spanish petticoats. A few years ago the first issue of the official bulletin of this organization appeared, in which the members published each other's mostly literary handiwork. Nothing has appeared since. Not much to give credence to here. But who pretends to foretell the future?

Fishman (1968) has pointed out that early studies of such aspects of corpus planning as codification and elaboration were wont to analyze the products of these efforts (the actual nomenclatures, dictionaries, stylistic guides, and so on), rather than the processes by which they were produced. This limitation is beginning to be surpassed by the work of such researchers as Garvin, Fellman, and Fishman himself, all of whom expose for us a picture of who the technical planners are, what they know, how they organize their work, what channels of communication (upward and laterally) they activate, their aspirations and aggravations, and so on. It seems to me imperative that those of us dealing with the corpus planning of U.S. Spanish give the broader picture, which Fishman has likened to structure-plus-content, rather than content alone. Among the reasons for this necessity is the weak status base upon which United States Spanish rises, the fact that authorized corpus planners of United States Spanish derive their authority from rather unique quarters, if they have any authority at all, and the more general fact that the truly sociolinguistic study of corpus planning must be no more socially in-nocent than is the study of language-status planning, since technical expertise alone never seems to be sufficient — there are always habits and attitudes and values and loyalties and preferences, not only in the target populations but among the planners themselves. Thus it is necessary, in establishing what language planners can learn from the Hispanic experience with corpus plan-ning, to attempt to answer such questions as how the corpus planners (if that's what we can call them in this case; actually 'handlers of the corpus' might be a better description) have actually worked, what they have re-cognized as their goals, how they have chosen between alternatives, and how they claim to have made the right choice. What we urgently need at this time is to analyze systematically what has been the process of Spanish corpus planning in each of the areas that I have described earlier as having attained some status in the United States: government, the mass media, the classroom, and the courtroom. Limitations of time and space do not permit this paper to cover all four domains. On the other hand, the remaining portion of this paper will address itself in some detail to what is clearly the overriding and most pondered issue: the corpus planning of Spanish as the language of instruction in the United States classroom.

The problem has been, which variety of Spanish to use in the classroom?

The anser has often been made in the form of one of two extremes. There are those who exalt the ethnic form of their locality and denigrate what the American Association of Teachers of Spanish and Portuguese (AATSP) has called 'world standard Spanish'. Conversely, there are those who exalt 'world standard Spanish', and denigrate the ethnic or folk form. The first group is often found in ethnic studies departments on the college campus, or in alter-native colleges, of which there are 15 or 20, mainly in the Southwest, and among the ethnic communities themselves, particularly among radical spokespersons for the Chicano or Boricua communities.

The second group has been well described by Rolf Kjolseth (1972). It includes the majority of Spanish teachers, both nonethnic and ethnic. Often the ethnic Spanish teacher fears the ethnic variety of the language as the stigma from which he or she has only recently escaped.

Of course, I am overgeneralizing this dichotomy. For example, the AATSP — the professional group of most importance in the United States — has made very sensible statements with respect to the potential domains of ethnic varieties of Spanish versus world standard Spanish. This is so because the AATSP has turned the question over to its professional linguists for public comment. However, the general membership of the AATSP tilts toward negative attitudes about United States varieties of Spanish. Let us examine the two extreme arguments, taking full cognizance in advance that there are other, more moderate, ways to do corpus planning.

First the exaltation of the vernacular. Joshua Fishman (1968) has made some cogent observations concerning the linguistic problems of developing nations and their relation to nationalism. These observations have been based on a substantial number of empirical investigations of sociolinguistic phenomena in Africa and Asia; nevertheless, they have relevance to the social movement being discussed here.

Fishman has shown that not all language differences that exist are noted. Language differences at the phonological, morphological, or syntactic levels that can be clearly distinguished by linguists may be consciously or unconsciously ignored by millions of native speakers. Moreover, those which are noted by native speakers may or may not be the basis for an ideologized position of divisiveness. The basic point is that divisiveness is an ideologized position and can magnify minor differences, or even manufacture differences, in languages. Similarly, unification is also an ideologized position which can minimize or even ignore seemingly major differences, whether these be in the realm of language, religion, culture, race, or other bases of interpersonal differentiation. Fishman sociolinguistically distinguishes between two forms of developing nations: those for whom the quest for nationism is paramount and those for whom the concern with nationalism is paramount. For those entities where nationalism is the major concern,

. . . that is, where populations are actively pursuing the sociocultural unification that befits those whose common nationality is manifest, the choice of a national language is not in question since it is usually already a prominently ideologized symbol. The major language problems of nationalism are language maintenance, reinforcement, and enrichment (including both codification and elaboration) in order to foster the nationalistic (the vertical or ethnically single) unity, priority, or superiority of the sociocultural aggregate. (1968: 43)

Conversely,

. . . among those for whom *nationism* is stochastically paramount *other* kinds of language problems come to the fore. The geographic boundaries are far in advance of sociocultural unity. Thus problems of horizontal integration, such as quick language choice and widespread literary language use, become crucial to the nation's functional existence per se, (1968: 43)

The social movements of Chicanos and Boricuas are analogous to the nationalistic goals of Asian and African peoples. Accordingly, among certain Chicano and Boricua radicals certain corpus policies are made with the goal of obtaining an official status for a local or regional language variety. In certain extreme-left sectors, United States minority movements take a form not unlike Fishman's concept of nationism except that, of course, the quest is not only linguistic but entails a geographic entity of one's own: witness the aspiration of some Chicanos to regain hegemony over Aztlán. Chicanos and Boricuas have attempted to validate culturally their tongues, their vernaculars; to convert them into the expressive instruments of their social identities and to have them generally accepted as such. This exaltation of the vernacular on the part of those Chicanos and Boricuas who radically embrace the notion of cultural pluralism is a powerful force and one that must be reckoned with by sociolinguists.

However, the notion of the vernacular may be quite different when entertained by a community spokesperson, the sociolinguist, or the general public. (Let us include most language teachers, both public-school and college, in this latter group). For example, Lozano (1974: 147) claims that 'the regional varieties of Spanish in Mexico and the [United States] Southwest which share virtually the same morpho-syntactic characteristics should be considered a binational macrodialect'. Lozano adduces solid linguistic reasons for subsuming Southwestern United States Spanish and Mexican Spanish, but in the sociopolitical arena his conclusions are nil. The Chicano is engated in combat not only with the 'Anglo establishment' but with the disapproving 'Mexican establishment', of which even such a distinguished Mexican linguist as Antonio Alatorre (1955) may be taken as a representative voice. Alatorre compares the Chicanos to the *mozárabes* of medieval Spain, intimating that the former, like the latter, have served to introduce many foreignisms into Spanish. He defines the Chicano (except that he uses the term *pocho*, which is pejorative in Mexico) as a Mexican who permits himself to be seduced by the American way of life and for whom Mexican ways are always contemptible and American ways unsurpassable. As for the language, it is the product of a border society 'that has created a type of dialect or creole in which elements of English and Spanish are fused' (1955: 11-15).

Naturally, the Chicano, when confronted with these sorts of stark expressions of prejudice on the part of Mexicans, is compelled to minimize systematically the Mexican element in the language and signle out systematically that which is autochthonous.

Let us look at the same phenomenon at the micro rather than the macro level. Troike (1968) points out that 'there are in fact several native dialects of Spanish spoken in Texas alone — even in a single city such as San Antonio or El Paso — and most of these are simple local varieties of the much larger regional dialect of North Mexican Spanish'. Troike goes on to observe the classroom implications of these differences, but once again the chances of implementing the fact of different subdialects in the Southwest into either a coherent corpus plan or a classroom pedagogy are obstructed by the over-riding ideological exigency that Chicano Spanish be one and the vehicle of Chicano self-identity. Thus Fishman's observation that divisiveness is an ideologized position must be recognized as a sociolinguistic fact, a fact that is more social than linguistic, but nevertheless a fundamental consideration in analyzing the development of in-group attitudes toward the vernacular. Moreover, these attitudes have had clear expression in the educational process. For example, Gaarder (1977) attests to the fact that many Chicano Studies programs actively denigrate what he calls 'world standard Spanish' and insist that for their purposes the only languages needed are English and 'barrio Spanish'.

Now let us turn to those who exalt the standard and denigrate the vernacu-lar. I shall be brief here because of the widespread familarity that linguists have with the types of arguments, pedagogically or politically, that are made in this regard. Kjolseth (1972) and also Steiner (1969: 212-213) have charac-terized this purist approach, which posits a single variety of language, or of culture for that matter, as 'correct', as one which involves 'deeducation': that is, the belief that the lower-class Chicano, Boricua, or Cuban-American child has to be deeducated before he or she can be reeducated. Kjolseth's graphic conclusion is strong but valid: these sorts of people liken themselves to priests of education busily civilizing the savages. In fact they are engaged in a type of self-arrogating educational colonialism.

In addition, I must note that there is in the United States a special, intense hostility directed toward non-English vernaculars which linguistically display the evidence of daily English-language contact. Specifically, I am referring to what in this country is popularly termed as 'Spanglish' — often used as a buzz word by 'vernacular denigrators' — analogous in its extreme negative connota-tions to terms such as 'barrio Spanish', '*caló*', '*pocho*', 'nuyorican', or 'Rican', which are often proferred as terms descriptive of a new, vibrant language emerging from the United States Hispanic ethnic communities by 'vernacular exalters'. Those who use the descriptive term 'Spanglish' for politico-pedago-gical purposes often take it to mean a pidgin, a hybrid, the illegitimate fruit of English-Spanish contact.

It is necessary, however, that we recongize the profoundly psychopolitical motivation behind the manifest antagonism to United States vernacular

Spanish. Alfonso Reyes, the Mexican thinker, once observed about his people, 'Pity us who are so removed from God and so near the United States'. It is especially painful for many Spanish-speaking persons to see the English language affect Spanish because of the obvious analogues with imperialistic exploitation. Yet, while we can understand some of the motivation as attributable to a feeling of anger and frustration directed toward what is seen as another instance of United States domination, what we cannot accept is the result: stigmatizing both United States vernacular Spanish and its legitimate speakers.

Between the two extremes there are those who chart a middle course. These tend to be sociolinguists and include such persons as Gumperz, Dillard, Kjolseth, G. Valdes, and Keller. For the sociolinguists the solution tends to be the fostering of bidialectalism. The world standard variety is to be added to the ethnic variety that the child already brings into the classroom.

This tug and pull with respect to differing language varieties as the medium of classroom instruction within bilingual education has had a profound effect on the actual creation of curriculum materials. In 1974 the National Institute of Education funded a project evaluating approximately 1,000 curriculum titles in Spanish bilingual education. I was the linguist for that project, the results of which were later published by the Educational Products Information Exchange Institute (popularly known as EPIE). The eight types of Spanish that we found to be in actual existence in 1974 in Spanish bilingual education programs were as follows:

1. Programs which use 'world standard Spanish'. The language is free of regionalisms. Some of the language may not be understood by United States Spanish speakers who use a regional or ethnic designation instead of the standard one (e.g. program uses *autobús* but not *camión*-[SW], nor *guagua* [NE].

2. Programs which use language specific to particular regions or social groups of the Hispanic world outside of the United States, such as Spain, Bolivia, or Chile. For example, these programs may use *micro* (Chile) or *autocar* (Spain), but not *autobús, camión,* or *guagua*.

3. Programs which use language characteristic of all the regions and ethnic varieties of United States Spanish. (e.g. program uses *guagua* and *camión* but not *autobús*).

4. Programs which use language characteristic of the eastern United States and the Caribbean (e.g. *guagua* but not *autobús* or *camión*).

5. Programs which use language characteristic of the western United States and Mexico (e.g. *camión* but not *guagua* or *autobús*).

6. Programs which use nonstandard non-Spanish (as in bad translations).

7. Programs which use both the regional or ethnic varieties of language and the 'world standard Spanish' variety (e.g. *camión* and *guagua* in addition to *autobús*).

8. Programs which use controlled 'world standard Spanish', using only language in the standard for which there are no alternate regionalisms or ethnic varieties (e.g. eliminates *camión, guagua,* and *autobús* from instructional materials).

Clearly there are types of Spanish now in use which are totally inappropriate with respect to United States bilinbual education. These include type 2 and, of course, type 6, which tends to be a bad translation of an English-language program. Yet even once we discard these two types, there surely remain too many corpuses. In addition, the viable corpuses that do exist are often found to overlap. They require the appropriate 'compartmentalization', to use a term that Fishman has advanced. Type 1, which is very common, in my mind is most compellingly used in more advanced Spanish-language courses, particularly in the content areas such as mathematics and the sciences. Types 4 and 5, for the relevant regions, recommend themselves for employment in transitional bidialectal education. When students enter the school system with a knowledge of only their ethnic or regional variety, it is logical to build upon their knowledge, at least for the first year or two, by teaching them what they don't know on the basis of what they are competent in. This is particularly true with respect to the pedagogy of beginning language arts, with its extensive use of sound-symbol and picture-symbol matching techniques, all of which are short-circuited when a child uses the ethnic term instead of the standard one, when the latter is expected by the pedagogy; for example, when the book expects the child to say *puerco* and the child says *chancho* instead. On the other hand, as a result of my participation in this massive evaluation, I hypothesized an eighth type, which at that time did not exist. Subsequently, a number of programs have been written in type 8, including one of my own. I believe they successfully deal with the miscues that crop up otherwise and are therefore able to teach decoding, encoding, word-attack and word-analysis skills in world standard Spanish without interference effects from the ethnic or regional variety. Finally, I find it hard to rationalize the use of either type 3 or type 7 programs. Under the guise of completeness or fairness, they offer mind-boggling numbers of synonyms for the same meaning. In this sort of program, to give one simple example, northeastern children are bombarded with southwestern Spanish in semantic domains such as the desert, agricultural communities, the mountains, the mines, which are simply irrelevant to them; the converse is equally true; to give an example, southwestern children learn the words *plátano, guineo, plátano dedo,* and other plants from the banana family, when for their language and culture only one term suffices. Unfortunately, this trend is being exacerbated. Attempting to be all things to all groups, publishers have tended to supplant pedagogical logic with synonymy or dialectal equivalence. Of course, from the publishers' point of view, it is wise to print a national edition, one that will sell everywhere. Perhaps the apotheosis of this trend can be found in the new Santillana program, *Aprendiendo en dos idiomas,* a slick, very expensive reading program which is marred, for me, irreparably by the fact that the reading lessons feature a teacher pointing out the lexical varieties for different meanings in different parts of the United States and abroad as well. I can't fathom to what positive purpose we should teach first and second graders eight synonyms for 'ballpoint pen' and ten for 'bus' when what we should really be engaged in is the expansion of their vocabulary to meanings that are totally unknown to them. To the extent that this synonymy proliferates in the classroom, we sacrifice language development.

Of course, the underlying problem, from the sociolinguistic point of view, is that presently there are too many Spanish corpuses being promoted in the classroom. On the other hand, while the classroom may have suffered for it, we have witnessed a remarkable surge of dictionaries, nomenclatures, and research studies into the characteristics of differing United States Spanishes on the basis of both regional and social dialects. There are as yet, of course, no grammars of United States Spanish. And in addition, the confusion and complexity that abound in the classroom have had a positive effect in teacher training and teacher certification. Virtually all colleges and universities that offer programs in bilinbual education require that prospective teachers take courses in sociolinguistics and be acquainted with the major analytic tools of that discipline, as well as the types of Spanish that exist in the Unites States. This situation is mirrored by state certification requirements for licensing as a bilingual-education teacher. At the very least, the massive, confusing babel that we are confronted with in the classroom has sensitized us to the sociolinguistic issues at the college level and in the state agencies.

One additional point should be highlighted before concluding this paper: the use of Spanish as the language of instruction outside of bilingual education, namely the variety of Spanish taught in the United States as a foreign language. A situation has developed whereby the bilingual-education and ethnic-power phenomena have profoundly influenced the instruction of Spanish as a foreign language. This should be highly instructive to a group of sociolinguists.

Prior to contemporary bilingual education, that is, prior to 1968, Spanish taught in the United States was very emphatically of the Castilian type; strongly suppressing standard Latin American Spanish, not to mention the varieties of United States Spanish. This is perfectly in accord with Fishman's 'Law of Anglo love of ethnic irrelavance', or the 'Disneyland preference for symbolic ethnicity', namely that the more locally irrelevant an ethnic language and culture is, the higher its social status, and the more viable it is locally, the lower its social status. As Fishman has put it, 'as long as these languages and cultures are truly foreign our schools are comfortable with them. But as soon as they are found in our own backyards, the schools deny them'. However, what is amazing is the total turnaround since 1968, or perhaps a bit earlier. Modesty aside, I must claim some credit in this task with my article (Keller 1974) on the systematic exclusion of Chicanos, Boricuas, Cuban Americans, and others from United States Spanish text-books. In the early 70's some textbook publishers were beginning to come around to the idea of teaching at least Latin American Spanish rather than the peculiarities of Castilian Spanish, and perhaps to give some attention to United States Hispanic culture as well. My 1974 article probably touched the publishers at perhaps the right moment. At any rate it received a great deal of attention in the publishing world and was generally circulated among editors, and most of its recommendations have now been implemented at the elementary, secondary, and college levels. These included teaching *loísmo* instead of *leísmo*; deemphasizing *vosotros* in the verbal paradigms; including the United States Spanish lexicon when items do not compete with standard Spanish items; and presenting the culture of United States Hispanos in a positive, nonstereotypical fashion. This then at the very least has been ac-complished by virtue of Spanish having acquired an official status in the United States: that in addition to the bullfighters, flamenco dancers, soccer and jai alai players, Cordoba peddlers, castanet clickers, Frito banditos, and all the other 'pop' or stereotypical or picturesque visions of the Hispanic world, the legitimate and authentic worlds of the Hispanic groups who live in the United States are getting some modicum of attention in the Spanish grammar books for Anglos.

In conclusion, let me return to the title of this paper: what, then, *can* language planners learn from the Hispanic experience with corpus planning? Among other things, we can learn that when the status of the language is only partially realized, or is temporary, indirect, crypto, or quasi, then the corpus planning that takes place will continue the struggle to realize, stabilize, make permanent, and, ultimately, enhance that truncated status. Or put another way, the Hispanic experience in the United States shows us that the contradictions left over in status planning will attempt to find their resolution in corpus planning, but that such resolution will be extremely difficult to achieve, at least in the short run, because effective corpus planning typically presupposes the conferral of power and authority on a group of corpus planners, rather than the converse, the struggle of this group or that to attain authority and stature.

REFERENCES

Alatorre, Antonio (1955), 'El idioma de los mexicanos', *Revista de la Universidad Nacional Autónoma de Mexico* 10: 11-15.

Fishman, Joshua (1968), 'Nationality-nationalism and Nation-nationism', in *Language Problems of Developing Nations,* ed. by Joshua A. Fishman, Charles A. Ferguson, and Jyatirindra Das Gupta. New York, Wiley.

Gaarder, Bruce A. (1977), 'Language maintenance or language shift: the prospect for Spanish in the United States', in *Bilingualism in Early Childhood,* ed. by Theodore Andersson and W.F. Mackey. Rowley, Mass., Newbury House.

Keller, Gary D. (1974), 'The systematic exclusion of the language and culture of Boricuas, Chicanos and other U.S. Hispanos in elementary Spanish grammar textbooks published in the United States', *The Bilingual Review/La revista bilingüe* 1(3): 227-235.

Kjolseth, Rolf (1972), 'Bilingual education programs in the United States: for assimilation or pluralism?', in *The Language Education of Minority Children,* ed. by Bernard Spolsky. Rowley, Mass., Newbury House.

Lozano, Anthony (1974), 'Grammatical notes on Chicano Spanish', *The Bilingual Review/La revista bilingüe* 1(2).

Steiner, Stan (1969), *La Raza: The Mexican Americans.* New York, Harper & Row.

Troike, Rudolph C. (1968), 'Social dialects and language learning: implications for TESOL', *TESOL Quarterly* 2: 176-180.

PART FOUR

Implementation of Language Planning

EINAR HAUGEN

The Implementation of Corpus Planning: Theory and Practice

This topic is basically one that ought to be handled by either a political scientist or a PR man. As I define the term, it is that long step which is taken between good intentions and actual accomplishment. 'Implementation' is that work of cajoling or enforcing compliance with decisions made in code selection and codification, which we usually leave to governments, or school systems, or any other agency that carries weight with the general public, such as the media, whether written or oral.

Since this is an area in which I am neither very competent nor very successful, I intend to talk around it rather than approach it directly. I am first going to place it in relation to other aspects of language planning in a theoretical section, and then I am going to report some examples of implementation that have come to my notice recently.

THEORY

As good a place as any to begin my consideration of language planning theory is Joshua Fishman's survey in his introduction to *Advances in Language Planning* (1974b). He calls it a 'state of the art' paper and regrets that the considerable body of research now available has not reached out to language planners and that they have not made use of it 'as a guide to their own procedures'. Perhaps I can contribute to the explanation of this asymmetry.

Fishman suggests that 'the major dimensions of language planning' are still those that I established in my article 1966a 'Linguistics and Language Planning' (written in 1964) and my book (1966b) *Language Conflict and Language Planning* (completed in 1965). He also refers to my Bucharest paper of 1969 (written in 1967). He is here referring to the fourfold problem areas, a model which I first put into matrix form in an article (1966c) in *American Anthropologist*, written in 1964 for Ferguson's summer seminar in Bloomington. I have fiddled a little with the terms since then, but I have seen nothing in the literature to make me reject the model as a framework for the starting points of language planners everywhere. They are starting points, since they say nothing about the end points, the goals to be reached, or the ideals and motivations that guide planners. In what I may call its 'classic' form the four-fold model includes (1) selection of norm; (2) codification of norm; (3) implementation of function; and (4) elaboration of function. Numbers (1) and (2) deal with the norm, (3) and (4) with the function. On the other hand, numbers (1) and (3) are primarily societal, hence external to the language, while (2) and (4) are primarily linguistic, hence internal to the language:

	Norm (Form)	Function
Society (sp)	(1) selection	(3) implementation
Language (cp)	(2) codification	(4) elaboration

After referring to my model, Fishman mentions that it has been 'slightly revised and refined by Neustupný (1970)' by the addition of a 'fifth consideration, namely cultivation' (1974b: 16). He further finds that Rubin (1971) has added the dimension of 'evaluation'. In an earlier essay (1973), reprinted in the same volume, Fishman has provided harmonization of my model with Neustupný's (1974a: 79). I agree that they lend themselves to harmonization, but I welcome the opportunity to provide my own. This is my first chance to respond in some detail to the valuable suggestions made by my fellow workers. It will be my contention that the procedures suggested by Neustupný and Rubin are provided for and to some extent foreseen within my original scheme.

Let me first explain that while the four steps in my model show a certain logical succession, they are not necessarily temporally successive, but may be simultaneous and cyclical.

Selection (status, acquis. policy)

Selection may include the decision to replace English with Irish in Eire, or French, German, Yiddish, or Arabic with Hebrew in Israel, or to replace urban with rural dialects in Norway. Selection or choice is necessary only when someone has identified what Neustupný has quite rightly called a *language problem.* Most problems can be identified as the presence of conflicting norms, whose relative status needs to be assigned. This has been called an *allocation of norms.* The selection may be preceded by lengthy wrangling in public or private, and it may be arrived at by some kind of majority decision. But it may also be decreed overnight, as when Ataturk changed Turkish spelling from Arabic to Roman. It may be resisted, as when Hassidic Jews persist in using Yiddish even in Israel. Over time a selection may be reversed. The common feature is that it is performed by society, acting through its leaders. It is a form of *policy planning,* which in this case establishes that a given linguistic *form,* be it a single item or a whole language, shall enjoy (or not enjoy) a given *status* in a society. While official government agencies are often involved, we should not limit the term 'planning' to such action, as I understand a proposal by Jernudd and Das Gupta (1971). Individuals make their selections, and they may be followed by voluntary groups, whose practice may become normative for a church, a political party, a province, or even a whole country.

2. Codification

Codification may also be the work of a single individual, who more or less informally, more or less knowledgeably, decides to give explicit, usually written, form to the norm he has chosen. It need not be his own; many languages have been codified by outsiders, from missionaries to masters. What Ferguson (1968: 29) has called *graphization* is often a first step. In areas where the concept of an alphabet, a syllabary, or a system of ideograms exists, a writing tradition can arise simply by the adaptation of a known system to the new language. In the early centuries of our era the Japanese began writing their language with the ideographic *kanji* of Chinese. In the eighteenth century the Faroese writer Svabo wrote his language for the first time, using the Danish form of the Latin alphabet. Even the simplest graphization requires many decisions and should in principle be done by a competent linguist.

Historically, most linguists came in after the fact, and to some degree linguistics owes its existence to the practical services linguists could offer as codifiers of language. They learned to extract and formulate the rules of correct grammar, a process we may call *'grammatication'.* Grammars were prescriptive from Panini to the present, at least the ones used in most schools. The extent to which they are also scientific depends on the skill of the linguist and the temper of the times. Beyond grammatication comes *lexication,* or the selection of an appropriate lexicon. In principle this also involves the assignment of styles and spheres of usage for the words of the language. The typical product of all codification has been a prescriptive orthography, grammar, and dictionary.

What the French knew as a *grammaire* or *dictionnaire raisonnée* was not a description of the real language, but of an ideal language that one was supposed to learn for admission to the world of learning. It could therefore become an instrument of national policy, a linguistic code corresponding to the civil and religious code. Like these it was of course regularly violated, and the degree of punishment depended on the kind of sanctions enforced by society. The grammarian was a lawgiver, and it was natural that his subject should become an important part of the basic education, the *trivium*. It is significant that grammatical deviations are still popularly known by terms of moral opprobrium: deviant forms are 'bad', 'wrong', 'incorrect', 'ugly', and 'vulgar'. Acceptable forms are 'good', 'right', 'correct', 'beautiful', and 'cultivated'. However meaningless such terms may seem to the scientific linguist, he is just as constrained in his usage of the language by the norms implied in these terms as is any other user.

Selection and *codification* appear in the same column because they both involve decisions on *form* and are part of what has been called *policy planning*. They correspond rather closely to the happy distinction introduced by Kloss (1969: 81-83) between *status planning* and *corpus planning*. But these go beyond the formal aspects and include the functional ones. *Selection* and *codification* remain mere paper exercises unless they are followed by *implementation* and *elaboration*, the former involving social status and the latter the linguistic corpus. To stay alive a language must have users for whom it performs useful functions.

Implementation

Implementation includes the activity of a writer, an institution, a government in adopting and attempting to spread the language form that has been selected and codified. Dealing, as we are for the most part, with written language, this is done by producing books, pamphlets, newspapers, and textbooks in the language. Those who have authority over schools or over mass media like radio and television introduce it as a medium of instruction and entertainment or at least as a subject to be taught. Laws and regulations are promulgated to encourage or discourage its use.

As long as a small, elite group has a monopoly on education, it is relatively simple to implement a given norm. But the spread of schooling to entire populations in modern times has made the implementation of norms a major educational issue. Nation-states are not necessarily chosen for their linguistic homogeneity (though attempts were made in this direction at the Treaty of Versailles in 1919 and in India more recently). The range of heterogeneity from an Iceland to a Nigeria is vast and disturbing. Each nation faces problems of its own.

Elaboration *(Ausbau) (includes Neustupný's cultivation)*

Elaboration is in many ways simply the continued implementation of a norm to meet the functions of a modern world. The major languages of Europe have set the standard here by their amazing inventiveness since the time of the Renaissance, when they undertook to perform the national and international functions of Latin. *Elaboration* is a useful English equivalent of *= Ausbau* Kloss's German *Ausbau*; it has been used for a somewhat related concept by Bernstein (e.g. 1971). A modern language of high culture needs a terminology for all the intellectual and humanistic disciplines, including the cultural underworld that runs from low to popular.

As far as I can see, my term fully includes whatever is meant by Neustup- *cultivation* ný in launching 'the cultivation approach'. (1970: 39; in revised form 1978: 258-268). He appears to think of it as either opposed to or added to 'language planning' and quite rightly indicates that it is more characteristic of 'developed' than 'developing' nations. He observes that terms for 'cultivation' are part of the terminology in this field in many European nations where it is desired to describe what academies and other guardians of the language claim to be doing.

In developing my model I was of course not unaware of this terminology, which is also well established in all the Scandinavian languages: in Swedish *vård*, in Norwegian (and the rest) *røkt*, both meaning 'care, cultivation', metaphorically taken from the tending of animals and plants, and corresponding to the German *Pflege*. I assumed it to be either a synonym of *language planning* or more specifically a part of that last phase which I called *elaboration*. I noted that this was not just a matter of developing a technical vocabulary but included also 'the extension of linguistic function into the realm of imaginative and emotional experience' (Haugen 1966b: 23). It is true, as Neustupný suggests, that 'cultivation' is more characteristic of the older, developed languages. But I, at least, felt that the metaphor involved is not entirely happy, in that it brings to mind an elitist view of 'culture' and 'cultivation'. It is not an established term in English, in reference to language, and *Haugen* lacks the neutrality that a scientific term ought to have. *against Neustupný's word cultivation*

Here it may be illuminating to ask what the Swedish Language Committee (*Svenska språknämnden*) actually does through its quarterly publcation *Språkvård* ['language cultivation']. By 1978 it had published a special series of brochures on spelling rules, pronunciation, place names, 'right and wrong in language', a guide to the dictionary of the Swedish Academy, word formation, inter-Scandinavian problems, transliterating Russian, the language of the mass media, bureaucratic gobbledygook, technical language, family names, medical terms, and descriptions of several urban dialects. In the periodical itself there are special articles on these and similar topics, as well as question-

and-answer columns on problems of correctness or language history. In short, Swedish (as a well-established standard language) has a continuing problem of *implementation* (by informing the public) and *elaboration* (by making decisions on novel problems, e.g. what should 'plastics' be called?). I suggest that 'cultivation' is merely that process of continued planning, here summed up as *implementation* and *elaboration*, which goes on in every language, once the basic form has been established.

Since for me the term *'language planning'* covers the entire process, I see no great need for Neustupný's term *'language treatment'*. If we assume with him that the process begins with the identification of a language problem, the natural solution is to make plans. 'Treatment', like 'cultivation', smacks of the metaphorical, in this case the sickroom. I find it a case of needless proliferation, a word that in itself is too vague. At least within our field, *planning* is now well established: we have a *Language Planning Newsletter*, a magazine entitled *Language Problems and Language Planning*, and a hefty volume entitled *Advances in Language Planning*.

Two other terms recently suggested may be regarded as valuable supplements to the model and can easily find their places within it. Neustupny's remarks on the need for *correction procedures* are well taken. Many of them are part of the natural acquisition of language, beginning with the parents and continuing with one's agemates. They are more consciously applied in school by teachers and textbooks, and eventually become self-administered through reading and general social acculturation. The need for *evaluation procedures* pointed out by Rubin (1971) is also clear. If we set out to reintroduce Gaelic into Ireland, one would hope that we should not forget to provide some way of evaluating the success of our program. When teachers correct pupils, they expect to evaluate the result by testing and giving grades. All of this is part of any good program of *implementation*, which should lead to successful listening and reading, or better still, speaking and writing.

For greater depth of detail in the discussion of theory I refer to Karam (1974) and the bibliography by Rubin and Jernudd (1977). The time has come for me to present a revised model as the conclusion of the theoretical section of my paper. I believe that in the revision shown in Table 1 I have incorporated the most important insights of my colleagues, without altering the basic outlines of my original plan.

Even with this revised model I cannot claim that it amounts to a theory of language planning. It provides a description of what language planners have done, but it does not tell us why they have done it, nor what goals they have hoped to attain. For some discussion of this problem I refer the reader to the section 'Criteria for Language Planning' in my 1966 article (Haugen 1966a: 60-64). Prague School theorists (as Garvin has repeatedly told us; cf. Garvin 1973) have proposed that a standard language should be 'stable' and 'flexible',

Handwritten note: Haugen's revised model (1983)

Table 1. *Revised model*

	Form (policy planning)	Function (language cultivation)
Society (status planning)	1. Selection (decision procedures) a. identification of problem b. allocation of norms	3. Implementation (educational spread) a. correction procedures b. evaluation
Language (corpus planning)	2. Codification (standardization procedures) a. graphization b. grammatication c. lexication	4. Elaboration (functional development) a. terminological modernization b. stylistic development

but as he has granted (Fishman 1974a: 73, note), this is a property of all language. The problem is how to build it into a formal standard language. It is a little like asking a disciplinarian to be both firm and gentle or telling a mother to spank her children lovingly. How stable and how flexible? In my model above, it is built into the tension between *codification*, which aims at stability, and *elaboration*, which requires flexibility. Writers have set up certain ideals for language, e.g. Ray (1963) with his 'economy', 'rationality', and 'commonalty', or Tauli (1968, 1977) with his instrumental efficiency, but these rarely appear to have played much role in the creation of standard languages (Haugen 1971). In any case, they are difficult if not impossible to define so that they will convince users to change their ways. Or why do we practical Americans continue to speak in four syllables of an 'elevator' when the impractical British do it in a single 'lift'? Yet we do need to continue exploring the problem, as I shall do in my examples below.

For the moment our discipline remains largely descriptive and has not reached a stage of 'explanatory adequacy'. Perhaps it is bound to remain so until we know more about the reasons for unplanned change in language. Fishman has called for a theory of language planning, without clarifying just how he thinks such a theory should look. It would surely have to be one that takes a stand on value judgments. We know there are many ways of writing a language; it is something else to say that method A is better than method B. Could we even reach agreement on whether it is better to write alphabetically, syllabically, or ideographically? Even alphabetically, we may ask if we should write phonetically, phonemically, or morphophonemically, and how much weight we should give to tradition and etymology. Where norms conflict, shall we plan for unity or for diversity, for 'transitional' bilingualism or for maintenance? Are we in favor of 'little' languages, and if so, what are we doing to save them? Or are we in favor of 'big' languages to promote world communication, and if so, shall we promote one of them or none, and in that case, opt for one of the many hundreds of Esperanto-type artificial languages? If ours is a species of cultivation, what species shall we cultivate? If we would cure linguistic ills, what are our remedies?

PRACTICE

As illustrations to some of the complexities involved, I shall outline some of the instances that have come to my notice in recent experience.

Example 1

The first problem relates to the trivial but irritating differences between British and American spelling, mostly established by Noah Webster in a burst of nationalistic separatism and rational reform. Just now it has surfaced in connection with the proposed introduction in the United States of the metric system, or metrication, as it is called. Having been a consultant to some of the planners involved, I draw from my file some details that will illustrate the implementation of corpus planning. It brings out some of the goals and motivations behind the process, as well as showing how much heat can be generated by even a minor change in our habits of English spelling.

Most Americans who know anything at all about the metric system have probably met with it, as I did, in my first science class. Invented at the time of the French revolution, it has by this time won acceptance throughout the world, except in the English-speaking countries, which have until recently clung to their feet and inches, quarts and gallons, pounds and miles. It took a world war and its aftermath to lead first Britain and now the United States down the metric path. In 1968 the Congress authorized a survey to study its effects, and three years later an official committee recommended 'that the United States change to the International Metric System through a coordinated national program over a period of ten years. . . ' (De Simone 1971: 85). The report was appropriately subtitled: 'A Decision Whose Time has Come'.

In 1975 the Congress adopted a Metric Conversion Act calling for voluntary conversion to the metric system (Public Law 94-168). We have all seen some of the effects of this program in the occasional appearance of metric signs on our roads, designations on our products, and temperatures in our weather programs. Not surprisingly, the changeover is slow; I have noted that in France it took 45 years (1795-1840) before it was fully accepted. Against a background of our need to buy and sell abroad, it seems inevitable: we are in for metrication whether we like it or not.

Curiously enough, this instance of social planning has raised certain questions of spelling. Since 1901 the official custodian of weights and measures has been the National Bureau of Standards (NBS) in Washington, which has its home in the Department of Commerce. The NBS responded to the 1968 recommendation of Congress by issuing an official translation of a French document entitled *Le Système International d'Unités* (NBS Special Publication 330, 1971). This presents an International System of Units (SI) adopted at a General Conference on Weights and Measures (CGPM) in Paris in 1960. The English translation came in separate versions for Britain and the United States, the latter being edited by Dr. Chester H. Page of the NBS. In a translator's note a special exception was made for the basic unit 'meter' (and presumably 'liter'), which was spelled in the British way as 'metre', 'in the hope of securing worldwide uniformity in the English spelling of the names of the units of the International System'. It was understood that a 'gentleman's agreement' had been made whereby the United States would accept '-re' in 'metre', as a *quid pro quo* for Britain's giving up the '-me' on the end of 'kilogramme'.

I do not know whether Dr. Page was aware of the hornet's nest he would stir up, but several American scientists at once spotted the deviation from the traditional American spelling. Here was indeed a 'conflict of norms' that called for 'status planning'; a selection had been made of a novel codification, and the question was whether American scientists and after them the American public would be willing to implement it. At least two of the English spellings that Webster rejected have crept into some American usage: 'theatre' and 'glamour'. The snob appeal of these spellings consists in equal parts of anglo- and francophile sentiment. But in the case of 'metre' and 'litre' we are dealing with an area of hard-headed, scientific practice, and as metrication grows, one that will affect the daily lives of every American who buys a liter of milk or a meter of cloth. All available American dictionaries describe the spellings with '-re' as 'chiefly British'.

One of the scientists who entered the fray with relish was Dr. John Howard, editor of *Applied Optics,* a journal of the Optical Society of America. He wrote his first editorial on this topic in his issue for August, 1971, reporting that at a meeting of the Publication Board of the American Institute for Physics (AIP) 'the editors of all the physics journals voted overwhelmingly not to yield the phonetic spelling of meter, liter, diopter in any such compromise with evil'. He was frank to say that the British spellings 'rankled' and caused hackles to rise. 'Our gram, meter, and ton are all more phonetic and logical than gramme, metre, and tonne, and we should not retreat from any phonetic English spellings just because the British have multiple errors'. Howard continued to beat the drum in his editorials for at least four years; I have ten of them down to 1975, but there may be more. I should add that Dr. Howard, although an optical engineer, admits to having taken college courses in the older Germanic languages, including Old and Middle English and Old High German (personal communication, June 20, 1974). Another active opponent of the British spellings came from Canada, rather surprisingly in view of Canada's having adopted '-re'. Albert Mettler, secretary of the Canadian Metric Association, put up a strong argument for '-er' in a *Metric Fact Sheet* of 1974.

My connection with the problem resulted from the fact that a former student of mine at Harvard, Susan P. Bryant, worked for Dr. Bruce Barrow, then of Waltham, Massachusetts. He was a member of the Standards Committee of the Institute of Electrical and Electronics Engineers, which had set up an American National Metric Council (ANMC) with offices in Washington, which in turn had a Metric Practice Committee (chairman, Russell Hastings). In the fall of 1973 Dr. Barrow was made chairman of a Task Force on Spelling and Pronunciation, which brought in a preliminary draft presenting arguments on both sides of the spelling controversy. In a poll of American scientists the vote was three to one in favor of American spellings.

Dr. Barrow decided to consult professional linguists, and Ms. Bryant suggested that I might have something to say on this topic. The first I heard of it was in a letter of January 21, 1974, to which I replied immediately, supporting his view in favor of the American spellings. I argued on the grounds of (1) usage (the '-re' would confuse learners and arouse resistance to metrication); (2) national unity (we might risk a splitting whereby the scientific community would write '-re' and the average layman '-er'); (3) phonology (syllabic 'r' is spelled '-er' in both British and American usage in the overwhelming majority of words, even those that are derived from French); (4) morphology (derivatives in '-Cr-' usually have bases in '-er', e.g. 'fibrous' from 'fiber', 'diametrical' from 'diameter', 'disastrous' from 'disaster', 'hungry' from 'hunger', etc.). I suggested that for the attainment of a unified spelling in English, it would make better sense for the less-numerous community (Great Britain) to adopt a more-rational spelling than for the more-numerous one to adopt a less-rational spelling.

Rather than depend on my (possibly uninformed) views alone, however, I recommended consultation with leading authorities on American English, specifically Professor Frederic Cassidy of the University of Wisconsin and Professor Albert Marckwardt of the University of Michigan, as well as the Center for Applied Linguistics, then headed by Professor Rudolph Troike. Troike brought in other linguists, including Professor Randolph Quirk from England. The opinion was absolutely unanimous in favor of '-er'. Even the old guardian of the Queen's English, H.W. Fowler, admitted in 1926 that 'the American usage is . . . more consistent. . . But we prefer in England to break with out illogicalities slowly. . . ' (Fowler 1926). In Sir Ernest Gower's revision of Fowler (1965) it is admitted that words like 'hexameter', 'diameter', and 'perimeter' are regularly written '-er' and that 'kilometer' is so written more often than not.

A revised draft (dated September 5, 1974) was written, incorporating the opinions of the linguists and the poll of the scientists. This led the Board of Directors of ANMC to change its policy (March 20, 1975) and issue a publication with the title 'ANMC Adopts Meter and Liter Spelling' (*Metric Conversion Paper* 8). Shortly after this, the Assistant Secretary of Commerce, Betsy Ancker-Johnson, issued a directive ordering the '-er' spelling in the Department of Commerce. In 1976 (December 10) this was followed by a *Federal Register* notice. Her successor, Jordan Baruch, has followed it up by advising Congressman Olin Teague that all Government agencies ought to write '-er' (*Congressional Record,* June 10, 1977). A new version of NBS Special Paper 330 was issued in 1977, changing '-re' to '-er'.

The story is still not complete, however. An organization that has a long history of prometric activity (going back to 1916) is the United States Metric Association. Its *Newsletter* for May, 1975 (Sokol 1975), included a spirited attack on the advocates of '-er' and defended the international and logical superiority of '-re'. After the Department of Commerce actions of 1977 the president and editor of the organization, Mr. Louis Sokol of Boulder, Colorado, published a whole brochure entitled *Statement on the Spelling of Metre* (1978).

Mr. Sokol describes the '-er' advocates as taking a 'chauvinistic attitude' trying to 'impose their will on the English speaking world' after the fashion of the 'ugly American' (1978: 6-8). He is liberal in his use of pejorative adjectives: his opponents are 'vociferous' and 'retrogressive', and he finds it suspicious that the ANMC committee members were all from 'east of the Mississippi'. The linguists cited are invariably referred to in quotation marks as 'linguists' and are said to have violated 'one of the principal ethics of a linguist which is, "a linguist does not prescribe a language, he describes it"' (1978: 7). Just to make sure, however, he brings his own linguist into court, a fellow Boulder resident, chairman Allan R. Taylor of the Department of Linguistics at the University of Colorado. Taylor, a specialist on American Indian languages, does not seem to have heard of language planning or in any case takes a dim view of it. He declares that the problem is trivial, that both spellings are phonetically adequate, that any literate person will recognize both, and that the question is purely political and sociological, hence prag-matic and nonlinguistic. He is backed up by Morris Halle of M.I.T., described as 'the dean of United States linguists' (1978: 8). It should perhaps be mentioned that Halle is on record as considering English spelling highly adequate.

There is no point in going into the argument further, particularly Sokol's feeble attempts to play linguist on his own. In the end it clearly appears that an important motivation is a fear by some American manufacturers that they may have to print a different label for goods going to the former members of the British empire. In return, American children should be forced to add another learning problem for their already beleaguered English teachers to overcome. But as language planners we may well be perplexed: shall our *selection* be national or international? Shall English *codification* follow the Germanic principle of writing '-er' or preserve a French spelling for historical and sentimental reasons? Shall the *implementation* be imposed by private scientific organizations or by a Department of the U.S. Government (who in turn dominate the publishing community)? Is all this purely political, as Taylor claims, or do linguists have a contribution to make?

Example 2

There is another body of functionaries who exert an enormous and probably growing influence on the shape of expository prose in this country. I am referring to the editorial staffs employed by American publishers, including (and perhaps especially) university presses. Most of them are women, well trained in the arts of rhetoric, and personally delightful. However painless they try to make the process, having one's manuscript edited by one of them reminds me of nothing quite as much as of going to the dentist.

For English language planning studies it would be most interesting and significant to do some intensive research on just exactly what they do in implementing what they understand to be the codification of standard English. As authors we realize of course that they are slaves to whatever style manual is adopted by their chiefs, whether it be the University of Chicago Style Manual or that of the Modern Language Association, which I understand has grown from a slim pamphlet to a big book. Of course we are happy as long as they limit themselves to appropriate punctuation, to catching errors in spelling and grammaticality, and to eliminating anacolutha and failures of congruence. Having been an English major myself and having some experience in writing, I dream of some day writing a book in which the editors will find no elementary errors to correct. But I write 'epochmaking' in one word and find it is hyphenated; I hyphenate 'step-sister' and get it back solid. I have learned that numbers below one hundred must be written out, only to find that this does not apply to percentages. Whenever I write 'that' as a relative pronoun, it gets changed to 'which' and vice versa. My pronouns seem crystal clear to me, but they are constantly being replaced by nauseatingly repetitive nouns. Editors replace my conjunction 'while' with 'though' because (although the dictionary records both), there is a rule that 'while' should be temporal. My sentence adverbs are shifted around, especially 'only' and 'here'.

But their special *bete noire* is my attempt to keep my style colloquial. If I write about a character that 'he decides to stick it out' or that two writers 'were running neck and neck', these are slashed or questioned.

My latest experience in the field, however, brought me up short before a solid wall of feminism. I was of course aware of the flurries over 'chairperson' and the sexist gender system of Indo-European, but I had not realized that there is already a set of guidelines adopted as policy by some of our presses. I have since been enlightened by the writings of an active worker in the field, Maija Blaubergs, of the University of Georgia, who is an educational psychologist and has kindly furnished me with two of her papers (1978a, 1978b). Again I have been struck by the importance of this movement for students of language planning. In the earlier article she conveniently lists many of the recommended devices for avoiding sexist terms: circumlocutions, indefinite and plural pronouns, sex-neutral nouns and suffixes, the creation of new terms, and the avoidance of such idioms as 'man overboard', 'good will to men', and 'man's best friend'. In her later article, a paper given at the World Congress of Sociology in Uppsala last August, she reports some of what she calls the 'misconstructions' placed on sex-neutral language planning, some of the counterarguments, including the nonargument of ridiculous overextension, some of which were new to me. I think my favorites, marked by a certain mad appropriateness, are the replacements of 'hysterectomy' by 'herterectomy' and of 'hernia' by 'hisnia'.

To return to my own experience: I had thought of myself as singularly unchauvinistic and had provided liberally for 'his and her' in my text. But I discovered to my shame that I had written of 'a poet who tries to reach his audience'; the 'his' had to go in favor 'an audience'. I had said that he wrote for 'all mankind'; but when this was systematically changed to 'humankind', I boggled and adopted 'humanity' instead. Without exactly writing a religious tract, I had said that 'Jesus proclaimed that all men were sinful'. Even sin we men cannot have to ourselves: I had to make it sex-neutral, I suppose 'people' or 'persons'.

My embarrassment was the greater since the book dealt with the dramatist who wrote the drama of women's liberation a century ago, *A Doll's House*. I had recently published a squib on '"Sexism" in the Norwegian language', in which I reported that in spite of this play Norwegian women today are just like American women in rebelling against the built-in chauvinisms of language (Haugen 1977). My view there (which would of course be disputed by Blaubergs and others) was that social injustice may be reflected in the language, but is neither caused by it nor seriously influenced by changes in it. Norwegian nurses have adopted the masculine form (*sykepleier,* rejecting *sykepleierske*), while Swedish nurses have retained the feminine (*sjuksköter-ska*), because the masculine (*sjukskötare*) would lower their status to that of an attendant in a mental institution (Andersson 1976). A recent news dispatch reported that the Pacific Coast Fishermen's Wives Coalition vigorously protested changing the occupational designation of their husbands from 'fishermen' to 'fishers' (Fleming 1979). The change had been made by the U.S. Commerce Department, basing itself on a *Dictionary of Occupational Titles* prepared by the Department of Labor.

No one can doubt that a social and generational change is in progress here and in other Western countries in the position of women. As we all know, not all the changes in terminology proposed are equally acceptable. The important thing is to eliminate all forms of negative discrimination, i.e. discrimination against women. I am all in favor of positive discrimination, i.e. discrimination between men and women. Whatever the merits of the case may be, we are in the midst of a process of language planning. Women have identified a language problem: the very language itself conflicts with their desired role in society, and they wish to make a new *selection* and *codification*, which some of them are trying to *implement* and *elaborate*. As with all innovations, many of the proposals will disappear as fashions change. Hopefully only the best will remain. An entirely different matter is the distinction between male and female registers, which I cannot take up here (Crosby and Nyquist 1977).

At this point I shall leave the English language alone, though there are numerous other issues one could broach. Joan Rubin refers to 'the need for a bridge between speakers of technical language and the common standard' (Rubin 1979: 3). Our government, which speaks to us in many voices, is one of the worst offenders in this regard, here as elsewhere. The Internal Revenue Service made a point in the 1978 blanks of the fact that their language was now adapted, I velieve, to the minds of twelve-year-olds. It somehow did not make the process any less painful for me; perhaps they haven't reached down to my level yet. But I call Joan's attention to a government publication entitled *Gobbledygook Has Gotta Go*. It is issued by the Bureau of Land Management in the Department of the Interior (1978). Written by one John O'Hayre, it is not only an entertaining example of its own doctrine, but provides numerous instances of how technical writing can be disambiguated (excuse the gobbledygook).

Example 3

Finally, I shall turn to a problem of *implementation* in Norwegian, the language whose problems first awakened my interest in the study of language planning (Haugen 1931). Just as background, let me remind you that since 1885 Norway has had the luxury of two standard languages, how known as *nynorsk* and *bokmal*. Purely for convenience I shall call the first N-Norwegian (NN) and the second D-Norwegian (DN). They are linguistically similar, but in Kloss's sense of *Ausbausprachen* they are distinct languages. All Norwegian children must learn to read both and, for entry to the university, write both. But only 16.4% of the school pupils have N-Norwegian as their primary written language, and they are all concentrated in the rural schools of western and midland Norway (Haugen 1975; latest figures from Bull 1978).

A major shibboleth is the suffix -*a*, which is absent from older D-Norwegian, but has a three-fold function in N-Norwegian:

	Def. art. (f. sg.)	Def. art. (n. pl.)	Pret. (wk. 1. class)
DN	*dor-en* 'the door'	*hus-ene* 'the houses'	*kast-et* 'threw'
NN	*dør-a*	*hus-a*	*kast-a*

We shall chiefly be concerned with the use of *-a* for the definite article, but the situation is analogous in the preterit. In Norwegian speech the suffix *-a* has long been (and in some circles still is) a heavily stigmatized form. In folk speech it is virtually universal (outside the city of Bergen and the rural dialects of western and midland Norway), but in elite speech it has been suppressed in favor of the Danish-derived *-en* and *-ene* (which coincide with the m. gender in each case). in the cities of eastern and northern Norway it is so common that even the children of the elite learned it and had to be corrected by their parents as part of their education, i.e. socialization into the upper class. Until 1907 it was forbidden in written DN in most words. Even Assen, creator of N-Norwegian, rejected it from his norm, preferring (for strong nouns) the suffix *-i* (*dør-i, hus-i*), both on historical (ON: *-in*) and social grounds. Not until after his death did NN officially permit *-a* as an alternative form, instead of the regionally very limited *-i* (which was felt to be remote and dignified).

In the halcyon years between the liberation of Norway in 1905 and its occupation by the Nazis in 1940 one of the chief thrusts of official planning was to fuse the two languages by selecting forms that were common to both. Here the suffix *-a* became a prime target, since adopting it in both languages would make N-Norwegian less regional and D-Norwegian less elite. Visionary language planners saw in the adoption of *-a*-forms in both languages the falling of one of the most important grammatical barriers separating the languages. The common ground was a form that was an unquestionable majority form but was felt to be vulgar by conservatives on both sides. At best it could be used in humorous or ethnographic contexts.

The *implementation* involved a progressive reeducation whereby both sides became used to seeing it in print. Private persons and enterprises were of course free to do what they pleased. But in all governmental and educational contexts a scale of usages was set up whereby the principle of obligatory and optional rules was established, long before Labov made it the cornerstone of his sociolinguistics. Rules were variable according to whether it was a question of textbooks or the pupils' own essays, in which greater freedom was permitted. By the reform of 1917 about 150 words were made obligatory in texts; they were mostly related to rural life or to concrete objects, where the *-a* was most natural. These often had no formal counterparts in Danish, and in that case were rather quickly adopted, e.g. *ku-a* 'the cow' (Danish *ko-en*), *barn-a* 'the children' (Danish *børn-ene*). In 1938 the number of obligatory nouns was raised to nearly a thousand. After the war a permanent Language Commission was established (1951), with the purpose of pushing this development to the point where both languages would become identical in a norm that could be called 'United Norwegian' (*samnorsk*).

But the postwar period brought some surprises for the planners. Norway had changed from an overwhelmingly rural nation to a predominantly industrial and urbanized one. By 1967 only 35% of the population lived in rural areas and only 20% were engaged in agriculture or fishing. A generation of Labor Party rule had moderated the nationalism of the interwar generation. The effects on the status of the dialect-based New Norwegian were catastrophic. Until 1944 its share of the school population had risen to a maximum of one-third (34.1%), but from then to the present its share has sunk steadily to the present one-sixth (16.4%). D-Norwegian has strengthened its position accordingly, and the Labor Party, which had actively promoted fusion (its members spoke 'folk' Norwegian), grew increasingly bourgeois and was becoming dubious about the whole policy. It was being attacked by some of its own staunch members and by a Parents' Coalition from the conservative D-Norwegian speech community, which organized demonstrations against the schoolbooks their children were having to learn from. Leading newspapers and publishers had established their own conservative norm, in which -*a*-forms were virtually excluded, and claimed for this norm the traditional name of D-Norwegian, *riksmål*.

In 1963 the Labor Party reversed its position and appointed a special 'language peace' committee headed by linguist Hans Vogt. On its recommendation the Language Commission was replaced by a Language Council, which started its work in 1971 and included representatives of all linguistic factions. Forced fusion by language planning was abandoned in favor of a policy of dual cultivation, i.e. a peaceful coexistence and rivalry, in which the rights of both would be respected. As of 1978 pupils are again permitted to write the old elitist forms in -*en* and -*ene*, even if -*a* is still favored in the textbooks, at least for nonliterary words.

As a footnote to this retreat from fusion it should be said that it may in fact be too late to stop the -*a*-forms from spreading, not only into writing but even into elite speech. A whole generation of youngsters is used to seeing them in print, and it is questionable whether they will enforce the old ban on them as their own children grow up. A democratically educated populace no longer recognizes the old distinction between vulgar and élite. A whole generation of school youth has adopted an antiestablishment view on language and is revelling in the use of broad dialect. The N-Norwegian movement is trying to make hay from this trend with the slogan, 'Speak dialect, write New Norwegian'. It is still doubtful how far they will succeed with either part of the slogan, but there is no doubt that academic young people are increasingly dialectal in their speech. Many of them bear the mark of the student revolt of the 1960s and are proud to wave the standard of 'leave your language alone'. Dialects flourish as academic conservatives lament the 'vulgarity' of young people. I have myself spoken with youths from upper-class homes who admitted that in order to be accepted by their friends they had to speak a 'less polished' language (Dahl 1977).

Language planning in Norway has therefore not resulted in the establishment of a new standard along the lines proposed by Ivar Aasen. He might be just as shocked by what he would hear in Oslo today if he were alive as are some of the conservatives. There is no doubt that the D-Norwegian form of speech and writing is too strong to be dislodged. But in many respects it is in competition not with N-Norwegian, but with the folk dialects of the cities, forms previously regarded as non- or substandard. It is a case in which planning has resulted in a surprising degree of tolerance of speech variation. The situation is different from that in Denmark and Sweden, even though one notes a certain loosening of standards there as well. Bengt Loman, the Swedish sociolinguist now teaching in Finland, has even advised the Swedish speakers of Finland to look to the example of Norway and relax some of their rigid prescriptivism. Perhaps it would make it easier to maintain Swedish against the inroads of majority Finnish (Loman 1976).

CONCLUSIONS

As each of the examples I have presented shows, language planning is a response to a social problem strongly felt by some particular social group. In the first we watched American scientists and engineers feeling themselves excluded from world markets by our traditional weights and measures. In trying to achieve uniformity they are unexpectedly faced with a spelling problem which could sacrifice national unity in a vain attempt to achieve international uniformity. In the second example feminists have found an obstacle to woman's equality in the very language they speak and now wish to recodify English into a nonsexist instrument. In doing so they are meeting with objections and obstacles, some of them perhaps inherent in the nature of language, some merely the usual attempts to ridicule and exaggerate anything novel. My third example shows how language-planning implementation is subject to political constellations and how any attempt to dislodge a well-established elite may result in backlashes and tectical retreat. What the examples have in common is the ultimate problem of how to balance the claims of uniformity and diversity. Only further research will increase our understanding of how much influence can be consciously exerted by the manipulation of sources of power and how much linguistic change is due to underlying and uncontrollable social forces.

REFERENCES

American National Metric Council (1974), January 4, 1974. *The Meter-Metre Controversy, First Draft*. ANMC Task Force on Spelling and Pronunciation, chairman: Bruce B. Barrow; Metric Practice Committee.

Andersson, Thorsten (1976), 'Manling sjuksköterska', in *Nordiska Studier i filologi och lingvistik: Festskrift tillägnad Gösta Holm*, 1-11.

Bernstein, Basil (1971), *Class, Codes, and Control*, volume one. London, Routledge and Kegan Paul.

Blaubergs, Maija S. (1978a), 'Changing the sexist language: the theory behind the practice', *Psychology of Women Quarterly* 2: 244-261.

_____(1978b), 'Sociolinguistic change towards nonexist language: an overview and analysis of misunderstandings and misapplications'. Paper presented at the IX World Congress of Sociology, Uppsala, Sweden.

Bull, Trygve (1978), 'Et vapenlager', *Dagbladet* (Oslo), October 23.

Bureau of Land Management (U.S. Department of the Interior) (1978), *Gobbledygook Has Gotta Go*. Washington, D.C.: Superintendent of Documents.

Crosby, Faye, and Linda Nyquist (1977), 'The female register: an empirical study of Lakoff's hypotheses', *Language in Society* 6: 313-322.

Dahl, Steinar (1977), 'Sprakskiftet i Oslo pa 60- og 70-tallet', *Dagbladet* (Oslo), March 12.

De Simone, Daniel V. (1971), *A Metric America: A Decision Whose Time Has Come*. National Bureau of Standards, Special Publication 345. Washington, D.C.: Superintendent of Documents.

Ferguson, Charles A. (1968), 'Language Development', in *Language Problems of Developing Nations*, ed. by J. Fishman, C. Ferguson, and J. Das Gupta, 27-36. New York, Wiley.

Fishman, Joshua A. (1973), 'Language modernization and planning in comparison with other types of national modernization and planning', *Language in Society* 2: 23-43.

_____, editor (1974a), *Advances in Language Planning*. The Hague, Mouton.

_____(1974b), 'Language planning and language planning research: the state of the art', in *Advances in Language Planning*, ed. by Joshua A. Fishman, 15-33. The Hague, Mouton.

Fleming, Patricia (1979), 'Article' in the *Boston Globe*, February 27.

Fowler, H.W. (1926), *Dictionary of Modern English Usage*. London, Oxford University Press. (Revised edition by Ernest Gowers [1965], London Oxford University Press).

Garvin, Paul (1973), 'Some comments on language planning', in *Language Planning: Current Issues and Research*, ed. by J. Rubin and R. Shuy 24-73. Washington, D.C., Georgetown University Press. (Reprinted in Fishman 1974a, pp. 69-78).

Haugen, Einar (1931), 'The origin and early history of the New Norse movement in Norway'. Unpublished dissertation, University of Illinois. (One chapter printed: 'The linguistic development of Ivar Aasen's New Norse', *Publications of the Modern Language Association* 48: 558-597).

_____(1966a), 'Linguistics and Language Planning', in *Sociolinguistics*, ed. by William Bright 50-71. The Hague, Mouton.

_____ (1966b), *Language Conflict and Language Planning: The Case of Modern Norwegian*. Cambridge, Harvard University Press.

_____ (1966c), 'Dialect, language, nation', *American Anthropologist* 68: 922-935.

_____ (1969), 'Language planning, theory and practice', in *Actes du Xe Congrès International des Linguistes, Bucharest, 1967*, ed. by A. Graur, 701-711. Bucharest, Editions de L'Academie de la Republique Socialiste de Roumanie.

_____ (1971), 'Instrumentalism in language planning', in *Can Language be Planned?* ed. by J. Rubin and B. Jernudd, 281-289. Honolulu, East-West Center and University Press of Hawaii.

_____ (1975), 'Language and society: a sociolinguistic profile of Norway', *Michigan Germanic Studies* 1: 9-46.

_____ (1977), '"Sexism" and the Norwegian language', *Studies in Descriptive and Historical Linguistics: Festschrift for Winfred P. Lehmann*, ed. by Paul J. Hopper, 83-94. Amsterdam, Benjamins.

Howard, John N. (1971-1975), 'From the Editor', *Applied Optics* August, 1971; December, 1971; February, 1972; April, 1972; June, 1972; October, 1972; May, 1974; January, 1975.

Jernudd, B.H., and J. Das Gupta (1971), 'Towards a theory of language planning', in *Can Language be Planned?* ed. by J. Rubine and B. Jernudd, 195-216. Honolulu, East-West Center and University Press of Hawaii.

Karam, Francis X. (1974), 'Toward a definition of language planning', in *Advances in Language Planning*, ed. by Joshua A. Fishman, 103-124. The Hague, Mouton.

Kloss, Heinz (1969), *Research Possibilities on Group Bilingualism: A Report*. Quebec, International Center for Research on Bilingualism.

Loman, Bengt (1976), 'Språklig folklore', *Språkvård* 2: 3-10.

Mettler, Albert J. (1974), 'The quest for logical spelling', *Metric Fact Sheet* 13, Canadian Metric Association, Fonthill, Ontario.

National Bureau of Standards (1977), *The International System of Units (SI)*. Special Publication 330. Washington, D.C., Superintendent of Documents. (Supersedes the 1974 edition).

Neustupný, J.V. (1970), 'Basic types of treatment of language problems', *Linguistic Communications* 1: 77-98. (Reprinted in Fishman 1974a, pp. 37-48).

_____ (1978), *Post-Structural Approaches to Language: Language Theory in a Japanese Context*. Tokyo, University of Tokyo Press.

Ray, P.S. (1963), *Language Standardization: Studies in Prescriptive Linguistics*. The Hague, Mouton.

Rubin, Joan (1971), 'Evaluation and language planning', in *Can Language be Planned?* ed. by Joan Rubin and B. Hernudd, 217-252. Honolulu: East-West Center and University Press of Hawaii. (Reprinted in *Advances in the Sociology of Language II*, ed. by J.A. Fishman, 476-510. The Hague, Mouton, 1972.

Rubin, Joan, and Björn H. Jernudd (1977), *References for Student of Language Planning*. Honolulu, East-West Center.

Sokol, Louis, editor (1975), *United States Metric Association Newsletter* (quarterly) 10(2). Boulder, Colo.

_____ (1978), *Statement on Spelling of Metre*. USMA Metric Practice Committee, United States Metric Association.

Språkvård: Tidskrift utgiven av Svenska språknämnden (1965), Stockholm.

Tauli, Valter (1968), *Introduction to a Theory of Language Planning*. Studia Philologiae Scandinavica 6. Uppsala, Acta Univ. Uppsal.

_____(1977), 'The theory of language planning', in *Issues in Sociolinguistics*, ed. by Oscar Uribe Villegas, 245-265. The Hague, Mouton. (Reprinted in Fishman 1974a, pp. 49-67).

DAYLE BARNES

The Implementation of Language Planning in China*

1. INTRODUCTION

Since 1949, when the People's Republic of China (hereafter, PRC) was established, the national educational authorities have initiated several programs intended to alter the form and function of language use in China. The potential scope of these activities is quite impressive.

Victor main→ pinging [handwritten annotation]

1.1. The promotion of PTH

In the southeastern inland and coastal provinces, the first language of nearly everyone is one of several regional languages, such as Cantonese, Fukienese, and Shanghainese. In addition to these, the North Chinese language (Mandarin; hereafter PTH) is spoken natively by the more than 70% of the ethnic Chinese population who live in the northeast, north, central, and southwestern parts of the country. The chief source of unintelligibility between PTH and the other regional languages lies at the level of phonology, and the differences can be considerable, involving consonantal, vocalic, and tonal variation. Such variation is also present in local varieties of PTH itself, implying the necessity for standardization within this vast language area as well. On the other hand, all of the regional languages for the most part share with PTH a common word order and lexicon.

*This paper comprises two parts. The first, a historical review of the PTH and PY language issues, is a summarization based on information published earlier (Barnes 1974, 1977a, 1977b, 1980). The reader is referred to these earlier publications for a fuller bibliography. The second part includes observations of language-program implementation gathered in China while I was a participant in the University of Pittsburgh's delegation to the People's Republic of China in July-August, 1979. The latter are presented as suggestive of developments in China rather than as the results of controlled field research. I am grateful to the following for financial support in the writing of this paper: the University Center for International Studies and the Asian Studies Program of the University of Pittsburgh.

In 1956, PTH was designated a 'common language' for purposes of communication among speakers of all the different regional languages in China. The principal responsibility for educating a new generation of Chinese capable of functioning in PTH across regional language barriers was assigned to the school system, which is nationally directed but locally financed and operated. If successfully implemented, PTH would eventually become the principal vehicle of expression among communicants with different language backgrounds.

1.2.   *Writing: simplification, vernacularization, phoneticization*

The Chinese written language has also been a subject of discussion and research over these years. The traditional character script has been evaluated in terms of its suitability as an instrument for mass education, as a vehicle for dispelling adult illiteracy, and as a medium for exact communication in the realms of scientific and technical activity. The most visible change in the appearance of materials published today in the PRC from those of the pre-1949 period is the substitution of structurally less complex, simplified character variants for traditional and frequently more complex ones. Conservatively, about half of the inventory of the most frequently occurring characters in general reading matter may now be written in simplified form.

In addition to the use of simplified characters, language authorities have also attempted to facilitate script acquisition by compiling lower-level reading matter using an inventory of characters having the highest frequency of occurrence. Simplification has also been advanced by proscribing further recourse to characters which are merely structural variants of one another, such as 'theater' and 'theatre' in English.

The increasing vernacularization of contemporary material published in China is relevant to any discussion of Chinese orthographic reform. However, this phenomenon is but the latest stage in a process begun in 1917 when social and political realities combined to force the retirement of the classical writing style in favor of its vernacular counterpart.

The final orthographic issue is the current function and future of the Phonetic Annotation System (*pinyin*; hereafter, PY) adopted in the PRC in 1958. By itself, the creation of a system of phonetic symbols to annotate the character script would be unlikely to attract much notice. The reason for the extraordinary interest generated in the past among Chinese and foreign observers alike by this phonetic system derived from continuing speculation that it may one day entirely replace the traditional character orthography for all but a few special purposes.

This paper will procede to examine two of these issues — PTH and PY — in greater detail. However, before taking up the matter of program implementation, the language policies themselves must first be reviewed.

This step involves some understanding of the several decades of discussions preceding the decisions made after 1949 in the PRC. It should also be appreciated that all the above-mentioned language issues had been discussed at some length, and some had even been implemented as state policies during that period. For example, the antecedents of the PTH program can be traced back to 1903, when a prototype of today's PTH was mandated for inclusion into the curriculum of China's first modern school system. A generation later, the Nationalist Government authorized, briefly, a modest plan which would have introduced simplified characters into all regularly published educational materials. And proposals for phonetic annotation systems, including those advocated as surrogates for the traditional script, antedate both of the others, having emerged in the early 1890s.

2. THE PTH PROGRAM

2.1. *The history of the question*

The origin of the PTH, or the common-language, question coincided with the Ch'ing dynasty's (1644-1911) earliest attempt to inaugurate a program of public education in 1903. This plan would have required that the spoken language of the capital in Peking, long used in the administration of state affairs, be incorporated as a component in mandated courses in the Chinese literature curriculum.

Although this plan was an expression of the imperial will, its realization was totally dependent on the initiative and the resources of local ducational administrations. The imperial government did not undertake training activities to prepare teachers, nor did it provide guidance with respect to instrucrional material. Some schools are recorded as having seriously attempted to implement the imperial directive, but the overall impact, especially in regional-language areas, was negligible.

Discussions relating to refinements in the new educational system, including the language component, continued through the years before revolutionary forces under Sun Yat-sen brought an end to the dynasty in 1911.

However, the events of 1911 resulted in a different climate of opinion regarding the inclusion of Pekingese in the school curriculum. Deprived of imperial support, the language plan turned out to have few real friends. This may at first seem incongruous, given the position of geographic and demographic dominance which PTH enjoys. Then, as now, the North Chinese language, of which Pekingese was the acknowledged representative, was spoken natively by two-thirds of all ethnic Chinese living in the densely populated eastern half of the country.

This incongruity lessens when one takes into consideration that the putative and the actual prestige of Pekingese differed significantly at that time. The relative prestige of the several Chinese regional languages had historically been measured by cultural rather than by geographic or demographic yardsticks. For centuries, men of ambition aspired to appointment as officals in the imperial civil service. Traditionally, only those candidates throughly grounded in the classical Confucian literature, as evaluated in Imperial examinations, could qualify for these positions. The status of each of the regional languages as an oral medium through which universal wisdom was acquired was derived and perpetuated by the countless acts of recitation and memorization undertaken in it by students of each new generation. Moreover, in the case of some of these regional languages, parts of this immense corpus of venerated literature could still be intoned in an approximation of its earliest recorded pronunciation — a factor which significantly enhanced its status. In North Chinese, however, regular processes of phonological change had made this impossible. The other regional languages, therefore, had a much stronger claim to represent the revered work of the culture's ancient teachers.

Indications of the disparity between the imperial government's early plans for Pekingese and the relatively low status it enjoyed among the literate elite were detectable even before 1911. In 1913, this qualified evaluation of Pekingese was reflected in the recommendations of the Conference on the Unification of Reading Pronunciation, convened by the Ministry of Education in the new Republican government. The conference recommended the promotion of a synthetic phonological norm based in the main on North Chinese but incorporating, in addition, several other sounds found in the regional languages which were considered historically significant by the traditional scholars who comprised the bulk of the delegates to this meeting.

The antiquarian orientation implicit in the recommendation of this conference was perhaps characteristic of the views of some conservative, traditional scholars, but unrepresentative of the younger intellectuals who contributed to the May Fourth Movement of 1919. Anticlassical, antitraditional, and promodern, this movement sparked a wave of reaction to the constraints inherent in traditional Confucian society. Unfortunately, these sociocultural changes which might have been favorable to the language issue in the years after 1919 were paralleled by a disintegration of national authority, which was only partially reversed during the years preceding 1949. During this period, state power was often shared uneasily among regional governors, depriving the central government of the freedom to pursue a full social agenda as well as the revenues to implement it.

The Communist Party in this period did not adopt a clear position relative to national language promotion. This was in part owing to practical considerations; except for a brief period in the early 1930s, organized Communist educational activities were before 1949 conducted chiefly in North Chinese-speaking areas of northwest China. Several of its members, however, were vocal in support of maximum cultural and linguistic autonomy for the regional-language areas. Strongly influenced by Soviet language policies of the time, these individuals advocated and contributed to the development of phonetic scripts suitable for use in the regional-language areas, urging their utility in literacy and educational work. Institutionalization of this activity would presumably imply acceptance of some role for the regional languages in the schools.

2.2. Planning the implementation of the PTH program

The two most important issues in connection with the implementation of the national PTH program were the following:

1. 'The Directives of the State Council Regarding the Promotion of the Common Language', issued February 6, 1956; and

2. 'The Directives of the Ministry of Education of the People's Republic of China Regarding the Promotion of the Common Language in Elementary, Middle, and Normal Schools', issued November 17, 1955 (hereafter, MOE Directives).

Although both documents relate to PTH promotion, each is addressed to a different segment of society. The State Council Directives embraced the entire adult society, particularly certain occupational groups whose work was considered of unusual relevance to PTH promotion. Separate sections of this directive appealed to the military, to the youth corps, to newspapers and news agencies, to public-health agencies, and to transportation, communications, and entertainment organizations. Each of these was directed to formulate plans for the incorporation of PTH in whatever public activities fell within its jurisdiction. Those branches of the central government which would share responsibility for the implementation of the PTH program were identified and their respective roles clarified. Only the linguistic activities of the ethnically non-Chinese national minority peoples were exempted from compliance with the requirements of this policy, although educational authorities in such regions were still charged with the responsibility for PTH promotion among Chinese living in their areas.

The impact of each of these groups on PTH promotion would necessarily be unequal. That of the broadcasting media, for example, would clearly be of great significance; that of municipal officals training streetcar conductors, less so. But it is evident that the purpose of these broadly focused activities was to encourage, even if only marginally, a climate of acceptance for PTH as well as a sense of public responsibility for its development. Without this kind of support from the local community, even accomplished learners of PTH might quickly discover the severe limits to its usefulness. It was essential for the adult community to behave linguistically in support of PTH promotion, even though it could never become its principal beneficiary, so that the development of new language skills among the young could be fostered.

The chief responsibility for the development of those skills was assigned to the school system, with special emphasis on elementary and normal schools. Wisely, educational authorities elected to allocate scarce human resources in a direct effort to teach the youngest and linguistically the most educcable group of learners, while at the same time devoting special attention to the preparation of teachers who would soon enter the classroom.

The MOE Directives stipulated that PTH would become the medium of instruction for the Chinese language and literature course in grades one through seven beginning in the fall of 1956. Teachers of all other subjects were, within two years, also to conduct their classes in PTH.

Special measures were taken to assist teachers who would begin to teach in PTH in 1956. A center was established in Peking to train selected teachers in PTH phonology and language pedagogy. Graduates of this center returned to their localities to assume responsibility for training other groups at the provincial, county, and municipal levels, who in turn instructed practicing teachers. Newspapers and radio stations contributed by broadcasting and printing, frequently in coordinated series, linguistic information of value to teachers with diverse language backgrounds struggling to function in PTH. Phonograph recordings in PTH were produced in large quantities.

In assessing the popular accpetance of the PTH program, it is interesting to note that official statements regarding the relationship between PTH and the other regional languages have always candidly predicted that the latter would eventually be replaced by PTH. However, the government has conceived its role as that of a midwife to history rather than a zealous extirpator of regional languages. It has supplied encouragement and avoided pressure or sanctions. Reasonable standards have been applied: students and language teachers are expected to excel; by contrast, the elderly are praised merely for trying. Officials serving in regional-language areas have been advised to learn the language of that region.

In one survey of Chinese youth who were educated in China but subsequently emigrated to Hong Kong, parents of the respondents were reported to have accepted their children's acquisition of PTH with at least equanimity, and often with enthusiasm, whatever their own attitude toward learning PTH themselves. Vocational displacement or discrimination on the basis of language competence was unknown among members of this group. It is note-

Canton!

worthy also that, during a period of relatively free criticism of government policies in 1957, the new PTH program did not become an item of controversy.

These data augur favorably for the continued expansion of the use of PTH. Marxist theory notwithstanding, the PTH policy does not necessarily imply the decay of the regional languages, and much may depend on the attitude with which native speakers come to regard them. What is interesting is to note the apparent acceptance in regional-language areas of the need for bilingual compentence by those youth whose grandfathers, just two generations earlier, would have balked at the choice of North Chinese to fill the role of a common language.

2.3. Observations regarding PTH program implementation

The conference for which this paper was prepared was held in 1979, the same year in which the United States and China ended three decades of diplomatic estrangement. In the summer of that year, I traveled through Canton, Shanghai, Sian, and Peking. In Canton and Shanghai I had several hours of talks with educational officers whose responsibilities include the implementation of language policies in the schools. This section contains a summary of these discussions, together with observations I was able to make along the way.

2.3.1. PTH promotion in urban areas

2.3.1.1. Canton. Canton is China's most populous southern city and the capital of Guangdong Province. The speech of this area is acknowledged as the representative variety of the Cantonese language. One of the several regional languages, Cantonese is the first language learned by the perhaps 48 millions of Chinese who are natives of the province.

The following paragraphs summarize the results of discussions about PTH promotion between the Head of the Department of Education for Canton City, the chief of the Department's Pedagogical Research Office, and myself.

There is in Canton considerable disparity between language policy and reality. Vigorously implemented between 1956 and 1958, the PTH program declined in intensity and in impact in municipal schools thereafter, and by the early 1960s was no longer aggressively pursued.

The original plans called for a steady progression in the use of PTH, culminating in its use as the medium of instruction in all elementary- and middle-school classes, beginning initially with the *yuwen* or language class. The reality is that PTH is employed regularly today only in the language class, and then only through the second year of elementary school. Thereafter, and

failure of PTH

uniformly in all other classes, the language of instruction is Cantonese. Instruction at the middle-school level, grades 7 through 12, is also in Cantonese.

Included among the factors contributing to this decline were (1) the inability of the educational sector to sustain the high level of promotional activity necessary to guarantee active support for the policy, (2) resistance from teachers with inadequate competence in PTH who insisted that they could only teach effectively and expressively through the medium of their regional language, and (3) the weak and fitful commitment of educational authorities in the central government. In this climate, the summer institutes for teacher retraining inaugurated in the 1950s were suspended early on and their staff reassigned to other work. As a consequence, contemporary noral schools are not equipped to prepare new elementary school teachers to teach PTH.

Nonetheless, almost all of the small number of people I happened to meet were capable of understanding and speaking PTH. These encounters included 18- to 20-year-olds in a bookstore, a 25-year-old student puzzling out an English text along the riverside, and the mistress of ceremonies at an evening magic performance. These individuals, of course, were all approximately the same age and probably enjoyed education through the middle-school level. Most of the hotel service staff could use PTH, which might be expected; however, several teenage floor stewards, doing unskilled work, could not.

2.3.1.2. Shanghai. Of all the varieties of the Wu language, Shanghainese is perhaps the most well known. As a group, Wu speakers probably number about 76 millions, or approximately 8% of all Chinese.

Language education in Shanghai is in the hands of seven or eight former teachers who received special training at a PTH institute in Peking between 1959 and 1966, after which time the central government suspended language-promotion activity until 1978.[1] The local branch of the Language Reform Commission, organizationally responsible to the highest level of municipal authority, comprises 30 members, but only four or five who are actually involved in the implementation of language programs and who draw their salaries from the Department of Education.

PTH is begun in the first term of instruction in elementary schools in Shanghai. First in Shanghainese and then in PTH, teachers model phrases essential to the conduct of the class. Six weeks later, they proceed to match their understanding of the sound values of PTH with the PY phonetic annotation symbols.

PTH promotion officials in Shanghai still do not feel able to take for granted the public acceptance of the language program among all segments of the population. The potential advantages of the program are not always immediately grasped, especially by new residents of the city who come from areas where other regional languages are spoken and where the need for PTH has not been felt.[2]

The types of people I happened to meet in Shanghai included (1) local guide-interpreters with the China Travel Service, (2) clerks in merchandise outlets, bookstores, post offices, and drug stores, (3) workers in a textile factory, (4) hotel service personnel such as floor stewards, gate guards, chauffeurs, (5) a streetcorner policeman, (6) Department of Education officials and middle-school teachers, (7) a Civil Airline flight stewardess, (8) operators of a *doujiangdian* [breakfast shop]. All of these contacts were over 30 years of age, and many of those over 30 could understand and speak PTH.

I have heard it said by a pre-1949 resident of Shanghai that PTH was, in consequence of the city's metropolitan character, better established there than in cities in other regional-language areas. Certainly the newspaper reports published between 1956 and the early 1960s pertaining to PTH promotional activity of the Shanghai municipal government were notable for their vigor and commitment, and many of the occupational groups listed above, who must deal with the out-of-town trade, were targets of PTH adult training classes during those years.

2.3.1.3. Sian. Modern Sian is the capital of Shanxi Province, and its speech belongs to the greater North Chinese language area.

I found PTH used routinely there along the streets, by caretakers at the renovated Bell Tower, clerks at the general merchandise store, a policeman, functionaries at the municipal Department of Education, a *youtiao* [breakfast roll seller], local travel-service personnel, and members of the hotel staff.

2.3.2. *PTH promotion in rural areas.* Since 80% of China's population is rural, much importance attaches to the development of educational institutions in this area. Thus far, the signs are not altogether encouraging.

2.3.2.1. Outside Shanghai. During a visit to North Bridge Commune, perhaps 20 miles southwest of Shanghai, members of my group were invited to examine the interior of a typical house. The occupant, a 24-year-old woman, answered our questions in a local variety of the Wu language, which was different from the Shanghainese of our tour guide. She implied that her inability to understand or to speak PTH was explainable by reference to the disruptions of the Cultural Revolution and the activities of the 'Gang of Four'. However, a 24-year-old individual in 1979 should have entered the first grade three to four years before political turmoil could have affected education in the countryside.

This individual also reported that her elementary-school language teacher's PTH was strongly accented, lending plausibility to the interpretation that she actually received negligible formal language training in school and apparently found little scope for its application in the local language area in which she lived.[3]

2.3.2.2. Outside Sian. The speech of a 20-year-old member of a commune northeast of Sian provided some indication of the probable linguistic diversity within the North Chinese language area. This man had completed elementary school, wrote attractively, and was literate. But although our conversation was governed by a common syntax, there were numerous consonantal and vocalic differences to overcome.

If this experience proves generalizable for other parts of North China, it would underline the very real importance of PTH promotion within this language area as well. Like the woman in the commune outside Shanghai, this man reported that his elementary teacher's PTH was also nonstandard, suggesting that the latter may well have been a native of the area near this man's school and perhaps was one of those who relied on phonograph records or special PTH radio broadcasts to augment his own control over PTH.

3.   THE CHINESE PHONETIC ALPHABET (PY)

3.1.   The history of phonetic annotation systems

As with the previous discussion of PTH, the proper place to begin the study of PY is with a review of its history in China.

Limited precedents for the use of phonetic scripts in China can be found in the sixteenth and seventeenth centuries, when Catholic and Protestant missionaries created them in order to facilitate their acquisition of Chinese. The creation of phonetic scripts by Chinese did not begin until the 1890s and was motivated by the conviction that the traditional character script constituted and would continue to constitute a major obstacle to the attainment of a literate citizenry. Only through literacy, this argument maintained, could China's population be mobilized to resist the political, economic, and military incursions of foreign powers.

The first Chinese phonetic script to appear during this period, in 1892, was based on the Latin alphabet and reflected the influence of similar scripts which had been developed in the latter half of the 19th century by Protestant missionaries in the regional-language-speaking portions of China. Greater interest was generated shortly thereafter by the appearance of another phonetic system constructed from bits and pieces of traditional Chinese characters, which became very popular in North China during the first decade of this century.

Previously, Chinese scholars had indicated the pronunciation of a character by reference to two other characters representing consonants, vowels, and tone. But rapid social change had rendered this system obsolete, and the need for a method to teach the complicated written language more rapidly eventually became obvious. The search for a phonetic instrument capable of convenient annotation of the character script culminated in the recognition of the National Phonetic Alphabet (hereafter, NPA) by the Ministry of Education in 1918. Based on components of characters rather than on Latin letters, the NPA reflected the dominant mood of the time in preferring familiar shapes embodying indigenous cultural values to those of manifest foreign origin. Nevertheless, many problems plagued the implementation of the NPA. Consensus on some aspects of the phonological norm was not actually reached until 1932, rendering uncertain its precise application. Within the educational community the NPA, designed to facilitate the acquisition of the character script, was consistently deferred at least until the third grade in approved school curricula — well after the introduction of the character script whose disparate regional pronunciations it was supposed to help standardize. Even had these pedagogical difficulties been resolved, a convenient method for large-scale publishing using annotated type fonts was unavailable until the mid-1930s. Finally, one cannot dismiss the impediment to educational innovation posed during these years by a fragmented political order.

Formal recognition of the NPA in 1918 did not discourage continued experimentation with Latin-letter phonetic systems. Two of these attained modest prominence in certain circles. One became the official romanization system of the Nationalist Government in 1928, but it has enjoyed only limited application.

The second, *ladinghua,* was developed explicitly to combat illiteracy among adults and was regarded by its proponents as a potential surrogate for the traditional character script. The instances in which *ladinghua* was promoted experimentally in literacy work, principally by the wartime Communist government in Yenan between 1940 and 1942, were apparently never formally evaluated, leaving unresolved the system's viability as a mature script.

3.2. The present PY policy

Ladinghua was the lineal precursor of the PY phonetic alphabet adopted in the PRC in 1958. In part for this reason, speculation continues in Chinese and foreign circles that the original intentions of *ladinghua's* creators may in the future yet be realized for PY. However, the current role assigned to PY, according to the late premier Chou En-lai, is more modest, extending to the phonetic annotation of characters, the transcription of PTH in dictionaries, the development of non-Chinese national-minority scripts, and the teaching of Chinese to foreigners.

Obliged, on the one, hand ritually to repeat Leninist predictions of an age when all languages will be written phonetically and, on the other, chary of appearing too partisan toward such a sensitive and potentially divisive cultural issue, the government officially postponed indefinitely further consideration of script phoneticization. Its position was best stated in a newspaper item written by Wang Li, an eminent Chinese linguist:

Many people mistakenly believe that the phonetic annotation system [*pinyin zimu*] is the same thing as a writing system [*pinyin wenzi*] .... That is not so. There is no hurry about resolving the question of whether [PY] will in the future replace characters. This is absolutely the case. After [PY] has been in use then we can, from an examination of the actual situation, determine whether or not it can fulfill the requirements of a writing system. Although there are people advocating the phoneticization of the written language, still there are difficulties in implementing such a proposal, and for the present it is still not possible to make any predictions. Currently the function of [PY] is about the same as that of [the NPA] – that is, it is a phonetic system for the annotation of characters. Earlier, when [the NPA] was being promoted, no one was worried that it would replace characters. Today, however, as [PY] is being promoted, many people are concerned that it will supplant characters. Why is this? I would say, first, because [PY] employs Latin letters. And second, because in the past some people advocated [*ladinghua*]. But if we make clear our present policy to the people, then there will be no further mis-understanding. If Latin letters are really superior to [the NPA], then we might as well use them. The government has never committed itself to im-plementing [*ladinghua*], and those who so advocate now are simply indivi-duals expressing their own personal opinion. (NFRB January 29, 1958)

3.3. Implementation of PY policy

Compared with the scope of the PTH teacher-training programs initiated in 1956, the implementation of the PY system in 1958 was allocated far fewer resources. PY teaching manuals were published, and newspapers and radio disseminated information on the correspondence between PY symbols and the PTH sound values with which most teachers had by then obtained some familiarity.

The addition of PY to characters in a variety of locations, including street and storefront signs and elsewhere, has also been attested.

It is possible that much of this early work may have been undone by the dozen or so years of the Cultural Revolution and its aftermath, beginning in the mid-1960s. During this period it was reported that street signs annotated in PY were removed and the PY annotations alongside the names of journals and newspapers were eliminated routinely by their editors. The temptation to attribute these reports to a militant xenophobic strain in Chinese culture should probably be resisted, because any visitor to China can see countless examples of PY annotation which survived the Cultural Revolution undistubed. It is perhaps safer to relate the shortcomings of PY promotion to the routine problems inherent in any educational innovation. Here, for example, one could cite the complaints that PY instruction was rarely pursued after the second grade, so that within a few years students lost all practical control of it.

3.4.   Observations relating to PY promotion

3.4.1. *Urban areas.* Despite the fact that my observations are limited to Canton and Shanghai and therefore cannot be taken as representative of the country at large, they are in general consistent with what has been reported about PY promotion in the past.

In Canton, the education officials confirmed that PY is a component of first- and second-grade instruction in the elementary schools but is not emphasized thereafter. This strongly implies that the present generation of elementary-school graduates will not differ significantly from the previous ones in its facility in using a phonetic annotation system.

The first requirement for the use of a phonetic system for all except the most limited purposes in schools is a sufficient phonological similarity in the spoken languages of correspondents so that the written record of one writer's speech is intelligible to others familiar with his language. As matters now stand, that requirement cannot be met in Guangdong Province because facility in PTH (the only regional language PY is authorized to represent) is not yet widespread. When asked how long a time may be necessary before that level of uniformity is achieved, the response was '190 years.'.

In terms of satisfying the PTH prerequisite, at least among the school-age segment of the population, Shanghai may be well ahead of Canton. Examples of the public use of PY are numerous, including virtually routine annotation of street and storefront signs in characters.[4]

In Shanghai elementary schools, PY is taught from the sixth through the twelfth week of the first grade. Symbols are presented singly at first, followed by morphological and word-level units, to students who have already been exposed to PTH sound values in the first six weeks of the term.

Beginning in January, 1979, the Shanghai Department of Education began to publish a monthly tabloid for teachers which is devoted to articles about PY promotion and always includes short items written exclusively in PY.

PY annotation can also be observed on library catalogue cards, such as those I noted in the Shanghai Jiaotong University collection. The librarian, apparently uncertain of the reason for their inclusion, suggested tentatively that (1) exposure alone might be a sufficient justification for use, or that (2) its presence would serve to promote more accurate PTH pronunciation. I suspect that neither rationale has much validity — catalogue users unfamiliar with PY must simply ignore it, and its mere presence cannot bring about a change in daily speech habits. A more plausible explanation is that annotation of cards now will facilitate a possible reorganization of catalogue filing along phonetic lines later.

3.4.2. *Rural areas.* Very little data is available about the extent of PY penetration in the countryside, but what is available is not encouraging. Just as in the case of the cities, the principal function of PY is still to advance the promotion of PTH; if the latter is proceeding at a glacial pace and with only marginal results, there is unlikely to be much scope for the use of PY. It is widely conceded that PTH, and therefore PY, promotion activities will require a longer and more stubborn commitment in rural areas, where allegiances to traditional cultural values, including the traditional forms of writing as well as local varieties of the regional languages, are likely to be firmly held, and innovation in whatever realm regarded with profound reservation.

It is not surprising, therefore, to hear educational authorities in Canton report that PY was not well received among adults in literacy programs. In the past, scattered references have occurred in the literature to adults whose ingrained veneration for the traditional character script disinclined them toward the use of an ancillary phonetic aid even though use of the latter would have accelerated their acquisition of the script. This is all the more interesting in discussing PY in Guangdong Province because a small stir was created in early 1960s when variations of the current PY system were developed for adult literacy activities and published in the local newspapers.[5]

My meeting with the young woman in North Bridge Commune outside Shanghai yielded information about PY as well as PTH. On that occasion I presented her with a short list of lexical items spelled in PY and, through the interpreter, attempted to elicit the equivalent forms in her own language. Some of the items in that list included *Mao Zedong* [Mao Tse-tung], *Hua zhuxi* [Chairman Hua (Guo-feng)], *shehuizhuyi* [socialism], and *zhonghua renmin gongheguo* [PRC]. This informant was unable to identify any of the items, although she insisted that she had been exposed to PY in elementary school.

4. PROSPECTS

4.1. The 1970 Hong Kong survey

The Chinese government has not, to my knowledge, published an evaluation of the results of PTH and PY promotion in regional-language areas. The only attempt known to me to assess these programs was a survey conducted by myself in Hong Kong in 1970. This survey indicated that students who had begun elementary-school educations in southeastern China after 1956 could, within the limits imposed by the level of their education, function in PTH. All of the 27 respondents who participated in this survey were judged capable of acceptable syntactic and lexical behavior in PTH.

The Hong Kong survey also investigated the respondents' familiarity with PY. The results of a very simple testing procedure revealed that 70% of the students interviewed were unable to recognize the phonological values of PY symbols, irrespective of whether the symbols were presented one at a time or were contextualized. Only three of the 27 interviewees were capable of understanding the contents of three short paragraphs written in PY, and their ability to do this was apparently related to the length of time during which they had been exposed to PY in school. In none of these three cases did the interviewee's abilities attain a functional level of competence adequate for independent reading or writing.

4.2. Reflections on PTH promotion

4.2.1. *Urban.* The findings of the Hong Kong survey have in the widest sense been upheld by observers of the Chinese language programs over the past decade. But certain of the most recent observations relative to PTH program implementation pose problems which that survey cannot answer.

The respondents in that survey were all native speakers of a regional language other than PTH, and almost all entered elementary school coincident with the beginning of the PTH program in elementary schools in 1956. As a group, their behavior is suggestive of possible levels of attainment in PTH prior to the mid-1960s but less reliable in determining the effects of events over the last 15 years. Thus, some of the practical difficulties involved in implementing the language program during these years raise questions which can only be answered by recourse ot a repetition of the earlier survey.

If in Canton, for example, the PTH program was reported in difficulty prior to the 1960s; and in Shanghai the most recent infusion of trained PTH instructors took place in 1966; and in both cities summer language institutes for retraining teachers and improving language skills have apparently been suspended; then what effect have these developments had in southeast China and how long are these effects likely to be felt? And what kind of PTH program implementation can the present PTH personnel maintain until new personnel are trained to assist them? These are the kinds of questions that PTH promotion will have to address in the nest few years.

4.2.2. *Rural.* The respondents in the 1970 survey who were educated in the countryside were less proficient in PTH than were their urban counterparts. Some of the urban respondents who had lived in the countryside corroborated this conclusion on the basis of their own personal experience. But these respondents were a minority of the whole survey group, as were respondents with rural educational backgrounds themselves. As a result, the survey could only hypothesize that, as of the early 1960s, PTH promotion might have been developing a limited momentum outside the cities.

But even this characterization would be too sanguine if indeed program implementation was never vigorous and subsided quickly in those areas soon after it began. The recurrent newspaper items citing instances of local coolness toward intrusions of nonlocal culture and language behavior attest to the strength of these indigenous traditions, and point as well to the fact that it may be difficult to make a convincing case for PTH in palces which are still linguistically self-sufficient in the local language. When the attitudes of some parents moving from the country to the city are reserved with respect to PTH instruction, it is hard to imagine why those whom they left in the agricultural sector would feel differently.

Until established by field investigation, however, these views must remain at the level of informed speculation.

4.3. PY promotion

The 1970 survey indicated that only a small proportion of the respondents interviewed had any facility whatsoever in recognizing PY symbols, and none could read it as one would his own orthography. The observations recorded in this paper do not contradict those findings in any way.

It is clear that attempts have been made to enhance the visibility of the PY system, but there is considerable doubt that it is read or is even readable by more than a handful of people. Students in schools seem to have negligible contact with PY after the first elementary grades, although many of them do develop facility in PTH. What factors might explain the tenuous status of PY throughout the years since 1958?

There are perhaps two possibilities worth exploring. One is that PY has had and will continue to have difficulty obtaining a following from all but a small although highly committed group, because it is an unmistakable foreign graft onto the Chinese cultural body. This possibility cannot be dismissed outright, but it has yet to be shown that PY has evoked significant antipathy among the population at large.

Another possibility is that language planners have not elaborated a methodology which would enable PY to play a larger role in the implementation of PTH. A parallel exists in the case of the MPA, which for more than 30 years after its formal recognition attracted only minor notice in educational circles, in part because the technological and pedagogical prerequisites for its use in the classroom went largely unrecognized. An examination of the actual situations in which PY is employed in the schools will help in understanding whether PY suffers from some of these same limitations.

NOTES

1. The resumption of central government leadership was marked by the Fifth National Conference on the Evaluation of PTH Instruction, convened in Peking, August 11-20, 1979. The conference focused national attention on PTH promotion by means of language contests featuring winners from provincial, county, and municipal competitions, and provided a forum for the exchange of information among teachers. The fifth such conference to be held in the history of the PTH program, it was the first of its kind since 1964 (GMRB August 8 and 23, 1979: 2).
2. This problem is likely to be more marked in rural areas where local sociocultural values militate against the use in public or in social situations of PTH learned by students in school (GMRB August 15, 1979: 3).
3. A three-year plan for the use of PTH in schools in another county in rural Jiangsu Province, beginning in the fall of 1978, established the same targets as the central government had previously hoped students might achieve nationally by 1959 (GMRB August 30, 1979: 4).
4. Distracting somewhat from this otherwise impressive display is so marked an absence of consensus in the handling of morphological and lexical spelling decisions that some PY annotations are patently perfunctory and are evidence of nothing more than an attempt to comply with local regulations. A striking example of this phenomenon was the storefront sign for the Huai Hai Road, Shanghai, women's clothing merchandise outlet for the Yangtze River Clothing Factory, which read, in uninterrupted PY annotation, exactly as follows: *changjiangfuzhuangchanghuai-hainushifuzhuang.*
5. The full text is in GDONB June 11, 1960; the first mention of this item in Western literature was in DeFrancis 1967: 149.

REFERENCES

Barnes, Dayle (1973 [1974]), 'Language planning in mainland China: standardization', in *Language Planning: Current Issues and Research*, ed. by Joan Rubin and Roger

Shuy, 34-54. Washington, D.C., Georgetown University Press. (Reprinted 1974 in *Advances in Language Planning*, ed. by Joshua A. Fishman, 457-477. The Hague, Mouton).

───────── (1977a), 'National language planning in China', in *Language Planning Processes*, ed. by Joan Rubin, Bjorn H. Jernudd, et al., 255-273. The Hague, Mouton.

─────────(1977b), 'To *er* or not to *er'*, *Journal of Chinese Linguistics* 5(2): 211-236.

───────── (1978 [i.p.]), 'Nationalism and the mandarin movement: the first half-century'. Paper presented at the Conference on Language Spread and Recession, September 12-14, 1978, University of Aberystwyth, Wales, sponsored by the Center for Applied Linguistics. (To appear in *Language Spread: Studies in Diffusion and Social Change*, ed. by Robert L. Cooper).

DeFrancis, John (1967), 'Language and script reform', in *Linguistics in East Asia and South East Asia*, ed. by Thomas A. Sebeok, 130-150. *Current trends in linguistics*, volume two. The Hague, Mouton.

Newspapers cited in the text

GDQNB: *Guangdong qingnian bao* (Guangdong Youth Daily News, Canton).
GMRB: *Guangming ribao* (Guangming Daily News, Peking).
NFRB: *Nanfang ribao* (Southern Daily News, Canton).

GLYN LEWIS

Implementation of Language Planning in the Soviet Union

THE TOTALITARIAN CONCEPT OF PLANNING

Like the development of literacy, of which it is an essential feature, language planning is an aspect of social change and, more especially, of the processes of modernization. Consequently the implementation of language planning depends not only on *agencies*, like the system of education, or *procedures*, like those which belong to linguistics, such as code selection, stabilization of the orthography, and control of lexical elaboration, but on the existence and influence of social, political, or economic *movements*. These may be defined as a series of actions which exemplify social tendencies and economic and political forces, as well as social and political principles or ideologies. It may be argued that such movements do not constitute aspects of planning but are simply the conditions under which planning is conceived and implemented. No doubt this may be true of many countries, but it is not true of the Soviet Union, where we have not simply an authoritarian but an entirely totalitarian society. This means not just that the society is completely mobilized and the activities of all its citizens controlled to a great degree, but that so far as possible all social, political, and economic activities are coordinated so as to ensure the success of a 'national plan'. The languages of the Soviet Union do not escape from the requirements of the 'national plan'.

Consequently in any description of language planning in the Soviet Union, unlike the planning of Amerindian languages in the United States, or of Welsh in Britain, we need to have regard to oblique or indirect implementation of language planning as well as direct planning. It is arguable that, in the last resort, such oblique processes of implementation have been more powerful than the direct intervention of linguists or even the work of educators, educational administrators, or writers. For instance, though induced migration of populations, industrialization, and urbanization are not planned primarily with linguistic changes in mind, it is true nevertheless that such social changes are expected to facilitate the rapprochement of nationalities, the possible merging of their languages, and above all else the supremacy of Russian. Deseriev acknowledges that the development and mutual enrichment of

Soviet languages are 'determined by the processes and rapprochement of socialist nations and nationalities and their cultures' (Deseriev 1966a).

Nevertheless, though it is true that changes in the social system, planned or unplanned, have a bearing on the development of the language, it is not true that there exists a necessary and automatic relationship between social and linguistic change. Certain aspects of social life, like education and the administration of justice, tend to change directly with changes in the economic system. Such aspects belong to the superstructure of society and reflect the changes in the basic economic foundation. But language is not an element of the superstructure. Consequently, compared with the immense changes which have occurred in the economic life and the political and administrative systems of Wales, over many centuries the Welsh language has changed relatively little. The same is true of other languages, like French, which has changed only slightly during periods of considerable upheaval. The Russian language as it stands at present, the language of Solzhenitsyn, is the language that served Russian feudalism and capitalism before the Socialist revolution at the beginning of this century.

It is more than a hundred years since Pushkin died. In this period the feudal system and the capitalist system have arisen. Hence two bases with their superstructures were eliminated and a new socialist basis has been created with its new superstructure. Yet the Russian language has not in this long span of time undergone any fundamental change and the modern Russian language differs very little from the language of Pushkin. (Stalin 1949-1952)

The same is true of other countries. Welsh society, its legal system, its economy, the pattern of political control, even its religion have all changed without changes of a comparable magnitude in the language. Therefore, though we argue that 'oblique' or 'indirect' influences have to be taken into account in understanding language planning, especially in certain types of political systems, we do not maintain that social, political, and economic changes are reflected automatically in linguistic changes. What I believe to be uncontrovertible is that such social changes motivate language planning and help to determine the aims and the direction which such planning takes, as well as ensuring that whatever planning is undertaken has some hope of coming to fruition.

Limited, elitist, or class literacy may emerge prior to national development, and we cannot ignore the efforts that were made prior to the Soviet regime; but these efforts were doomed because they were not able to take advantage of fully mobilized nations. For instance, as early as 1802 the Tsarist administration of education gave two of its six commissioners of education responsibility for the education of national minorities. By the fourth quarter of the nineteenth century the system of education was organized into 15 districts with varying ethnic and linguistic patterns including five Asian, Turkestan, and Amur Pacific coastal areas. In 1869 the Minister of Education, D. Tolstory, appointed Ilya Ulyanov, Lenin's father, as school inspector for the multiethnic province of Simbirsk in the educational district of Kazan. He introduced native languages as media of instruction into very many of the 450 schools (Alston 1969). But such schools catered for relatively few children, and whatever the level of standardization of any of those languages, the opportunity of using them as bases of literacy was extremely restricted.

Modernization (of which the social and political mobilization is one aspect) is therefore a prerequisite of the success of language planning. Though, naturally enough, Soviet linguists accept this postulate, they identify modernization with the development of socialism. Thus they argue, 'the development of national languages (and therefore literacy) in socialist and capitalist societies is very different' (Guxman 1960). The process of ensuring a national base for literacy reflecting unified literary norms by means of press, radio, and educational institutions, it is claimed, 'is most intense in socialist countries'. In fact, however, the development of both a unified literary medium and a particular system of society are independent though parallel developments in a process of modernization. Contrary to the claims of Soviet linguists, universal literacy as an aspect of language planning has nothing to do with socialism as such.

AIMS OF PLANNING IN THE SOVIET UNION WITHIN THE CONTEXT OF MODERNIZATION

If language planning is influenced so much by social change in the Soviet Union, it is equally the case that changes in the languages are meant to facilitate social change. The problem of language change, like the problem of bilingual education, is synonymous in some aspects with the problem of the distribution of political power. The planning of minority languages is only superficially a purely linguistic exercise: it is basically one of the means of promoting the political and economic interests of the minority. Thus planning may be positive or promotional on the one hand, and on the other negative or adversative. Ignoring a minority language, or prohibiting its use in any social context, is as much an aspect of planning as providing it with an alphabet. The French Academy indulged in negative planning when it sought to eliminate dialects of the French language in 1794, and it adopted this stance because it believed dialects were a hindrance to a unified political system. The same is true of the Soviet Union in respect of several minority languages, and some languages like Yiddish and Hebrew which have a world-wide role. The aim is to ensure that political power is not spread more than can be helped.

Similarly, changes in the geographical spread and community restructuring (urban or rural), as well as class and occupational spread of particular languages, are some of the aims of those concerned with language planning in the Soviet Union, particularly as it affects the Russian language positively and the minority languages negatively. Migration is encouraged from Slavic to Central Asian areas and the beneficiary is the Russian language. The movement of industry into the virgin lands means the urbanization of rural communities as well as increased linguistic heterogeneity, to the benefit of Russian. Upward social mobility, and particularly status within the ruling hierarchy, depend on the acquisition of Russian.

These are aspects of the modernization of the Soviet Union, and it is necessary to stress the dependence of the development of language planning on the processes of modernization because the aspects of the growth of 'national' as distinct from 'folk' or 'nationality' languages reflect the intensification of modernization. For instance, it is not surprising that there has been such phenomenal growth of literacy in several languages when we remember the equally rapid growth of urbanization, especially in the Central Asian areas. Related to this fact is the choice of urban dialects or urban groups of subdialects as the bases of national languages, as we shall have occasion to note later in the case of Uzbek. Urbanization is also a factor in the improvement of the channels of language planning, the most important being the schools. The positive correlation of language planning and urbanization is not coincidental, partly because the standard of education in rural schools does not compare favorably with the standard in urban schools. It was reported in 1973 that while the rural schools of Kazakhstan cater for 50% of the child population, the education given them in those schools 'does not come up to contemporary requirements'. Similar comments have been made about most of the other Republics (*Uchetelskaya Gzeta* 1973).

Second, language planning in the Soviet Union reflects the scientific, technical, and secular aspects of modernization. The work of early language planners such as Ilminsky was related to the demands of religion. Although he was Professor of Languages at Kazan Theological Academy, Ilminsky was first and foremost a missionary who strove to extend the use of Chuvash, Mari, Udmurt, and others. Again, slowness in introducing the Latin alphabet in Turkic countries was explained by the Chairman of the All-Union Committee for the new Turkic Alphabet (VTsKNTA) as being due to the religious associations of Arabic, which made a decision to learn a new alphabet tantamount to an affront to Islam and a sin before God (Vsesoyuznogo Tsentral'nogo Komitet 1929). For the Soviet regime, however, language planning is important 'because it is part and parcel of the work of the Communist Party (*Okuticiliar Gazetasi* 1968). Language planning leads to literacy and so opens the way to an understanding of Marxism. Lenin maintained 'an illiterate person is outside politics and he has to be taught his ABC. Without this there can be no politics' (Lenin 1918).

But having emphasized the necessity of including such political and kindred considerations in analyzing Soviet language planning, we must acknowledge that such considerations alone do not constitute language planning, and for that reason the more obvious, though not the most fundamental, aspects of such planning are the concern mainly of linguists and educators. These comprise code selection, terminology and alphabetic reform.

Code selection

Within the Soviet Union the discussion of the specifically linguistic aspects of language planning has a preponderantly sociological orientation. The possibility of universal as opposed to elitist or class literacy depends on the development of 'national' as distinct from what is termed 'folk' language. The fundamental characteristic of a developed national language compared with a folk language is that it is a single standardized literary language (a common national literary norm) which is shared by the entire nation, which functions in all aspects of communication, and which was formed from a folk base. The existence of folk language does not necessarily rule out a written literary language. But a distinctive feature of such a literary fōlk language, if it exists, is the limitation of its currency to a very select group. Literacy, which is the aim of language planning in the USSR, requires a national language which is defined as 'examplifying the most highly developed, stable and socially acceptable linguistic norms' (Guxman 1960: 295-320). It emerges only at certain points in the history of a people, namely the 'stage of nationality formation and development and the stage of national formation and development' (Konrad 1960). For language planning to have any hope of fruition or practical effect, therefore, the full potential of the nation must have been or be in process of mobilization: 'a national language is formed when it becomes a unified common national language for the whole society' (Konrad 1960).

Social and economic development, by ensuring that the results of planning have a reasonable promise of being implemented nationally and of being effective, can only lay the foundations of the promotion of literacy. The linguistic analysis has been very intensively pursued in the Soviet Union since the early days of the regime, and some of the descriptions of languages have been made available for the first time. Such studies are complicated by the dialectal patterns of large numbers of Soviet languages. For instance, before the stabilization of Khakass there existed only several separate spoken dialects – Beltir, Sagay, Kachin, Koybal, and Kyzyl. The choice of Sagay-Kachin as the base of literacy and school instruction was dependent on field studies – work involving several dialects (Juldasev 1959).

Uzbek is a good example of the problems facing language planners in the initial stages of the regime. Its dialects, classified according to their locale, include Central Uzbek from around Tashkent, a variant spoken in Samarkand and its environs, and another group of dialects spoken in the Ferghana Valley, which are in close contact with dialects of the Andizhan area. Then there are the North Uzbek dialects spoken around Chimkent and north of Tashkent as well as in the southern areas of Kazakhstan. There are also the Kazakh dialects of Uzbek, and finally the Turkmenised variants spoken in the area surrounding Khiva. This distribution of Uzbek dialects has to be explained in terms of the ethnic processes under which the Uzbek nation was formed. Certain local dialects have retained clear traces of linguistic interaction between members of various Turkic groups during different periods of their coexistence. Individual dialects retain pronounced phonetic, lexical, and grammatical differences, and the distribution of these features does not always coincide with the geographic distribution of the dialects.

Tadzhik is usually regarded as possessing at least five groups of dialects, of which the Northwestern, spoken west of Ferghana near Samarkand and Bukhara, is the best known. Its most northerly variant is spoken northeast of Tashkent. The second group, the Southwestern, are spoken by the Mountain Tadzhiks of the Badakhshan-Goron area. Farsi, the Central Asian form of Persian, and the Yagnobi dialects are two other groups, and there is a collection of dialects spoken by Beludzhi, Kurds, and Afghans on the frontiers. The standard literary Tadzhik is based on the Northwestern variant.

There are at least three approaches to language planning. The first approach is, realistically perhaps, to be content to allow languages to die, or, the more extreme exemplification of the same attitude, actually to create conditions leading to the extinction of a language. Examples of languages to which the approach of the planners is at best only neutral are, first, the Buduck and Khinalug languages spoken in Azerbaydzhan by 3,000 and 1,000 people respectively. The two languages are gradually becoming extinct, their place being taken by Azerbaydzhan. The Batsbi language occupies a similar position. It is spoken in only one village in the Georgian Republic, Zemo-Alvani, and Georgian is gradually assuming the role of native language for nearly all the inhabitants. The second approach is negative or at least highly critical and subversive of the norms of an existing 'literary' language. Many of the languages of the Soviet Union possessed such historical literary languages but many 'of the old literary languages were based on medieval dialects remote from the living spoken language of the people' (Deseriev 1966b). Consequently, one of the priorities of the linguists was to attack the artificial literary norms: 'one characteristic feature which is invariably present in such controversies (with regard to the creation of a national language) — the object of attack has always been the written literary language, characterized as reactionary and feudal' (Konrad 1960). In Uzbek, for instance, there had been an attempt to create an artificial literary language based on the old book-language which was wedded to the use of Arabic and Persian (Baskakov 1973). Part of the efforts of the Soviet linguists was to eliminate Persian lexical, phonological, and grammatical elements in Uzbek (Resetov 1960). The development of the eastern variant of the Armenian national literary language was also facilitated by such critical approaches, first of all to Grabar, which, because it was in the early periods restricted to the Church, became a cult language and ceased to be intelligible to the mass of people. Out of this critical phase grew *Ashkharhabar* [lay language], which was well defined by the fourteenth century and was still current in the nineteenth century. It too, in turn, underwent a vigorous critical appraisal and in consequence the grammar of the new literary language which emerged after the 1880s was purged of dialect forms; its lexicon was 'purified' of more recent Arabic, Turkish, and Persian importations. The same processes were promoted in the case of the west Armenian literary language.

The third approach to the selection of a code and its stabilization at all levels, lexical, phonological, and grammatical, is creative, guided by clearly defined criteria of judgment and selection. The first criterion is a continuous historical tradition of speaking a particular dialect. The choice of the Tashkent-Ferghana dialect as the base for Uzbek was determined partly by the fact that it 'can be traced back to the linguistic community of the Karkhanid period, and which genetically speaking is related to the Uygur language. Together they form a single and unbroken line of development' (Resetov 1960). But the choice of a historically authentic dialect is not necessarily synonymous with the selection of the 'most pure dialect'. If that had been the case the original choice of the South Kazakhstan dialect of Uzbek as the base for the literary language would have prevailed. Its possession of full vowel harmony was more in character with historical Uzbek than the modified urban dialects of Tashkent, where the vowel system had been modified and had approximated more and more to Tadzhik or to the vowel system of the Samarkand-Bukhara dialects, which replicate the vowel system of Tadzhik.

In any case, in some instances it is difficult to be precise about the authenticity of an indigenous historical development of the language. Thus, in Gagauz, the literary language is formed 'on the base of the Central Comrat and Chayrlung dialects and has retained the traces of its most ancient state' (Baskakov 1952), but it is also characterized by considerable importations from Slavonic, Romanic, Greek, and Turkish. In syntax and morphology it has much in common with Turkish, but there are characteristic morphological innovations from Greek as well. The impact of Slavonic is the analytical manner of forming the components of the Gagauz verb. The influcnec of other languages on the phonetic and lexical systems of Gagauz is even more pronounced. It would be difficult, therefore, to employ the criterion of 'linguistic purity' or even historical authenticity at all strictly in selecting and stabilizing the norms for the literary form of Gagauz.

A third criterion for selecting a dialect base is that it should be the most widely representative, not alone in geographic terms but also, perhaps mainly, to the extent that it represents the total complex of dialectal features. For instance, in the case of Bashkir, in 1921 after the Kuvakan dialect had been selected as the main base for literacy it was realized that far from all the characteristics of Kuvakan were represented in other dialects. These dialects had been influenced by Tatar and consequently they tended to exert an alien pressure on literary Bashkir. In turn, Kuvakan could not steer those dialects into the main stream of Bashkir linguistic development – in other words the choice of Kuvakan did not ensure a stable set of norms. Only by combining characteristics of Kuvakan and Jurmatin could a sufficiently widespread acceptability be ensured. It is one of the corollaries of the complexity of the dialectal patterns of Soviet languages and of the requirement of maximum national acceptability of the standardized norms that planning should be flexible and eclectic. For instance 'the formation of the phonological system of the Kalmyk literary language was directed toward blending the sound phenomena which are characteristic of leading dialects', especially the Torgut and Derbet dialects. Literary Kalmyk is a synthesis of dialectal features (Deseriev 1973). Ashkharhabar, the historical literary base of contemporary Armenian, shows a blend of elements from various dialects. Such syntheses are facilitated by the historical development of local dialectal koines (Konrad 1960), the consequence of natural convergence. In the case of Armenian it produced the northeast Armenian, the *um* dialect, and the *ke* dialect of the south and southwest. The consolidation of these two sets of dialects facilitated the rise of the two national literary variants of Armenian. In Bashkir the Kuvakan dialect became the msot suitable base fot he literary language because of the convergence of the related subdialects (Juldasev 1960).

Perhaps the most important criterion used in code selection is the degree to which the proposed dialectal base represents the norms of the spoken language. In the Soviet view the historical development of a literary language, whether 'folk' or 'national', is characterized by closer approximation to colloquial forms. Thus, it is argued, the 'historical life of the old Armenian literary language flowed along two lines – written and spoken. The written language was preserved for centuries almost without undergoing change . . . .

The need for a written language for lay purposes . . . resulted in the rise of a variant of the written language which reflected the spoken language and was significantly different from Grabar, the historical literary language' (Garibian 1960). In Bashkir, too, the movement for greater incorporation of colloquial forms may be observed. As in Armenian, there were two streams, the folk-colloquial and the written language which 'for the entire duration of its history up to the Soviet revolution differed from each other considerably. When in the eighteenth century changes were made in the written language it was with a view to bringing it closer to colloquial Bashkir and to a greater recognition of the norms of the spoken language' (Juldasev 1960). However, in spite of the invariable tendency toward closer identification with the spoken language, it is generally recognized that 'the literary norms of the written language always represent the results of a certain isolation from the colloquial base' (Guxman 1960), so that however well-judged the selection of the code may be it is never entirely or finally stabilized. There is a continuing need to maintain the closest contact between the written literary norm and the spoken language.

Whatever phase of the approach to the stabilizing process we are concerned with, negative-critical, or positive-creative, and notwithstanding the occasional statement that 'the development of languages in the Soviet Union proceeds from natural, spontaneous tendencies' (Deseriev 1960a), there is general agreement on the vital role of planning on all levels of linguistic analysis, phonology, grammar, and lexicon. Developments under Soviet conditions are 'not so much spontaneous as regulated by a system of measures that facilitate the greatest possible expansion of the literary languages' (Terenteva 1972). Guxman is among the most emphatic in this view:

The formation of a new type of literary language, expressive of a common national unity, is impossible without conscious normalization, without theoretical comprehension of the norm and codification of definite rules . . . . The common national norm in the literary language is never the result of a spontaneous process of language development, but to a certain degree the result of a artificial selection and interference with this spontaneous process. (Guxman 1960)

Nevertheless, however deliberate, conscious, and theoretically well founded the selection of the code may be, it is impossible to eliminate the possibility of continuing controversy about the appropriateness of the selected norms. This is true, as wel shall have occasion to note in discussing alphabetic reform, but it is no less true of other aspects of language planning. Thus, 'the standardization of Bashkir has been criticized because the features selected from Kuvakan and Jurmatin, the twin bases, tended to be mutually exclusive, nor do they correspond to features of any of the other dialects'. The new norms, in addition, are not distinguished by sufficient consistency inasmuch as they are essentially a mechanical mixture of the rules of several dialects (Juldasev 1960). Consequently, certain aspects of the standardization of Bashkir continue to be matters of controversy. The same conclusion is arrived at by Wurm in his discussion of Baskakov's treatment of the planning exercise which has been proceeding for several decades in respect of other Turkic languages (Baskakov 1960). Neither close approximation of the written language to common speech, nor devotion to explicitly stated and conscientiously pursued sociolinguistic criteria and guidelines are sufficient to ensure stabilization of the code, necessary to the growth of universal literacy, without continuous adjustment.

Terminology

Vocabulary is undoubtedly the aspect of language which is most immediately affected by social change, and this is one of the reasons why N.Y. Marr gave such prominence to terminology – the linguistic aspect of the future. Changes in terminology arise partly from the need to enrich the language with the lexical items required by the economic and cultural revolution, partly by the politically motivated desire to eliminate from Soviet languages vestigial lexical items which link them to prerevolutionary and genetically related languages – for instance, Arabic and Persian. A third cause of the insistence on encouraging lexical change was the wish to ensure that the national languages were able to cope with translation demands from Marx-Engels-Lenin and Stalin. These issues were raised at the Congress of Workers' Education in 1924. A special commission was set up, following the Congress of Turkology at Baku in 1926, to initiate work on dictionaries and lexicons for new political and scientific developments. By 1933 this commission had produced several minimum lists for science and technology (Dimanshtain 1933). The Baku conference also confronted the problem of the 'basic common stock' of the lexicons of Soviet languages, but this commonality was alleged to be pan-Turkic and it was disapproved. In 1962 the development of a common stock in more comprehensively Soviet terms was favorably argued at the Alma Ata Conference on the Development of Literary Languages.

Apart from the Soviet-wide commissions on terminology, many Union Republics created their own commissions. In Armenia, the Speical Terminology Commission by 1950 had approved over 18,000 medical terms and 13,000 legal terms. In Latvia, 40,000 terms were approved between 1947 and 1949 (Mordvinov 1950). A permanent Terminology Commission of the Soviet Ministry of the Bashkir ASSR was created in the 1940s and its efforts were subsequently continued by the Bashkir branch of the Academy of

Science of the USSR (Juldasev 1960). It produced the first normative dictionary, which included sociological and philosophical terms as well as lexicons for botany, chemistry, mathematics, physics, linguistics, and medicine. A second series, concerned with the same and additional subjects, such as chemistry and forestry, was published later (Juldasev 1960). Similar work has continued in most of the other languages. For instance, the Terminology Commission of the Kirgiz Academy of Sciences has been systematizing the lexicology of nearly all branches of science and has produced nearly 70 lexicons (*Sovetskaya Kirgizia* 1973a).

Such advances in lexicology have been governed by certain theoretically sound principles, though in the matter of foreign importations (as we shall note) there is some ambivalence. The first principle is that 'the maximum possible use should be made of native resources' (*Sovetskaya Kirgizia* 1973b). The processes of exploiting these resources, involving extension and restriction of meaning, word composition, derivation, abbreviation, and loan translation, are well known to linguists. The development of native resources has not invariably been uncomplicated. The several dialects of Bashkir often diverge in respect of vocabulary, not so far as the inclusion or exclusion of particular items is concerned but in the semanticity of words which are common to several dialects, especially those terms which concern kinship and other distinctive features of local customs and different cultural orientations. Very often, too, the same words may have different meanings in different dialects, for instance, *qasik* 'pilgrim' in the Jurmatin dialect but 'spoon' in the Northwestern.

The maximum use of native resources entailed the introduction into the literary language of elements of dialects and subdialects. In Uzbek, for example, 'archaic words and expressions were gradually deleted and replaced with words and expressions existing in the spoken language (Resetov 1960). It entailed in the second place the elimination not simply of archaisms but of foreign importations. Thus lexical derivations from Arabic into Uzbek amounted to a significant factor in the development of the language historically, in view of the protracted Arab rule of Maverannakhra and the spread of Islam. Although importations from Tadzhik were fewer, the influence of that language was also considerable. Every effort was made to eliminate these substratum influences (Resetov 1960). In Armenia the languages of greatest influence were Arabic, Turkish, and Persian, and Armenian was 'freed' of words borrowed from these sources. There can be no doubt that part of the rationale for such 'purifications' was political. Non-Russian foreign importations proclaim the historically close relations of Uzbek as well as Armenian with the disapproved sources. For the same reason Tatar words, of which Bashkir has very many, have been progressively removed (Juldasev 1960).

In this respect the attitude to Russian importations is inconsistent. That language is at least as foreign to speakers of Central Asian languages, and for that matter to speakers of Armenian, as Arabic and Persian or Turkish are. Indeed in the 1920s and 1930s there was a similar disinclination to allow the importation of Russian terms. Gradually the attitude changed: 'the experience of the peoples of the USSR has shown', it was claimed 'that the Russian language has played and will play a historically important role in the development of their languages. Thanks to its richness the Russian language is the main source of borrowing . . . . In most of the languages of the USSR 70-80% of the new terms have been borrowed from Russian, (*Vushka* 1972). An analysis of a sample of Uzbek periodicals between 1933 and 1940 shows that, while the percentage of Arabic and Persian words has declined from 37% ro 25% the Russian element increased from 2% to 15% (Kari-Nyazov 1968). In 1950, 18% of the items in a Uzbek/Turkic dictionary were of Russian origin (*Kizil-Uzbekistan Quarterly* 1952), while a Tatar dictionary contained twice as many Russian loan words in the 1958 edition as there were in the 1929 edition (*East Turkic Review* 1960). Because of this extent of Russian infiltration a merging of the lexical content of the national languages and the Russian language has occurred and through this 'a merging of the lexicons of the national languages themselves' (Baskakov 1952).

The Russian influence is more pervasive than this indirect contribution suggests, since the Russian language has become the accepted model as well as a main source of lexical enrichment. First, Russian is the intermediary for most words introduced from non-Soviet linguistic sources, English or French or German for instance. Second, the broad application of calquing, mainly from Russian sources, has expanded considerably. For instance, in Bashkir we now have *kultura-ayarti ese* [culturally instructive work], *kultura-politik ayarti* [cultural-political education], *xeomat geroizmi* [labor heroism] (Juldasev 1960). Third, derivatives are formed from Russian by the addition of native affixes. For instance in Bashkir there are now *buntarliq* [rioting], *novatorliq* [innovation], *bol'sevistik* [bolshevik], *kulturahid* [uncultured], etc. Lithuanian may be taken to exemplify the very wide range of types of indirect Russian influence upon a national language. For instance, Lithuanian follows in its own way the Russian practice of abbreviation and contraction, acronym formation. Thus, as in Russian *spec* for specialist the Lithuanians have created *specas* from *specseminiras* [special seminar] and *speckyrius* [special division]. The Russian characteristic of prefixes and compound words has influenced the creation of similar words in Lithuanian: the Russian *soavt* is the analogy for Lithuanian *bendeaautoris* [joint author]. Productive suffixes such as *-yste* are used to produce words on the analogy of Russian, such as *nacetcik*, the Lithuanian *prisiskaitelis* [well-read]. Hybridization of Russian and Lithuanian terms has become a fruitful source, as in *energotraukinys* (Russian *energopopojezd*) [mobile track for railways]. Lithuanian words have developed new and more specialized meanings while retaining traditional meanings, mainly because of Russian influence. For instance, the verb *uzastrinti* [to sharpen] has come to acquire an abstract or metaphoric meaning on the lines of Russian *zaostrit* [to refine or to stress an argument]. Finally, international words borrowed through Russian help in restricting or refining native or traditional meanings. For instance *plenumas*, meaning 'special political meeting', is now available in addition to the native *pilnatis*, which means 'plenary session' (Salys 1967).

Alphabetic reform

The Soviet Union is not simply multilingual but multigraphic as well, and was even more so at the commencement of the Soviet regime. At one time the main alphabets were Arabic and Cyrillic, but there were some examples of the use of a Latin script, especially in the Baltic countries; while Georgian and Armenian were each of them unique alphabets within the USSR. Other nationalities had been given modified Russian scripts, Abur, as far back as the fourteenth century by missionaries like St. Stephen of Perm. These were the Finno-Ugrian group of the Volga Basin, Mari, and Komi. The motives for alphabetic reform were several: it was claimed that Arabic was unsuited to some of the Central Asian languages, but in these cases it was even more the case that it was felt that Soviet languages should be separated as far as possible from non-Soviet and independent speakers of related languages. There was the imperative requirement to diminish the degree of heterogeneity which existed in the USSR, though its abolition, official statements notwithstanding, has never been a feasible proposition, in view of the existence of such historically rich and powerful nations with unique alphabets such as Georgia. But even if radical changes in the alphabets had not been contemplated, it was generally agreed that the alphabets of several languages needed reforming. For instance, changes had been introduced into Armenian, the need for which arose entirely from the intrinsic dialect situation of that country. In 1927 a new orthography was introduced, and so far as East Armenian is concerned this involved the omission of two traditional signs − *o* and *t*. The appearance of the East Armenian dialect became significantly different from that of West Armenian, with consequent marked mutual unintelligibility. In 1940 the two signs were reinstated in order to bring the two dialects together once again. Similar internal stresses occurred within the Arabic alphabets and their reform was proposed, both in Turkey and among the Turkic peoples of the USSR, as early as 1862.

With the inauguration of the Soviet regime, the demand for reform became widespread. In 1919 a special section of the Department of National Minori-

ties of the USSR Commissariat of Education was created to develop textbooks and literature with the help of local teachers, and this necessitated the
development or adaptation of scripts. By 1922 the adoption of latinization
was receiving approval, exemplified for instance by the report of the Second
Conference of Uzbek Education Workers, who fiercely opposed any suggestion of Cyrillic innovations as smacking of Russification (Polivanov 1928). In
the meantime Azerbaydzhan was already revising the existing latinized script,
New Road (*jeni jol*) and was attempting to substitute it for the Arabic alphabet (Winner 1952). The first Azerbaydzhan periodical in the latinized alphabet was issued with 200 copies in 1922. By 1926 the circulation had risen to
6,000 (Guxman 1960). Between the two dates the latinized script had been
accepted, though with some reservations, all over Central Asia. The discussions culminated at the First Turkic Congress in Baku in 1926 which, after
heated argument, accepted the principle of the superiority of the Latin over
the Arabic alphabet.

The new Latin alphabet was named the Unified New Turkic Alphabet
(*Novogo Tyurkskogo Alfavita-NTA*). By order of the Supreme Soviet of the
USSR (UTsIK), a permanent organization was established to undertake
research and to organize the introduction of the new alphabet, namely the
All Union Central Committee on the New Turkic Alphabet (*Vsesoyuznyy
Tsentral'nyy Komitet Novogo Turkskogo Alfavita* [VTsKNTA]). The initial
impulse was to unify the 17 latinizing projects, but at the second plenary
session of the VTsKNTA in 1929 it was agreed that this was impracticable
because of the considerable differences between the phonetic systems of the
various languages (Guxman 1960). Nevertheless, sufficient unity was achieved
to satisfy the political demands for a means of drawing together the various
Soviet nationalities. By 1928 all Union Republics were using NTA and
schools were becoming acquainted with it (*Novy Vostok* 1928). By 1930,
36 nationalities with a total of 30 millions accepted it. At this point the
VTsKNTA ceased to function as a specifically Turkic-oriented commission
and a new department, a direct organ of the central government, was sub-
stituted, with responsibility for promoting latinized scripts for all peoples,
Turkic and non-Turkic. This was the *Vsoyuznoyy Komitet Novogo Alfavita
pri VTsIK SSSR* (VTsKNA pri VTsIK SSSR) (Korkmasov 1955).

However, the promoters of NTA were already in difficulties because the
Russian Cyrillic script was preferred by some nationalities, and by 1937 there
were clear indications of a radical switch of policy. The first adumbrations
were sensed at the Seventh Plenary Session of the VTsKNA itself, when it
was found necessary to agree that the Kabardo-Balkars should be allowed to
adopt the Cyrillic script. In 1939 Daghestan adopted Cyrillic, and by 1940 it
had spread to most Republics, more than 68 languages having been supplied
with scripts and over 25 millions, it was claimed, able to use them. In all these

developments at least five different but related aspects have to be distinguished. In the first place there was the creation of alphabets of any kind for some languages; and this, in the abstract, was the main contribution to literacy made by the linguists. Second, there was the decision to have as far as possible a unified base, whether this was Latin or Russian. This had conduced to the gradual involvement toward a homogeneous Soviet society, though it was not necessary to the creation of any national language. The third aspect is concerned with the choice of Latin, which meant severing the connection of some languages with the written form or related languages outside the USSR. The fourth is the change from Latin to Cyrillic, which was brought about not so much to improve literacy in any national language but to facilitate the acquistion of literacy in a second language, Russian. Finally, whatever alphabet was used, Russian or Latin, it meant, for very many languages that they were able to compete for the first time with major languages, whether Russian or the languages of Union Republics other than Russia, and could be the basis for expanded social functions which, in theory at least, if not in practice, could be fully comprehensive.

THE GROWTH AND DIFFERENTIATION OF LANGUAGE PLANNING

Fundamental language planning

The main agencies for promoting language planning have been the schools and the mass media. In 1969 the number of students in general-education schools in the whole of the USSR had increased by five times since 1914. In some nations of the Union the increase had been very much greater – Uzbekistan 1,300% Tadzhikstan 1,000% Kirgistan 900% and Turkestan 600%. In addition, schools were established for illiterate adults. In Uzbekistan 51 points were established in 1924, and this number increased to 82 in the following year. Corresponding to this rise in the provision of formal education there was a similar development of printing and publishing in Russian and in the national languages. The greatest impact was made on the Turkic people, who prior to the Revolution had no publishing houses to speak of, and where publishing was severely restricted. Between 1913 and 1963 the number of titles appearing in Kazakh rose from 40 to 187. By the following year the number was 500 and by 1966 the figure was 557. The story of the other nations is very much of a piece (Lewis 1972).

The consequence of the increase in educational provision and books has been a remarkable rise in the level of fundamental literacy in both the lingua franca and the national languages. The campaign to develop vernacular literacy has to be seen against a dark background of deprivation. In 1897 only 28%

of the whole population was able to read at all. By 1926 the general level for the then-Empire had risen, in respect of those between ages 9 and 49, to 56%; by 1938 the level was 87% and by 1970 the figure had risen to 99.7%

Functional language planning

Fundamental language planning, however, is not the entire story – there is the equally important question concerning the opportunities to use the skill available to those who are literate in non-Russian languages. Here the position is somewhat ambiguous. First, there can be no doubt that the work of linguists in the USSR has expanded the range of social functions for very many languages. Languages which, prior to their standardization and graphicization, were confined to limited geographic areas and to a limited range of functions are now, potentially, in a position of equality with any of the major languages, even Russian. However, the Russian language is expropriating the most prestigious and socially significant functions. Even the basic roles of the national languages, exemplified by use among members of the family, are being superseded: more and more non-Russians claim Russian as their native language, 18% in the case of Udmurts, 12% of Uygurs, and 33% of the peoples of the north, for instance (Lewis 1975). In the area of primary and secondary education, Russian is the dominant language even among 'nationalities', and it is almost the exclusive language of major courses in institutes of higher education. In industry the most sophisticated operations demand the use of Russian, which takes over at even the lower levels of industry, where the degree of ethnic heterogeneity makes it convenient to do so. In science and technology as well as in state administration, Russian is coming to exercise an increasing functional prerogative, although national languages are more assertive at severely local levels. In the domains of mass communication, national languagages are used in newspapers and periodicals, on radio, and in films, but their use is localized, and more readers are turning to Russian, partly because it is easier to obtain Russian publications than publications in local languages. Face-to-face oral communication enables national languages to play their part, and for that reason non-Russian languages play an important part in local public services. But so far as recording transactions go, Russian is the most frequently used language. In the administration of justice all languages are guaranteed a role, and this is strictly observed. But only Russian is current in all courts of law and at all levels of justice.

These aspects of the functional differentiation of Soviet languages, as it affects the use of the skills of reading and writing, may be illustrated in the case of Yakut. Although this nation has a 96.3% literacy level and 16% of the population has attended secondary school, the language is used only in primary schools. Russian is used in the administration of justice, in science and technology. The shift to Russian literacy is accelerating: in 1939 less than 1% claimed Russian, by 1959 the figure was 3% and by 1970 it was 4%. Similarly, Abaz, spoken by approximately 20,000, was alphabeticized in the early 1920s, but it has not been promoted as a language of instruction in secondary schools. School books of only the most elementary sort have been produced in the language. Even when Russian and the national language overlap in their functional roles, there is considerable difference in the frequency or intensity of their employment. For instance, Russian and Georgian are used in the Georgian SSSR for the teaching of physics. But because it is claimed that Georgian writings on physics have not covered all aspects of the subject in the past, the use of Russian is far more frequent and popular.

REFERENCES*

Alston, B.L. (1969), *Education and the State in Tsarist Russia*. Stanford, Stanford University Press. (English)

Baskakov, N.A. (1952), 'The Turkic peoples of the USSR: the development of their language and writing', *Voprosy Yazykonaniya* (June) 2.

_____(1960), *The Turkic Languages of Central Asia: Problems of Planned Culture Contact. Appendix 1*. Soviet Affairs Study Group, St. Anthony's College, Oxford.

_____ (1973), 'The scope of abstract influences on a language functioning in complicated intra-ethnic relations'. Paper presented at the IXth International Congress of Anthropological and Ethnological Sciences, Chicago.

Deseriev, Yu (1966a), 'The development and the mutual enrichment of the languages of the USSR, *Kommunist* 13(2).

_____ (1966b), *Patterns in the Development and Interaction of Languages in Soviet Society*. Moscow, Nauk.

_____ (1973), 'Social linguistics', *Language in Society* 1: 5-40.

Dimanshtain, S. (1933), *Principles Governing the Introduction of New Terminology in National Languages*. Moscow, Moscow University Press.

East Turkic Review (1960), 'Editorial', *East Turkic Review* e(1): 38. (English)

Garibian, A.S. (1960), 'The Armenian national language', in *Problems of the Formation and Development of National Languages*, ed. by N.M. Guxman. Moscow, Nauk.

Guxman, N.M., editor (1960), *Problems of the Formation and Development of National Languages*. Moscow, Nauk.

Juldasev, A.A. (1959), 'The Bashkir language', in *New Written Languages of the Soviet Union*. Moscow and Leningrad, University Press.

_____(1960), 'Problems of the formation of Bashkir', in *Problems of the Formation and Development of National Languages*, ed. by N.M. Guxman, 1-25. Moscow, Nauk.

Kari-Nyazov, T.N. (1968), *Studies in the History and Culture of Soviet Uzbekistan*. Moscow, Nauk and Tashkent University Press.

*Unless otherwise stated, all References are Russian texts.

Kizil-Uzbekistan Quarterly (1952), 'Article', *Kizil-Uzbekistan Quarterly* (April): 5.

Konrad, N.I. (1960), 'On the literary language in China and Japan', in *Problems of the Formation and Development of National Languages*, ed. by N.M. Guxman, 3-48. Moscow, Nauk.

Korkmasov, D. (1955), 'On the alphabets of the literary languages', *Revolutsiya i Natsionalosti* 9 (Moscow).

Lenin, V.I. (1918), *The State and the Revolution*. Berlin, Wilelmsdorf Verlag die Aktion.

Lewis, E. Glyn (1972), *Multilingualism in the Soviet Union: Aspects of Policy and its Implementation*. The Hague, Mouton. (English)

——————— (1975), 'The soliological bases of the relationships of Soviet languages', *Forum Linguisticum* 7: 1-27. (English)

Mordvinov, A.E. (1950), 'The development of national languages in the USSR', *Voprosy filosofii* 3: 358-369.

Novy Vostok (1928), 'Article', *Novy Vostok* 28: 289.

Okuticiliar Gazetasi (1968), 'Article', *Okuticiliar Gazetasi,* July 14.

Polivanov, Y.D. (1928), 'Formation of the Turkic language in the Soviet Union', *Novy Vostoka*: 23-24.

Resetov, V.V. (1960), 'The Uzbek language', in *Problems of the Formation and Development of National Languages*, ed. by N.M. Guxman, 7-26. Moscow, Nauk.

Salys, A. (1967), 'The Russification of the Lithuanian language under the Soviets', *Litanus* 13(2). (English)

Sovetskaya Kirgizia (1973a), 'Article', *Sovetskaya Kirgizia*, April 10.

——————— (1973b), 'Article', *Sovetskaya Kirgizia*, April 28.

Stalin, J.V. (1949-1952), *Collected Works*, volume three, volume fifty-six. (Supplementary volumes: Hoover Institute, Stanford University, 1967).

Terenteva, L.N. (1972), 'Some aspects of ethnic processes in the Volga and Ural regions and in the European north of the USSR, *Sovetskaya Etnografiia* 6: 38-51.

Uchetelskaya Gzeta (1973), 'Editorial', *Uchetelskaya Gzeta*, November 20.

Vsesoyuznogo Tsentral'nogo Komitet Novogo Tyurkskogo Alfavita (1929), Unpublished Proceedings of the Plenary Session of the Vsesoyuznogo Tsentral'nogo Komitet Novogo Tyurkskogo Alfavita: 190. Baku.

Vyshka (1972), 'Editorial', *Vyshka*, June 20: 2-3.

Winner, Tog. (1952), 'Problems of alphabetic reform among the Turkic peoples of Central Asia 1920-1941', *Slavonic and East European Review* 3: 133-147. (English)

PART FIVE

Evaluation of Language Planning

JOAN RUBIN

Evaluating Status Planning:
What Has the Past Decade Accomplished?

It hardly seems possible that ten years have passed since some of us met in Honolulu to consider language planning from a multidisciplinary perspective. At that time the term 'language planning' was barely known. The term, while not a household word, has by now achieved some measure of acceptance as an approach and as a field of study. Nonetheless, it still has a long way to go.

At the Language Planning Conference held in Honolulu in 1969, I presented a paper which attempted to show how evaluation (that is, providing information to planners) was a necessary component of good planning, and I related evaluation to a particular model of planning. Many of my views expressed in this paper have not changed. I still feel strongly that good planning must be based on information, serious consideration of alternatives, and forecasting of outcomes. Further, I am even more convinced that we must separate our understanding of this kind of decision-making *process* (i.e. language planning) and what it can and cannot achieve from global consideration of all language changes. Scholars must recognize that changes in language may be the result of many causes, only one of which can be called 'planning'. In contrast to the above views, since 1969 a great deal has happened to the planning field as a whole and especially to the field of social planning. As a result, I have come to consider whether the particular planning model used in the 1969 paper can be the sole one selected to provide for good planning.

The planning model used was one which Allison (1971) has called the 'rational' model. Among the several assumptions which it makes are, (1) that there is a *unitary* plan made by a *unitary* national actor, and (2) that it is possible and normal to consider all the alternatives and to select the very best one. While Allison believes that the rational model can explain some of the decisions taken in planning, he argues that it leaves much to be explained. Rather than settling on one plan for a problem, Allison suggests that there are a 'large number of partial choices in a dynamic stream' (1971: 33). Further, he shows that in fact there is no signle person whose job it is to make the right decision; rather, decisions are often fractured and fragmented. Allison shows that decisions are not based on the best alternative but rather on such constraints as 'Simon's satisficing' (that is, taking the first alternative that seems acceptable), avoidance of uncertainty, and standard operating procedures.

Other students of social planning (Pressman and Wildavsky 1973; Sabatier and Mazmanian 1977; Bardach 1977; and others) have shown how important it is to include specifications and constraints on the implementation process in policy formulations. Further, they argue that it is important to involve as many types of participants as early as possible in the planning process and to try to have someone troubleshoot if planning is to be successful.[1]

After 20 years of relying only on the 'rational' model, social planners have come to realize the need to view planning as one continuous integrated event rather than as one with a strong separation of planners and implementers and targets.

If evaluation is to provide information for planning, there must be an awareness of the changing view of the planning process.

I see my assigned topic, 'evaluating status planning: what has the past decade accomplished?' as having two interpretations, both of which I will discuss in this paper: (1) has the nature of/act of/focus of status planning changed? and (2) have the techniques of/measures of evaluation changed?

NATURE OF/ACT OF/FOCUS OF STATUS PLANNING

I think it is reasonable to say that many changes have occurred in the nature of/act of/focus of status planning in the past 10 years; some of the major ones will be discussed below.

Ten years ago, most status planning was being done by new or developing nations, whereas for the developed/older nations, the language-status question seemed secure and unquestionable. At that time, it was Indonesia, Israel, the Philippines, Ireland, and Tanzania that we saw as examples of countries facing, or having faced, major status-planning problems.

However, in the past 10 years, many seemingly monolingual, developed, and older nations and regions have begun to reconsider the status of minority or nonofficial languages and in many cases made efforts to change the status and allocation of use of these languages.

A principle example is, of course, the United States. Until the passage of the Bilingual Education Act in 1968 and the subsequent discussions of language use in the courts, in voting, and in other public services, the official language of the United States was English, and no one dared challenge it. Today, as a result of changes in allocation of use in several domains, there are frequent challenges to the appropriateness of having a single language as the only official language.

Another example of recent changes in the status of the languages of a developed nation is that of Canada. Although Canada has had two official languages for many years, many French-speaking citizens felt that the two languages were not on an equal footing and that the situation required legal clarification. After the work of the Bilingual/Bicultural Commission, the Official Languages Act was passed in 1969, spelling out in great detail when and where a citizen could expect to be able to use French (as well as English) and providing for increased use of French in government offices.

Even more remarkable has been the stauts planning of the Province of Quebec. In the past decade, the Province has passed a series of legislation challenging the language status of English and promoting that of French (Bill 85, Bill 63, Bill 22, and Bill 101). With the passage of Bill 101 in 1977, the Province made its strongest statement, by trying to make French the only language of the area. The Province has been quite successful in its planning, as D'Anglejan (1979) testifies: 'More has been done during the past decade to enhance the position of the French language in Quebec than in the previous 200 years' (1979: 1).

We can note that even homogeneous Scandinavian countries have begun to give consideration to the status of some of the minorities within their boundaries. Most of Scandinavia has begun to recognize the language rights of the Lapps. In 1971, the Sami Language Board was established, functioning as the Secretariat for all Sami Language Committees in the Nordic countries. Each Nordic country has its own Sami organization as well. In addition to attention to the Lapp language rights, children living in Sweden whose home language is not Swedish are now entitled to regular instruction in their home language for prescribed periods each week. Whereas many Nordic countries either did not have or paid little attention to their linguistic minorities 10 years ago, considerable change can now be seen in the stauts of their languages.

Finally, The Netherlands presents an even more complex case of recent attention to language-status planning. According to Professor Guus Extra (personal communication), there are five separate types of groups for which changes in language status have been requested or actually made. Frisian, a regional language with an established written tradition, has achieved the highest status. As of four years ago Frisian is permitted to be used as the transitional language in the schools. It is the only 'minority' language with quite elaborate facilities for corpus planning. Extra states that speakers of other dialects in Holland, seeing the success of Frisian, have begun claiming their rights. After the position of the Moluccans was finally clarified by the Dutch refusal to support Moluccan claims in 1977, the Dutch began to discuss the need to teach Moluccan children in their own language. Throughout Europe the status of the guest worker has been a problem. In 1968, the

Dutch government took the first step and began to teach these workers' children Dutch as a second language. It is interesting that the Moluccan situation became clearer once the guest-worker problem was faced. Extra indicated that a discussion of what should be the language of education of guest workers has also begun. Finally, immigrants from Surinam and the Antilles are being taught Dutch as a second language. There is, however, no question of bilingual education for these people at the present time.

These examples show that many developed nations have begun to consider the possibility of changes in language status within the past 10 years. (For further information on the guest-worker situation, see Dittmar et al., 1978, for changes toward the language of immigrant children in England; see also Centre for Information on Language Teaching and Research, 1976).

Another change in status planning that can be observed is that new domains are being planned for. Ten years ago, education was the domain for which most status planning was done, and many felt that this was the domain most susceptible to planning (cf. Alisjahbana 1971). The most striking example of a new and important kind of status planning is the current efforts of the Province of Quebec to make French the language of work. Unitl recently, English was the predominant working language of business. If French speakers wanted to advance themselves in industry and business, it was they who had to become bilingual (D'Anglejan 1979). In passing first Bill 22 (1974) and then Bill 101 (1977), the Province is attempting to shift the economic power base away from the English-speaking community and to make French the sole official language at all levels of business and industry.

Bill 22 required professionals (engineers, doctors, nurses, social workers) to demonstrate a working proficiency in French to obtain certification. But, according to D'Anglejan (1979), 'Bill 101 is more explicit and rigorous in imposing the use of French at all levels'. Bill 101 states that by 1893 all business establishments having more than 50 employees must have obtained their 'francization certificates'. Companies failing to obtain such certificates are liable to sanctions: inability to receive governmental subsidies, contracts, etc.; substantial fines; and other sanctions and denunciations likely to result in a loss of clientele and revenue. The Office de la Langue Francaise is working hard to implement this bill; its effectiveness in doing so will remain for future evaluation.

Another area which has not been planned for in the past is the legal sphere. However, in the United States, consideration of the need for status planning in the courts has begun to receive some attention. In 1978, Congress passed the Court Interpreters Act (PL 95-539), which established standards for court interpreters and made some provision for their fees. Similar recognition of the need to provide for better translation for participants in court proceedings has occurred in California (Chang and Araujo 1975).

A third domain of incipient status planning (incipient because the problem has only been identified; decisions have not as yet been taken) is the need to provide for transfer of technology. Both Sweden (Dahlstedt 1976) and Germany (Michael Clyne, personal communication) have noted that the variety of language used by technocrats prevents popular participation in policy decisions. The suggestion is made that findings should be translated in a regular way into standard popular language.

All three of these examples indicate some new domains that are now the focus of status planning. It is probable that we will see more status planning for the legal and medical domain in the future as the research of sociolinguists reveals new areas of communication stress.

Another trend in status planning in the past 10 years is the changing view of language problems. Whereas formerly the tendency was for planners to consider the status of language types (national, vernaculars, languages of wider communication) separately, increasingly there is a trend to see the process of language allocation as a complex consideration of all language types in a nation or region. Some examples of this trend are to be found in Indonesia, Quebec, and Australia.

Since Independence, the language-planning agency in Indonesia has been concerned with the development and spread of Indonesian and incidentally with recording information about vernaculars. With the reorganization of the agency in 1972, all three language types were brought under one organization so that their interaction can be considered together.

The writers of Bill 101 in Quebec also seem to have realized by looking at the relationship between French and English that if French is to be fully accepted then French and English cannot be on equal footing. Bill 101, through the regulations of the language of work, but more particularly through the limitations on admission to English-language schools, is an attempt to prevent the growth of the English-speaking community and to diminish its status.

In 1978, an Australian scholar, Ingram, called for a national language policy which would consider all the language resources of the nation, indicating that if a language policy 'is to meet the nation's needs, it must be coherent and comprehensive, embracing the whole society and all the linguistic issues pertinent to the society' (1978: 1). In his report, Ingram chides prior reports for having considered only a piece of the picture; for example, the place of language learning in education, language problems of the aboriginal community, or language problems of migrant communities.

The language-planning literature also contains criticisms of decisions taken or research which has not considered the relation among the several types of languages in a nation or region. Jernudd (1979) criticized the Jordan English-language survey for assessing only the role of English without considering the role of other languages used in Jordan. He suggests that the policy advocated ignores some segments of society that might influence future policy toward English. Jernudd suggests that planning for English or other LWC's be related to the functions of other kinds of languages in a country.

Khubchandani (1974) chides planners for using a historical rather than an ecological (spatial) view of language use. He observed that by separating standard Hindi from other language varieties in northern India, an artificial speech situation was created, with unforseen consequences. Khubchandani suggests that planners need to consider the functional distribution of language varieties.

While Khubchandani (1974) and Serpell (i.p.) call attention to language situations where movement from variety to variety is relatively easy and fluid and planning should take this configuration in account, in Quebec the status question is more marked, and planners there, who feel that coexistence leads to subordination, have worked to change this relationship through language laws.

In all these cases, the idea of the speech community as an important unit of analysis seems to have pervaded the planning literature.

As indicated in the introduction, planning theory 10 years ago was based on a model which assumed that experts (and politicians) made decisions for an entire population (called mechanically the 'target population'). That is, planning was based on the assumption that centralized decision making was the best way to achieve success. Since that time, social planning has recognized that in dealing with unclear goals and in trying to identify new technologies to deal with the complex set of goals facing them, involvement of implementers and clients was essential to successful planning (Webber 1978).

While involvement of implementers and clients has occurred in some language-status planning, it has been relatively rare. However, there do seem to be some signs of greater involvement of clients in status planning. One concrete example of such involvement is the decentralization of language-teaching units in the Canadian federal government. Before 1977, all of the teaching of official languages to federal employees was handled by a unit in the Public Service Commission. As of 1977, each federal agency was expected to establish its own language unit, suited to its own communication needs (Treasury Board 1977).

Unfortunately, in sharp contrast, the American bilingual-education program has operated with standardized goals and procedures and with relatively little attention to the requirements of the characteristics of each environment. Particularly unfortunate has been the implementation of the Lau regulations according to the standardized requirements of what constitutes 'language dominance' and 'bilingual education', regardless of the sociolinguistic situation. The reaction of several communities to the rigid imposition of

Lau regulations has been (1) to comply minimally without really intending to change, and (2) to challenge the regulations in court. The centralized approach to status planning seems destined to fail, especially in as complex and decentralized a country as the United States.

Abdulaziz, an African language-planning scholar, has also been concerned with the lack of involvement of communities in planning. In a review of the East African Language Survey, organized by American scholars and funded by the Ford Foundation, Abdulaziz (1975) suggested that as many local people as possible be involved in the planning and administration of surveys, and that when surveys are intended to influence official policy, local authorities should be involved as much as possible in setting goals, proving funds, and selecting personnel. Abdulaziz suggests that even in the identification of a problem, the initial stage of planning, implementers and clients should be involved.

There is some indication that another major change in the nature of status planning has occurred in the past 10 years, a change in the methods used to implement language-status changes. Two examples stand out. The Canadians have experimented with the creation of an ombudsman to receive and report on complaints regarding language use by official government services and to try to see that the source of such complaints is removed. The first yearly report of the Commissioner of Official Languages was issued in 1970-1971. To date there has been no assessment of this approach to encouraging compliance to policy, but the method is innovative.[2]

Another change in the nature of status planning may be an increase in the use of coercion in status planning. In implementing the Lau regulations, the U.S. Office of Civil Rights has threatened withdrawal of all federal funds to noncomplying school districts. In Quebec as well, although the Province is trying to use negotiation and persuasion to get companies to change the language of work and to acquire their 'francization' certificates, they too have very strong threats which they can use to promote compliance, namely ineligibility to receive government contracts, subsidies, etc.; fines and moral sanctions; and public denunciation likely to result in loss of clientele and revenue. Another form of coercion in Quebec is the education section of Bill 101, which greatly limits who can be educated in English (D'Anglejan 1979).

It may be that coercion (or negative sanctions) has always been an important part of status planning; however, the threat of strong sanctions seems more pronounced than in past years.

In summary, it can be noted that there have been a number of changes in the nature of/act of/focus of status planning over the past 10 years.

CHANGES IN THE TECHNIQUES OF/MEASURES OF/EVALUATION OF STATUS PLANNING

Rubin (1971) indicated that language planning and evaluation had often been neither very specific nor systematic enough to be useful. Has the situation changed — do planners now use more information in doing status planning?

There does now seem to be more interest in gathering information on the scope of language problems. Although census figures of mother tongue and language use were used extensively 10 years ago in status planning for countries like India, they were not that common. More recently, their use is on the increase. Particularly notable is the use of the census on mother tongue carried out in Belgium in the early 1970s, which provided the basis for a division of the country into language areas. Similarly, with considerable pressure from several ethnic groups, the 1980 U.S. census will ask about language usage for the first time. The responses are intended to help in planning for children with limited English ability. The National Center for Educational Statistics has already carried out a sample survey in 1976 to estimate current language usage as well as language background (Waggoner 1978). The results of this survey will probably become the new basis for program planning in bilingual education.

Certainly the U.S. needs more information on the subject of children with limited English. At the time the Bilingual Education Act was passed in 1968, it seems clear that Congress had little notion of what the range of the problem was. They did not know how many children were involved nor even how to measure their abilities. Only with the *Lau* vs. *Nichols* decision did it become necessary to provide for all children of 'limited English'. Only at that time did the need to establish criteria to assess the scope of the problem become crucial. The period following the *Lau* va. *Nichols* decision has shown how little able we still are to really assess the ability of children to function in monolingual classrooms.

At the same time that censuses are becoming a tool for problem definition, others (Khubchandani, forthcoming) have pointed out that responses to census questions do not always reflect usage; rather, they may reflect an individual's posture *vis à vis* his social identity. If the major purpose of status planning is to correct communication inequities, using censuses to establish allocation of languages may increase rather than decrease the problem.

In addition to an increase in the use of censuses, there is also more interest in surveys and other kinds of needs assessment for status planning. A forerunner in the needs-assessment field was the Philippine Language Survey. In particular, this survey asked about attitudes toward the use of language in particular domains (Otanes and Sibayan 1969). Since the Philippine survey, there have been several major surveys intended to provide information for

status planning. The Committee on Irish Language Attitudes Research reported in 1975 on the results of a national survey of the ability to use Irish and
on attitudes toward Irish. Germany and The Netherlands have both conducted extensive surveys to ascertain needs for foreign-language training. In the
case of Holland, the survey was directly related to recent education laws. The
government of Jordan commissioned a survey (1975) to ascertain its needs
for the English language prior to establishing policy. After a pilot survey of
language knowledge and usage by Jernudd (1979), the University of Khar-
toum, Sudan, embarked on a large-scale survey of language knowledge and
usage.

The United States has also begun to use language surveys to define need.
As a result of the Lau regulations, the Office of Civil Rights has asked many
school districts to define the home language of its students and to ascertain
language-dominance patterns. However, unlike the above-mentioned surveys,
which were done by professional researchers, our school districts were not
equipped either financially or technically to conduct these surveys. In order
to minimize costs, schools have used tests whose major characteristics were
that they were easy to administer by volunteer labor. School districts like
Hawaii had a difficult task thrown at them. Language-testing technology was
not prepared to meet their requirements: the Hawaiian school district wanted
a single test which would be usable for the 15-plus languages spoken in the
Islands and for ages k-12, and administrable in less than half an hour by
volunteer workers. With advice from evaluation specialists (who were not
trained in sociolinguistics), the test finally chosen had many of the same
kinds of problems Labov (1970) noted in assessing the speaking competence
of black children, namely that silence or poor performance did not indicate
incompetence but rather inhibitions related to the test setting and the task.

Similar problems in surveying have occurred in several other states. I am
particularly familiar with the home-language questionnaire used by the
California schools. The lack of technical expertise in writing the form can
be surmised by the astounding fact that it lists Egyptian and Arabic as
separate languages in the home survey (Form 14, November, 1977). Further
evidence of the lack of linguistic sophistication is the listing of Sri Lankan
and Singhalese as separate languages, while there is no mention of Tamil.

Hence, although there is an increase in the use of surveys and censuses in
status planning, there is still a serious problem with the collection and
analysis of language-proficiency and language-use data.

One can ask whether more information has been used in deciding on and
promoting implementation of status decisions. Unfortunately, as yet, there
seems to be little conscious use of information gathering in the implementation process in status planning.

The lack of research on alternative implementation procedures was noted by Troike (1978) in his review of research on bilingual education. An earlier review by Engle (1975) of the literature on two basic approaches — the Native Language Approach and the Direct Method Approach — showed that all the studies examined displayed significant conceptual and/or methodological weaknesses.

Canada, Quebec, and Belgium have all established ombudsmen to report on deviations in the implementation process. However, there is no clear indication that this sort of reporting does improve the process or is in fact used to improve the process.

It is notable that only one book in progress, by Colman O'Huallachain (personal communication), begins to identify some of the bureaucratic procedures which may impede policy implementation. This has already been discussed in the more general planning literature. Allison (1971) noted how the role of the agency designated to implement policy may distort such policy. O'Huallachain's insights into the implementation process *vis a vis* Irish status planning is a welcome innovation.

Further, we may ask whether status planners try to obtain information to ensure that the results meet their goals. It seems that this is only rarely done and, when done, is fraught with problems. The evaluation of results is not usually based on prestated goals with a predefined time frame; that is, when policies are established, rarely do bureaucrats or politicians indicate in specific-enough detail what is to be accomplished by specific dates.

The lack of evaluation of results is related to a number of problems. Perhaps the most important problem is that the very nature of language and social problems is different from that of problems of a more technical nature. City planners (Rittel and Webber 1973) point out that, unlike mathematical or other 'technical' problems, which can be clearly stated and whose answers can be clearly established, in the case of social planning we are dealing with 'wicked problems'. 'Wicked problems' in contrast to 'tame problems' are those where the goals of planning are difficult to establish because of the complex network of cause and effect. Rittel and Webber claim that defining and locating the 'real' problem is difficult. Further, once one has defined the problem, the solution is obvious because it is isomorphic with defining the problem.

'Wicked problems' have other characteristics: there is no stopping rule, whereas in solving a problem in a game such as chess the problem-solver knows when he has done his job. But with 'wicked problems', there are no criteria to ensure sufficient understanding and no ends to the causal chain; the planner can always try to do better. Hence, 'there is no immediate and no ultimate test of a solution to a "wicked problem"' (Rittel and Webber 1973: 163). Every wicked problem can be considered a symptom of another problem. There is nothing like a natural level of a wicked problem.

All of these characteristics make the process of providing information (evaluation) a very subjective and evolving one. There seems to be no beginning and no end to the process, only better or worse information.

While Rittel and Webber point out how hard it is to establish goals, they also show how hard it is to establish solutions. One must not assume that, because they observe these difficulties with 'wicked problems', they do not espouse using a planning approach — rather, they discourage a too-pompous attempt to establish the 'right' answer using 'objective' criteria. As they indicate, 'solutions to wicked problems are not true or false, but good-or-bad' and reflect the planner's point of view.

Assessing the success of language planning has always been difficult. For one thing, in addition to Rittel and Webber's comments, most language planning does not have a time frame, and planners are rarely specific in stating what their projected outcomes are. Second, there is the problem of actual versus stated goals. I once thought that the Irish Language Reform was a failure, because I though the main purpose was, as stated, to make Irish the language of everyday communication. I now feel it can be considered a success, since the real goal seems to have been to establish the State of Ireland, and the language only served as a symbolic rallying point. Third, it is often difficult to know if planning directly caused the outcome or whether other intervening variables really made for success. Perhaps Rittel and Webber are right in thinking that every solution to a wicked problem is a 'one-shot operation because there is no opportunity to learn by trial and error, that is, every attempt counts significantly' (1973: 163). One other problem makes assessing planning results difficult: this comes from the fact that planning is a continuous process with everything always in flux. Hence, perception of problems continously changes and it is difficult to know whether the outcome should be related to earlier or later problems.

Despite all of the above problems, language-status planning should make greater use of evaluation in all stages of planning, throughout the entire process. Although the outcomes cannot always be predicted, the process of establishing goals, setting up better implementation processes, and assessing results can be improved through provision of better information.

SUMMARY

In summary, the focus of status planning has changed more than measures of evaluation of status planning. With the heightened awareness around the world of the functional nature of linguistic variation, status planning has begun to move from its monolithic posture. Although focusing on communication problems is still not high on anyone's priority list except as they permit or promote political or economic change, there is beginning to be some awareness of the need to look at communcation problems in status planning.

Although there is relatively little change in the use of evaluation in status planning, some countries are using more information in defining problems. The lack of use of information in implementation or in evaluating results seems due to three reasons: (1) crisis management still seems to be the most expedient mode of decision making, especially in the United States; (2) status planning is a 'wicked problem' and hence very complex, hard to define, and hard to resolve; and (3) many persons seem not to be aware of the need for more information and argumentation in order to improve the decision-making process for resolving communication problems. It is to be hoped that this situation will change in the near future.

POSTSCRIPT: STATUS VS. CORPUS PLANNING: A USEFUL DISTINCTION?

In 1969, Kloss suggested the dichotomy, status vs. corpus planning, as exemplifying two different focuses on planning. Although these terms have been widely accepted and used, I wonder whether they are the best set to use for those interested in the theory of language planning.

In working on the volume, *References for Students of Language Planning* (1979), Jernudd and I often found that much planning was not concerned with the status (i.e. importance) of a language; rather it was concerned with the allocation of use, or corpus planning. It is true that in the implementation of changes of use, such changes might be more quickly made by enhancing the status of the language variety. Since one of Kloss's principle concerns was language rights, it is understandable why he chose this term, but it is misleading and awkward to try to include all cases of language allocation under the term 'status planning'; rather, status planning should be put under language allocation.

Secondly, language planning has continued to move toward the identification of language problems as motivated by social interaction and communication problems arising from social change (Neustupny 1978; Rubin 1978). Earlier views of language planning focused on the need to make changes in language based on some standard or ideal view of what a developed language should be like (Tauli 1968).

Kloss's dichotomy seems to be somewhat intermediate between these two views. On the one hand, Kloss's dichotomy seems to focus on language for its sake. Problems are identified in terms of whether the planner is concerned with the whole language or just one aspect of it. On the other hand, Kloss's distinction may be used by those concerned with problems *vis à vis* some domain — status planning may refer to changes needed in the status of some language for some sociopolitical or economic purpose. However, the dichotomy seems to be used more in the older language-centered view rather than for the newer communication in interaction concerns.

Finally, the distinction between status planning and corpus planning may be blurred. Doesn't a change in spelling or grammar often constitute a change in status? Does a change in variety belong to status or corpus planning in fact?

I suggest that we consider using the dichotomy 'allocation of use' and corpus planning as more representative of two distinct kinds of planning foci which are on the same level of abstraction.

NOTES

1. For a fuller discussion of the application of the insights of social planning to language planning, see Rubin 1979.
2. Professor Richard Wood has recently called my attention to the existence of a similar commission in Belgium, established in 1932. It also publishes a yearly report.

REFERENCES

Abdulaziz, M.H. (1975), 'Methodology of sociolinguistic surveys — problems of interpretation and implementation. Paper presented at the International Conference on the Methodology of Sociolinguistic Surveys, Montreal, Canada, May 19-21.

Alisjahbana, S.T. (1971), 'Some planning processes in the development of Indonesian-Malay language, in *Can Language Be Planned?*, ed. by Joan Rubin and Bjorn Jernudd. Honolulu, University Press of Hawaii.

Allison, Graham T. (1971), *Essence of Decision: Explaining the Cuban Missile Crisis*. Boston, Little, Brown.

Bardach, Eugene (1977), *The Implementation Game: What Happens After A Bill Becomes A Law*. Cambridge, Massachusetts Institute of Technology Press.

Centre for Information on Language Teaching and Research (1976), *Bilingualism and British Education: The Dimensions of Diversity*. Papers from a conference on Bilingualism in British Education convened in January, 1976. London.

Chang, Williamson B.C., and Manuel U. Araujo (1975), 'Interpreters for the defense: due process for the non-English speaking defendant', *California Law Review* 63: 801-823.

Committee on Irish Language Attitudes Research (1975), *Report* (Tuarascail) (Main Report: Priomh Thuarascail). Submitted to the Minister for the Gaeltacht (in English).

Dahlstedt, Karl-Hampus (1976), 'Societal ideology and language cultivation: the case of Swedish', *International Journal of the Sociology of Language* 10: 17-50.

D'Anglejan, Alison (1979), 'Quebec language policy: ici on parle francais', *Journal of Communication* 29: 2.

Dittmar, Norbert, H. Haberland, T. Skutnabb-Kangas, and U.U. Teleman, editors (1978), *Paper from the first Scandinavian-German Symposium on the Language of Immigrant Workers and their Children.* Roskilde, Denmark, Roskilde Universitetscenter.

Engle, Patricia Lee (1975), *The Use of Vernacular Languages in Education.* Language Medium in Early School Years for Minority Language Groups, Papers in Applied Linguistics, Bilingual Education Series 3. Arlington, Va., Center for Applied Linguistics.

Harrison, William, Clifford Prator, and G. Richard Tucker, editors (1975), *English-Language Policy Survey of Jordan. A Case Study in Language Planning. With an Introductory Essay by Thomas P. Gorman.* Arlington, Va. Center for Applied Linguistics.

Ingram, D.E. (1978), 'The case for a national language policy in Australia'. Paper presented to the 1978 State Conference of the Modern Language Teachers Association of South Australia, Adelaide, October 27.

Jernudd, Bjorn H. (1979), *The Language Survey of Sudan. The Phase: A Questionnaire Survey in Schools.* Acta Universitatis Umensis, Umea Studies in the Humanities 22.

_____ (1979), 'Review' of *English-Language Policy Survey of Jordan. A Case Study in Language Planning. With an Introductory Essay, by Thomas P. Gorman,* ed. by William Harrison et al. (1975). *Language in Society.*

Khubchandani, Lachman M. (1974), 'Fluidity in mother tongue identity', in *Applied Sociolinguistics: Proceedings of the Association Internationale de Linguistique Appliquee* (Third Congress, Copenhagen, 1972), ed. by A. Verdoot, volume two: 81-102. Heidelberg, Julius Groos.

_____ (forthcoming), *Explorations in Language Demography: Selection of Papers Presented at the 'Language Census' Session, Eighth World Congress of Sociology, Toronto, Canada, 1974.*

Kloss, H. (1969), *Research Possibilities on Group Bilingualism: A Report.* Quebec, International Center for Research on Bilingualism.

Labov, William (1970), *The Logic of Nonstandard English.* Georgetown University Round Table 22. Washington, D.C., Georgetown University Press.

Neustupny, Jiri (1978), *Post-Structural Approaches to Language: Language Theory in a Japanese Context.* Tokyo, Univeristy of Tokyo Press.

Otanes, Fe T., and Bonifacio P. Sibayan (1969), *Language Policy Survey of the Philippines, Initial Report.* Manila, Philippine Normal College, Language Study Center.

Pressman, Jeffrey L., and Aaron B. Wildavsky (1973), *Implementation.* Berkeley University of California Press.

Rittel, Horst W.J., and Melvin M. Webber (1973), 'Dilemmas in a general theory of planning', *Policy Sciences* 4: 155-169.

Rubin, Joan (1971), 'Evaluation and language planning', in *Can Language Be Planned?*, ed. by Joan Rubin and Bjorn Jernudd, 217-252. Honolulu, University Press of

_____ (1978), 'The approach to language planning within the United States', *Language Planning Newsletter* 4: 4.

_____ (1979), 'Do the Lessons of city planning apply to language planning?' Paper presented to Spring Seminar on Language Planning and Ethnicity: Theories, Cases and Approaches, May 15, University of Washington.

Sabatier, Paul, and Daniel Mazmanian (1977), *The Implementation of Regulatory Policy: A Framework of Analysis.* Davis, Institute of Government Affairs, University of California.

Serpell, Robert (i.p.), 'Learning to say it better: challenge for Zambian education, in *Language and Education in Zambia,* ed. by L. Omondi and Y.T. Simukoko. Institute for African Studies Communication 14. Lusaka, University of Zambia.

Tauli, Valter (1968), *Introduction to a Theory of Language Planning*. Uppsala, University of Uppsala.

Treasury Board (1977), *Guidelines on the Planning and Evaluation of Official Langues Programs*. Ottawa, Canada.

Troike, Rudolph C. (1978), *Research Evidence for the Effectiveness of Bilingual Education*. Washington, D.C. National Clearinghouse for Bilingual Education.

Waggoner, Dorothy (1978), 'Non-English language background persons: three U.S. surveys', *TESOL Quarterly* 12(3): 247-262.

Webber, Melvin (1978), 'A difference paradigm for planning', in *Planning Theory in the 1980's A Search for Future Directions*, ed. by Robert Burchell and George Sternlieb. New York, Rutgers University Press.

BJORN H. JERNUDD

Evaluation of Language Planning — What Has the Last Decade Accomplished?*

I have been spared the task of finding 'natural' clines or points of beginning in the historical flow of events by the title's limitation to the last decade. The editors of this book saved me from having to make a choice of when to begin. But they did not save me from having to make a choice of whom and what topics to discuss: ought I to cultivate the reacers' understanding of Eastern European *kul'tura jazyka* networks? of Scandinavian *sprakvard* circles? or do I discuss German critique of *Sprachkritik*? The fact that an explicit American focus accompanied the general ambition of reviewing 'language planning' helped me decide to concentrate my evaluation on American-oriented scholarly networks; I bring in others in order to characterize the American one better.

PROFESSIONAL LIFE

The International Conference on Language Planning, which was held at Skokloster, Sweden, in October, 1973, made recommendations to enhance the flow of information about language-planning activities in different countries, about language-planning research efforts, and about training. I shall begin by talking about professional networks.

I shall refer to a member of the 'international group on language planning' as an iglp-er. This 'group' is very loosely constituted, and comprises students of *language planning*. The iglp has met only once since Skokloster, at Montreal in May, 1975, to discuss the function of sociolinguistic surveys in language planning (Center for Applied Linguistics 1975) but informal contacts continue. It should be noted that the iglp network, although the only specialized international network of its kind, does not include all those who work on language-planning problems. (Study of membership of this network

*I am grateful to Dr. Mary M. Slaughter, Dr. Jiří V. Neustupný and Dr. Geoffrey White for their critique of manuscripts of this paper; and Mrs. Barbara Bird for helping with bibliographical searches.

demonstrates one of the problems we face in the field; and I shall say more about that later in this paper.)

For the most part iglp-ers meet in smaller groups in a larger context which has motivation other than language planning, e.g. in the context of an international sociological association convention. The *Language Planning Newsletter* is the iglp-ers' 'house organ'. No journal is exclusively theirs, but the *International Journal of the Sociology of Language* publishes 'review articles on language-planning processes or language-planning research' as does the quite new and mildly Esperantist journal *Language Planning and Language Problems*. Some attention is given to language planning in e.g. *Language in Society* (particularly the review section), *Anthropological Linguistics,* and *Babel.* The *Linguistic Reporter* continues to be an additional news channel for the discipline.

The *Language Planning Newsletter,* guided by the very able editorship of Dr. Joan Rubin and supported by the Culture Learning Institute of the East-West Center, reaches about 1,000 addressees in 90 countries. About one-third of the addressees live in the United States. They represent mainly academic disciplines (primarily linguistics, English language (native and EFL, ESL), foreign languages, area studies, and the social and behavioral sciences). I estimate that just about one in five addressees works outside an academic institution. Without substantial change in format the *LP Newsletter* could accommodate a much wider range of readers and institutions; it could cater for readers at newspapers and in publishing companies, in industry, in public office, at schools, at native (other than English) language centers, as well as for technical writers, information specialists, terminologists, and lexicographers. As concerns the foreign addressees, a very major accomplishment by the *LP Newsletter* is to link together national-language academies and other language-planning agencies. Although it would be difficult to measure, I am convinced that because of the *LP Newsletter,* information now flows between representatives of national cultures who would be rather unlikely otherwise to share information, between scholars both in the United States and abroad, and across professional and disciplinary boundaries. I know of two other newsletters on corpus planning for an international public: the *INFOTERM News Letter* and the *TERMDOK Bulletin.* The 46th issue, dated December 5, 1978, was, however, the last issue of the *TERMDOK Bulletin*: 'any future communication to an international public on the development of the TERMDOK system will be directed through *International Classification,* a journal devoted to concept theory, organization of knowledge and data, and to systematic terminology'. The *TERMDOK Bulletin* dealt exclusively with the development of computer facilities for term processing and exchange of term information between processing agents. It was produced by Eric Sundström at the Swedish Centre of Technical Terminology (TNC). The *INFOTERM*

News Letter is issued by the International Information Centre for Terminology. INFOTERM was established in 1971 with UNESCO sponsorship within the framework of the UNISIST program. It works in liaison with the Technical Committee 37, 'Terminology (principles and co-ordination)', of the International Organization for Standardization (ISO). INFOTERM is affiliated to Österreichisches Normungsinstitut, where it is also physically located. A section entitled 'Infoterm News' in the Journal *International Classification* is compiled from data in the *INFOTERM News Letter*.

The Skokloster conference also recommended that a directory of language-planning agencies and individuals involved in language planning or research should be prepared. (Rubin 1979b) Although the first edition of the *Directory of Language Planning Organizations* (Rubin 1979b) lacks some information which perhaps could have been retrieved and suffers from some inconsistencies in coverage, it nevertheless represents a first attempt at a comprehensive listing of language planning organizations. There also exists a comprehensive listing of language planning organizations. There also exists a directory on term-planning organizations, which, however, also has its selective biases, emphasizing particularly agencies in the INFOTERM network (Krommer-Benz 1977).

At Skokloster it was further recommended that Jernudd and Rubin revise their annotated reading list on language planning (1971). This recommendation was first implemented by Rubin's selected bibliographies in the *Linguistic Reporter* (1974a, 1974b, followed by a preliminary edition of Rubin and Jernudd's *References for Students of Language Planning*, prepared in time for the Linguistic Institute 1977 in Honolulu. The preliminary edition has been revised with the help of iglp-ers and students, and should appear shortly as a Culture Learning Institute publication.

Detailed bibliographies for term planning are available through INFO-TERM and associated agencies.

Other recommendations at Skokloster concerned training in language planning. Jernudd, Molde, and Rubin agreed, it says in the Proceedings, to prepare papers on 'this general topic'. Molde has been active in Sweden conducting training courses in Swedish language cultivation and presenting papers there on corpus-planning work, cooperation, and training (see particularly articles and chronicle of events in the Swedish language cultivation journal, *Språkvård*). The language-planning program at the Culture Learning Institute of the East-West Center, which Dr. Joan Rubin directed, culminated in an intensive summer of language-planning courses as part of the 1977 Linguistic Institute program. Jernudd has begun to write a series of papers on conditions of training in the form of a critique of the language professions (1977a; n.d.). Language planning has found a place in American University curricula and summer institutes, but after Rubin left Georgetown University, where she conducted courses on language planning, and after the East-West Center affirmed its problem orientation (which thus excludes disciplinary development and training in principle, although it accommodates application of language planning), only Professor Molde remains in close contact with university-level training opportunities.

In the absence of a systematic overview, my impression is that language planning has a place subordinate to sociolinguistics course components, yet increasingly informs Ph.D. dissertation topics. language planning is probably very much at the mercy of individual iglp-ers' opportunities at their home institutions.

In term planning, courses have been conducted for professional term planners and for term-planning users, e.g. in Sweden by TNC and in Denmark by Nordic term planners. An impressive series of meetings has been held by members of the INFOTERM network (Felber 1977).

In training its own internal personnel, TNC has courses covering the following topics (Sundström 1978):

språkliga elementa [linguistic basics] ;
skrivning av definitioner [writing definitions] ;
administration av projektarbete [administering project work] ;
terminologiarbetets teknik [methods of term work] .

TNC has a short course of 27 teaching hours over three days, intended primarily for term users and for term planners outside specialized agencies like TNC. It covers the following topics (TNC 1978):

terminologins roll i samhälle och språkbruk [the role of terminology in society and language use] ;
sökning av terminologisk information [searching for term information] ;
det språkliga tecknet: term, begrepp, företeelse [the linguistic sign: term, concept, phenomenon] ;
definitioner [definitions] ;
relationer mellan begrepp [relationships between concepts] ;
institutioner med terminologiverksamhet [term-planning agencies] ;
litteraturreferenser [literature] ;
information on TNC [information on TNC] .

The list of participants in TNC's November 1978 course is interesting in that it illustrates who could participate, should someone take the initiative to bring people together on equivalent work done in the United States; these participants represented the following:

an industrial translation firm,
the government medical-care planning institute,
L.M. Ericsson's standards unit,
a commercial business information company,
a university technology department,

a textile research institute,
the construction industry's information center,
a government construction industry authority,
a metal norms center,
a defense standards bureau,
the hydreoelectric authority,
the government accountancy office,
a government defense aviation agency,
a private technical firm,
a defense materials department,
a business investment company, and
the government planning authority.

Rondeau at the Université Laval in Quebec is apparently also organizing an 'international committee responsible for planning and developing a basis for training terminologists'. (*Language Planning Newsletter* 4: 4).

While the iglp-ers' short tradition has progressed from rapid realization that language planning is not coterminous with solving language problems of developing nations — although initial motivation came very much out of a concern to be of assistance in the LDCs and to understand development processes (cf. Fishman et al. 1968) — to the recognition that language is subject to evaluation and development any time, anywhere, it still remains isolated to a degree from term planning in its European manifestation (e.g. from INFOTERM), from disciplinary linguistics, and from practitioners in the United States. Yet, rather than lament such relative isolation of language planning, one ought to emphasize the rapid and promising growth that language planning has undergone, readying itself to link up with other networks and schools of thought. Most iglp-ers are academics whose primary business today is to teach sociology, political science, sociolinguistics, anthropology, etc.

By contrast, INFOTERM, which is also young (Felber 1978), has grown through cooperation between individuals and agencies engaged in practical work with terminology. INFOTERM works with people from linguistics, logic, ontology (philosophy), information science, and fields of application such as chemistry, physics, medicine, etc. In many of the latter, there were already established regional and international networks. (I reproduce the organizational chart of the network which INFOTERM services in Appendix 1, according to Felber.) INFOTERM has UNESCO, therefore government backing. The iglp has had the backing of the Ford Foundation, the East-West Center, and American universities.

Term planning has begun to develop theoretical models and is adding to its practical principles a realization of the complexity of its working environment. Term planning has found that 'Term work is carried out at every level

of human activity and is fundamental to information and documentation'
and has found the '. . . importance of the widest possible consultation in this
work' (as stated by the evaluation panel for INFOTERM's project of a network, Felber 1978: 180). Language planning has made good progress toward
understanding the range and complexity of language problems that are
attended to in any speech community, and has meanwhile managed to build
a fragile but inspiring network of practitioners and theoreticians. But the lack
of mutual reference between the term-planning network today and the iglp is
striking (as any bibliography shows). In the United States I believe there is
good potential for bringing iglp corpus-planning interests together with
terminological interests, some of which are perhaps already part of IN-
FOTERM. The fact that Canadian linguists and other language-treatment
personnel already participate in both networks may facilitate a link-up.
Another bridge is Fred Riggs's COCTA, a voluntary organization which
concerns itself with social-science terminlogy and is in close contact with
INFOTERM organizations (Riggs 1978).

Although language planning discovered European language cultivation, it
has yet to penetrate the Great Traditions of language treatment in South Asia
and in the Arab world. In the United States, such varieties of language treatment as, among others, the practice and theory of native-language teaching,
foreign-language teaching, translation, and linguistics still remain to be understood in their mutual relationships and motivations. Term planning is weakly
organized in the United States, translation too perhaps, but some of the
other varieties of language treatment are well networked. As study of the
Language Planning Newsletter distribution list shows, people with interest in
language planning are mostly English-language teaching, foreign-language
teaching, and linguistics specialists.

Yet language planning has not appreciably influenced linguistic thought;
we know that there exists a small, reasonably identifiable group of people
with a strong interest in language planning, and that many of them are
linguists; bibliographical study indicates than an even smaller group of them
publish regularly to develop and communicate their discipline. As one
measure of the *impact* of language planning *on* linguistics, one could see
whether established linguistics bibliographies and journals include language
planning publications? I decided to look at mention of *language planning* in
Language, a journal which ought to be considered to be at the core of the discipline of linguistics, and also to see which and how many publications appeared with a *language-planning* description (and here I biased the inspection
in favor of language planning) in the LLBA and ERIC abstracting services.

ERIC lists a total of about 260 entries, for which language planning appears as one descriptor among others from 1966 to January 1979. These
entries include publications on bilingual education, language policy, language

situations (including opinions on the best solution for 'my country'), and so on. I did not analyze these ERIC listings to determine which were corpus and which were status entries.

From 1972 to date, LLBA lists one book on corpus planning as a main entry, namely Rabin et al. on language planning in Israel. It lists the two bibliographies by Rubin (1974a, 1974b) and one other by Bar-Adon (1973). Only a handful of papers by people outside the usual group of iglp-ers are included, namely Stone (1972) on Russian corpus planning, Barkman et al. (1974) on medical information retrieval and language code problems, Valdman (1975) on Creole, and also a couple of AILA (1978) papers. About 10 papers authored by iglp-ers were listed, most printed in Fishman's journal *IJSL*; an example is Dahlstedt (1976). There were 19 reviews of 13 different books and collections of articles by an even smaller number of people: Das Gupta (1970), Haugen (1972a), Rubin et al. (1977), Fishman (1972, 1974), Rubin and Shuy (1973), Ferguson (1971), Rubin and Jernudd (1971), Zgusta (1971), Schweizer (1971), and two others, Girke and Jachnow on Soviet linguistics (1974) and one Hungarian collection (Sauvageot et al. 1971). The selection of available literature is limited. The number of entries is low.

When inspecting *Language,* the picture is depressing. As is reflected in a review of a survey of applied linguistics (*Language* 54(4): 999), language planning didn't make it: 'The editors comment that they considered for inclusion, but rejected, many deserving topics such as translation, psycholinguistics, experimental phonetics, and language policy . . . .' Discussion of 'language policy', a term which antedates language planning, continues on the review pages of *Language,* but extension to 'language planning' is not represented. I looked at issues from 47(4) in 1971, to volume 54, number 4 in 1978. There is a total of eight mentions of 'language planning'. And all are in reviews or booknotes! (See Appendix 2 for a complete account.)

BASIC ISSUES 1: PLANNING AND TREATMENT OR LEAVE LANGUAGE ALONE

The Skokloster meeting raised a number of basic questions concerning definitions, typologies, and ideologies of language planning. One question reads: 'Should language be "left alone" as much as possible or is it the responsibility of society to maintain and improve its language?' Another question reads: 'How does language planning fit in with the broader phenomena of "language treatment" which include other ways the speech community deals with its language?'

Perhaps it is already clear from the above that I consider there to be consensus in the discipline that language is not 'left alone'. One cannot find a speech community where language treatment does not occur in some form or other. Questions concerning responsibility should therefore address what duties scholars may have, given the fact that speech communities minimally recognize language treatment 'experts' and the fact that speakers correct inadequacies whether they like it or not. An attempt was made in 1968-1969 (Jernudd and Das Gupta 1971, Jernudd 1971a) to formulate how a normative theory of public intervention could be constructed particularly to meaningfully pose the question of when *planning* might be appropriate as distinct from other possible approaches to solving language problems and form the point of view of explicit criteria (as then defined and still according to my preference, i.e. as an ideology which 'is committed to the belief that development can be brought about or accelerated by government intervention' [Myrdal 1968: 709; cf. also Jernudd and Das Gupta 1971: 195-196]). This attempt has not been followed (see, however, Sabourin 1978). In my own case, discovering and describing an exploding universe of correction and treatment of individual communicative acts and communication systems became more important. Now that Neustupny has provided basic terms in a model of correction of inadequacies in an individual's speaking, a fundamental question to be given some priority in research would seem to be, under what conditions, how, and with what consequences can an individual be assisted with correction of his/her own inadequacy in speaking? This is an empirical question. It includes the question of when *planning* might be appropriate.

BASIC ISSUES 2: THE CORRECTION MODEL

Neustupny explains how his model of correction came about (1978: 32):

. . . I commenced developing a much wider framework (for language treatment), based on the concepts of "inadequacy" and "correction" . . . . This framework places language treatment within a more general class of correction processes such as simple reissuance of a speech act, proof reading, automatic foreign language acquisition, language teaching, translation, etc. It also *claims that these correction rules form a system which parallels and supplements the more widely discussed system of generation rules.*

He says that 'by establishing the concept of language correction I hope to have provided a number of steps which connect a simple act of grammatical correction with a language reform' (1978: 35). Postulation of 'inadequacy' and 'correction' does not perhaps by itself go much beyond earlier discussion of correction of error (Swedish: *felrattning*) in Scandinavian language cultivation debates (cf. Teleman 1978) or the discussion of 'adequacy' (Swedish: *andamålsenlighet*) as a principle in language cultivation, or, for that matter, much beyond discussion of, for instance, Haugen's criteria for making language decisions.[1] But it *does* make a difference if Neustupný can (make us) connect language correction (therefore treatment, etc.) with generative models in linguistics.

In any communicative act a speaker may be judged deficient because he/ she has not mastered the behavioral conventions — whether pronunciation, vocabulary, sentence formation, gestures, turn-taking, specking at all perhaps, or what have you — and any speaker has strategies to handle this possibility, which I take to be Neustupný's central point.

A speaker may proceed in the wrong variety or style, in which she expresses herself quite clearly, yet suffers negative evaluation and correction by others; she may have used vernacular expressions, for isntance, when 'standard-language' expressions ought rather to have been used. Teleman (1978) classifies this kind of speaking 'error' when committed by pupils in school as instances of 'norm conflict' (Swedish: *normkonflikt*). Or a speaker may simply not possess an adequate way of expressing herself, vernacularly or otherwise; Teleman classifies this kind of 'error' as instances of 'norm gap' (Swedish: *norm lucka*). He takes as examples spelling rules, vocabulary in public language (or to use 'thingamebob', 'whatchamacallit' as default words). We could vaguely add to these examples 'gaps' that we know exist when we struggle to dress new thought in language, at any level of linguistic elegance or proficiency. There is after all such a thing as precise language, esthetically pleasing language, efficient language.[2] The third kind of speaker difficulty, following Teleman's classification, is getting on the wrong track in generating utterances. Syntactic structures may become too complex for successful outcome. Teleman refers to this kins of 'error' by pupils at school as the 'machinery going wrong' (Swedish: *maskineriet strejkar*).

Inadequacies are normally located in the speaker and may come about because she cannot 'fit the pieces together', lacking mastery in the communicative system, or because she has not acquired others' varieties of received expressions.

Inadequacies can be seen to be located in the language system, too. Correction then involves such diverse activities as reaching agreement on spelling (in which expert linguists often have a hand) or stylistic (grammatical) innovation at the highest intellectualized and artistic level, as in the writing of James Joyce.[3,4]

This is how I understand Neustupný's model: generative rules (production rules) have to be used in a particular way (the limiting case is that one doesn't have any, in which case 'correction' may supply the generative ruels) for the speaker to make sense and to fit expectations on communicative behavior, whether it be one's own or another's expectations. To 'manage' the selection from all available generative possibilities within one's language faculty — since 'inadequacies' inevitably appear — including the most general decision on which generative system, i.e. language, to use, there has to exist some system of rules. Neustupný refers to these rules as 'correction rules'. But perhaps it would be convenient to separate out the actual 'corrective' function of this management device from its 'evaluative' function. Then we could propose that when evaluation detects either a 'wrong path' (*maskineriet strejkar*) or an 'inability' to express oneself ('norm gap') it assigns inadequacy marking which may or may not trigger correction. This is in fact what Neustupny has in mind when he makes a distinction between 'marking rules' (1978: 246) and correction in a narrow sense, 'correction rules' (1978: 248). We face rather a terminological than a conceptual problem: Neustupný uses the term 'correction' in both a broad sense, including evaluation, and a narrow sense, excluding it.

Individual inability to correct may cause the speaker to seek help from other members of the speech community, or intervention by the hearer. An answer may already be available in manuals, dictionaries, or personal insight as communicated by telephone from a member on call at the High Language Advisory Council . . . . Or the Advisor may in turn convene a meeting to discuss the matter; minimally to eliminate repeated misunderstanding or uncertainty by encouraging an arbitrary ruling through bringing about user agreement or through imposing a ruling by authority. (The former is, I believe, not uncommon in general language cultivation of public language.)

Evaluation determines whether what was purported was communicated 'adequately'. Would we not otherwise blabber disconnectedly? Evaluation provides a grammaticality, an acceptability, an efficiency, an esthetic check on discourse. It is also perfectly possible that a speaker who evaluates his/her own utterance as inadequate from some point of view (absence of objective case marking of 'whom' perhaps) nevertheless discovers that the communication was successful.[5] By removal of the inadequacy marker, then, there is 'language change'. The speaker might be challenged to defend her decision in discourse, she might not. Given that others model their speech on this speaker, the 'deviation' spreads. When the speaker produced this 'deviation', she brought into use a new communicative feature which is made acceptable by the absence of an overt correction act. Or acceptabilities are restructured through uncorrected use of previously 'vernacular' vocabulary items in communicative settings which demand public language. (Isn't this what's happening with 'rip off' or 'hassle'?)[6]

The following exemplifies how evaluation triggers correction: when I speak English in formal situations I anticipate difficulties with syntax and coherence of discourse; in Swedish technical-academic discourse, I similarly anticipate difficulties with vocabulary. Evaluation 'indexes' those generative rules which I am going to employ that involve syntax and 'fluency' in the former, vocabulary in the latter. Before articulating, I check for inadequacies. This is what Neustupný terms 'pre-correction'. Often as not, in- and post-correction still become necessary (Neustupny's terms; cf. also Laver 1973: 141-142). Gradually I am becoming more proficient in English, and could also, given enough communicative opportunity, reach such proficiency in Swedish technical-academic discourse that 'pre-correction' becomes unnecessary. Alternatively, I could refuse to entertain others' protests that my technical vocabulary is 'all English'. I could routinely engage in code-switching whenever I fail to anticipate a Swedish term and employ the automatized English term instead. I then place the evaluative burden on the others, who may demand correction, either in a mild form by asking what such-and-such a term corresponds to in Swedish or by disapproving of my discourse. On the other hand, correction may not be requested.

I shall try to make Neustupný's correction model more concrete by applying it to the treatment system of foreign-language learning and teaching. Neustupný says about foreign-language acquisition,

Language pedagogues or so-called applied linguists normally tell us what learners *should* do. However, little information has been available on what people *actually do* when they teach or learn languages. The description of these rules of language acquisition as a type of correction rules is the primary prerequisite for an improvement in our language teaching and learning strategies. (1978: 33)

Rubin (1975) is a good beginning along this new road. And it works.

Not only are decisions concerning varieties to be acquired and social systems of language teaching a matter of language treatment, but all rules of 'how to teach' . . . and how to learn are language correction rules . . . . Some of these rules are highly metalinguistic and rigorous, but in many instances, such as the instance of an unaided immigrant, foreign language acquisition is conducted without much metalinguistic guidance; much of the native language learning certainly remains without any rigorous metalinguistic intervention at all. (Neustupný 1978: 33)

Since the beginner-learner obviously doesn't know the foreign language he is about to study (sic!), he has to find at least a speaker who does (who can be a teacher), approach him for communication, revealing, excusing, or at least cushioning the fact that his purpose is acquisition rather than 'purposeful', natural communication (cf. Slama-Cazacu 1973: 294). This is the stuff out of which correction for learning a language is made.

The speaker of the target variety can also serve as a source of model speech, but the more important function is for him to decode inadequacies, feed this back to the learner, and (possibly) correct. One does not normally pester another person with communicative nonsense (not knowing the language at all or very badly) or categorically demand exclusive attention to one's learning need (one's inadequacy in the entire variety!) other than in agreed settings or with understood consequences for one's social role. (Doesn't a language-learning adult get treated as a child some places?) These settings are language-teaching settings, with which corrective behavior that results in language learning is congruent. Designing models of presumed efficient settings for language learning and applying them is the job of language-teaching treatment systems.

Neustupný (personal communication: letter of July 27, 1979) mentions that 'traditional' language-teaching situations (in the classroom, etc.) are now in disrepute. Correction in classroom situations appears to be rather inefficient, although precise explanations as to why that is so may be difficult to offer. In 'contemporary' foreign-language teaching the following is normally provided for the learner, says Neustupný:

1. opportunities for unconscious self-correction: through nondirected correction situations, such as natural conversation with target-language speakers, television viewing, reading, etc.;

2. opportunities for conscious self-correction: through instructions on how to use nondirected situations for self-direction (self-instruction), e.g. to consciously reflect on segments of conversation by an interlocutor, to make use of television commercials for acquiring utterances, etc.;

3. conscious correction by others: situations directed by interlocutors, etc.

What is so amazing is how little we know about individual language-learning behavior and about motivations of language-teaching systems. We know little about communicative interaction in such settings through which, e.g., a learner who is immersed in a target speech community gradually gains participatory use of generative rules through self-correction and communicated correction by others.

My discussion so far has addressed another two questions posed at Skokloster, namely 'Is there a fundamental difference between an internal linguistic theory ("teleology") in language planning and an external sociological theory of implementarion?' and 'What is the relation between language planning as a soucre of linguistic innovations and other processes of language change?'

SOME CONTEMPORARY ISSUES FOR CORRECTION

In *stable* speech communities,[7] language use is backed up by dictionaries, grammatical description, and other means in a variety of treatment systems. In *emerging* speech communities, social institutions of treatment and individual conventions of correction become restructured to fit a new developing evaluative order. In *transient* speech networks, those that are formed by communicating through marginal or pidgin languages in their early stages of development (although the latter may have had a long chronological tradition of use), there is considerable tolerance for individual variability and inventiveness in finding expressions that get a message across.

MIGRANTS' LANGUAGE PROBLEMS

In immigrant speech networks there is often little possibility of enforcement of evaluation of migrants' native speech through treatment systems. What is often important is to speak the adopted society's language well. That language normally has strong support in treatment systems, e.g. a compulsory school education in and about its language. Migrants may work hard to further develop their skill at using the adopted society's language. When among themselves they may use their own native language; and it may be regarded as appropriate to do so. But what is important then is not to 'speak correctly' but to express solidarity with one's own group. What is minimally required is at least not to speak the adopted society's language. Evaluation concentrates on maintaining this minimal distinction. The native language has been severely restricted in range of communicative situations to which it can be applied by migration into another society with another language, and speakers have lost contact with the treatment systems that helped support the language in the old country. What remains is individual corrective resources. And the individual migrant is under strong pressure to adopt the adopted society's language in new contexts of speaking. Therefore, nonnative language expressions enter rather freely into the vernacular. For others, to correct a speaker under such generally adverse circumstances, when at least he makes an effort to speak the 'old language', is difficult. Therefore the native variety of speaking moves even closer to the adopted society's language until only some features remain to mark this migrant group's 'peculiar dialect'.

On the other hand, others will correct discourse in the host variety if the social relationship permits: my wife who is American does, immigrant parents do to their children. Often such correction draws on very limited information about what *is* correct, because the migrant-corrector has limited access to evaluative sources. Therefore, migrant transition to full proficiency in the host society's variety may be slowed down; or generational differences in language use can become quite sharp if children go to schools that successfully correct norm conflicts and norm gaps.

But the language situation is not always like the above. Different immigrant groups place different value on maintaining their varieties — Hebrew and Arabic are God's languages and must therefore be maintained literally, in religious function. The Jewish holocaust places an infinite value on maintaining Yiddish. Neustupný says (1978: 247):

As far as acts containing violations of communicative rules are concerned, the inconvenience resulting from such cases will again be judged differentially in different societies. It seems to me that some societies allow for more variation in this respect than others. In any case, empirical studies of this problem will be needed.

Neustupný (1975: 7) derives a host of questions from his correction model[8] to inform policy toward immigrant groups in Australia:

Which migrant communication rules are marked as inadequate by native speakers of English? Which Australian English rules are marked as inadequate by the individual migrant groups? Which correction rules operate for migrant English? Which inadequacies exist in communication by migrants in their own languages, and which correction mechanisms apply in this sphere, etc.?

Relationships between migrant groups and host societies may, however, change: I assumed assimilatory pressure above. I suspect that current attention to minority ethnicities', guest-workers', and migrants' language, not only in the United States but also in Germany, Sweden, the United Kingdom, Australia, and many other countries, which is now principally directed toward languages, may well be followed soon by attention to language-corpus issues. Then how does one evaluate the English, German, Swedish varieties of these groups? With what consequences? How does one evaluate German varieties in Australia? Perhaps the question has already been raised as to how one evaluates Canadian French? In Scandinavia, the Same community faces issues of coordination and overall development of Same speaking, first to reach agreement concerning 'standardization' for educational purposes (a direct result of the ethnic-rights movement), but simultaneously covering cultivation of the dialects. There are attempts at evaluating and legitimizing nonnative English varieties not only for domestic use (Filipino English in the Philippines, etc.) but also for international communicative situations, i.e. attempts to reach agreement on tolerance and to institute corrective systems.

The plain-language movement

Another contemporary issue is how, in many speech communities today, distribution of highly intellectualized, automatized speech is called into question in the name of democratization of speaking. Thus, there is discussion of *Fachsprachen*, 'bureaucratese', and 'officialese'. There may be less willingness in many contemporary communities to interpret foregrounding of technical *into* popular or wider-audience speaking, thus the burden of making the discourse intelligible (however accurate and clear it is) is shifted onto the speaker; a decade ago it might not have been.

Dahlstedt says (1976: 28):

The gulf between official Swedish and colloquial spoken Swedish causes a communication barrier between the authorities and the citizens, especially those who lack higher education and linguistic training. This serious inconvenience to democracy and equality has been attacked by left-wing radicals during the 1970's, but it has also − for decades − been a focus of interest for influential language cultivators. The opening up and equalization of official Swedish is, without doubt, a major task for modern Swedish language cultivation. There are, of course, in public administration special concepts which in themselves are difficult to interpret or explain to outsiders. The democratization of a language is not as easy as, simply, turning society upside down . . . Before long any new authorities will necessarily develop a linguistic variety, which is appropriate to their conceptual sphere and professional occupation . . . (The) goal must be to modernize official Swedish, i.e. to clarify and simplify its syntax until complete syntactic transparency for every normal native adult Swede is achieved, and to lower its abstract qualities as much as the semantic content of each text admits.

Havránek cites the case of 'the professor who uses the language of science in ordinary conversation. [He] is a well-known humorous figure; neither workaday technical speech nor the style of written expression can properly be sued in plain conversation' (1964: 12). This is being rediscovered in today's 'plain-language movements'. There is a deep difference between Havranek's then and our now, though: the professor who uses technical language outside his offices is no longer tolerantly seen to be a humorous figure in today's society but one who gives offense or is to be rejected with ridicule.

BASIC ISSUES 3: LANGUAGE PLANNING AND CITIZENSHIP

Another set of questions raised at Skokloster ask, 'Is language planning basically a "technical" activity to be kept removed from politics or is it intimately involved in the political processes of a nation?' 'Is the difference between a "value" orientation and an "instrumental" orientation of importance in language-planning processes?' It is true that one can choose a perspective of study and analysis that keeps 'political', 'sociological', etc., aspects constant and that therefore may appear to be 'value' neutral or that by design disregards technical concerns of term planners. Such modelling (cf. Harvey 1969: 158-161 on models) may be highly efficient for the express purpose of understnading a particular subset of relationships. But it remains partial, because sociolinguists know that (differential) use interacts with (differential) knowledge with (differential) attitude (Fishman 1971: 330-335); we know that when communicating, we can concurrently comment on the communicative act and the system that makes it possible (Hymes 1974: Chapter 1). Even 'technical linguistics' is neither 'value' neutral nor 'politically' neutral. However harmless grammar-writing and description of communicative behavior may seem or how far basic research on language may appear to be beyond judgment in that its target is deeper understanding of man, such pursuits have their social, political, economic settings. Moneys are allocated to particular linguists with particular methods at particular linguistic topic to begin studying and as to who shall publish the findings in what format (cf. Hymes 1974: Chapter 10).

Perhaps the Skokloster questions aimed at clarifying something more 'specific'? In specific terms, then, an example of 'value' orientations in language planning is 'purism'. The IRPLPP demonstrated how opinion on the most appropriate source of terminology (native, classical, or foreign) varies in strength by social characteristics of populations studied, by the professional field of respondents, and by country (Fishman 1977, Rubin 1977b, Jernudd 1977). In his historical study of purism in White Russia and the Ukraine, Wexler (1974) shows how puristic zeal fluctuates according to the political mood of the period, how external sociopolitical events motivate the opening or closing of the language system to native and nonnative sources, respectively through prescriptive intervention. The link between language corpus planning and 'political processes' is obvious in Wexler's study. Haugen's case study of Norway forced me

. . . to speculate that a society can play a game of pseudo-issues of language as a surface manifestation of political and social affiliations, thus registering and scoring power-points, with little explicit relationship to the reality of language ostensibly rallying the forces around discussion and decision. And the deep reasons for much of the Norwegian discussion are yet to be found. Initially the language movement was based on national feeling "which called for self-realization in language as in other matters" (116). Later it became a playground for group politics, with a less systematic motivation by real communication problems. (Jernudd 1971b: 492)

Perhaps it was naive of me ever to have thought otherwise.

Das Gupta's work in IRPLPP demonstrated

. . . how the political context and pattern of authorization of planning, the political objectives of planning and the choice of the administrative form have affected the course of planning . . . . They had a demand to meet and they knew that this demand primarily emerged from political prescription rather than from the expressed need of a specific user population. (Das Gupta 1977a: 77; cf. also Neustupný 1968: 291-292)

A serious issue in the critique of language-treatment systems is therefore to understand whether in a given instance it is motivated more by political interest, thus using and even creating language encounters; and even in the latter case whether 'norm conflict' is 'value'-triggered, in the sense of the Skokloster question.

Neustupný emphasizes (1975) how there are attempts to cover up social problems by pushing to the fore the politically less sensitive language problems: like money appropriations for Aboriginal language studies rather than for sociological studies, support of English learning for migrants and for use of migrants' ethnic languages in Australia rather than attention to the more vital social problems of inequality and social mobility, etc.

Another serious issue is to rid language-planning discussion and practice of any illusion that it can remain 'technical'. It cannot (Jernudd 1977a: 54-56). A 'sentimental' orientation analytically distinct from an 'instrumental' orientation (Kelman 1971; Haugen 1971) ought best to be seen as an ever-present duality which bears on any correction act. With what strength either manifests itself is an empirical question in a given setting. Generalizations are undoubtedly possible; Gumperz hypothesizes (1969) that membership in coterritorial social groups who share verbal repertoires made up of different 'languages' is expressed not by syntactic-semantic grammatical difference but by the morphonology and lexicon. This hypothesis relates directly to the fact that puristic judgment and nativistic principles appear to be applied particularly to vocabulary. The obvious alternative to this hypothesis is that vocabulary is much more accessible for comment, so it, rather than the inaccessible syntax, becomes the object of *Sprachkritik*, whatever its content. The other extremely accessible language system feature is orthography (cf. Fishman 1977a).

BASIC ISSUES 4: DEVELOPMENT

Early language-planning work by iglp was quite clearly motivated by concern with development (cf. the Airlie House conference on 'Language Problems of Developing Nations', Fishman et al. 1968). As a result of better descriptive knowledge of diverse language-treatment systems, a broader perspective which takes into account contemporary European practice and attempts to isolate what is developmentally unique both currently and through time by typologizing and generalization, corpus planning has made significant progress in understanding the fourth Skokloster question: 'Are language-planning processes significantly different in developing countries and advanced, industrialized countries, or is the difference between "emerging" languages and relatively "stable" languages more important?' (for terms, cf. note 7). At any historical moment, communicative systems may undergo intensive change responding to intensive change in society. The concepts of *emerging* and *stable* speech communities address consequences of such change for relationships between repertoire and treatment system (Jernudd 1977c: 48-49).

Stages of language development

Neustupný's seminal paper on corpus planning, 'A theory of language problems' (1978: Chapter 12), summarizes his typology of the developmental stages of correction systems (1978: 255):

. . . within the recent period of history at least three stages must be considered. The Early Modern stage of socioeconomic history corresponds to so-called *macro-modernization* processes, and these in their turn require a *policy* approach to language treatment and the *grammar-translation* variety of foreign language teaching. (In linguistics pre-structural linguistics corresponds to this state.) The Modern stage of socioeconomic development produces so-called *micro-modernization*, paralleled by the *cultivation* variety of language treatment and the *audio-lingual* methods in foreign language teaching. (Structural linguistics corresponds to this stage.) The character of the correction processes which correspond to the Contemporary stage of socioeconomic development still awaits clarification. Within the metalinguistic sphere we are witnesses to the development of *language planning*. (Post-structural linguistics is emerging as a replacement of structuralism for this period.)

Relatively detailed discussion of these stages in Japanese communicative development are found in Neustupny (1978: Chapters 8, 9, 13, and 14; and of 'linguistic variety' in Chapter 1). In these papers the societal and language-variety features that constitute the typological dimensions are presented (cf. also Jernudd's hypothesis about consequences on language of macro-economic change in 1971a: 272-275 — which, however, remain untested).

Several important IRPLPP findings can be understood in developmental perspective as indicative of stabilization of a speech community's treatment system. Das Gupta finds that in their accounts of success of programs, Hindi language-planning agencies in India make 'few statements concerning the actual impact of these [dictionaries, glossaries, the annual turnover of terms, translation, textbooks, etc.] products on the official or general language situation' and that 'a crude, output-centered orientation appears to characterize the initial stages of planning in less developed countries' (1977b: 76). These findings specify the macromodernization kind of linguistic correction. Quite compatible with this stage of Hindi's development is the fact that 'Language planning, besides satisfying a sense of nationalist pride, created a level of control over national and regional languages that considerably expanded political authority over national affairs' (Das Gupta 1977b: 77).

Khubchandani (1972) analyzes how premodern 'undeveloped languages' and 'speech as an *integral activity* in a (premodern) society' with its unique characteristics of fluidity of verbal repertoires conflict with assumptions of language-development ideals in modernization. 'Less fortunately placed speech varieties' (1972: 100) and their speech communities may suffer as a result: Unable to meet the challenges and the aspirations in our plural society, this approach [that of the modernizing "language reformers"] can generate only discord and rivalry among people, as is all too evident now' (cf. also Scollon, forthcoming, on fluidity of language boundaries as a characteristic of premodern speech communities). Das Gupta, however, takes the more optimistic view that, at least in some Indian states and at the level of 'dominant languages' (to employ Khubchandani's term), politics of language development help create and maintain democratic decision making:

If the information and analysis which have been presented in this paper succeed in partially bridging this gap, they may be of service to all participants in the Indian language policy process. Such a bridge is particularly important in the case of policy processes which utilize democratic decision making and put a premium on plural demands and negotiated settlement. (1977b: 192; cf. also Das Gupta 1970, Jernudd 1972.)

French Polynesia, a colony of France, when given an opportunity to discuss a future course of language-corpus planning, convened a Colloque des langues polynesiennes in December, 1978. The setting was the Assemblee Territoriale; the Colloque was opened with the first speech to be delivered in Tahitian before the French Haut-Commissaire inside the Assemblee. In addition to an agenda which dealt overtly with status- and corpus-planning issues for Tahitian and its relationship to 'dialects' on other islands, my definite impression was that the meeting served the function of creating local-political channels and of defining local-political networks. This, it could be suggested, is typical of the first stage of present-day modernization of communication in the LDCs.

Fellman and Fishman contrasted the actual working relationships of two terminology committees in Israel to the 'higher authority of the Academy' and to the respective professions they served. Their conclusions were that

Although the problem of indigenousness/internationalness of terminology
was far more severe in one field, both committees [Librarianship and Inorganic Chemistry] attempted more or less successfully to "hold the line" in
favor of indigenous or indigenized roots and constructions insofar as possible.
Both reveal the recurring problem faced by language planning bodies constrained to pursue modernization within the general framework of an indigenous Great Tradition which frowns upon foreign influences in language
if not in behavior. (1977: 94)

Specifically, the Chemistry Committee

. . . accepted and retained all Hebrew chemistry roots customarily in use,
although actually there are only a small number of these. They also accepted
all international roots customarily used in Hebrew and now felt to be part of
Hebrew. However, there still remained to be considered many international
roots and word-coinages which did not as yet exist in Hebrew, and it was
decided to transfer them directly into the language rather than to translate
them into Hebrew. Even then two questions of integration arose, namely
the problems of affixation and transliteration. (Fellman and Fishman 1977:
91-92)[9]

But 'Israeli students, teachers and textbook writers did not favor Hebrew as
a source language, which conflicts with the views held by members of the
Hebrew Academy . . .' (Jernudd 1977b: 232) *and*

. . . as a matter of fact, the Hebrew Academy itself has moved to solve the
conflict between the "linguistically liberal" proposals that come from committees preparing terminologies (where technical people are in the majority)
and the "linguistically conservative" (i.e. Hebraizing) screening of proposals
by members of the Academy in the Academy plenum. Instead of the plenum
passing or rejecting the technical terminologies, a standing committee on
terminology makes the decision. Members of this committee are selected for
their understanding of professional needs, rather than of ideology. Thus, the
conflict is being checked by internal administrative means. (Jernudd 1977b:
221)

I believe that what we witness in Israel is transition from the macromodernization to the micromodernization stages, accompanied by a decentralization
of term planning which considerably alleviates and routinizes term processing
within the professions and thus stabilizes the speech community's treatment
system. The latter presupposes reasonable agreement on a public Hebrew
norm.

That teachers 'make functional/situational distinctions with respect to the necessity for indigenous vocabulary' was a major finding for the countries that IRPLPP studied. 'Their own professional reading, writing, and meetings with foreign colleagues incline them toward such differentiations and, indeed, their students are already closer to them in this respect than they are to white-collar adults in general' (Fishman 1977b: 211). The goal conflict between stress on indigeneity as an expression of Israeli/Hebrew authenticity and demands of professional interaction within networks that are not uniquely indigenous (particularly for inorganic chemistry) in a technically rather forward society such as Israel led to administrative restructuring of term-planning decision making. (Jernudd 1977b: 235)

IRPLPP gave 'an impression of crucial generational . . . differences' (Fishman 1977b: 210):

It would seem (particularly in Israel) that the populations most positive attitudinally towards LPA activity (teachers, parents) are not at all necessarily the ones that are most 'approved' usage-oriented, while the populations most in control of Approved Word-Naming (students) are not necessarily attitudinally/informationally most positive.

Fishman concludes (1977b: 212):

. . . in the three countries reported upon in this paper the attitudinal/informational goals of language planning tend to be best approximated by an older generation of users (who were themselves young adults when language planning activity may have been less routinized and more ideologically embedded), whereas its approved usage goals often tend to be best approximated by a younger generation of users (who acquire the new terminologies as part of normal and institutionalized educational experiences with much more minor attitudinal/informational overtones). Although significant between-country differences and country-by-population interactions exist in all of these connections, the regularity and size of the between-group differences encountered is suggestive of recurring routinization trends as language situations that initially elicited ideologized central planning slowly normalize and stabilize, and as languages of wider communication formerly viewed locally as competitors for various official or unofficial functions are no longer as widely regarded as such.

Ideology of indigenization as a driving force in modernization and generalized social change becomes less motivated as corpus treatment systems get established: macromodernization features are replaced by micromodernization features.

Term and vocabulary planning at different stages of development

Term planning serves distinctly different purposes in speech communities at different stages of development. If specialists from developing countries seek to share 'techniques' through, e.g., INFOTERM study tours or international discussion, one will have to recognize this fundamental fact. A term-planning agency that maximally supports the use of an indigenous language (and the ideology of indigenization) or indigenized terminology could pay much less attention to term formation and term systmaticity, definitions, etc., than a term-planning agency in a modern, stable-speech community. In the former, a demonstration effect through publication of volumes of lists and perhaps texts (maybe critically selected for impact) should be the goal. In the latter, coordination of usage and agreement on definitions dominate, and will be achieved through intensive interaction between planner and user and careful preparation of highly specialized reference works, often containing only a modest number of highly elaborated term entries[10] (see for example TNC 1971, a term list for industrial engineering).

Promotion of a standard language implies not just codification of a public norm for speaking but growth of 'functional differentiation of standard language norms' (for discussion, see Rubin 1977: 163ff.). In order for vocabulary or terms to become standardized by agency action we require a style-differentiated language system; in other words, a texture of language variation. Standardization implies choice, and a choice can only be expressed relative to a context. Other competition between vocabulary items would be expressed in terms of, e.g., purism, to the exclusion of one item. A somewhat extreme suggestion arises from the above, namely that parallel promotion of several word lists should perhaps be attempted by a language-planning agency in order to hasten style differentiation and in order to implement 'standardization'. Parallel promotion of many words for 'the same thing' may encourage specialization (contextualization) of usage of one set of terms. If there is but one term which is used by the general public as a general vocabulary word, more words will inevitably be made up.

Corpus planning cannot proceed uniformly throughout all networks in a national speech community; Neustupný shows (1978: 170) how in Japan a 'considerable amount of Early Modern non-functional variation in the sphere of microsociolinguistics has . . . survived'. He offers as one of several examples the word 'constant':

As early as 1950 the White Paper of the National Language (Kokugo shingikai 1950) turned attention to the fact that it was rendered as *joosúu* in mathematics and physics, *kansúu* in chemistry, *teisúu* in engineering, and *fuhensúu* in economics. Similarly, the terminology of ikebana varies considerably according to the school, and an analogous situation can be found in many other areas.

At each stage of corpus development, subject specialists will differ as to when they accept what kind of indigenizing and standardizing pressure. Accepting planned terminologies in a professional field would also seem to imply that — particularly given the absence of their own language terminologies at an earlier stage — previous use of general vocabulary in the indigenous language is replaced by specialized vocabulary which can then only be acquired by special study. Different subject areas may also be differentially receptive to employing terms that derive from general vocabulary. All these considerations may interact to explain the startling between-country and between-subject-field differences that are reported from IRPLPP:

. . . interesting between-country differences appeared in connection with the intercorrelations among the three Approved Word-Naming scores obtained for all teachers and students (see Tables 6 and 7). In Israel all three scores were consistently positively related to each other. In India, on the contrary, they were consistently negatively related to each other. Finally, in Indonesia, a different pattern emerged for teachers and students. Among teachers the Approved Word-Naming scores in [SL] grammar and in civics were positively related to each other but negatively related to Approved Word-Naming in chemistry. Among students consistently positive interrelationships were obtained. The first mentioned pattern (that in Israel) indicates the most generalized response to academy-approved nomenclatures whereby individuals either utilize or fail to master them regardless of whether they be in one's own specialized field or not. The second pattern mentioned (that in India), on the other hand, reveals the most specialized response to academy approved nomenclatures. In this pattern the more one utilizes such approved nomenclatures in one's own field, the less one masters them in any other. The third pattern mentioned (that among Indonesian teachers) is intermediate between the foregoing two. In this pattern the humanities/social sciences are on one side and the natural sciences on the other. The more humanities and social sciences specialists utilize their own and each other's approved specialized nomenclatures, the less they master those in the natural sciences and, similarly, the more natural science specialists utilize approved terminology in their own field the less they master those in either of the others. (Fishman 1977b: 206-207)

An interesting observation about specialist-language vocabulary in Japan noted by Neustupny is that

Strangely enough, it seems to be only the problem of *development* of lexicon and of the modern scientific and other functional styles which did not attract much conscious attention. While the most important changes in the Japanese vocabulary occurred in the Meiji period . . . , it was not until the 1930's that planning processes were initiated . . . and to my knowledge the planner's intervention has never been very intensive. (Neustupný 1978: 166)

If this is true also for European language development in its early modern stage, this fact could demonstrate the validity of making a distinction between content of corpus development at present and at an earlier (prewar?) period.

WHAT LANGUAGE CAN BE PLANNED?

Finally, 'What is the relation between language planning about public policies of language *use* and language planning about the actual *forms* of the language?' (Skokloster, too). (These two phases or stages were referred to as language policy or status planning and language cultivation or code or corpus planning.) Perhaps a more meaningful formulation of the question might be, what minimal communicative characteristics must a variety have to become subject to status planning? On the one hand, in Papua New Guinea (Wurm 1974) or in Africa (Spencer 1974; Welmers 1974) a lot of different kinds of language work precede attention to 'policy' by national legislatures and central administrative organs, and some of the varieties which are developed in the process may never become subject to governmentally authorized planning. On the other hand, if guest-worker speech attracts the attention of language-planning authorities in Germany, even marginal varieties of speaking can become subject to planning. Pidgins and creoles, we know, qualify for corpus planning; so do subsystems of languages like morphology and vocabulary, even across languages, as internatinal coordination of scientific terminology demonstrates. My suspicion is that the question must remain trivial. We can, after all, create language. From a different perspective, even an ♀ over *a* (although this same *a* is doubled in the competing spelling) can temporarily raise the public temper so much as to accuse fellow citizen-reformers of a language sell-out to another nation! (Galberg-Jacobsen 1973: 150-156, including Figure).

SUMMARY

Enquiry

Language planning has made progress in delimiting a corpus, a data set, with which to work. Historical studies and political analyses and one international

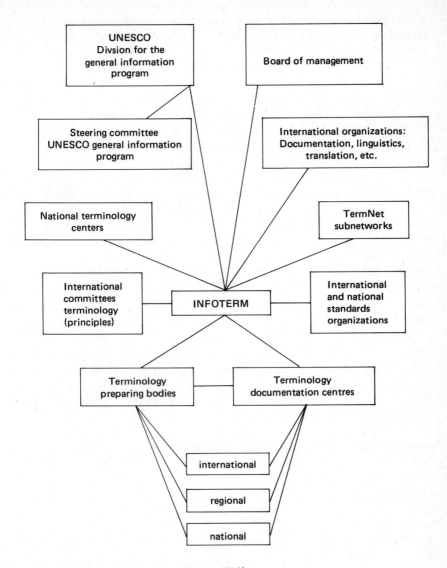

Organization chart TermNet (from Felber 1978)

comparative study provided this data. By projecting problems and treatment systems that were found to exist in other countries, primarily in Europe, onto the United States, we have begun to come to grips also with American data; the ethnic-rights and plain-language movements which reflect societal problems require that the facts of usage and treatment be uncovered before correction and restructuring can take place.

Though

Less progress has been made in theory. Some rough-cut terminological distinctions between speech communities in motion or at rest and a bold typology of sequential developmental stages have been proposed. The most promising idea is Neustupný's attempt to link up linguistics with correction, by challenging linguists to account for correction behavior as a rule-governed and necessary part of speaking. The term 'inadequacy' has great appeal. Unfortunately, theoretical efforts in linguistics have hardly been affected at all by language-planning thought.

Application

There is we hope, a growing interest among practitioners — much as a result of very determined efforts by some iglp-ers — in formulating language-planning theory. Some practitioners participated in the 1977 Linguistic Institute. The *Language-Planning Newsletter* is gaining more readers. In regard to term planning, there are well-organized networks of practitioners who interact with expert *terminologists* in a tradition of applying *principles* of term formation to the production of term lists; language planners have not yet found a place in that treatment system.

Professional life (social system and idiom)

The world of language correction is a fascinating mixture of the serious and the funny, of systematicity and ad hoc-ery. Some treatment systems, as for instance foreign- and English-language teaching, are internationally organized so that not only one but several competing structures reach the individual language teacher wherever he may work. Yet the discipline which takes correction systems as its object of study has only just begun its long journey toward academic respectability. There is a newsletter; there are a couple of journals in linguistics and the sociology of language, in translation, and in information science, that accept language-planning articles. Language planning is noted in several bibliographies; it can organize subsections at a sociological and an applied linguistics convention. Both in the United States and abroad some universities offer courses and accept dissertations on language-planning topics. This volume takes the discipline of language planning another step forward on a journey which offers a unique combination of intellectual excitement and practical relevance.

NOTES

1. Cf. Jernudd and Das Gupta's interpretation (1971: 199) of Haugen: 'An alternative for solving a language problem is effective, in our definition of the term, when it is expected to accomplish what we want it to accomplish. When making a prognosis, planners take into account the "acceptability" of possible alternatives. The alternatives are formulated because a linguistic phenomenon is felt to be less "adequate" (see figure 1).

2. "One point of interest to future investigation is the concept of language planning as a means to strengthen the faculty of abstract reasoning in language. It is commonplace to practised language planners that linguistic expressions relating to individual objects and actual phenomena require much less attention than those relating to classes of objects and categories of phenomena. Language planning can, probably fruitfully, be viewed as efforts to alleviate the generalizing faculty of language and thus to promote innovative thinking' (TNC 1972).

3. The very loosely organized public language treatment system in the United States (cf. Rubin 1978, 1979) is now looking for a word for unmarrieds cohabiting for long periods (why not 'marvin' or 'paramour'?). And a system inadequacy of great importance which I believe it will take long to settle is *gender* in American English and in the languages of many other contemporary speech communities. Cf. TIME Magazine April 2, 1979: 'Chairman's Lib – The British draw the line':

   '"Chairman" is fine, but "chairperson" isn't, according to one of the language's most respected arbiters, the Oxford Unviersity Press, whose new 770-page paperback dictionary states crisply: "The word chairman may be used of persons of either sex."

   'The dictionary, which serves as a guide to British, rather than American usage, was compiled by a woman, Joyce M. Hawkins, 50. Aware that "chairperson" and its kin (*e.g.*, "spokesperson") are incresingly accepted in the U.S., she notes, "In this country, chairperson is treated with mild amusement." The huge *Oxford English Dictionary* first included "chairman" a century ago, and, as Hawkins points out, its original usage made no sexual distinction. Still, Hawkins' dictionary tolerates "chairwoman," which it defines as a "female chairman."

   'Reflecting the inconsistencies and quirks in usage, the Oxford paperback views "salesman" as exclusively masculine (with "saleswoman" its feminine counterpart). In this case, the dictionary also bows uncomplainingly to civil authority, defining without derision the term "salesperson," required by law in nondiscriminatory help-wanted advertising'.

   A closely related problem is a matter on which language planning is expended in Sweden, namely democratization of address (cf. Neustupny 1978: Chapter 10). English has this most marvelous 'you' in the second person, both singular and plural, which Swedish lacks. The former prime minister, Palme, put his weight behind generalizing *du* and it may yet succeed (Bratt-Paulston 1976; Ahlgren 1978). Replacing the Swedish *du/ni* opposition by *du* asserts equality in speaking encounters. Yet some people seem blissfully ignorant of the fact that economic and social inequality remains regardless. Perhaps it is better not to be constantly reminded in discourse of one's factual lack of power and assets?

4. One of the most severe problems in practical work, but evidently also in theory, is for the language planner to maintain a realistic perspective on inadequacies in the system. Systematic linguistic insight may be valuable as data for a terminological work group, e.f. *Rechner* [German for 'computer'?] might not be as desirable (to the working group in session) as *Rechenanlage* or *Rechenmaschine* [German for 'computing machine'] because transparency is lost (semantic motivation is not immediately apparent from the morphology) and *Rechner* could be animate, by reckoning of the language system, not just inanimate; while on the other hand *Rechner* may be convenient, not quite as cumbersome, as the more transparent alternatives. (From Nordisk terminologikurs 1978: 237) But the same author who offered the preceding observations cannot resist (1978: 240) listing this set of alternative expressions to illustrate a kind of 'term-formation error' as he continues his exposition; that if the working group select *Rechner* it commits an 'omission of characteristic feature (a too severe abbreviation)'. The author in question may not have intended to establish universal rules of term formation; but why then use such words as 'term-formation error' and 'omission' at all? Transition from real to irreal is only too easily made: 'Too much, sofar, has been said on how language should be evaluated. Little is known about the actual processes of evaluation in language situations around us' (Neustupny 1978: 248; cf. also Jernudd and Das Gupta 1971: 197).

5. A very interesting paper by Jefferson (1973) has shown how speakers deliberately generate speech which requires inadequacy marking and application of a correction rule: '. . . When thu ku- officer . . .', says somebody in front of a judge in traffic court, with the implication that 'I know that in this situation one says "officer", not "cop".' Correction is used as 'an interactional resource' by the speaker.

6. Application of generalized correction models also brings about language change, as Rubin shows by citing examples from Sango (a prestige model) and Haitian Creole (Gallicizing) (1977a: 264-265).

7. By *stable* speech community I mean, 'as long as a speech community can anticipate, through its treatment system and with self-perceived success, most of the language problems they have recognized and will recognize, then it is stable' (Jernudd 1977: 49).

8. Neustupný's correction model can accommodate Havranek's theory of automatization and foregrounding in the stand language (Havránek 1964). It is conceivable that generative communicative rules could be quite unstructured for use, that is to say, not yet 'automatized' nor 'intellectualized', in that grammatical generative resources have not been developed. Speaking in a complex society would, if neither, require constant evaluation, thus be most energy-consuming and difficult. When 'foregrounding' – opposing automatization – is employed in speaking, we set aside automatized expectation in breaking styles or using metaphorical switching and we signal that correction is not invited. We are deliberately not correcting what is an obvious breach of language use toward a purpose which legitimizes our behavior. The relationship between what is corrigible by another and what is permissible to use in foregrounding is indeed vague; deliberate calling into question of one's style (most speaking is neutral) itself signals employment of metaphorical switching but may be subjected to correction by others and even to postcorrection by oneself if there's misunderstanding or unfavorable comment.

Havránek says, 'In a scientific treatise the author uses, on the one hand, words and phrases which have accurate meaning for specialists in the field, by scientific definition or codification or convention, so that he doesn't have to worry about their meaning, that is, automatized expressions. . . . If, however, such expressions and modes of expression are included in utterances designed for non-specialists, they lose their original automatization in the new context (which in the old context we might have called "technical"), and become either unintelligible, if they are devices totally alien to the layman, or they become automatized in an entirely different way, if, indeed, they are not foregrounded' (Havránek 1964: 10).

9. What is 'felt to be part of Hebrew' is itself variable; what it means to say that 'international roots . . . did not as yet exist in Hebrew' is problematical. All languages originated in Turkish, after all; and much of Swedish is still Greek to me.

10. Perhaps this is the distinction that Noss intuitively has in mind when he dismisses 'gazetting discipline vocabulary' as a means to 'establish discipline vocabulary' in Southeast Asian languages (Noss 1974: 7).

APPENDIX 2: Language planning as a term in *LANGUAGE* 47(4), 1971, through 54(4), 1978:

47(4), 1971, page 985	Review by Gilbert of Moser, *Sprachnorm, Sprachpflege, Sprachkritik*: 'The term language planning was invented by Einar Haugen in 1959. The German equivalent, *Sprachplanung*, occurs only once . . .'
50(3), 1974, page 600	Review by Moravcsik of Sauvageot, *L'edification de la langue hongroise*: '. . . cannot be looked upon as a conscious act of language planning . . .', '. . . it provides a historical study of language planning in. . .', '. . . offers data for comparative studies of language planning as envisaged by Fishman et al. 1971', *and* '. . . and a rich source of data for theorists of language planning'.
51(1), 1975, page 236ff.	Review by Neustupny of Haugen, *The Ecology of Language*: extensive discussion.
53(2), 1977, page 478-479	Review by Gilbert of Haarmann, *Soziologie und Politik der Sprachen Europas*: '. . . distinction between language planning ("Sprachplanung") and language cultivation ("Sprachpflege", 176-177): the former is an integral part of the social policy of central governments (largely a 20th

Century phenomenon), while the latter is an activity of private persons or associations. . .'; 'There is abundant material in this book for the study of sociolinguistic universals of language development, standardization, and planning'.

53(3), 1977, page 730   Booknote by Kaplan on Ohannessian et al., *Language Surveys in Developing Nations*: 'There are also papers dealing with India, Latin America, the Philippines, and the three countries (Indonesia, India, and Israel) covered in the International Research Project on Language Planning Processes reported in Fishman's paper', 'It might have undertaken to explain, to interested officers of government, the advantages of language planning; that's where the rub most often lies'.

54(1), 1978, page 160   Review article by Grimshaw on four 'Language in Society' texts: "In contrast to Robinson, T. gives fairly detailed attention to studies of language change, language conflict, and language planning'. [T is Trudgill].

54(1), 1978, page 244   Booknote by Hinnebusch on Herbert, *Patterns in Language, Culture, and Society: Sub-Saharan Africa*: reproduces the titles of three articles in this collection in which the words 'language planning' occur.

54(1), 1978, page 229   Review by Clyne on Schutze, *Sprache soziologisch gesehen, I*: 'language planning' occurs in the title of one of the references.

54(3), 1978, page 774   Booknote by Kaplan on Harrison et al., *English-Language* Policy Survey of Jordan: 'Anyone interested in language planning and sociolinguistic surveys really should read it'.

REFERENCES

Ahlgren, P. (1978), *Tilltalsordet Ni. Dess semantik och användning i historiskt perspektiv*. Uppsala, Acta Universitatis Upsaliensis.
Bar-Adon, A. (1973), 'Language problems of developing nations: a selected bibliography', *Hebrew Computational Linguistics* 7: 89-180.
Barkman, B., L. Cousineau, G. Tanguay, and L. Bernier (1974), The translation of S.N.O.P.: 'a first step toward the construction of an automated medical lexicon', *Meta* 19(1): 28-42.

Bratt-Paulston, C. (1976), 'Pronouns of address in Swedish: social class semantics and a changing system', *Language in Society* 5(3): 359-386.

Center for Applied Linguistics (1975), *Conference Proceedings with a Paper on Sociolinguistic Surveys: State of the Art.* International Conference on the Methodology of Sociolinguistic Surveys, Montreal, Quebec, Canada, May 19-21.

Dahlstedt, K.-H. (1976), *Societal Ideology and Language Cultivation.* Publication 11, Department of General Linguistics, University of Umea. (Also in *IJSL* 10: 17-50.)

Das Gupta, J. (1970), *Language Conflict and National Development: Group Politics and National Language Policy in India.* Berkeley, University of California Press.

_____(1977a), 'Language planning in India: authority and organization', in *Language Planning Processes*, ed. by J. Rubin et al., 57-78. Contributions to the Socidogy of Language 21. The Hague, Mouton.

_____(1977b), 'Language associations in India', in *Language Planning Processes*, ed. by J. Rubine et al., 181-192. Contributions to the Sociology of Language 21. The Hague, Mouton.

Felber, H. (1977), 'Terminological symposia held in different countries of the world from 1967 onwards'. Unpublished course materials from the Nordisk Terminologi Kursus, June 20-30: 35-38.

_____(1978), 'Organization of terminology work on an international scale'. Unpublished course materials from the Nordisk Terminologikursus, June 20-30: 171-190.

Fellman, J., and J. Fishman (1977), 'Language planning in Israel: solving terminological problems', in *Language Planning Processes*, ed. by J. Rubin et al., 79-96. Contributions to the Sociology of Language 21. The Hague, Mouton.

Ferguson, C. (1971), *Language Structure and Language Use: Essays by Charles Ferguson.* Stanford, Stanford University Press.

Fishman, J., C. Ferguson, and J. Das Gupta, editors (1968), *Language Problems of Developing Nations.* New York Wiley.

Fishman, J. (1971), 'The sociology of language: an interdisciplinary social science approach to language in society', in *Advances in the Sociology of Language*, ed. by J. Fishman, 217-404. The Hague, Mouton.

_____(1972), *Language in Sociocultural Change.* Stanford, Stanford University Press.

_____, editor (1974), *Advances in Language Planning.* The Hague, Mouton.

_____, editor (1977a), *Advances in the Creation and Revision of Writing Systems.* The Hague, Mouton.

_____(1977b), 'Selected dimensions of language planning: a comparative analysis', in *Language Planning Processes*, ed. by J. Rubin et al., 195-214. Contributions to a Sociology of Language 21. The Hague, Mouton.

Galberg-Jacobsen, H. (1973), *Sprogrogt i Danmark i 1930rne og 1940rne.* Dansk Sprognaevns Skrifter 6. Copenhagen.

Girke, W., and H. Jachnow (1974), *Sowjetische Soziolinguistik: Probleme und Genese.* Kronberg Taunus, Scriptor.

Gumperz, J. (1969), 'Communication in multilingual societies', in *Cognitive Anthropology*, ed. by S. Tyler, 435-449. New York, Holt, Rinehart and Winston.

Harvey, D. (1969), *Explanation in Geography.* London, Edward Arnold.

Haugen, E. (1971), 'Instrumentalism in language planning', in *Can Language Be Planned?*, ed. by J. Rubin and B. Jernudd, 281-289. Honolulu, Univeristy Press of Hawaii.

_____(1972a), *The Ecology of Language.* Stanford, Stanford University Press.

_____(1972b), *Studies by Einar Haugen*, ed. by et al. E.S. Firchow, The Hague, Mouton.

Havránek, B. (1964), 'The functional differentiation of the standard language', in *A Prague School Reader on Esthetics, Literary Structure, and Style*, ed. by P. Garvin, 3-16. Washington, D.C., Georgetown University Press.

Hymes, D. (1974), *Foundations in Sociolinguistics: An Ethnographic Approach*. Philadelphia, University of Pennsylvania Press.

Jefferson, G. (1973), 'Error correction as an interactional resource', *Language in Society* 2: 181-199.

Jernudd, B. (1971a), 'Notes on economic analysis for solving language problems, in *Can Language Be Planned?*, ed. by J. Rubin and B. Hernudd, 263-276. Honolulu, University Press of Hawaii.

_____(1971b), 'Review' of *Language Conflict and Language Planning: The Case of Modern Norwegian*, by E. Haugen, *Language* 47(2): 490-493.

_____(1972), 'Review' of *Language Conflict and National Development* by J. Das Gupta, *Kivung* 5(1): 62-67.

_____(1977a), 'The study of language and language problems', in *Sprakvitenskapens forhold til samfunnsvitenskapene*, 53-75. Oslo, Norges almenvitenskapelige forskningsrad.

_____(1977b), 'Linguistic sources of terminological innovation: policy and opinion', in *Language Planning Processes*, ed. by J. Rubin et al., 215-236. Contributions to a Sociology of Language 21. The Hague, Mouton.

_____(1977c), 'Prerequisites for a theory of language treatment', in *Language Planning Processes*, ed. by J. Rubin et al., 41-54. Contributions to a Sociology of Language 21. The Hague, Mouton.

_____(n.d.), 'Critical factors in planning language treatment'. Unpublished manuscript'.

_____, and J. Das Gupta (1971), 'Towards a theory of language planning', in *Can Language Be Planned?*, ed. by J. Rubin and B. Hernudd, 195-215. Honolulu, University Press of Hawaii.

_____, and J. Rubin (1971), 'Some introductory references pertaining to language planning', in *Can Language Be Planned?*, ed. by J. Rubin and B. Jernudd, 311-323. Honolulu, University Press of Hawaii.

Kelman, H. (1971), 'Language as an aid and Barrier to involvement in the national system', in *Can Language Be Planned?*, ed. by J. Rubin and B. Jernudd, 21-52. Honolulu, University Press of Hawaii.

Khubchandani, L. (1972), 'Language policy for a plural society', in *Towards a Cultural Policy*, ed. by S. Saberwal. Simla, Indian Institute of Advanced Study.

Krommer-Benz, M. (1977), *World Guide to Terminological Activities/Guide mondial des activities terminologiques*. INFOTERM Series 4. Munich, Verlag Dokumentation.

Laver, J.D.M. (1973), 'Detection and correction of slips of the tongue', in *Speech Errors as Linguistic Evidence*, ed. by V.A. Fromkin, 132-143. The Hague, Mouton.

Myrdal, G. (1968), *Asian Drama*. New York, Pantheon.

Neustupný, J. (1968), 'Some general aspects of "language" problems and "language" policy in developing societies, in *Language Problems of Developing Nations,* ed. by J. Fishman et al., 285-294. New York, Wiley.

_____(1975), 'Language planning for migrant languages in Australia: a theoretical framework'. Paper presented at the Conference on Migrants, Migration, and National Population Enquiry, Monash University, October 24-25.

_____(1977), 'Language planning for Australia', *Language Sciences* 45: 28-31.

_____(1978), *Post-Structural Approaches to Language*. Tokyo, University of Tokyo Press.

Nordisk Terminologikursus (NTK) (1978), Skodsborg, Denmark, 20-30. juni. Unpublished course materials.

Noss, R. (1974), 'Scientific and technological vocabulary in the less common languages: some solutions in search of a problem'. Paper presented at the Eighth World Congress of Sociology, Toronto.

Riggs, F. (1978), 'The committee on conceptual and terminological analysis (COCTA)', *International Classification* 5(3): 166-167.

Rubin, J. (1974a), 'Selected bibliographies 3', *Linguistic Reporter* 16(4): 7-10.

_____(1974b), 'Selected bibliographies 4', *Linguistic Reporter* 16(5): 7-10.

_____(1975), 'What the "good language learner" can teach us', *TESOL Quarterly* 9(1): 41-51.

_____(1977a), 'New insights into the nature of language change offered by language planning, in *Sociocultural Dimensions of Language Change*, ed. by B. Blount and M. Sanches, 253-269. New York, Academic Press.

_____(1977b), Texbook writers and language planning, in *Language Planning Processes*, ed. by J. Rubin et al., 237-254. Contributions to a Sociology of Language 21. The Hague, Mouton.

_____(1977c), 'Language standardization in Indonesia', in *Language Planning Processes*, ed. by J. Rubin et al., 157-180. Contributions to a Sociology of Language 21. The Hague, Mouton.

_____(1978), 'The approach to language planning within the United States', *Language Planning Newsletter* 4: 4.

_____(1979a), 'The approach to language planning within the United States', *Language Planning Newsletter* 5: 1.

_____, editor (1979b), *Directory of Language Planning Organizations* (an East-West Culture Learning Institute publication).

_____, and B. Jernudd, editors (1971), *Can Language Be Planned?* Honolulu, University Press of Hawaii.

_____, and R. Shuy, editors (1973), *Language Planning: Current Issues and Research*. Washington D.C., Georgetown University Press.

_____et al. 1977. *Language Planning Processes*. Contributions to a Sociology of Language 21. The Hague, Mouton.

_____, and B. Jernudd (1977), *References for Students of Language Planning* (preliminary edition; revised edition in press). Honolulu, East-West Culture Learning Institute.

Sabourin, C. (1978), 'Aspects économiques de la planification et des politiques linguistiques'. AILA paper.

Sauvageot, A., P. Hajdu, and L. Lorincze (1971), *A Magyar Tudomanyos Adademia nyelv- es irdodalom- tudomanyok osztalynak Kozlemenyei*. Budapest, Editions de l'Académie.

Schweizer, A. (1971), *Problems in the Sociology of Language*. Leningrad.

Scollon, R. (forthcoming), 'The context of the informant narrative performance: from sociolinguistics to ethnolinguistics at Fort Chipewyan, Alberta'. To appear in *National Museum of Man*, Mercury Series, Canadian Ethnology Service.

Slama-Cazacu, T. (1973), *Introduction to Psycholinguistics*. The Hague, Mouton.

Spencer, J. (1974), 'Colonial language policies and their legacies in sub-Saharan Africa', in *Advances in Language Planning*, ed. by J. Fishman, 163-176. The Hague, Mouton.

Stone, G. (1972), 'Language planning and the Russian standard language', *Transactions of the Philological Society* 165-183.

Sundström, E. (1978), 'Terminologiutbildning i Sverige'. Unpublished course materials from the Nordisk Terminologikursus, June 20-30: 448.

Teleman, U. (1978), 'Sprakriktighet i och utanför skolan', *Rolig Papir* 11. Roskilde UniversitetsCenter, Lingvistgruppen.

TNC (Swedish Centre of Technical Terminology) (1971), *Produktionsteknisk Ordlista*. TNC 49. Stockholm.

_____(1972), 'Comments on IRPLPP-DRAFT'. Unpublished manuscript: ESu.

_____(1978), 'Kompendium. Kurs i terminologi. Norrtalje 6-8 November'. Unpublished manuscript: TNC P pro 1 1978-11-02 KA.

Valdman, A. (1975), 'Creole et francais en Haiti', *French Review* 49(2): 174-184.

Welmers, W. (1974), 'Christian missions and language policies in Africa', in *Advances in Language Planning*, ed. by J. Fishman, 191-204. The Hague, Mouton.

Wexler, P. (1974), *Purism and Language: A Study in Modern Ukrainian and Belorussian Nationalism (1840-1967)*. Bloomington, Indiana University Press.

Wurm, S. (1974), 'Language policy, language engineering and literacy in New Guinea and Australia', in *Advances in Language Planning*, ed. by J. Fishman, 205-220. The Hague, Mouton.

Zgusta, L. (1971), *Manual of Lexicography*. The Hague, Mouton.

Journals used extensively for reference

Anthropological Linguistics (Indiana University).
Babel (International Federation of Translators).
ERIC.
INFOTERM News Letter.
International Classification.
International Journal of the Sociology of Language (*IJSL*).
Language.
Language and Language Behaviour Abstracts.
Language in Society.
Language Planning and Language Problems.
Language Planning Newsletter.
Linguistic Reporter.
Sprakvard.
TERMDOC Bulletin.

Conclusion

JOSHUA A. FISHMAN

Progress in Language Planning:
A Few Concluding Sentiments

Empirical research and theoretical formulations pertaining to language planning have benefited substantially from a rather small number of seminal conferences and projects during the past 15 years. This series starts off with the 1966 Airlie House Conference (Warrenton, Virginia) on 'Language Problems of Developing Nations', proceeds to the 1969 conference on 'Language Planning Processes' at the East-West Center (Honolulu, Hawaii), reaches a crescendo with the manifold publications and meetings that grew out of the 1969-1972 'International Research Project on Language Planning Processes' which focused on Israel, India, Indonesia, and Sweden, continues to reverberate to this very day through the *Language Planning Newsletter* which that project fathered, attracted the attention of a large number of Western and Third-World students at the 1977 Summer Linguistic Institute (held at the University of Hawaii, Honolulu) which was largely devoted to courses and seminars on language planning, and now, in this volume, attempts to focus primarily on the more modern world via papers prepared in 1979. This brief retrospective glance clearly reveals that in a very few years language planning has fully established itself as a recognized topic not only within the sociolinguistic enterprise (both theoretical and applied) but also within the fields of linguistics and social theory more generally. It would be a foolhardy linguist indeed who would now dare to discuss *language change* without attending to language planning as well, just as it must be a foolhardy sociologist who would work on *social change* in ignorance of social planning. Such foolhardiness still exists, of course, but it is becoming ever rarer, particularly among the generation whose academic socialization occurred during the 15-year period sketched above.

As befits a conference that is held after many years of related prior work, this conference was based on a theoretical grid derived from earlier endeavors. Accordingly, it focused on the Americas and Europe (to disabuse us even further of any simplistic notions about any purportedly required link between language planning and lack of econo-technical or politico-cultural advancement), on the one hand, and on differential language-planning goals (status planning and corpus planning) and *foci* (decision making, codification, implementation and evaluation), on the other hand. Our purpose was obviously neither to 'settle' value issues nor to 'recommend' policies for any given language community, but, rather, to indicate how both values and policies, carried out as they are by established ethnic, political, social, and economic systems, influence language-planning processes at every step, whether in status planning or in corpus planning.

It is more difficult for the last in a series to be as innovative as the first, but it is clear that there has never before been a language-planning conference (nor a subsequent collective volume) with quite as many papers on the Americas. This is progress, indeed, particularly from the perspective of American academia, since up until now it has preferred to examine language planning in distant contexts rather than close to home. Similarly 'progressive' are the emphases on developing further those very research topics on which particular investigators have labored for many years (in this way, language planning avoids being a mile wide but merely an inch deep), the attempts to summarize the general state of the art in whole areas of language-planning endeavor, and the attempts to relate language change and language planning more explicitly than has hitherto been the case.

Several topics were mentioned by more than one investigator but from rather different perspectives. Among these is the 'common man's view' that 'proper language' is a cause of 'proper thinking' and 'proper behavior', the assumed relationship being referred to both in order to foster language planning and in order to resist it (the latter, when 'proper language' *is* viewed as natural and untrammeled). The descriptivism-prescriptivism dichotomy is also related to this issue, since some linguists (and particularly older Anglo-American linguists as well as other English language 'spokesmen' or 'caretakers') still view language planning as immoral, unprofessional, and/or impossible. Another theme that is frequently encountered in this set of papers is the growing awareness that language planning operates at morphosyntactic levels rather than 'only' at lexical ones. Finally, although the status planning/corpus planning distinction did not find favor in at least one participant's eyes, it was generally correctly appreciated as being the two interdependent sides of a single coin, two stages linked via a feedback cycle.

From various papers, it became increasingly clear that the complexities and subtleties of status planning still evade parsimonious conceptualization, particularly in the USA and other more democratic and relatively decentralized settings where organized identity planning and culture planning are also unknown. It is particularly in these settings that laws are very far from determining social processes (*legis sine moribus vanae*, as the ancients knew full well). Laws are merely an indication of official position or *pro forma* permission; they are more enabling than causal. The tension between modernity and tradition must still be 'worked through', between econo-technical universality and humanistic/philosophical ethnoauthenticity, between constant innovation needs, on the one hand, and constant continuity needs on the other, even when enabling legislation is passed. Language-status planning thus quickly runs into some of the major ideological dilemmas forstered by the last two centuries of accelerated Western modernization. Another dichotomy often mentioned in our deliberations is not unrelated to the foregoing and pertains to the distinction between the personality principle and the territoriality principle as the legal bases for status planning. The focus on individual rights (personality principle) does not easily provide ethnolinguistic minorities with strong status-planning protection for their collective cultural processes and institutions. On the other hand, the focus on group rights (territoriality principle) often leads not only to the violation of individual rights but to dangers for the overarching (interethnic) political enterprise. Thus, individuals, minorities, majorities, and totalities may represent incommensurable interests such that even solomonic status planning (were we able to engage in it) could not simultaneously satisfy them all.

We recognized that language planning itself is often but the plaything of larger forces. It is not language planning that keeps the varieties of English from flying off in totally incomprehensible different directions. It is not language planning that makes educated Indian English more understandable to American ears and eyes than uneducated Black English within the USA itself. It is not language planning that keeps the 'pathological language switching' in some bilingual communities from forging altogether new languages. While we did not pause once again to define language planning, no one used it in such a way as to see it in each and every act of language choice or use (an all-encompassing definition being a useless definition), just as no one used it in such a way as to imply that it takes precedence over more basic social, economic, political, and cultural forces. Indeed, it was our constant effort to see how these forces influence language — even in connection with our much vaunted English — that gave our status-planning deliberations whatever underlying unity they attained and that provided even our corpus-planning inquiries with rather more societal perspective than such inquiries have commonly revealed heretofore.

Much still remains to be done — to be asked, demonstrated, and understood — in the language-planning area. Nevertheless, these papers represent 'progress' in those very respects. If 'good deeds beget other good deeds', as the *Sayings of the Fathers* claim, then, certainly, 'progress begets further progress' (in the intellectual domain above all others). Since the language-planning field is currently an active and exciting one on all continents, even further progress in connection with our understanding of it will certainly not be long in coming. It is to be hoped that our contributions in this volume will have a ripple effect that will be noticed in volumes yet to appear.

Contributions to the Sociology of Language

edited by Joshua A. Fishman

This series brings to students, researchers, and practitioners in all of the social and language-related sciences the best book-length publications dealing with sociolinguistic theory, methods, findings and applications.

Scott B. Saulson **Institutionalized Language Planning**

Documents and Analysis of the Revival of Hebrew

vol. 23, 1979, VIII + 204 pp. DM 62,–; US $28.25

Originally published in Hebrew, the present volume makes available to the English language reader the most important documents describing the history of the Hebrew language and the attempts made to make Hebrew a modern vernacular. Varying in kind from minutes of long-forgotten meetings to fundamental lectures and essays, these documents recall bitter polemics and decisions on the government level; they deal with sub-categories such as vocabulary semantics, style, grammar and language-teaching. A lengthy supplement applies the theoretical knowledge of the young field of language planning to modern Hebrew.

Robert Henry Billigmeier **A Crisis in Swiss Pluralism**

The Romansh and Their Relations with the German- and Italian-Swiss in the Perspective of a Millennium

vol. 26, 1979, XIV + 450 pp. DM 90,–; US $41.00

This study of Swiss pluralism presents the life history of the Romansh people from the beginning of their cultural evolution in the Roman province of Raetia to the present. Tracing the impact of economic, demographic, and political changes upon the Romansh-, German-, and Italian-speaking communities in what is now canton Graubünden, the present volume shows the forces which have led to a sharp erosion of the position of the Romansh language and the strength of the Romansh cultural life, and the efforts which have been made to maintain and strengthen the place of the Romansh in the culturally pluralistic society of Switzerland.

Madeleine Mathiot **Ethnolinguistics:
Boas, Sapir, and Whorf Revisited**

vol. 27, 1979, X + 324 pp. DM 80,–; US $36.50

In an attempt to deal with the question, "what meanings are communicated through language?" the contributors to this volume revive the tradition begun by Sapir, Whorf, and Boas, by attempting to analyze referential meaning. These contributions advance the study of empirical semantics in the following ways: (1) the usefulness of an approach to the study of referential meaning in which translation, paraphrase or folk explanation are used as data is confirmed; (2) a systematic investigation of lexical meanings is added to that of grammatical meaning; (3) further insights are gained into how referential meaning reflects world views and how it relates to the rest of culture; and (4) the development of a more flexible theoretical framework of reference, in which the whole range of phenomena between the universal and the language-and-culture specifics find their place, is furthered.

Prices are subject to change without notice

mouton publishers

■ Berlin · New York · Amsterdam ■

Contributions to the Sociology of Language

edited by Joshua A. Fishman

This series brings to students, researchers, and practitioners in all of the social and language-related sciences the best book-length publications dealing with sociolinguistic theory, methods, findings and applications.

Bud B. Khleif Language, Ethnicity, and Education in Wales

vol. 28, 1980, XIV + 332 pp. DM 85,–; US $38.75

A study of the interrelationship of language, ethnicity, and education in Wales, a Third World region within the First World. Not only does this book have implications for Great Britain, but also for all modern nation-states with culturally and linguistically distinct outlaying regions.

J. L. Dillard (Editor) Perspectives on American English

vol. 29, 1980, VIII + 468 pp. DM 110,–; US $50.00

Twenty-seven essays providing some essentially historical perspectives for the study of American English, including recent studies on the early influence of nautical terminology on American English as well as the variations used by the Pennsylvania Germans, Yiddish-speaking groups, and those speaking Puerto Rican "Spanglish," Black English, and Pidgin English.

Peter G. Forster The Esperanto Movement

vol. 32, 1982, XIV + 413 pp. DM 120,–; US $54.75

Research monograph examining the history of the Esperanto movement from a sociological and linguistic perspective, from its beginnings in late 19th century Russian Poland to its growth into an international movement. The present volume offers the first in-depth treatment of the movement for those unable to read Esperanto, but curious to explore the movement's tendency to appeal to wider values in support of Esperanto.

The author relies principally on printed documents, supplemented by participant observation and questionnaires to show the variations in the orientation of Esperantists during the history of the organized movement and the difficulties these pose for categorizing the movement sociologically. Consideration is given both to the dynamics of the movement within the broad context of European international relations and in the particular context of British society. Included in the appendices is a summary of the Esperanto-grammar.

Prices are subject to change without notice

mouton publishers

Berlin · New York · Amsterdam